United We Stand

ALASTAIR J. REID

United We Stand

A History of Britain's Trade Unions

ALLEN LANE
an imprint of
PENGUIN BOOKS

ALLEN LANE

Published by the Penguin Group

Penguin Books Ltd, 80 Strand, London WC2R ORL, England

Penguin Group (USA) Inc., 375 Hudson Street, New York, New York 10014, USA

Penguin Books Australia Ltd, 250 Camberwell Road, Camberwell, Victoria 3124, Australia

Penguin Books Canada Ltd, 10 Alcorn Avenue, Toronto, Ontario, Canada M4V 3B2

Penguin Books India (P) Ltd, 11, Community Centre, Panchsheel Park, New Delhi – 110 017, India

Penguin Books (NZ) Ltd, Cnr Rosedale and Airborne Roads, Albany, Auckland, New Zealand

Penguin Books (South Africa) (Pty) Ltd, 24 Sturdee Avenue, Rosebank 2196, South Africa

Penguin Books Ltd, Registered Offices: 80 Strand, London WC2R ORL, England

www.penguin.com

First published 2004

1

Set in 10.5/14 pt PostScript Linotype Sabon
Typeset by Rowland Phototypesetting Ltd, Bury St Edmunds, Suffolk
Printed in England by Clays Ltd, St Ives plc

ISBN 0-713-99758-3

Contents

PART TWO

The 1820s to the 1870s

PART THREE

The 1870s to the 1920s

CONTENTS

PART FOUR

The 1920s to the 1970s

Epilogue

Introduction

Most previous discussions of the history of trade unions in Britain have portrayed a unitary figure of 'the working class' in either a heroic or a sinister light, implying that its members came from somewhere different from the rest of the population and may indeed have been not quite human. What follows in this book has been informed instead by the alternative idea of 'working people' who were an integral part of the society in which they lived. Each of the main chapters therefore begins with an individual life story, subject to its own combination of local influences and its own unanticipated twists and turns of events. Similarly, the analysis of patterns of collective behaviour assumes that groups in different occupations and different parts of the country had their own distinctive experiences, attitudes and expectations. British trade unionists were not a uniform army marching towards a single goal under a disciplined leadership, but rather a cross-section of the working population attempting to meet their immediate needs by whatever means lay at hand, and consequently acting in different ways and at different times.

Within this diversity it is possible, at the risk of some over-simplification, to identify three main types of occupational experience, each producing its own outlook and form of organization. The first of these types consists of those workers mainly concerned with assembling products from a number of components, for example in the medieval making of clothes, in the early-modern printing of books or in the modern building of machinery. Such workers needed an accurate idea of the final product, consequently tending to be better able to read plans and instructions, and generally better educated. They usually lived in long-settled urban areas and were well paid and individually mobile. On this basis they were able to support their own welfare funds and a distinctive type of organization usually referred to as craft unionism, confident of looking after most of its members' interests without any outside assistance. In some contrast, the second type consists of workers who were mainly concerned with processing a single raw material through a variety of stages, for example in the mining of minerals, in the smelting of metals or in the spinning of textile thread. These workers needed only a mastery of the particular process for which they were responsible, picked up their skills and gained seniority by observation on the job and could be replaced relatively easily by anyone else who had the opportunity to observe them. They usually lived in concentrations of recent housing around the plant in which they worked, were relatively poorly paid and found it more difficult to move between employers. They therefore found it hard to maintain welfare funds and permanent trade unions, giving rise to a distinctive type of organization which in this survey will be called seniority unionism, usually dependent on government intervention to achieve anything lasting. The third main type consists of workers who performed general manual labouring tasks, basically variations on fetching and carrying on roads and quaysides, or inside other workplaces. These workers needed only to be strong, willing and minimally observant, and were not only easy to replace but often employed on very short-term contracts, by the day or even by the hour. They were usually recent migrants from the countryside, receiving the lowest pay and living in the worst housing. This highly vulnerable situation gave rise to a distinctive type of organization which gradually evolved into what here will be called federal unionism, always dependent on outside assistance either from better-off sympathizers or from massive national organizations.

Given this view of trade unionism as a response to occupational circumstances, it would seem reasonable to expect significant continuities within each of the types outlined. And indeed, although there was also some adaptation to changing times, much of the outlook and behaviour of engineers, coal miners or transport workers in the 1970s would have been quite familiar to their forerunners in the 1870s or even in the 1770s. The engineers and other craft unions mainly wanted to be unimpeded in looking after their own affairs, which gave them a strong commitment to what has come to be known as a 'voluntarist' system of industrial relations, in which employers and employees were largely left to sort out their differences among themselves. In contrast, the coal miners and other seniority unions constantly found themselves weaker than they would have liked in such free collective bargaining and so tended to press for measures of government intervention in their industries, culminating in the nationalizations of the 1940s. The transport workers and other federal unions were equally in need of outside support but were not usually concentrated in single industries, so their pressure tended to be for government regulation of the national labour market to secure reasonable minimum standards of working hours and wages. Partly because of this diversity of aims, and partly because the organizations of the assembly workers were older and stronger, it was their model of voluntarism which became the basic underpinning of wider labour politics in Britain. Indeed, even the forms of state intervention favoured among the process and general workers can be seen as having a marked voluntarist quality, for they were the result of pressure from particular unions rather than of coherent central planning, and they varied between cases according to government assessments of the balance of forces in particular industries at particular points in time. Thus it will be less surprising to find that well into the twentieth century the mainstream of trade-union involvement in politics in Britain was connected not with socialism but with forms of progressive liberalism.

However, to point to long-term continuities need not always involve denying the existence of significant changes, and one major focus in this survey will be on periodic fluctuations in trade-union strength. While each body continued to press for what can be seen as its typical demands, it was not always equally capable of achieving them and at times may even have found its very survival under threat. The immediate cause of this was the recurrence of severe fluctuations in the level of employment. For years of prosperity produced more job security and higher wages, making it easier to put pressure on employers and pay union subscriptions; while years of depression led to less job security and lower wages, making it more difficult to see any point in industrial organization or find the financial resources to support it. Thus collective bargaining power and trade-union membership fluctuated in relation both to short-term trade cycles of roughly seven years in length and to longer-term economic waves of roughly fifty years in length. Indeed, it is the latter which have been the most decisive for trade unions in Britain since the eighteenth century: producing four distinctive phases of expansion, in the 1790s to 1820s, 1850s to 1870s, 1890s to 1920s and 1950s to 1970s, separated by equally marked phases of instability and decline, in the 1820s to 1840s, 1870s to 1890s, 1920s to 1940s, and then once again from the 1970s to the 1990s. These long waves also seem to have important social and political dimensions. For example, investors' confidence has always played a role in determining levels of business activity, and more recently government policy has emerged as a major determinant of levels of employment. Similarly, the long periods of economic prosperity have been accompanied by more generous social provision and more expansive democratic reform, while the long periods of economic depression have been accompanied by cuts in social spending and a contraction in opportunities for popular political participation. We may then be observing long waves in wider social psychology, with periods of steady progress in all spheres eventually producing excessive optimism and ambition, and thus provoking counter-reactions towards traditional sources of power and status, accompanied by wider pessimism and retreat. A brief review of the features of each of the main periods may help to illustrate this, as well as setting the scene for the more detailed narratives in subsequent chapters.

In the early period we will see trade unions emerging over a longer period of time than has often been realized and already becoming a widely accepted part of British society in the late eighteenth century. Indeed, they were never straightforwardly illegal even under the notorious wartime Combination Act of 1800. However, they were still widely dispersed across the country and organizing among very different groups of workers. On the one hand, the craft unions in the larger cities had a degree of strength and independence derived from their roots in the medieval guilds and in long traditions of urban economic calculation. On the other hand, the seniority unions in the new industrial districts were significantly weaker, especially in the post-war slump after 1815. They therefore pressed harder for protective legislation and on occasions became involved in significant incidents of violence, though even they were far from revolutionary but were just using different methods in pursuit of similar limited and sectional goals. It was this uneven combination of growing confidence on the part of the craft unions and persistent insecurity among the seniority unions which produced the first burst of political radicalism after the French Wars. What may be striking is that this had nothing whatever to do with socialism: some of the demands were highly traditional, in particular the real popularity of some members of the royal family, and as a more modern radicalism began to form it cohered around constitutional reform to ensure a non-interventionist state.

In the middle period we will see the first clearly marked long cycle between the relative economic depression of the 1820s to 1840s, with its attendant unemployment, trade-union weakness and desperate social movements, and the sustained economic boom of the 1850s to 1870s, with its expanding unions and realistic, and frequently successful, demands. The craft unions in particular achieved a more settled local membership as well as a significant status as a pressure group in national life. Their central demand was for the recognition of collective bargaining, in which they were largely successful by the end of the 1860s, when their broader ambitions were increasingly accepted as a legitimate social movement by progressive middle-class opinion. Meanwhile the seniority unions were still having a harder time. They suffered more setbacks during the depression years, took longer to recover and still found it hard to maintain national industrial organizations during the mid-century boom. Their central demand was therefore still for protective legislation and, through coordinated pressure on Parliament and the support of a number of friendly MPs, they too achieved an accepted place on the national stage by the 1860s. The wider political development from Chartism in the 1830s to Liberalism in the 1870s therefore requires more careful consideration than it has often received. For, while Chartism was indeed the first large-scale mobilization around the radical programme of constitutional reform, it emerged in a period of economic depression and trade-union defensiveness, and it failed. Meanwhile Liberalism initially looks more moderate because it operated within the bounds of the constitution, but it emerged in a period of economic prosperity and union confidence and it succeeded in achieving at least some of the earlier radical demands. Based in particular on the craft tradition of non-intervention, it was therefore the Gladstonian Liberal Party that became the first main vehicle for trade-union participation in electoral politics.

The next phase might be called the classical period because in it we will see the first examples of more than half the workforce being recruited in key sectors, as well as the formation of an independent political party representing the trade-union interest. However, if the middle period sees the first clear long cycle, the classical period sees the first clear conflict between progressive ambitions and a sharp counter-reaction. The craft unions in particular achieved a much more powerful collective bargaining position in the long period of prosperity which began in the 1890s. On many occasions this was fuelled by local pressures against unfavourable national procedures, and it was significantly strengthened by the First World War. However, the prospect of a new, more cooperative approach to industrial relations was undermined by a counter-attack on the part of the employers after 1918, followed by their hard-nosed exploitation of their position of advantage during the next long depression. Meanwhile, the seniority unions, having barely managed to survive the previous long depression from the middle of the 1870s into the early 1890s, also experienced a major surge in strength. They managed to establish national organizations capable of mass strikes and since they were operating in key sectors of the economy they received a good deal of attention from the public and from the government. This even led to the first serious discussion of the possibility of nationalization of the coal industry in 1919, but once again this was quickly swept away by the employers' reassertion of their traditional attitudes. Another development which gives this period a 'classical' feel is that trade-union organization achieved a more complete coverage with the setting up of the first permanent organizations for general workers. They, however, did much less well than the longer-established bodies. They were still highly volatile and vulnerable in 1913 and it was only the labour shortages and public control of the First World War which guaranteed their survival. Meanwhile, the overwhelming impression of wider labour politics in this period is still of a marked continuity with nineteenth-century popular Liberalism. Moments of excitement over 'class struggle' and the 'revival of socialism' were brief exceptions and those active in them were generally reabsorbed into the mainstream pursuit of a more cooperative 'new social order'. Thus the newly established Labour Party made its gains before 1914 as part of an alliance with the Liberal Party, and the growing rivalry between them after 1918 was due much more to the latter being compromised by its running of the war effort than to any conversion of the unions to a new ideology.

When we look at the modern period its proximity may make events seem more dramatic and the unions seem more powerful, but really the story of these years is as much one of continuity as it is of change. Thus among the assembly workers there was once again a long upturn in trade-union strength after 1945, to be seen partly in the growth of formal bodies but even more strikingly in the growth of informal shop-floor bargaining. However, this had very little to do with any mood of revolutionary revolt, being more the unintended outcome of employers' strategies in the new sectors of engineering. The workers concerned were normally pursuing ordinary economic demands in new ways, and even when they resisted government intervention they and their leaders were acting squarely within the long tradition of craft-union voluntarism. In some contrast to this dynamic response to new challenges, the story among the seniority unions was a rather gloomy one of long-term decline, so that the post-1945 nationalization of their industries was as much a form of social welfare as of economic restructuring. Thus even the miners' famous mass strikes, impressive as they were, were less a result of popular insurgency than of the excessively confrontational attitudes of those managing the industry: in this case then we may have a rather old-fashioned sense of trade unionists living in a world they had not made and did not want. The story among the general workers this time is more like that among the assembly workers, with new job opportunities, new challenges and dynamic trade-union responses. Again this included a good deal of local unofficial action, in this case as a result of the sheer size of the general workers' massive federations, which made it hard for them to contain the sudden emergence of newly confident groups among their ranks at the end of the post-war boom. In wider political terms the Labour Party remained a vehicle for moderate trade unionism. Despite its increasing use of the word 'socialism' from the 1930s, and despite the scale of post-war reconstruction immediately after 1945, Labour in government remained a party of piecemeal social reform and some sensitivity to traditional libertarian issues. The big change was in its increasing sense of responsibility for the economy, leading to recurrent frictions with the trade unions, but after each of these storms blew over the close relationship between the party and the unions reappeared intact. Thus in the 1970s there was still a real possibility of constructing a new 'social contract' around responsible collective bargaining in exchange for further rounds of political and social reform. However, this depended on every group within the nation being prepared to cooperate, and, as with the missed opportunities of the early 1920s, too much will be left out if we focus only on disorder among trade unionists and neglect the sharp counter-reaction of short-sighted employers' pursuit of immediate profits and conservative politicians' cynical manipulation of public opinion.

Finally, in the most recent period we will see a process of regrouping. For the unions began to work together more effectively to ensure their survival during a long period of high unemployment and unusually hostile governments in the 1980s and 1990s. This was achieved partly through the formation of even larger federal bodies and partly by keeping the Labour Party afloat and steering it back towards more moderate policies. Thus we will be able to appreciate that the title of 'New Labour' has been part of an effective process of re-branding rather than the design of a different product. For the new leadership's preference for piecemeal reform rather than systematic planning has been a constant feature of Labour in government, and even its preference for a rhetoric of 'radicalism' rather than 'socialism' has deep roots in the party's earlier years and even deeper roots in the history of British trade unionism.

Looking at this overall story, there is indeed a sense of a more focused 'labour movement' in the classical period of the late nineteenth and early twentieth centuries, when the greater spread and depth of union recruitment along with the formation of a new Labour Party produced high hopes for a breakthrough of some sort. However, in the immediate aftermath of the loss of so many lives in the First World War, the employers' industrial and political counter-attack confirmed

British trade unionists in their sense of social exclusion and their need to cling tightly to traditional adversarial attitudes. Even though the modern period saw a revival of union strength during the long post-1945 boom, by this time their members had experienced more serious setbacks than expected as well as the further suffering of a second world war, so perhaps it is not surprising if they began to seem more cynical and self-centred. By the late 1960s and 1970s the craft, seniority and federal unions were all strong enough to bring down governments which did not suit them, even Labour ones, something which would have been unthinkable fifty years before. With the two wings of the 'labour movement' frequently at loggerheads, idealistic hopes of creating a really new type of society had largely evaporated.

There is also a sense in which political representation was gradually becoming detached from everyday trade unionism. In the early period the relationship was a fairly pure one: small bands of demonstrators protesting outside the building. In the middle period it was still relatively straightforward: the social movement was now inside the building but still pressing for basic rights. However, in the classical period the formation of a new party required adjustments to the constraints of electoral opinion and the behaviour of other parties. Then in the modern period there was the addition of the heavy responsibilities of forming national governments. By this time the political party had largely taken over from the social movement, though it was sometimes able to regain some of the latter qualities when in opposition. Thus even 'New Labour's' sometimes rather cynical pragmatism and its preference for a greater distance from the unions are both part of longer-term trends.

However, while one of the most important lessons of history is to teach us not to exaggerate the novelty of contemporary events, an equally important one is to teach us not to assume that there is an inevitable line of future development. If the current trends in the Labour leadership's strategy and its relationship with the trade unions do not meet the needs of the majority of the membership, they can be changed. And, while the study of the past may not produce a set of cast-iron predictions, it does provide us with a fairly good idea of the menu from which the future is likely to be chosen.

Prologue

I

From Medieval Guilds to Modern Trade Unions

The people of London eat a lot of meat; this makes them very robust; but at the age of forty or forty-five they die.

There is nothing as awful as the streets of London; they are very dirty; the paving is so badly maintained that it is almost impossible to go on it in a coach, and one ought to make one's will before going out in a hackney cab . . .

In London there is liberty and equality. The liberty of London is the liberty of decent people . . .[1]

These were among the first impressions of the French landowner and man of letters Charles Louis de Secondat, better known by his family's noble title of Montesquieu, during his two-year stay in England from the autumn of 1729: he began as visitors often do with the novel and threatening aspects of diet and urban life, and moved on to a growing fascination with the differences in deeper attitudes. The longer Montesquieu stayed the more he came to believe that the much-talked-of liberty of the English was not just a hollow phrase but an important social reality, and the more of his time he spent making observations and reflections on this theme. It seemed to him that the aristocracy and the clergy had lost their wealth and power as a result of the discovery of overseas colonies, the influx of new money, and a resulting decline in land rents. This was reflected in social behaviour in the unusual modesty of the English gentleman, whether well educated or not, and the declining value placed on courtly politeness, noble honour and religious belief. And it was reflected in the political system in the monarch's increasing financial dependence on the resources of ordinary citizens through regular grants of the House of Commons. This in turn resulted in a constitutional balance of power which gave an unusual degree of liberty to the whole population, particularly striking and even shocking to a continental observer in the outspoken criticism of the government to be found in the press and in parliamentary debates. Having started out as a convinced republican, a practical comparison of Venice and Holland with England had convinced Montesquieu that modern republics were not immune to corruption and petty tyranny, and that the proponents of classical civic virtue should adapt their principles to the realities of the modern world:

> England is at present the freest country in the world, not excluding any republic; I call it free, because the prince has no power to do any harm at all to anybody, because his power is controlled and limited by an act of parliament; but if the lower house was to become the ruler, its power would be unlimited and dangerous because it would also have the executive capacity; whereas at present unlimited power is spread between the parliament and the king, the executive capacity with the king, whose power is limited. A good Englishman must therefore try to defend liberty against its violation both by the crown and by the House of Commons.[2]

These first-hand observations were to become the basis of the more extended analysis of the British constitution which Montesquieu presented twenty years later in his comprehensive survey of *The Spirit of the Laws* (1748), particularly influential for the argument that political liberty and personal security required the separation of the powers of the executive, the legislature and the judiciary, and the establishment of a set of checks and balances between them. In addition Montesquieu made a more systematic compilation of reflections on the consequences for a nation which enjoyed such liberty, including on the one hand the likelihood that it would be formidable in defending itself because of the willingness of its people to submit to high levels of taxation and public borrowing to do so, and on the other that there would be a suspicion of the pursuit of military glory through conquest and a focus instead on civilian pursuits, particularly commercial ones. Indeed Montesquieu himself already had considerable experience of this commerce, having for many years been involved in the export to England of wine from his estate in Bordeaux.

As a result of these observations and reflections Montesquieu became one of the early pioneers of the modern study of the interaction between governing institutions and social behaviour, shifting the focus of political thought away from the discussion of abstract principles and towards the comparative study of concrete developments: in effect a form of historical sociology or social history. In the case of Montesquieu this was based on acute first-hand observation of the distinctiveness of early-eighteenth-century England, where limited monarchy was leading both to political liberty and to economic prosperity. Moreover, this particular combination of historical circumstances was also leading to the emergence of a distinctive form of popular organization: British trade unionism. For the dispersal of political power had inhibited government intervention in the affairs of the old local guilds and corporations, and the new economic opportunities were producing widening gaps between large employers and increasing numbers of skilled urban workers. As these manifested themselves in the decline of effective guild regulation of production and the emergence of new forms of economic self-organization, the government generally continued to stand back and allow this process to take its course.

This was in some contrast to the rest of Europe, where states were much more interventionist in economic and social life. In Germany guild regulation was viewed in a positive way by governments keen to maintain social stability: at first it was made an integral part of small-town administration, but the effectiveness of this system in excluding outside influence came to be seen as a major obstacle to the building of larger states. However, when local corporations were suppressed in the early nineteenth century their powers of economic and social regulation tended to be transferred from the local to the national level, with the Prussian government for example taking over direct policing of the trades in 1810–11, and workers' self-organization being illegal and severely repressed. In France governments were less consistently positive about guild regulation but always keen to interfere with it in one way or another: at first it was supported as a fruitful source of tax revenues for the absolutist state, but it came increasingly to be seen as a major obstacle to economic growth. As in the case of Germany, the abolition of local corporations during the Revolution in 1791 was quickly followed by the transfer of their powers to the level of the national government, for example through the compulsory 'labour books' of 1803 which regulated mobility, and workers' self-organization was to be disrupted repeatedly by cycles of revolution and repression throughout the rest of the nineteenth century. Taking a longer and broader view, British trade unionism can thus be seen less as the development of something radically new and more as the survival of the kind of sectional rights and privileges which had been common throughout medieval Europe but which were removed elsewhere by the concentration of power in the hands of modern nation states. The independent behaviour of Britain's working people, which was to lead to the relatively greater strength and assertiveness of the country's trade unionism, was thus integrally linked to the developing tradition of liberalism in national government.

THE LEGACY OF THE GUILDS

Local guilds had first been extensively documented in the south of England by a royal inquiry of 1388–9, concerned about popular self-organization in the aftermath of the 'Peasants' Revolt' of 1381, but they had undoubtedly emerged out of earlier forms of village association probably stretching back before the Norman Conquest. The most numerous in the late fourteenth century were the social or parish guilds, in effect what would later be called friendly societies, providing support for their members in periods of poverty, sickness, old age and death, as well as a framework of regular social occasions including annual gatherings and processions to the local church. These associations were organized on democratic lines, with fines for absence from meetings, for bad behaviour when present, and for refusing to take one's turn in office. In urban areas where there were enough people in a given trade they began to form craft guilds along parallel lines, promoting each other's well-being through welfare funds and social occasions, through the exclusion of outsiders and then, on the basis of this monopoly, through the regulation of product standards and conditions of work. As time went on they were also gradually incorporated into local government as their full members became entitled to the 'freedom', or citizenship, of the town.

The 'masters' who organized the workshops in this period generally operated on a small scale, training their own and their relatives' children through live-in apprenticeships of seven years, during which the trainees lived with their masters, received little or no payment, and picked up the practical skills of the trade by working alongside them. On the completion of apprenticeship the young adults would then normally have worked for a period as 'journeymen', customarily for three years, earning a daily wage while saving enough money to set up their own workshops. In a sense the real employers were therefore the merchant middlemen who emerged between craftsmen and customers as the towns grew larger and trade between towns increased. The early craft guilds were generally quite small bodies, with half a dozen to a dozen members, among whom the masters were both the most numerous and the most influential. But in any case, the masters, journeymen and apprentices usually found themselves on the same side in protecting craft practices against the pressures of the merchants for higher output and lower costs, and they were in addition all classed together by such measures of government intervention as the royal inquiry of 1388–9.

Apart from their welfare and social activities, the craft guilds had three main trade functions: to maintain standards of training, to fix the prices of the manufactured products, and to set the journeymen's wage rates. Masters and journeymen would have had a shared interest in maintaining the standards of training, the former to ensure that the workers were truly competent, the latter to restrict the number of trained adults competing for employment and eventual mastership. Masters and journeymen would also have had a shared interest in maintaining high prices for their products, as this would have increased the amount of the revenues to be divided between them. However, there was clearly the potential for conflicts of interest over how large the share of each should be, and in the larger towns where there were growing numbers of journeymen, above all in London, this led to increasing differentiation within the guilds.

On the one hand, in order to contain the pressure from the journeymen, they were permitted to establish 'yeomanries' within the guilds, and these bodies increasingly took over the responsibility for dealing with new arrivals in the area, collecting dues and distributing welfare benefits. As early as 1434 the yeomen of the Blacksmiths' Company had secured an agreement that:

From henceforth when any stranger cometh to London to have a service, any of the servants . . . [who] knoweth that he will have a service shall bring him to a master to serve and to warn the warden that is their governor that he may be at the covenant making.[3]

On the other hand, the richer masters began to establish 'liveries', entitled to wear elaborate costumes on special occasions, to attend exclusive dinners, to own and manage property, and to admit merchants who were prepared to purchase membership, most notably in the cases of the Merchant Tailors and the speculative Masons. The liveries within the larger guilds increasingly acted to preserve their privileged position, by postponing the age at which journeymen could set up as masters and pushing the smaller masters down into the yeomanry. Naturally there were disputes between the yeomanry and the livery sections within these guilds, especially over elections to offices and the control of welfare funds, and these began to intensify from the middle of the sixteenth century as rising demand led the richer masters to admit more apprentices and adult outsiders than the traditional regulations permitted and, especially in the clothing trade, to organize large numbers of home workers outside the city walls.

The main recourse of the journeymen under the guild charters was the 'power of search' to identify irregular workmen in the shops, including those who had no apprenticeship and those who came from other districts or other occupations. Among the London building trades the huge demand for labour during the rebuilding of the capital after the 'Great Fire' of 1666 reduced the effectiveness of the yeomanries among the masons and carpenters in their attempts to use the power of search. However, in the cases of the more numerous and more powerful London yeomanries, such as those of the weavers and the tailors, a combination of expulsion and the extension of membership enabled them to establish effective closed shops in the second half of the seventeenth century. The weavers were even able to prevent the use of new engine looms with multiple shuttles in the London area by using the power of search and the custom of the destruction of 'deceitful' goods to engage in extensive machine-breaking in the 1670s. By the end of the century the distinction between the activities of the yeomanry and livery ends of such trades was so great that they began to part company amid protracted legal disputes over the control of the guild funds, such as that among the tailors in 1696.

Among the smaller London trades the yeomanries had had so little power that they had tended to make earlier breakaways from the guilds to set up their own independent chartered corporations of journeymen and smaller masters engaged directly in manufacturing processes, within which the masters tended to be subordinate to the more numerous journeymen: the glovers had broken away from the leathersellers in 1638, and the feltmakers (hatters) had broken away from the haberdashers in 1667. Outside London, where the journeymen had neither the numbers nor the financial resources to secure incorporation, similar breakaways led to the establishment of more unambiguously plebeian 'box clubs', for example among the Devon woolcombers, the Bo'ness seamen, the Newcastle keelmen and the Edinburgh tailors. These bodies aimed to provide welfare funds against sickness, old age and funeral expenses, at first relying on the masters to deduct contributions from their wages and look after the money but soon, finding this unsatisfactory, beginning to make their own collections and payments at regular meetings.

THE EMERGENCE OF TRADE UNIONS

Whatever the precise form of organization and order of priorities, by the late seventeenth century the yeomanry sections of the guilds were increasingly being transformed into independent associations of wage-earners. These frequently still included small masters as full or partial members, but on different principles of organization: dominated by the journeymen, with less of a spirit of fellowship between all members of the trade, and less of an appeal to a common framework of trade regulation. However, despite their growing sense of independence, most of these journeymen's associations emerged in the course of re-thinking and re-organization within the old crafts and they retained many of the centuries-old procedures and symbols of the guilds. On the more open side were the welfare funds and committees, common seals and emblems, tipstaffs, colours and public processions. On the more closed side were the rites requiring blindfolded walks before the officers and the swearing of oaths in front of bones or weapons, in return for which applicants were initiated into secret passwords and signs which gave them access both to workshops and to society meetings.

In other occupations which were growing up outside the older urban centres and the framework of guild regulation, the regular meeting of men at work which had originally produced the guilds was now operating once again to promote social and economic association. The daily life of most workplaces would normally have included chatting, debating, singing and reading the newspaper; weekly rhythms would have been marked by paydays and the more or less regular celebration of 'Saint Monday' before returning to work on Tuesday; these routines would have been punctuated by special occasions such as the end of a young man's training or the birth of a colleague's child; and from time to time there would have been the passing round of the hat for those in extreme need. In addition to such natural sociability most work groups also evolved customary practices to guide individual behaviour to the mutual advantage of all their members, covering such matters as the arrangement of the workplace and the allocation of tasks to men of different ages and abilities. Even in workplaces which were outside the scope of formal craft regulation there were informal sanctions to exclude untrained interlopers, by 'sending them to Coventry', sabotaging their work and generally making their life so unpleasant that they would rather leave. Similarly among the coal miners there were pit 'brotherings' when the colliers who had come of age were admitted as full men, which acted as a check that they had learned the skills necessary to work in safety and initiated them into the customs of the group, involving such practices as stopping work for the day after any accident, however small. Thus out of natural sociability and customary practices emerged a habit of cooperation around common interests which could easily become the basis of 'combination' to improve conditions of work and rates of pay, whether or not it gave rise to formal organization.

Women had for long played a subordinate role in the domain of paid work, and the processes of economic development were producing an increasing segregation of the sexes. For population growth and movement was releasing most of the bottlenecks in the supply of labour for the craft sectors, thus reducing female access to the apprenticed trades. Meanwhile more strength and stamina were required for the expanding non-craft sectors, thus tending to exclude female labour from the highly skilled tasks in factories and mines. As a result, women were increasingly confined within clearly defined areas of employment, usually in work which resembled household chores: above all domestic service in other people's houses, but also needlework, ancillary textile work and light metalwork. Female workers were always poorly paid and usually widely dispersed, well away from the main centres of trade-union activity. To add insult to injury, male workers then began to protect their own positions by struggling to keep women out of their skilled labour markets and organizations. The old craft unions in the urban trades adopted an openly exclusive attitude; the new seniority unions in the factory districts only accepted parallel female organizations if they remained subordinate. Women continued to play an important role in the paid workforce and a supportive role in the conduct of collective bargaining, both as individual house-hold managers and as members of mass demonstrations, but they were largely excluded from direct participation in the world of trade unionism until the last quarter of the nineteenth century.

Among both the journeymen's associations and the growing numbers of male non-craft workers an increasingly characteristic form of pressure in pursuit of their demands was unilateral direct action: 'turning-out' or 'striking off work', frequently accompanied by pro-cessions through the streets with flags, drums and music to maximize its impact. The clothing industry seems to have been a particularly fertile soil for this kind of activity, with a local strike for higher wages recorded among the woollen workers of Trowbridge in Wiltshire as early as 1677, where, in the words of one of the local employers:

Goeing forth he saw a great company of men ffollowing a ffidler and one of them made a kind of Proclamacon that 'whosoever was of their side should ffollow them'. Afterwards, hearing that they were att an Alehouse neere the bridge he went thither with the Constables where he heard Aaron Atkins say he was the man who made the Proclamacon and that the intention thereof was to engage as many as he could for the raising of their wages sixpence per weeke and that Samuel Bowden (and others) affirmed the same and were with him in the streete upon the same designe, and Atkins said he had a sword and wished that he had had it with him.[4]

In the absence of continuous documentary records kept by formal organizations there is something of a bias in our knowledge of these early associations, as it arises mainly from employers' complaints about them or attempts to secure legal sanctions against them, and thus highlights the moments of conflict at the expense of less dramatic welfare provision or peaceful collective bargaining. However, in the absence of other evidence these reports of disputes are an indispensable guide to the extent and effectiveness of early trade unionism.

The London tailors were already organized in a widespread network of local clubs in the first decades of the eighteenth century and a major strike for higher wages in 1720 led their employers to secure parliamentary legislation prohibiting such acts of combination. However, as the masters continued to complain about the journeymen throughout the century they were clearly unable to control their behaviour. Further recorded conflicts over wages began to increase from 1744, reaching a peak between 1767 and 1771, by which time over forty local London tailors' clubs were affiliated to a delegate conference known as the House of Representatives which in turn elected an executive committee known as the Grand Committee for the Management of the Town. Indeed the tailors' organization became something of a model for others among the London trades, which between them were responsible for around 30 per cent of the country's industrial disputes in the eighteenth century. Among the other occupations the hatters were particularly well organized, making successful wage demands in 1772 and 1775 through a town-wide body known as the Congress. Similarly in Edinburgh the tailors were active in pressing for higher wages at times of high demand for mourning clothes for royal funerals in 1702 and 1727, and were able to organize a major wage strike in 1748. Despite the masters' success in obtaining a legal indictment against them, it proved impossible to control their behaviour: between 1757 and 1761 they were involved in a rash of disputes, and in 1767 in another strike for higher wages, which spread to include the building trades and the shoemakers. In Dublin too the tailors were pioneers of industrial organization, with a strike over apprenticeship in 1728, and bursts of activity over wages between 1747 and 1754, when they were emulated by the weavers, woolcombers and hosiery workers, and again in 1769–70, when they were emulated by the weavers, bakers and coopers.

Outside the major cities, the woollen industry was another centre of assertive trade unionism, particularly in the West Country, which accounted for another 10 per cent of the country's industrial disputes in the eighteenth century. From 1717 the woollen weavers were increasingly effective in organizing themselves to restrict the number of apprentices, and to regulate prices, wages and working conditions, frequently resorting to physical intimidation. The employers secured a royal proclamation against them, followed by an act of 1726 prohibiting combinations, but as in the case of the tailors such legislation was ineffective in preventing industrial action: there continued to be at least two major disputes in each decade with a rapid escalation in the early 1750s. Meanwhile the shearmen in the West Country were organized on a parochial basis from at least the 1740s, with a federation covering Wiltshire and Somerset evident during a dispute in 1769. Similarly, powerful local woolcombers' organizations were recorded in the south-west, the east Midlands, Yorkshire and the north-east of Scotland from the 1740s.

The third large cluster of strongly organized workers in the eighteenth century covered the seamen and shipyard workers, whose vital contribution to both commercial wealth and national security brought them a good deal of public sympathy and more respectful treatment from the authorities. The seamen were on strike for higher wages in Southampton in 1739, with an escalation of disputes beginning in 1746 and reaching a peak between 1768 and 1775 on the Thames, the Clyde and the Tyne. Meanwhile, among the shipyard workers, there were disputes in the naval dockyards on the Thames in 1729 and 1739, with an escalation between 1755 and 1775 focusing on the shipwrights. This latter group was particularly noted for its independent attitudes, forming a breadmaking cooperative on the Thames as early as 1758, and flying a blood-red flag of defiance the following year to celebrate the failure of legal action against it for undercutting commercial bakers' prices. Taken together these occupations accounted for around another 10 per cent of the country's industrial disputes in the eighteenth century.

In addition to these outstanding cases, examples of disputes have been found for most of the other occupations and most of the other regions of eighteenth-century Britain, rising from an average of one to two significant cases reported in the press each year in the first quarter of the century, to four to five each year by the third quarter. Even taking a fairly strict definition of trade unionism as continuous formal association, the evidence now suggests there were at least fifty such bodies in the skilled trades by the end of the eighteenth century. However, given that even in the late nineteenth century trade unionists amounted to under 10 per cent of the workforce, it is important to bear in mind that, widespread as it was, eighteenth-century trade unionism still involved only a small proportion of its potential membership: perhaps 5–10 per cent as a maximum in the more prosperous years of the period.

THE STATE, EMPLOYERS AND COLLECTIVE BARGAINING

There had already been large numbers of wage labourers in medieval Britain, both as journeymen in the urban crafts and increasingly as farm servants, and the state had first become involved in setting their wages in the aftermath of the 'Black Death' of 1348. This disaster had reduced the number of workers and thus led to an increase in wages, so the Statute of Labourers of 1350, extended to all occupations by 1373, had laid down maximum wages and attempted to restrict labour mobility, and thus become one of the grievances behind the 'Peasants' Revolt'. Since national Acts of Parliament had proved too rigid in the face of regional variations and frequent fluctuations in prices, local Justices of the Peace had been given the power to set wages from time to time. This had been paralleled in Scotland from 1426 by the right of magistrates, first only in the royal burghs but gradually extended to all the others, to fix the prices of the local craftsmen's products.

Statutory regulation became more systematic in the early-modern period, above all through the Statute of Artificers of 1563 which consolidated the custom and practice of the previous two centuries, with particular attention to the rapidly growing woollen textile and clothing trades. The length of apprenticeship was set at seven years, the number of apprentices was regulated at one for every three crafts-men, and Justices of the Peace were given the power to set wages. Whereas in the fourteenth century there had been a labour shortage and the setting of wages had tended to establish a maximum broadly in the interests of the masters, by the sixteenth century population growth meant that there was now a labour surplus and the setting of wages tended towards the establishment of a minimum broadly in the interests of the men. Along with the regulations for long apprentice-ships and limited numbers of apprentices, this made the Statute of Artificers popular with the journeymen. On the other hand Justices of the Peace were also given powers to restrict labour mobility to those with a permissive certificate from their previous employer, and to prohibit 'confederacies and conspiracies' of workmen in pursuit of their interests through strikes, and this seems to have made the statute acceptable to the masters. It was later imitated in Scotland by acts of 1617 and 1661 which gave powers to Justices of the Peace to make annual settlements of wage rates, though in this poorer part of Britain the relative shortage of skilled workers led to an absence of apprentice-ship regulations along with a greater emphasis on the restriction of labour mobility. The implementation of these statutory regulations always varied considerably between districts, and even before the eighteenth century there is little evidence of prosecution of either employers or employees for giving or accepting wages different from the assessments, so it seems that where they were active the magistrates were adjusting their assessments to the realities of local labour markets.

By the 1700s this general legislation was largely falling into disuse, but the eighteenth century still saw nine special English Acts of Parlia-ment aimed at regulating conditions in particular trades. The first of these 'Combination Acts' was that of 1721 aimed at the London tailors: it set maximum wages and minimum hours to be reviewed from time to time by the Justices of the Peace, prohibited any collect-ive action to change them, and enforced individual completion of contracts; moreover, prosecution was to be by summary procedure of two Justices of the Peace, without any need for the normal processes of trial by jury; and the standard punishment was to be two months in prison. Soon afterwards, in 1726, a similar statute was aimed at the weavers in the woollen trade throughout England, with the extension of the standard prison sentence to three months and the addition of provisions to make violence to person or property a felony, punishable by transportation in the case of the former and execution in the case of the latter. A second cluster of legislation along these lines can be found in the middle of the century, starting with an omnibus act of 1749, which began by addressing problems among the hatters but went on to cover a wide range of other occupations in the clothing industry. This was followed by revisions of the weavers' and tailors' acts in 1756 and 1768, as well as new legislation for the Spitalfields silk weavers in 1773 and for the hatters in 1777. Finally a third cluster of particular legislation came in the 1790s, with the revision of the Spitalfields act in 1792 and an act directed at the papermakers in 1796, which for the first time reduced the number of Justices of the Peace required for the summary procedure to one. Since these acts were usually passed by Parliament in response to pressure from masters faced with relatively well-organized and assertive groups of workers, they provide a good overview of the position of trade unionism in the eighteenth century, broadly confirming the pattern of disputes reported in the press: organization was relatively stronger among the London tailors and silk weavers, and outside the capital among the woollen weavers and the hatters; and it was more assertive in the early 1720s, the 1740s to 1770s, and then again in the 1790s.

Because the distinct Scottish legal tradition recognized the legal identity of associations, the English statutes against combination could not be applied in an unamended form; however, on some occasions Scottish judges did rule that combinations were illegal, especially when they involved coercion of employers to go against earlier court rulings. By contrast Ireland's still separate Parliament was able and willing to pass legislation against combinations, beginning in 1729 with an act aimed at the situation in brickmaking, followed by more general legislation in 1743 and 1763. The latter act provided for particularly severe physical punishments, leading in 1770 alone to two weavers being whipped through the streets of Dublin for combining, and a publican being pilloried for allowing tailors to meet on his premises. Indeed the Irish employers' pressure for legislation was strong enough to secure a further general act against combinations in 1780, in the face of a widely supported journeymen's campaign of resistance.

The main attraction to the employers of such special combination acts was the ease and speed of securing the punishment of troublesome workers through summary proceedings to enforce statutory rules, but they were ambiguous in their impact. On the one hand, they were clearly intended to suppress associations of workers which took direct action against their employers in pursuit of improved contracts; on the other, they restated the powers of magistrates to set wages and permitted the formation of associations of workers to petition for improvements through this channel. They were, then, an attempt not so much to suppress trade unionism altogether as to replace strikes with compulsory arbitration, and as the unions became increasingly well organized in the middle decades of the century this point was made increasingly explicit in press commentary on legal actions:

> ... if the Masters and Journeymen would, amongst themselves, settle proper and reasonable wages, and leave that settlement to the judgment of the Court, to be established or altered as they in their wisdom should think proper, journeymen of all kinds must be inexcusable, and would be highly punishable if they take any steps to distress the trade to which they have been brought up, as they have so friendly a Court to apply to.[5]

Outside the capital the public authorities tended to evade their responsibilities when wage rates caused controversy: in the West Country woollen industry, for example, when the magistrates were petitioned by the weavers to set new piece-rates in 1756 they initially complied, but when this led to a serious dispute the government responded by repealing the wage clauses of the 1726 Combination Act. However, in London the more strongly organized trades tended to be more successful in their petitioning, with the first of the particular combination acts itself giving higher wages to the tailors in 1721. This success grew as the magistrates began to make concessions to their demands in order to maintain public order in the capital, most notably in the cases of the seamen, coal heavers and tailors at the time of the 1768 demonstrations in support of the reformer John Wilkes. Indeed, following several years of serious disorder in the Spitalfields district of the East End, the Combination Act of 1773 aimed at the silk weavers gave the magistrates more powers to fix wage rates and they tended to do so to the general satisfaction of the workmen. This ambiguity in the impact of the law was paralleled in Scotland in the case of the continued powers of the burgh magistrates to regulate conditions in the craft trades, which could result in the imposition of controls on troublesome workers but also in successes for journeymen's campaigns. It certainly encouraged the growth of their associations, especially among the Edinburgh tailors, who fought an unsuccessful case for improved mealtimes through the courts in 1761, followed by a successful one in 1770.

Although normal court cases would generally be more expensive than summary jurisdiction, as well as having less predictable outcomes due to the central role of juries and the uncertainties of case law, the employers who wished to control their workers' behaviour began to turn to the common law of conspiracy. Emerging out of the crime of confederation to pervert the course of justice, conspiracy had come to cover a range of confederations to cause harm to others even though it was never clear why the charge of conspiracy was necessary in addition to that of the illegal act itself. Then in the case of the Cambridge tailors in 1721 the definition of conspiracy was significantly extended to cover cases where the act itself need not be a crime when carried out without the group agreement. This remarkable judgment may be better understood in its context of the immediate aftermath of the 1721 statute aimed at the London tailors, as a way of using case law to extend the illegality of combination to the rest of the country, and it set an important precedent: almost thirty prosecutions of workers for criminal conspiracy have so far been traced between 1721 and 1800. Among the most important additional precedents were the cases involving the Liverpool tailors in 1783, which confirmed that the offence lay in the agreement not in the action, and that involving the London shoemakers in 1799, which accepted their society's rules as evidence of such a criminal agreement. With convictions resulting in sentences ranging from six months' to two years' imprisonment, these common-law conspiracy cases allowed significantly more severe punishment than that provided for by the combination acts, which was presumably another reason for employers' choice of this option. Considered as an overview of eighteenth-century trade unionism the common-law pattern broadly confirms that of statutory intervention and press reports of industrial disputes: the most frequent cases involved the tailors, shoemakers and clothing workers; and they increased most rapidly in the early 1720s, the 1740s to 1770s, and then again in the 1790s.

However, even this more punitive legal sanction was not particularly effective in the face of well-organized groups of journeymen. First, like the combination acts, it was aimed only against unilateral direct action in breach of contract and not against association as such: judges frequently discharged offenders with warnings, made statements in court approving the welfare functions of the journeymen's clubs, and urged groups of masters and men to reach voluntary agreements. Secondly, when it came to industrial action itself, strikes among the major London trades like the tailors and seamen could involve up to 15,000 men and, apart from the practical difficulty and political sensitivity of arresting them all, giving them all substantial prison sentences would only have closed down the employers' businesses for even longer than the strikes themselves. Finally, in those cases which were pursued, delays of up to a year before they came to court meant that the disputes which had provoked them had frequently already resulted in a settlement, often favourable to the men. Thus the threat of legal action was most effective as an initial deterrent, and once it was clear that a large body of journeymen was prepared to take strike action the masters were usually reluctant to make martyrs of a few of their leaders at the risk of embittering industrial relations for years to come.

With the legal system proving to be such an unreliable ally, the employers frequently formed their own independent associations to combat strikes, particularly among the master tailors, who advertised for replacement labour during disputes in London in 1720–21, 1744, 1756 and 1764, and in Edinburgh in 1760. The problem with this was that, while local employers might come to an initial collective agreement to resist wage demands, such pressure was more likely in periods of increased output and they were then likely to break their agreements in order to secure the increased labour they required for their own businesses. There were also divisions of interest between groups of employers in this period, with the smaller masters frequently advising the journeymen's associations on when to press for higher wages from the larger masters, in order to maintain a standard rate throughout the trade. For example, the London magistrate John Fielding observed in 1760:

The Master Taylors in this metropolis have repeatedly endeavoured to break and suppress the combinations of their journeymen to raise their wages, and lessen their hours of work, but have ever been defeated, notwithstanding the excellent provision of the above statute; and this has been in some measure due to the infidelity of the Masters themselves to each other; some of whom, taking advantage of the confusion, have collected together some of the journeymen, whose exorbitant demands they have complied with, while many other Masters have had a total stop put to their business, because they would not be guilty of a breach of so necessary a law; but the success of the journeymen in these disputes, and the submission of their Masters, is chiefly owing to the custom the Masters have now got, of charging extra wages in their bills, by which means they relieve themselves, and the imposition is thrown entirely on the public . . .[6]

Thus even at the level of the individual firm the employer was not necessarily stronger than a combination of his workmen. In theory the employer could last for longer without his immediate profits than his men could last without their immediate wages, but in practice it would only be sensible to do so when demand was falling and the men were resisting downward pressure on wages: when demand was rising it usually made sense to give in to the workmen's pressure in order to benefit from brisk trade and to prevent skilled men leaving for other employment. Moreover, it was clearly also the case that the employer was likely to be facing an organized body of men, who were not only agreeing to withdraw all their labour at once, but who would in many cases have built up some financial reserves to keep them going and might be making use of the sophisticated tactic of the 'strike in detail' or the 'rolling strike', when the workmen in a district would agree to pick off the employers one by one, with those still at work supporting those on strike. Moreover, it was not unknown for strikers to get sympathy and financial support from other sections of the community, sometimes from other trade unionists, sometimes from public sub-scriptions, sometimes even from Poor Law officials. Finally the work-men could use intimidation against strike-breakers from among their own ranks, against substitute labour brought in from outside, or even against the employer himself. The methods used in the eighteenth century were usually the customary rituals for the expression of popu-lar disapproval: especially 'cool-staffing' or parading the offender around the town on a pole and then ducking him in a pond, and 'rough music' or making a great commotion outside someone's house. However, striking workers were beginning to develop their own specific form of intimidation by the sheer presence of very large numbers, or 'picketing': either touring the district to persuade others to come out and join them, or standing in front of a workplace to scare substitute labour away.

In the course of the eighteenth century British employers were there-fore dealing with a legal system increasingly willing to accept aspects of workers' association even in the drafting of combination acts and the adjudication of conspiracy cases. Moreover, despite the employers' own counter-association and individual efforts they were increasingly unable to prevent their workers from engaging in effective industrial action. By the end of the century, then, trade unions had established themselves as a permanent element in the country's social framework, and the pressures in favour of the acceptance of collective bargaining were growing.

Two spirits which, if not altogether contrary, are at least very diverse, seem to hold equal sway in England.

The one prompts people to pool their efforts to attain ends which in France we would never think of approaching in this way. There are associations to further science, politics, pleasure, business.

The other prompts each man and each association to keep all advantages as much as possible to themselves, to close every possible door that would let any outsider come in or look in . . .

. . . I cannot completely understand how the 'spirit of association' and the 'spirit of exclusion' both came to be so highly developed in the same people, and often to be so intimately combined. Example a club; what better example of association than the union of individuals who form the club? What more exclusive than the corporate personality represented by the club?[7]

This was one of the many questions posed by the French landowner and man of letters Alexis-Charles-Henri Clérel, better known by his family's noble title of Tocqueville, during the second of his short visits to England in 1833 and 1835: he had a penetrating insight into social attitudes and organization, and in this case identified a paradox which has continued to puzzle students of British trade unionism to the present day. However, Tocqueville himself, like Montesquieu 100 years earlier, was primarily interested in England as a model of liberal government and a free society. During his first stay he had been most concerned about the changing balance of power between the aristocracy and the people and had concluded that developments in Britain would continue to be gradual rather than revolutionary, largely because the aristocracy was not an exclusive and widely hated caste but instead was open to the recruitment of new men of wealth and included a significant reforming faction within its own ranks. However, Tocqueville had no doubt that the future of Britain lay with its democratic and egalitarian forces, and had been especially impressed by the performance of an unknown speaker from the floor of a public meeting in support of the Poles:

His speech, addressed to the upper classes of society, maintained those formulas of respect that ancient usage had consecrated. But what immense and rebellious pride in those simple words which followed his noble sentiments: 'However, I am just a simple worker!' With what satisfaction and superb humility he continued to add, 'A worker in the lower grades of industry.' When men appear so happy and so proud in their lowliness, those above them should take alarm.[8]

By the time of his second visit Tocqueville was more concerned about the close connection between the rise of democracy and the increasing centralization of political power, and was worried to find evidence of this even in the English case, particularly in the parliamentary reformers' dislike of such aristocratic institutions as the local Justices of the Peace, and in their urgent pressure for economic and social reforms before the construction of new forms of local government. It was in the latter that Tocqueville placed most of his hopes and, in a development of Montesquieu's ideas about the separation of powers, argued that it was now necessary to include decentralized administration by locally elected officials as a counter-balance to centralized legislation by the national parliament, with any conflicts between the two being resolved by individual appeals to the courts for public judicial review. At the same time Tocqueville continued to inquire into alternative sources of power in society, and it was this which brought him into contact with the paradoxical features of English voluntary associations. By the time he wrote his prophetic second volume of *Democracy in America* (1840) these first-hand observations had become the basis of one of his most characteristic ideas about the safeguarding of liberty in modern democracies. This was that the trend towards centralization could be checked not only by local administration but also by influential combinations of private citizens:

An association for political, commercial, or manufacturing purposes, or even for those of science and literature, is a powerful and enlightened member of the community, which cannot be disposed of at pleasure or oppressed without remonstrance, and which, by defending its own rights against the encroachments of the government, saves the common liberties of the country.[9]

Tocqueville had made few direct contacts or observations among the urban working classes and therefore did not himself apply this principle to trade unions, which were in any case still rather weak, but by the early twentieth century the notion of trade unionism as a way of limiting centralization in modern democracies was widespread among progressive liberals. Thus, if by the end of the eighteenth century trade unions had been able to emerge out of the old guilds as a result of the opportunities provided by the tradition of liberalism in Britain's national government, the course of the nineteenth century was to see them growing to a position where they could themselves contribute to the development of liberty by acting as intermediate institutions between the central state and the individual citizen. Whether, as an increasingly important element in a complex network of public institutions, British trade unionism might become so powerful as to pose a threat to the balance of the constitution would then become a much-debated issue.

PART ONE

The 1770s to the 1820s

2

Local Organization among the Assembly Workers

Some time before I was married I became a member of the Breeches Makers Benefit Society, for the support of the members when sick, and to bury them when dead. I paid my subscription regularly, but I never attended at the public house at which the club was held excepting on the evenings when the Stewards were chosen. The club, though actually a benefit club, was intended for the purpose of supporting the members in a strike for wages. It had now in the Spring of 1793 about £250 in its chest which was deemed sufficient a strike was agreed upon and the men left their work.[1]

The author of this memoir, Francis Place, was later to become one of the first effective national spokesmen for British trade unionism, but at this time he was just starting out in his career as a young craftsman in London and his involvement in the strike was to be connected with a great deal of personal suffering. The root cause of the dispute was the disorganized nature of the trade:

It was a badly paid badly conducted trade, a good workman who was constantly employed might earn a guinea a week, but scarcely any one was fully employed; it required from an hour to an hour and a half when two were employed to cut out and get ready a pair of Leather Breeches, and as no one master had an arrangement so complete as to have work always ready, and as the whole was piecework, the masters were regardless of the loss and inconvenience the men suffered, the men in the best shops could not therefore earn more than eighteen shillings a week, and in all the others much less; they had therefore resolved to strike for wages which would put them as to earnings on a level with other trades.[2]

As it developed it became clear that the dispute would be a battle for position around the craftsmen's accumulated war chest. Their own calculation was that, though long-term employment in leather breechmaking was in decline, many of them had already moved into the newer line of cloth breechmaking and the proportion of men to work was favourable: they therefore expected their fund to support them until the masters had to give in, if they were to be able to take advantage of that year's high demand for new spring clothes. However, the London masters not only took care to publicize their own case and to persuade their customers to wear cloth breeches for a time, but also took the unexpected and severe move of dismissing all the members of the craftsmen's club known to have moved into cloth breechmaking, including Place himself, in order to prevent them from giving financial support to their striking colleagues. Thus the pressure of springtime demand on the masters had been eased, and the craftsmen's fund had to support more men than had been anticipated. Place responded by taking a leading role in the organization of the craftsmen's campaign, during which they publicized their own case, sent as many as were willing to look for work out of London, and made their war chest last as long as possible by setting up a small workshop to make cheap leather breeches and generate some income. However, even this could not last indefinitely and after three months they had to call the strike off without any wage increase.

Most of the men involved were taken back by their employers, but their households would have suffered a great deal during three months on half pay. For the more active on the craftsmen's side the consequences were even more desperate:

The masters in their turn punished the men as much as they could, and as the whole number of masters was small, and the whole number of men few it was by no means difficult for the combined masters to effect their purpose. All who had been in any way active in the strike were not to be employed so long as any other man was unemployed, I and another young man named James Ellis were never again to be employed in any way whatever, by any master breeches maker.[3]

Not surprisingly Place was aggrieved about this, as he had not been among those who had initiated the strike, having only been brought into it by the masters' own decision to lock out the club members making cloth breeches. Moreover, this episode became a particularly important turning-point in his life, as near the beginning of the strike his father had died of gout and old age, almost immediately followed by his own infant daughter's death from smallpox. After the strike he and his wife

made many efforts to procure some sort of employment, but were wholly unsuccessful, we suffered every kind of privation consequent on want of employment, and food and fire . . . Our sufferings were great indeed. As long as we had any thing which could be pawned we did not suffer much from actual hunger, but after every thing had been pawned, but 'what we stood upright in', we suffered much from actual hunger. My wife was a fine hand-some young woman and I was most affectionately and sincerely attached to her, notwithstanding the ebullitions of temper I have noticed, and when I sometimes looked at her, in her comfortless, forlorn and all but ragged condition, I could hardly endure our wretched state . . . I made up my mind to endure whatever I should be compelled to suffer, and resolved to take advantage of every thing which might occur to work myself into a condition to become a master myself. I never afterwards swerved in the least from this resolution.[4]

Place did eventually find work in the trade again, the craftsmen's club was kept going and a new fund built up, and two years later, in the spring of 1795, another strike over wages was threatened. The masters had probably suffered financially themselves during the first dispute, for they now granted the wages demanded and started to organize their businesses better, in order to cope with the dual pressure from the craftsmen and the increasing competition from cloth breeches. In the long run Francis Place did succeed in his aim of becoming a master, and worked so hard and well at it that he was able to retire at the age of forty-seven and devote the rest of his life to campaigns for social and political reform.

This first-hand account of late-eighteenth-century industrial conflict in London suggests much about the ambiguous experience of the skilled craftsmen. On the one hand they had a relatively strong bar-gaining position based on their indispensable skills: during the strike the masters had not been able to bring in substitute labour, but only to adopt the high-risk strategy of advising their customers to buy alternative products, and after the strike most of the men had been taken back by their previous employers. As a result the craftsmen could approach industrial relations on the basis of fairly sophisticated calculations: they kept themselves well informed about the state of the labour market and the state of consumer demand, and they worked out when their employers would be most vulnerable to strike action. This in turn depended on their skills being not only indispensable to the masters but also restricted to a limited body of men. In the past this had been ensured by local controls on the number of apprentices, through either guilds or statutes, which was why the craftsmen were still so attached to these old regulations even though they were becoming increasingly ineffective. In the absence of craft unions strong enough to enforce their own regulation of apprenticeship throughout the whole of their trades, it seems likely that the overall supply of skilled labour in particular occupations was limited in this period mainly through individual choices: youths would only enter a trade which seemed to have good prospects and, if as adults they found they had been mistaken, they would transfer their skills into a neighbouring one. All this implies that the craftsmen were living in an urban environment in which there was a range of alternative types of employment, well-developed networks of information, and a culture of economic calculation. It was on this basis that they were able to obtain wages high enough to allow them a small margin for saving for illness and old age, and, as the collective bodies which emerged tended to take an occupational form, also for industrial action to secure better wages.

On the other hand it is important not to exaggerate the strength of the craftsmen's position. Though their skills were indispensable they were still employees dependent on wages and, as a result both of genuine seasonal and cyclical fluctuations in demand and of the inefficiencies of their masters, they were subject to serious irregularities in employment. As a result their weekly incomes were usually significantly lower than their piece-rates might have suggested, and those rates themselves were subject to reduction by the masters in periods of slackening demand. At the same time, the erosion of guild and statutory regulation of the number of apprentices left the craftsmen vulnerable to an excessive supply of skilled labour and yet another downward pressure on their wages. If they took industrial action to improve their position, they would be bound to suffer a significant loss of income during the strike or lock-out, and if they took a leading part in organizing it they might suffer even more from victimization after the dispute was over. Thus Francis Place's determination to become a master was not an expression of material greed or social ambition, but rather of desperate self-assertion in the face of a hostile world; and though he did eventually succeed it was only after many years during which he, and sometimes also his wife, worked sixteen hours a day, seven days a week. Without this sort of heavy family commitment and self-restraint even the small masters' position was highly vulnerable: among Place's own early employers one ended up in jail for debt, one committed suicide after being financially ruined twice, and one had bouts of melancholy and ended up in a madhouse. The world of the craftsmen, though it may have been close to the world of the small masters, was not a secure one and they had hardships enough to face to give them a real understanding and sympathy for those even less well-off than themselves, and to make them take a leading role in wider social and political movements.

LOCAL CRAFTSMEN'S CLUBS

There were local craftsmen's trade clubs in most towns and cities by the end of the eighteenth century, usually with a few dozen members each. As the members of the local craft guilds had done for many centuries before, they met frequently in public houses within easy walking distance of the main workshops, these pubs often taking their names from the trades with which they were most closely connected, and in addition to food and drink providing other useful services such as free newspapers and secure postal addresses. There the clubs also had periodic business meetings in the evening, in the days of the guilds quarterly, among the early craft organizations usually on the first Monday of each month. These were held in upstairs rooms let free by the landlords, with free candles, in the expectation of considerable purchases of beer by the large number of members present during the meeting.

As indicated by Place, these local craftsmen's clubs were in the first instance occupational friendly societies and should therefore be seen as merely one aspect of an urban network of plebeian savings associations, all of which met in public houses and were vigorously self-governing, rejecting both upper-class patronage and government intervention. These included short-term associations such as clothing clubs and boot-and-shoe clubs, and longer-term associations such as the 'sick-and-draw' clubs which, like the parish guilds long before them, aimed to provide protection against accident and illness, a decent funeral and a framework of social occasions. By the late eighteenth century these latter, the friendly societies proper, were particularly strong in the newer northern manufacturing districts: there were reckoned to be around 7,000 of them, including up to 25 per cent of adult men at a time when the trade clubs would have included only 5–10 per cent, and they were formally recognized by Parliament under the Friendly Societies Act of 1793 which gave them a legal status and protection for their funds. Their rules and procedures were almost identical to those of the trade clubs, with which their activities often merged, particularly as the 1793 act provided a safe front for other potentially illegal activity. As a result many of the earliest open unions in the early nineteenth century indicated their friendly-society origins in their titles, particularly in the newer metal-working trades based in the north: the Friendly Society of Ironfounders (Bolton, 1809), the Mechanics Friendly Union Institution (Bradford, 1822), and the Friendly Union of Mechanics (Manchester, 1826).

Meanwhile, the craftsmen's trade clubs functioned only at the most respectable end of their occupations, generally restricting their membership to those who had served a full seven years' apprenticeship and who, on its completion, had been given certificates signed by the senior members of the society. If formal apprenticeship was no longer universal in the occupation, the club would enforce some other condition concerning the length of experience, for example having worked in the trade for five years, with candidates then being vouched for as competent workmen by some existing members and elected by a majority of all those present. Since it would be rare for clubs to include all the local men in their trades, they were not in a position to use this insistence on apprenticeship and skill to control the local labour market as a whole. However, by including only the best-qualified men they were able to function as local 'houses of call', or informal employment exchanges, where employers looking for men could be sure of finding highly skilled applicants in strict order of rotation from the 'vacant book' kept behind the bar. Simultaneously the craftsmen's clubs were able to put pressure on employers by only allowing their members to work in shops they approved of and recognized as 'legal' (with reference to the Statute of Artificers), particularly in terms of the ratio of apprentices to journeymen and the rate of wages.

The craftsmen's trade clubs were highly democratic in their internal organization, following the lines laid down during the centuries of experience of the local friendly societies and the craft guilds. There were fines for those absent from meetings, a president chosen for the evening, and elected longer-term officers: a secretary, a treasurer, a small executive committee, and rotating benefit stewards. In the larger London societies there were further arrangements for consulting the whole membership. For example, in the case of the London Society of Brushmakers, which met at the Craven Head in Drury Lane, votes on important matters were taken before meetings by circulating a tin box around all the workshops: each shop was allowed four hours to read the papers, discuss the issue and cast its vote, and it was responsible for the safe delivery of the box, with no papers of its own added, to the next stage on the round, all subject to substantial fines for breaches of procedure. If a club belonged to a wider formal association it would also elect a delegate to attend the committee meeting of that body. It was still unusual for local clubs to hand over sizeable proportions of their own funds to wider associations on a regular basis, but there were often one-off donations and loans to other clubs in difficulty, not by any means always in the same occupation or even the same town.

The clubs generally focused on providing significant welfare benefits to their own members, in particular for sickness, old age and burial, unemployment being catered for either by tramping around the country or by special voluntary 'petitions' for needy cases. To pay for their regular provisions the clubs required regular subscriptions, usually paid at the monthly meeting and often at a high rate, with the aim of maintaining all the members in a state of independence from the Poor Law and private charity. This drive to secure a position of independence through the ups and downs of the economic cycle and the inevitable physical deterioration of ageing lay at the root of group solidarity in the early craft societies, and welfare provision remained central to their functioning even as they developed into national trade unions. As a result a major problem, which lasted well into the nineteenth century, was how to protect their funds against malpractice on the part of their own officials when there were no means of legal redress, and the early trade unions were vulnerable to unreliability, heavy drinking and embezzlement on the part of their officers. Following the example of the local friendly societies, it was common to have a substantial box, to leave it in the custody of the landlord of the pub, and to secure it with three locks and three separate keys, one in the hands of the landlord, and the others in the hands of the society's two benefit stewards. The landlord, indeed, often served as the treasurer of the society and would even tide it over with loans in periods of bad trade, so, if not himself already a member of the trade who had set up a pub to provide a service to his colleagues, he would be very carefully vetted before being taken into this position of trust.

However, though this was a valuable precaution against unreliable individual officers, it also tied the clubs even more strongly to public houses and long-standing popular customs of social drinking. Many of the spontaneous bonds of the workplace could be barriers to formal organization, for they were invariably connected with heavy drinking: alcohol was cleaner and safer than water, when it took the form of beer it had a nutritional content popularly associated with physical strength, and whether beer or whisky it functioned as a pain-killer and mood-enhancer for those working very long hours. Clearly, however, if this social drinking got out of hand, it could lead to erratic behaviour and bankruptcy, both on the part of individuals and on the part of associations. It is therefore interesting to note that it was common for the craftsmen's trade clubs to have drinks stewards and to allocate some of their funds for alcohol as an aid to conviviality and good fellowship, but simultaneously as a way of limiting consumption. The London Brushmakers' rule book, for example, allowed money for three pints of beer for each man present at meetings, but also limited consumption to those three pints and laid down strict rules about behaviour:

If any member dispute on politics, swear, lay wagers, promote gambling, or behave otherwise disorderly, and will not be silent when ordered by the chairman, he shall pay a fine of 1s. Any member coming to the society intoxicated shall be fined 1s, and be ordered to withdraw. Every member speaking shall stand up, under a fine of 6d, and address the chairman, who shall call him to order if he does not speak to the point in hand.[5]

Since these clubs were organized by the most skilled and steady men in the trades it is not surprising that, from the earliest years, they regulated the amount of drinking allowed at their own meetings, restricted the other social drinking customs of the work group to the bar downstairs, and frequently campaigned against any tendencies towards dependence on alcohol among their colleagues.

THE LONDON TRADES

By the late eighteenth century London was Europe's largest centre of urban consumption, generating considerable employment for skilled workers in tailoring, shoemaking, furniture-making and building, mostly still in numerous small workshops but frequently concentrated in distinct districts. London was also the nation's largest port, generating considerable employment not only for dockers and sailors but also for skilled workers in shipbuilding and related trades along the riverside. Taken together this probably came to a total of around 100,000 craftsmen in 1800. As a result of the much greater numbers and concentration of skilled trades in London there had long been a strong basis for occupational self-regulation and city-wide cooperation among its craftsmen. Since the metropolis was the attractive goal of ambitious youths from the provinces, as well as the obvious refuge for those dismissed for trade-union activity elsewhere, there had also long been plenty of energetic organizers available. Moreover, the two decades of the French Wars from 1793 to 1815 strengthened these tendencies, for they saw greatly increased demand for labour as well as rapidly rising food prices, thus providing the basis and the motivation for more intensive organization in pursuit of higher wages, which reached its peak of success in 1811–12. As a result, closer links were built up between clubs in the same trade and there were increasing examples of cooperative contact between the trades throughout the capital.

The London tailors, drawing on the long-standing strength of their yeomanry guild organization, had shown the ability to organize on a wider basis throughout the eighteenth century and were able in the 1790s to strengthen their federation still further under the leadership of a committee now known simply as the Town: they paid out unemployment benefit and secured repeated wage rises in 1795, 1801, 1807, 1810 and 1813. One of the men's representatives during the last of these movements later recalled:

Our demands were moderate, and were made in the shape of a request, giving our reasons for making them. They were made in writing, a copy being left with each master for his private consideration, and a time being named when his answer would be looked for. They saw by the simultaneousness of their respective workmen's movements that they were acting in concert, although in a respectful manner. They therefore soon proposed a conference, at which, after some little hesitation on the masters' side, and a good deal of trouble to keep the wrong-headed among the workmen from behaving offensively, the advance of wages was agreed upon, and was thenceforth freely paid.[6]

Similarly, in the London printing industry, the compositors, who had successfully pressed for a wage rise in 1785, were able to secure rises in 1793, 1800, a consolidated scale of piece-rates in 1805, and another rise in 1810, which remained as the basis of further negotiations for the rest of the nineteenth century. As in the case of the tailors their strength was based on their city-wide organization, coordinated in this case by the Phoenix, or Society of Compositors at the Hole in the Wall, Fleet Street, with around 500 members in the 1790s, charging a substantial subscription, providing welfare benefits, and presenting moderate demands in writing for meetings between their representatives and those of the masters. Yet another trade experiencing a similar pattern was the London cabinetmakers, many of whom were working in larger shops of 50–100 workers by this period, and who were able to secure wage increases in 1793, 1803, 1805 and 1811. The work of the shoemakers was significantly less skilled as a result of a larger market for standardized products, but even they were able in 1804 to enforce a closed shop in the larger London firms with a degree of control over the ratio of apprentices to journeymen.

The nearby Thames shipbuilding industry focused on highly skilled work, partly in repairs and partly in very large yards producing sophisticated vessels for the East India Company and the Royal Navy, for which there was rapidly growing demand during the French Wars. In order to cope, the yard owners offered high piece-rates and bonuses to attract and motivate their labour, and this allowed the craftsmen to establish increasing numbers of friendly societies, most notably among the shipwrights, who formed the St Helena Benefit Society in 1794 and the Hearts of Oak Society in 1811. However, this also led to major confrontations at home when the decline in overseas hostilities produced a collapse in demand and downward pressure on wages. Firstly during the temporary truce of 1802, when the shipwrights were strong enough and united enough to defend their position effectively through a major strike; and then after 1810 when the naval side of the war effort began to run down and the shipwrights attempted unsuccessfully to establish a formal London-wide union to control piece-rates. Having experienced very prosperous periods during the wars but still been unable to establish an effective trade union, the shipwrights were particularly interested in, and prone to be involved in, cross-trade labour movements.

Particularly towards the peak of the wages movement in 1810–12, such contacts between the trades were on the increase, usually to provide financial assistance in the form of grants or loans during industrial disputes: the goldbeaters, for example, gave or lent over £200 to other trades in these years. One particularly important focus of inter-trade cooperation was a legal battle with the employers over the apprenticeship clauses of the Statute of Artificers. Thus between 1809 and 1812 an attorney named William Chippendale, presumably acting on behalf of a coordinated group of craftsmen's clubs, brought cases over breaches of the apprenticeship clause against nineteen masters across thirteen trades. However, this was not only expensive but also produced poor results: twelve acquittals and, when cases were won, the lightest of penalties the law permitted even when the offences were admitted to be serious. As a result the network of craftsmen's clubs came out into the open as the Artisans General

Committee, or United Artisans Committee, campaigning for parliamentary legislation to restate and extend the old apprenticeship regulations. Among the London trades sixty-two affiliated and provided financial support to the committee, with a particularly high participation from among the shipbuilding trades; moreover there was some response from another seventy places throughout the country, with particularly effective parallel organization in Bristol. The initial petition presented in 1813 claimed over 32,000 signatures and for a short while a Sunday newspaper called the *Beacon*, and probably connected with the committee, was issued in London. This extensive campaign secured a select committee to hear evidence and initially looked set to secure the passage of a bill. However, it then met the counter-organization of the employers, faced with a major wave of increasing trade-union strength throughout the country and determined to resist any attempts to tighten up the application of the regulations contained in the Statute of Artificers. In resistance to the pressure of the handloom weavers, their employers secured the repeal of the wage-fixing clauses of the statute in 1813, then in resistance to the wider craftsmen's pressure their masters, led by a group of London engineering employers, secured the repeal of the apprenticeship clauses of the statute in 1814.

However, the London craftsmen now had the experience of playing a leading role in a national agitation over labour legislation and they were not to forget it. In 1818, when they were attempting to repair the damage to their wage rates inflicted in the immediate aftermath of the war and rapid demobilization, an attempt was made to federate all the London trades under a committee led by John Gast of the shipwrights: known as the Philanthropic Hercules, this had links with a parallel body in Lancashire. Then in 1824–5 the London craftsmen played a major role in a national movement to repeal all the laws against combination and, as this coincided with a general economic recovery, it produced a wave of strikes during which they managed to secure wage increases, set up new unions and again establish better links between existing societies. The shipwrights formed their first effective London-wide organization, the Thames Shipwrights' Provident Union, with delegates elected in each yard and John Gast as its overall secretary: it was able to enforce a standard minimum daily rate, to exclude non-apprenticed labour, to make contact with ship-wrights in other ports and to win recognition from the employers following a major strike. Meanwhile the carpenters were coordinating joint action between their five separate London societies, and the sawyers were establishing a federation of London branches and making contact with equivalent organizations in the north of the country.

THE TRAMPING SYSTEM

Strong personal links had already been established between local groups of craftsmen throughout England as a result of the 'tramping system'. For it had long been traditional for skilled men on finishing their apprenticeship to go 'on tramp', walking about the country from town to town seeking employment and wider experience of both life and the skills and practices of the trade. As early as the fourteenth century the local craft guilds or their yeomanry sections had been regulating the admission of travelling 'strangers' into their locality, usually involving a trial period of work, an entrance fee, and initiation into the local rates and customs. In sixteenth-century records of the masons there is evidence of a system of helping strangers to find accommodation and work, or to travel on to the next lodge and, as this had out of necessity always been one of the most mobile crafts, it may be assumed that these practices had been in operation for some time, along with secret signs and handshakes to prove the genuineness of the applicant. Gradually this practice of hospitality to legitimate 'travelling brothers' began to spread to other occupations, first to the weavers and combers of the wool and silk trades in the seventeenth century, then more generally among all the craftsmen in the eighteenth century.

By the early nineteenth century this had evolved into a system of relieving local unemployment among adult members of the craftsmen's clubs by tramping to nearby towns, presenting a trade card or 'blank' at the local clubroom, sometimes also still using a secret password or sign, and claiming a brief period of hospitality while looking for a job in a 'legal' shop. The strongest trades, such as the masons and the boilermakers, were able to retain many shop foremen within the ranks of their clubs and thus to guarantee a regular allocation of work to members of the craft on the local vacant book or on the tramp. If no such job could be found the man would be given some money (eventually fixed at either a half penny or a penny a mile) to tide him over while he walked on to the next port of call, these being listed in a prescribed order and each man having the right to make a complete 'turn' of up to forty local clubs once every six months. One detailed account of an individual experience of tramping emerged during the trial of a sawyer for union activities in Ashton later in the nineteenth century:

Thompson ... had left Hull on December 6 and after working at Goole, Doncaster and Sheffield, he came to Ashton at 8 o'clock on Wednesday. He went to the Stag's Head, saw the relieving steward and many other sawyers and slept at the house that night. The following day he went to get a job at the first yard along the Stalybridge Road, after trying the next yard, he went back to the Stag's Head, had twopennorth of stew and went away to Oldham which he reached about three o'clock and went to the club house . . . On the following day, Mr Richard, timber merchant at Oldham, saw Thompson in the sawpits of his own yard with the men. On hearing an unusual noise or kind of loud laugh among the men, who were drinking beer which had been sent out for by them, he went to inquire the cause and they said it was an old shop mate of whom they were glad to see from Manchester.[7]

This system was designed not only to provide some possibility of relief from unemployment for the individual concerned, but also to remove him from the local labour market before he was tempted to take work under inferior conditions, thus undermining the position of all the other 'legal' men in the area. Once it was established, tramping could be brought into operation during local disputes, to disperse as many as possible of those on strike throughout the rest of the country, and many societies issued special strike cards, often green, which entitled their holders to more generous hospitality. Moreover, it could be adapted to spirit away local leaders or key witnesses if they were threatened by legal action, or to ship in pickets who could act more freely as they were unknown in the area. In calmer times, tramping functioned as an important channel of communication about prices and wages in other towns, thus providing the necessary basis for calculations about local wage demands and the risks attached to engaging in local disputes. The tramping artisans, as a particularly independent and experienced body of men, were often responsible for setting up new trade organizations in localities where they did not already exist, and the personal links established by all these features of the system provided a firm basis for closer cooperation between local craftsmen's clubs throughout the country.

Highly organized tramping networks were recorded for the following trades during the 1790s: tailors, hatters, weavers, woolcombers, curriers, brushmakers, millwrights, compositors, papermakers and calico printers. It has been estimated that by 1800 there were substantial inter-town contacts of this type in at least seventeen trades, and by 1820 in at least twenty-eight trades. Though some networks did spread as far as Ireland, especially in the case of the printing and bookbinding trades, the tramping system was focused mainly in England, for it was not until the late nineteenth century that there were more than scattered pockets of craftsmen in Wales, and the Scottish craftsmen tended to take their unemployment benefit at home. The administrative requirements of effectively managing the tramping system soon led to increasingly elaborate inter-club coordination: for example, the organization of clubs into 'divisions', the issuing of a common rule book, the establishment of a headquarters branch, the 'equalization' of funds between branches to ensure the universal operation of the system, and the calling of periodic meetings of local representatives. Thus it was out of the age-old system of travelling in search of work that the notion of wider regional or even national 'unions' of the craftsmen's trade clubs began to emerge in the early nineteenth century, and for these workers the word 'union' therefore implied not so much a submersion of individuals within a collective mass as a federation of already existing societies which had strong traditions of local self-government.

3

Problems of Organization among the Process Workers

In 1818 we turned out, among the rest of our fellow-spinners of this town [Manchester], for an advance of wages, which had been previously promised to us. During the continuance of the struggle, it pleased Mr Peter Ewart, and some of his minions, to charge us with being present at *but not taking part in*, an affray, when some 'knobsticks' were forcibly prevented from going to work in his mill at the reduced rate of wages; and on this charge, we were sentenced . . . under the late combination laws . . . for merely being present at a slight disturbance, in which not the slightest injury was done to any living creature.[1]

The author of this account, John Doherty, was later to become one of the most prominent leaders of early-nineteenth-century Lancashire trade unionism, but at this time had only recently arrived from Ireland to work as a cotton spinner and his involvement in this strike was to lead to a number of years in prison. The root cause of the dispute and the way in which it was conducted was the increasingly sharp polarization between employers and workers in the industry. As Doherty recalled of his early experiences in the cotton mills:

We have ourselves felt the full force and severity of the system in its worst days; we have been subject to all the petty tyranny and vulgar arrogance which insolence, ignorance and cupidity combined could practice or assume. We are practically acquainted with all the vexatious restrictions and illegal exactions which are constantly practised upon the poor, the feeble, and defenceless operative. We know what it is to be victims of robbery which we have so feebly, we fear, attempted to describe and denounce. We have been shut up as prisoners in the 'hellish and stinking and health-destroying bastiles', to unremitting toil while our ears have been stunned and our understanding insulted by the fraudulent and empty boast of the 'blessings of free labour'! We have seen men so terrified at the casual approach of an employer, as to drop down speechless, and almost lifeless, and others stand motionless and petrified, lest they should incur his displeasure. While all these things are fresh in our recollection, it is impossible we could speak with calmness and temper of the system.[2]

As the 1818 dispute developed it became increasingly violent. At the beginning of July the Manchester spinners considered that the time had come to demand the restoration of an earlier wage reduction which had been promised by the masters and that, as food prices were now rising sharply, they had no alternative but to strike when this was refused. They organized an effective town meeting, with two representatives from each mill electing an executive committee of twelve to oversee the distribution of the strike fund and the organization of picketing. Despite financial support, not only from spinners in the surrounding towns who were still at work, but also from other trades throughout the country, the large number of strikers involved meant that the amount of relief available was less than 1s. a week for each spinner, with nothing at all for their assistants who were also deprived of earnings by the dispute. The situation was made even worse when their treasurer ran off with over £150 from the common fund. Thus when, under pressure from the Home Office, which was concerned about the possibility of widespread political unrest, the masters declared their mills reopened at the end of August, many of the men were desperate to return to work. Inevitably this led to conflict with those who wished to stay out on strike, leading to a number of incidents involving the reading of the riot act, the intervention of the military, and finally, again under Home Office pressure, the arrest of the strike leaders by the local magistrates. Under such concerted pressure from the employers and the state, the spinners were forced to return to work at their old rates early in September.

Doherty himself played a leading role in the attempted intimidation of 'knobsticks' or 'blacklegs' by the assembly and parading of pickets outside the mills, this generally being carried out by men from other factories so that they could not be identified by the master concerned. However, the masters counteracted this by turning up together at certain mills to identify the pickets, and it was this method that led to Doherty's detention under dramatic circumstances: a crowd of several thousand attempted to free him from his initial arrest, the constable had to take refuge inside the mill with his prisoner and then be rescued by the intervention of a company of the 95th Regiment, and the day was capped off with a minor riot outside the prison to which Doherty had been taken. Along with two other spinners arrested during the disturbances around the reopening of the mills, Doherty was eventually tried for conspiracy in January 1819, found guilty and sentenced to several years' imprisonment with hard labour in Lancaster castle. Here he was supported by the activities of a relief fund which provided him with books, paper and pens, and small sums of cash, and he later wrote to the local members:

I owe you a debt of gratitude, which, I am afraid I shall never be able to repay. The support which you so generously gave me, whilst inured in a dungeon for two long years, has made an impression on my heart, which nothing can erase while that heart remains warm. None of you can know, who have not experienced the same hardship, the value of that support, under such circumstances.[3]

Otherwise, however, the industrial organization of the Manchester spinners was rendered largely ineffective for the next five years: around 250 other men had been blacklisted for their activities, the funds had been depleted by the strike and the ensuing trials, and while the organizing committee had eventually been released without trial, this had been in return for abject submissions and sureties of £100 each. On his own release from prison, Doherty was able to find work again despite his reputation: he played a significant role in the revival of the Manchester spinners' union around the time of the repeal of the combination laws in 1825 and served as its secretary in 1828–30 and again in 1834–6. The celebrity he had acquired through his imprisonment also allowed him eventually to set up as a small printer and bookseller and to become increasingly prominent in wider movements, including those for factory legislation and parliamentary reform.

This first-hand account of early-nineteenth-century conflict in the cotton industry suggests much about the distinctive experience of the rapidly growing numbers of workers in the factories and mines of the new industrial districts. In the first place, their working conditions were significantly more brutalizing than those of most of the skilled craftsmen: they were confined for long hours in noisy and dangerous situations, they were often subjected to tyrannical supervision, and many of them were recent rural migrants, often from Ireland, and thus especially frightened and vulnerable. Moreover, instead of scattered small workshops with the possibility of the men moving between towns, shifting between trades, or even becoming small masters themselves, the new industries were throwing up larger workplaces in what were virtually single-trade districts with fluctuations in employment affecting all the towns at the same time, and virtually no possibility of the men acquiring the amount of capital required to set up in business for themselves. There was, therefore, no solution for the men in mobility or advancement, no bond of common experience between men and masters, and little room for peaceful negotiations based on a shared sense of independence and mutual respect. The men responded by building the widest possible organizations and mounting district-wide strikes, sometimes even supported by financial donations from other areas. The masters responded by coordinating their own activities, trying to divide their opponents and using whatever coercive tools were available, including the local magistrates and police, and sometimes even the army. Thus, finally, the government was more likely to become involved in disputes in these industries, for there were rapidly escalating incidents of violence among large populations concentrated in new areas of settlement, and fears that this might spill over into wider political unrest.

This confrontational, even military, quality of many of the disputes in the new industrial districts does not, however, mean that they were examples of revolutionary class struggle. On the contrary, the demands which lay behind them were simply for higher wages and better working conditions, the workers' organizations were still restricted to particular occupations, and their effectiveness was still severely limited by a number of problems which arose out of the nature of the work involved. As industries processing a single raw material, mainly cotton or coal, they tended to be located near the sources of that material and the power required, and also to employ a range of workers of varying levels of skill on closely adjacent aspects of the processes involved. This led to a marked concentration of workers within localities in which organizing strikes meant finding financial support for very large numbers, and any uncertainty about this in the course of a long dispute was likely to lead to a drift back to work. It also led to the most skilled workers being vulnerable to replacement by their assistants or ancillary workers who had been able to observe them at work for some time. The skilled workers in the new industrial districts were thus faced with two serious challenges which had to be overcome if they were to realize the potential of their bargaining position: effective coordination of wide organizations, and the inclusion of less skilled workers within them. In the absence of solutions to these problems they would always be vulnerable to substitute labour, either from among their own number or from neighbouring groups. It was this problem which lay behind most of the violence in these industries: the local police and the army may have moved in to maintain order, but the initial physical conflicts were usually not between men and masters but rather between men who wanted to strike and men who wanted to work.

THE CHALLENGE OF ORGANIZATION

The textile spinners had a relatively easy transition to the new factory system. Neither the increasing concentration on cotton nor the sequence of eighteenth-century mechanical innovations, culminating in a machine known as the 'mule' because of its combination of a number of earlier improvements, led to any reduction in the need for skill or strength. Indeed, if anything the larger machines and longer hours required more attention and endurance. Even when the factory owners, frustrated by their continued dependence on skilled manual labour, began to pursue further steps towards automation from the 1820s, the resulting 'self-acting' mule still required considerable atten-tion, was only really suitable for the coarser yarns, and even on these was only introduced slowly. Thus from the late eighteenth century onwards cotton spinning was increasingly the preserve of adult men with skill, stamina and experience who recruited and paid their assis-tants, usually from among their own children and relatives, to 'piece' the broken threads, replace the spindles and keep the machinery and the work area clean. Their closest assistants were the 'piecers': the 'big piecer', who was a teenager picking up the skilled work, able to take the spinner's place when necessary, and looking forward to advancing to fully skilled status when he came of age; and the 'small piecers', who were children waiting to advance to big-piecer status in due course. The spinners and their assistants therefore comprised a tightly bonded work group on which the mills were completely dependent for their operation. Potentially this gave them a very strong bargaining position, but the work group was not without its ambiguities. On the one hand, its younger members were kept in check by the expectation of promotion in due order of seniority; on the other, being well acquainted with the work of the adult men, they made up a large and threatening pool of replacement labour. Something of this problem can be appreciated from the size and composition of the workforce. The typical cotton mill employed between 200 and 500 people, and this branch of the industry had over 100,000 workers by 1815, both of which would seem to have made it a fertile breeding ground for workers' organization: however, only around 10 per cent of these people would have been skilled adult spinners. A similar ambiguity can be found in the development of the typical settlements. On the one hand, the mills were moving from isolated rural locations near sources of water power and dominated by a single employer who usually provided the housing, to urban centres using steam power where workers found their own accommodation and were becoming increasingly independent. However, on the other hand, the workforce was growing very rapidly on the basis of rural migrants with low levels of literacy and little tradition of organization.

Early organization among the spinners had a tendency towards exclusiveness, perhaps in imitation of local craftsmen's clubs: there were attempts to organize closed shops of society members, to work only under conditions approved of by the society, and to provide substantial welfare benefits to members. The spinners were then able to use the tighter labour market and higher demand for their product during the two decades of the French Wars from 1793 to 1815 to establish town-wide organizations from which they never retreated even if their effectiveness varied between periods. Given the large numbers of men employed in each workplace, there was a tendency for these unions to be based on representative democracy rather than universal participation: delegates were sent to town meetings and then, to preserve secrecy in a period when striking was illegal, even smaller executive committees were elected. The first friendly societies among the Lancashire factory spinners were recorded in 1792 in Manchester and Stockport, also taking an active interest in trade matters: the Manchester spinners were successful in striking for higher wages in 1795, 1802 and 1813; while the spinners in Stockport, Bolton and Preston were able to catch up in 1813–14. Similarly in the west of Scotland the Glasgow Operative Cotton Spinners began to organize in the early 1800s with a more explicit emphasis on the control of working conditions and the establishment of a local closed shop, which was said to be in operation by 1810. The wartime expansion of the industry also encouraged attempts to establish links between the factory towns within each region, which was harder than might at first be imagined, for these areas encompassed a wide range of conditions in coarse-, medium- and fine-spinning towns, as well as strongly felt local loyalties. Nevertheless, in Lancashire a General Union was initiated by the Manchester spinners in 1810 with the aim of protecting their own higher wages by bringing the country districts up to the same level, and the 'rolling strike' was pioneered in the summer of that year, during which each district took it in turn to come out with financial support from those still at work. However, this tactic was defeated by a sudden trade depression and coordination among the masters to lock out the working districts, thus cutting off the flow of funds, forcing the men back, and undermining the wider federation.

Under normal peacetime conditions the spinners were unable to make much progress in the early nineteenth century. In both Lancashire and the west of Scotland they struggled stubbornly against wage cuts in the aftermath of the Napoleonic Wars, but the early 1820s saw a rash of town-wide strikes ending in defeat as the employers were able to find willing replacement workers even in the face of violent picketing action, and the self-discipline required to organize regional rolling strikes was absent in the face of imminent wage reductions. As Doherty observed acutely in 1829 during the next major attempt to construct a wider organization:

... the one great error of the former union which had been established in England was, that all were at liberty to turn out, if a reduction was offered to them. It certainly must be mortifying to men to be obliged to submit to a reduction, more especially while they were in the act of subscribing to uphold others against the same evil. But, painful as it would be, he was well convinced that if men were to come out, district after district, even against reductions, they would soon be overwhelmed with the number they would have to support.[4]

This experience of a strong wartime bargaining position, followed by increasing ineffectiveness and frustration in peacetime, led some of the spinners' leaders to take an active interest in even wider organizational links. The Manchester spinners seem to have been particularly interested in this, beginning with their strike in 1818 when they tried to set up a supportive network called the Philanthropic Society, aiming to attract all the trades in Lancashire into a common strike fund with a small weekly subscription and a federal executive committee. Contacts were soon established as far away as Liverpool, Birmingham, Nottingham and even London, where it stimulated John Gast's formation of the parallel Philanthropic Hercules. However, impressive as these early national links were, they were largely restricted to providing financial support for the Manchester strike and once that had been defeated the wider network also collapsed. A similar pattern was repeated during the wave of strikes after the repeal of the combination laws in 1824, though this time in reverse as the Manchester spinners, with John Doherty now in a leading role, attempted to provide support for other groups of workers. For example, delegates were sent to support the spinners in Glasgow during a district strike there, with £142 and a proposal for a national union of cotton spinners and a permanent strike fund. However, even this focus on building wider organization in one occupation soon foundered on regional differences when a public meeting of the Manchester spinners made it clear that the leadership had acted ahead of its local members, and neither the aims of the Glasgow strike nor their own delegates' actions had found general approval. The challenge of organization among the spinners had still to be met successfully, but the potential, the determination and the willingness to learn from experience were all clearly evident in the first decades of the nineteenth century.

The textile weavers experienced a much more traumatic transition to the new factory system due to the late mechanization of their branch of the industry, as a result of which there was an enormous expansion and then a sharp contraction in handloom work. As technical innovation in cotton spinning saw a surplus of lower-cost yarn from the 1770s, there was initially a high demand and a willingness to pay for the skills of the handloom weavers. This led to a shift of the bulk of cotton weaving away from its traditional rural locations, where incomes had been supplemented by seasonal agricultural pursuits, towards the new industrial towns, where high levels of immigration led to an expansion of the number of weavers. Moreover, higher levels of pay led to the brief flourishing of an independent culture in the late eighteenth century, with impressive levels of literacy and, particularly in the west of Scotland, individual cases of real poetic achievement. However, in the medium term the handloom weavers' position was vulnerable to the over-stocking of the labour market as levels of rural migration into the towns remained high during the French Wars, the newcomers were increasingly prepared to take lower wages and part-time work, and the labour market was then flooded with demobilized soldiers in 1815: all this leading to a workforce of over 200,000 at its peak in the early nineteenth century. This was possible first because the basic operations of plain cotton weaving could be picked up in three to six weeks, and could be carried out efficiently by women and children as well as by adult men; and second because it was virtually impossible to exercise effective labour-market controls in a home-working trade, in which both the small employers and the weavers themselves were engaged in an increasingly intense competition for work. In this period the handloom weavers' position was maintained to a degree by the employment of other family members to maintain total household incomes; however, in the longer term it was quite untenable as by the 1820s, after many years of experimentation, power-driven machines were developed which were up to four times more efficient than handlooms, were capable of producing better quality cloth, and could be operated by young women and children. Thus after the trade depression of 1826 the cotton handloom weavers entered a terminal decline and were absorbed into the new mills, shifted into the handloom weaving of more specialized textiles, or found other employment in the expanding industrial districts.

The initial strength and independence of the handloom weavers was particularly marked in the west of Scotland, where there is evidence of local food-retailing cooperatives and defensive action to protect wages as early as the 1750s to 1760s, an attempt to form a regional association as early as the 1780s, and a dense network of local friendly societies offering generous benefits and able to support large-scale industrial action in the 1800s. Similarly in Lancashire the handloom weavers were prominent in the explosion of local friendly societies after the enabling act of 1793, and these provided financial backing for industrial action with particular centres of strength in Manchester, Bolton and Stockport, where there were large regional strikes for wage increases in 1808 and 1818. However, after the end of the French Wars the handloom weavers became increasingly dependent and disorganized: the dispersal of ever-increasing numbers in their own homes and small workshops made it difficult to coordinate activity, and their earnings were becoming too low to permit the funding of effective societies or strikes. In Manchester repeated attempts to form an open union after the repeal of the combination laws in 1824 all failed; and in Glasgow, although the weavers were initially more successful in rebuilding their organization during this revival in union activity, they were defeated in a wage strike in 1825, their union was broken up in 1829, and their fresh attempts at organization in the early 1830s were equally short-lived. Unfortunately, as increasingly poorly paid and casual workers, the handloom weavers soon found themselves being tempted into acting as strike-breakers in other branches of textiles, and thus became increasingly isolated from the trade-union networks developing in their regions.

The underground workers in the coal industry were engaged in one of the most demanding tasks to be performed by large numbers of people in modern Britain. The central figures were the adult male colliers or hewers, whose work had hardly changed since the earliest times: it required highly physical but also skilful labour to get the coal down from the face in cramped, dusty and often life-threatening conditions, which created deep feelings of interdependence and mutual respect among the men involved. Thus, in a parallel to the cotton spinners, the coal hewers comprised a tightly knit occupational group on which the mines were completely dependent for their operation, with the additional advantage in this case of being able to meet in secret in their underground workplaces. Potentially this gave them a very strong bargaining position, but it was not an unassailable one, for there was a range of other underground tasks, from opening and closing the ventilation doors, through loading and hauling the wagons to the pit bottom, to maintaining the roadways and passages. Known as 'oncost' work, this was carried out by two distinct groups. First by the sons of hewers who entered the pits at around the age of eight as 'trappers' on the ventilation doors, and were gradually promoted over the next twelve years through various aspects of haulage work, to end eventually at the coal face itself. And second by some men, and in the older fields occasionally still some women, who were restricted to the ancillary tasks either because they had aged or because they had entered the mines as adults and consequently were regarded as less skilled. Both types of oncost workers were familiar with underground conditions and made up a threatening pool of replacement labour, something of the scale of which can be appreciated from the size and composition of the workforce. In the smaller pits, employing under twenty people, the hewers carried out much of their own oncost work; however, in the larger pits, employing 200 to 500 people, where the potential for hewers' organization was greater, their proportion could fall to as little as a third of those underground. The industry as a whole was employing around 50,000 workers by 1800 but, taking account of both oncost and surface workers, the hewers probably accounted for only around 25 per cent of these people. Because of this relatively restricted supply of fully experienced underground workers, the employers used various forms of constraint to secure an adequate labour force, their most-favoured device being the long-term contract, or 'bond', of at least a year, which could be enforced in law and could be reinforced by the provision of company housing and credit in company shops. And they also tried to restrict labour mobility by insisting that applicants for jobs should present 'discharge notes' indicating their previous employer's permission to leave. However, these were far from perfect methods of control: the signing of the annual bond soon became an occasion for collective bargaining and demands for bonuses, and the discharge notes tended to become ineffective whenever sharp increases in the demand for labour revived the competition between individual employers. Further ambiguities in the position of the coal miners can be found in the development of the industry's settlements. On the one hand, they were often isolated from other groups in semi-rural locations, and always brought together around each pit where common employment, residence, religion and perhaps above all the dangerous conditions of work created a close family-like atmosphere. However, on the other hand, their wider organization was quite seriously inhibited by their dispersal across a multitude of pits in which working conditions varied enormously, not only between but also within coalfields.

Again in parallel to the spinners, early organization among the hewers had a tendency towards exclusiveness: they set a minimum starting age for miners' sons, imposed high fees and minimum training periods on new adult entrants, and aimed to provide generous welfare benefits. Indeed, among the Scottish hewers these practices were underwritten by oaths and rituals showing strong signs of Masonic influence. As the demand for coal for other industries increased in the eighteenth century, the bargaining position of the hewers began to grow as the employers competed for their labour: particularly during the French Wars a rapid increase in output and a marked shortage of labour led to an equally marked increase in miners' wages, accompanied by an increase in pit-level organization and strike action throughout the coalfields. In Lancashire and Yorkshire the enabling legislation of 1793 encouraged the formation of numerous miners' friendly societies, no doubt functioning from time to time as fronts for illegal strike action. In Scotland the unions seem to have been more open and the employers responded by reforming their unpopular system of lifetime bonds, enforced by Acts of Parliament dating back to 1606, with a bill which was intended simultaneously to attract an influx of new labour and impose new statutory regulation of wages and enforcement of the discharge note. However, the restrictive clauses were removed under the combined pressure of the miners and the employers in the expanding districts, and the legislation of 1799 became known in the Scottish pits as the 'Emancipation Act'.

Under normal peacetime conditions the hewers were put on the defensive by recurrent employers' pressure for wage reductions. This provoked stiff resistance and an increase in wider organization, with the large numbers of men involved leading to the early adoption of representative democracy: delegates were sent from each pit to meetings of county associations, and there is evidence of coordinated activity between counties early in the nineteenth century. However, these initial attempts at wider trade unionism were undermined by two main problems: first, the variations in conditions between pits, and second, the ready availability of substitute labour. For example, strikes against wage cuts in Scotland in 1817–18 were successful in Lanarkshire but failed in Ayrshire. Then there was a resurgence of organization throughout the coalfields following the repeal of the combination laws in 1824, during which the Scottish miners began to establish links of mutual financial support between the western and eastern coalfields, and both the Scottish and the Lancashire miners made pioneering attempts at the coordinated restriction of output to reduce the reserve stocks of coal. However, the employers were still able to achieve repeated victories by simply replacing their hewers with other underground workers, and there were as yet no signs of any major figures on the miners' side with a clear understanding of their problems of organization.

Given the traumatic disappearance of the handloom weavers under the combined impact of an over-stocked labour market and late mechanization, the process industries came increasingly to be dominated by employment based on seniority. Thus in both cotton and coal, teenagers began as ancillary workers and assistants, gradually picked up the necessary skills through close association with the older men, and constituted a large reserve army available for recruitment. However, though the spinners and the hewers were making real efforts to establish wider district organizations and even experimenting with sketchy national coordination, they still made no attempt to organize the less skilled workers near at hand. Their collective bargaining position thus remained distinctly fragile, with every advance in periods of prosperity being liable to a sharp reversal as soon as markets turned down, and they therefore began to look for other methods of defending themselves.

PROTECTIVE LEGISLATION

The increase in the spinners' bargaining power during the long period of the French Wars was accompanied by the emergence of an interest in securing favourable parliamentary legislation. The first Short-Time Committee was recorded in Manchester in 1814 as an offshoot of trade-union organization, launching a campaign to limit the hours of work of children in the mills. Though the union's ulterior motive was to pave the way for a limitation of hours for the adult spinners as well, the humanitarian appeal of the focus on children was hard to resist and the campaign received the support of some leading local employers. Sir Robert Peel in particular introduced a bill into the House of Commons in 1815 to limit hours for those under eighteen, and this was eventually passed in an amended form in 1819. However, while this first factory act prohibited the employment of all children under nine, it only limited the hours of those under sixteen to twelve a day and was not very effectively enforced. A further campaign during the revival of trade-union activity in 1824–5 led to a slight improvement in the 1825 Factory Act, reducing the nominal upper limit by half an hour a day.

Meanwhile the pressures of sharp fluctuations in employment led the handloom weavers to launch a parallel movement for protective legislation. In 1799 the Lancashire weavers petitioned for a statutory minimum wage along the lines of their colleagues in the Spitalfields silk industry, arguing in an 'Address to the Public' that:

It is vain to talk of bad trade, for if goods are actually not wanted they cannot be sold at any price; if wanted, twopence or threepence per yard will not stop the buyer; and whether does it appear more reasonable that twopence or threepence per yard should be laid on the consumer or taken from the labourer? A single twopence per yard would increase wages from eleven to twenty-one shillings . . . consider how little it would affect the one, and how important to the other. How impressed with gratitude must that man be with five or six small children when informed that Government has devised certain measures, that where he now received only eleven shillings he might receive about twenty shillings for his work.[5]

55

Although this widespread agitation formed part of the background to the passing of the 1799 general Combination Act to restrict strike action, the government was not totally unsympathetic to the weavers' economic plight and also passed a special act in 1800 permitting the use of arbitrators in disputes over cotton workers' wages. However, this attempt to resolve the problem proved rather ineffective, as the employers tended to evade the act by appointing arbitrators too far away to be consulted, while for their part the weavers began to coordinate their recourse to arbitration to establish standard regional wage rates: it was therefore amended in 1804 to reintroduce the previous powers of the local magistrates. In the face of the employers' resistance to any legislation, the survival of the Arbitration Act even in this truncated form was a testimony to the wartime strength of the weavers, and they then went on to revive their petitioning for a statutory minimum wage, only to be turned down by Parliament in 1808 and again in 1811.

The initiative then passed to Scotland, where the previous setbacks led to ever more determined organization. Having formed a federation based in Glasgow, the handloom weavers first attempted to secure local government intervention to regulate wages and then, advised and represented by the outstanding Whig lawyer Henry Cockburn, they mounted a successful legal action in the Glasgow courts in 1812. The local magistrates decided that their wage demands were reasonable, and the Scottish appeal court confirmed the magistrates' powers to fix wages, but failed to include any compelling clauses: as a result the employers concerned continued to pay the old rates and this provoked a Scotland-wide strike of up to 40,000 men over three months in pursuit of what they regarded as their legal rights. The effectiveness of the weavers' organization allowed them to conduct the strike with the minimum of intimidation and it ended peacefully when their funds ran out; however, in a further court case fourteen of their leaders were given prison sentences under a rather confusing interpretation of Scottish common law to render simple combination illegal. Moreover, in order to forestall any further challenges through the courts, the old statutory framework was completely repealed by Parliament in 1813. Thus despite their best efforts the weavers' assertive campaign for protective legislation was completely defeated, and this demoralizing result was soon underlined by the onset of the crisis of over-supply in their labour market caused by post-war demobilization in 1815.

Thereafter, the handloom weavers' pressure for protective legislation had an increasingly futile quality about it, and particularly after the introduction of the power-loom in the 1820s they came to be seen more as an object of public concern and charity than as a group of independently organized workers. The Lancashire weavers had a powerful champion in the radical MP for Oldham, John Fielden, the Scottish weavers had their equivalent in the Whig family of the Maxwells of Pollok, and they began to press for local 'boards of trade' to fix minimum wages by agreement between a majority of employers and workers. However, though two sympathetic inquiries were eventually secured in 1834–5 and 1837–41, Parliament's conclusion was that the economic position of the cotton handloom weavers was irretrievable and that they had better look for employment elsewhere.

The war years had also led to pressure for legislative protection among the woollen workers, arising in particular from the Peace of Amiens in 1802, which temporarily reduced the military demand for cloth and released large numbers of soldiers into the labour market. A Woollen Cloth Weavers' Society was set up in Gloucestershire to pursue large numbers of cases against 'illegal' men under the apprenticeship clause of the Statute of Artificers. However, this only provoked the counter-organization of the master clothiers, who successfully petitioned Parliament for the annual suspension of the statute as applied to the wool trade from 1803 until its final abolition for that trade in 1809, five years before the general repeal. Other frustrated groups among the textile workers included the Lancashire calico printers, too recent a trade to have been included in the old statute, who campaigned unsuccessfully for inclusion; and the east Midlands hosiery and lace workers, who petitioned unsuccessfully for parliamentary regulation in 1811 and 1812.

Given the problems the process workers faced in establishing an effective collective bargaining position, campaigning for protective legislation was an obvious alternative form of activity. The cotton spinners achieved a degree of success by focusing on the issue of child labour, securing the support of some employers and creating a new humanitarian consensus among the country's legislators. In some contrast, the older textile trades were consistently frustrated in their attempts to revive neglected regulatory statutes, and indeed by reminding Parliament of their existence only speeded up their repeal. This failure then led to their increasing adoption of a third and more desperate form of activity: direct physical coercion.

INTIMIDATION AND VIOLENCE

In considering the widespread use of coercive tactics by workers during industrial disputes in this period it is important to distinguish between three main types of activity. In the first place, there was the destruction of manufacturing equipment as a result of clear opposition to technical innovation: this would be the classic type of hostile 'machine-breaking'. In the second place, there were actions taken against manufacturing equipment or other workers during strikes for improved wages and conditions: this would include both the interference with equipment to render it unusable, which might extend into permanent destruction in some cases, and the interference with substitute labour through picketing. In the third place, there were assaults on persons or property arising in the heat of industrial disputes, which moved out of the area of intimidation and into that of criminal violence. The first two of these types of activity had significant precursors in the rights of the guilds to seize and destroy 'deceitful' goods and to enforce the closed shop through the search for and expulsion of 'illegal' men, and this may have contributed to the feelings about their legitimacy among many groups of workers in this period. However, despite the widespread assumption that popular resistance to industrialization was common, clear-cut examples of hostile machine-breaking were comparatively rare. It can be found in many scattered local cases of initial resistance to new equipment before it had been explained and the terms of its operation agreed upon, but some of the more serious cases turn out on closer examination to have been examples of temporary interference in the course of strikes over wages and hours.

As already described above, the cotton spinners depended heavily on picketing against 'knobsticks' or 'blacklegs' during strikes, which tended to turn increasingly violent when it became clear that defeat was imminent. Meanwhile, strikes among the miners were occasionally pursued through interference with vulnerable pit-head equipment, particularly winding gear and pumping engines, but the most common form of coercion was intimidation by large assemblies of men, both to bring neighbouring pits out on strike and to prevent the importation of substitute labour.

Among the cotton weavers there was a stronger tradition of industrial sabotage, beginning with temporary interference but turning towards more hostile machine-breaking as the spread of power-looms made their position increasingly desperate in the early nineteenth century. In Glasgow in 1787 the handloom weavers unsuccessfully attempted to resist wage reductions by cutting the webs from the looms of non-strikers and burning the warehouse stock of their employers. Similarly, during the Lancashire dispute in 1808 they sabotaged the looms of non-strikers by removing the shuttles, and there were incidents of mill-burnings with overtones of hostility against power-looms in Manchester in 1792 and in Bolton and Stockport in 1812. However, it was not until April 1826 that the position of the weavers in the smaller north Lancashire towns had deteriorated so much that they engaged in a three-day outburst of clearly hostile machine-breaking against the power-looms, including rioting and leading to military intervention, ten transportations and thirty-three jail sentences.

Among the wool workers in the west of England there were also protests against new machinery in the middle of the 1770s and again in the early 1790s, but these were soon overcome by negotiations and the expansion of production, especially during the French Wars. As a result the 'Wiltshire Outrages' of 1802 mainly involved intimidation of non-strikers and assaults on employers' property during disputes over wages and hours, escalating into personal attacks only after the employers themselves had resorted to violence. Meanwhile in Belfast the actions of the muslin weavers in the downturn after 1815 fell into the more brutal pattern of Irish industrial relations when protests against wage cuts led to attempts to set fire to the house of one of the employers, in turn resulting in two hangings, two public floggings, a transportation and soon afterwards the shooting of the union's president, allegedly by a local employer.

Undoubtedly the most famous case of physical coercion during industrial disputes in this period was 'Luddism', an intense wave of activity in 1811–12, so-called after the widespread use of threatening letters to employers signed by the invented character 'Ned Ludd', or sometimes 'General Ludd'. It attracted a great deal of attention at the time because this suggested underground coordination and was combined with a parallel wave of food rioting in the north and Midlands, leading to fears of uncontrollable popular unrest in the middle of the French Wars and a large-scale, though not very effective, mobilization of the army to maintain domestic law and order. Something of this combination of circumstances, and the escalation of feelings as the protest was repressed, can be seen in the following extract from a letter sent by General Ludd to the Prime Minister in February 1812:

That in consequence of the great sufferings of the Poor – whose grievances seem not to be taken *into the least consideration by government*, I shall be under the necessity of again calling into action (not to destroy many more frames) but —— —— my brave Sons of Shirewood [*sic*] who are determined and sworn to be true and faithful avengers of their and Country's wrongs. I have waited patiently to see if any measures were likely to be adopted by Parliament to alleviate distress in any shape whatever; but that hand of conciliation is shut and my poor Suffering Country is left without a ray of hope: The Bill for Punishing with death has only to be viewed with contempt and opposed by measures equally strong; and the Gentlemen who framed it will have to repent the act: for if one man's life is sacrificed !blood for !blood.[6]

Exaggerated threats and reactions aside, the extent of the industrial sabotage was impressive: it began in 1811 in the Nottinghamshire hosiery industry, where 1,000 stocking-frames were reckoned to have been destroyed, and it spread first to the Nottinghamshire lace industry, and then in 1812 to the West Riding of Yorkshire woollen industry, where the workers broke shearing-frames and set fire to mills. Clearly each of these actions required a good deal of local organization and the spread of common tactics implied some coordination between districts, even if only of an informal and occasional kind. However, that should not obscure the presence of a number of different occupational grievances sparked into simultaneous outbreaks by the conjunction of high wartime food prices and a temporary disruption of manufacturing exports which had led to widespread wage reductions. The Nottinghamshire hosiery and lace workers were in situations similar to the contemporary handloom weavers: relatively easily learned trades using traditional methods combined with over-stocked labour markets and declining bargaining power, leading to workers' interference with manufacturing equipment during disputes over wages. The Yorkshire woollen workers, on the other hand, had more in common with the handloom weavers' later behaviour in the 1820s, for here the finishing workers, or 'croppers', were genuinely hostile to technical innovation. Indeed they had organized trade-union resistance to it for some time and where that had been most successful, as in Leeds, there was little Luddite activity in 1812. Thus the hostile machine-breaking was concentrated in the remoter rural areas where the croppers' previous resistance had been least effective, and it spilled over into criminal assaults only after one employer's defence of his mill led to the deaths of two of the protesters.

Among those working in agriculture, violence had been in evidence in Scotland as early as 1724 when small tenants in the south-west, building on the strong local tradition of the Covenanters' revolt against state interference in religious life, had attacked the property and cattle of their landowners in the course of a campaign for the 'levelling' of rents. However, this had been a brief and isolated event and it was not until the early nineteenth century that rural intimidation became more endemic as well as increasingly focused among the agricultural labourers. The Napoleonic Wars led to rapidly rising food prices, the extensive cultivation of marginal lands, labour shortages and rising wages; all, however, sharply reversed when the wars ended, wartime over-production led to rapidly falling prices, and over 300,000 discharged soldiers came on to the labour market. Discontent over wage cuts focused on the new threshing machines, which were seen as causing higher levels of winter unemployment in the cereal-growing regions, leading to incidents of protest against them in East Anglia in 1816 and 1822, and finally to an intense wave of wage demands and hostile machine-breaking which started in Kent in 1830 and spread throughout the southern counties of England over the course of the next three months. These riots were named after the invented character 'Captain Swing', who appeared widely as the signatory of threatening letters to employers, and, though there was as little formal coordination of the movement and as much local diversity of grievances as there had been in the case of 'General Ludd', their rural location led to a significantly more severe repression: 2,000 arrests leading to nineteen executions, 500 transportations, and over 600 imprisonments. This then provoked a turn towards criminal violence among the understandably resentful labourers, particularly in the form of arson and sheep-stealing, which was to last for many years, especially in the counties of East Anglia.

Taking all these cases together, it would seem that major outbreaks of hostile machine-breaking were confined to three cases: the Yorkshire wool croppers in 1812, the Lancashire cotton handloom weavers in 1826, and the southern agricultural labourers in 1830. Moreover, given the concentration of the first two of these cases in the smaller outlying country towns, it would also appear that violent opposition to technical innovation was confined to declining occupations in rural districts. After all, machinery rarely leads to net reductions in either skill or labour requirements: it usually replaces manual rather than mental labour in the processes concerned and it is generally introduced during expansions in production which simultaneously absorb any temporarily displaced workers. Thus, though individuals might experience uncertainty and disruption, organized groups of workers rarely oppose the introduction of labour-saving machinery in principle, though of course they are always concerned about the wages and hours involved in its operation. The exception to this rule in early-nineteenth-century Britain seems to have been in rural areas, where isolation and lack of alternative employment opportunities weakened the workers' collective bargaining position and led on occasion to unusually desperate resistance to innovation.

If there were fewer serious cases of hostile machine-breaking in these years than is often thought, then perhaps there was also more continuity in trade-union methods among the process workers than is often assumed. As their workplaces became more sophisticated and more enclosed, interference with industrial equipment in the course of disputes may have become more difficult, but the use of picketing against substitute labour remained a key tactic during strikes. Such cases then had the potential to spill over into incidents of criminal assault, especially when the employers were prepared to sanction the use of force themselves. Thus the seniority unions remained concerned about the legal definition of acceptable behaviour during picketing and increasingly attempted to restrain their own members during disputes, in order to avoid the tarnishing of their public image which could occur so easily as a result of incidents involving criminal violence.

4

Trade Unionists and Extra-parliamentary Radicalism

It appeared to him that Sir Samuel Romilly was not only entitled to support of the opulent, but, perhaps in a more peculiar degree, to the support of the poor and working classes of the freemen, inasmuch as he had always been the advocate of humanity, the friend of his country, and, as he conceived, the true friend of the working classes. While the system of the present Ministers was extending pauperism all over the land, he thought the honest and able exertions of such men as Sir Samuel could alone check so destructive a system. He himself had left Bristol at a very early age, to seek a residence where he could be free from oppression, and where he could better encourage the generous feelings which he thought became a free-born Englishman.[1]

When he made this speech in 1812 John Gast was already forty years old and established as a leading figure among the London shipwrights, in which role he was to become increasingly prominent in wider radical politics over the next two decades. There is evidence that he had already been a regular reader for several years of the *Independent Whig*, the main radical paper of the day, which stood for the tradition of the 'Glorious Revolution' of 1688, above all individual liberty, and for its extension through the abolition of slavery, Irish emancipation, and further instalments of parliamentary and legal reform. Because Gast had served his apprenticeship in Bristol he was entitled to vote as a 'freeman' in the general election for the two seats there in 1812, and because of his radical convictions he played an important role in organizing London residents in a similar position in support of the Whig gentleman Sir Samuel Romilly, who also had a significant following among the local craftsmen's clubs in Bristol, especially the carpenters. Once the election was under way a further candidate emerged in Henry Hunt, a local Whig brewer and supporter of more advanced proposals for parliamentary reform along the lines of the household suffrage, and there is evidence that both the London-based freemen electors and the Bristol craftsmen, while continuing to support Romilly, became particularly enthusiastic about Hunt. However, this joint ticket was defeated by a large majority, amid allegations from Hunt, supported by Gast, that their opponents had engaged in electoral corruption and intimidation to secure their victory.

Gast's next major political appearance was during the post-war unrest six years later, by which time Hunt was emerging as the leader of a radical movement which was becoming increasingly national and increasingly assertive: its demands now included manhood suffrage and the introduction of an income tax to replace taxes on consumption, and its methods now focused on mass demonstrations for these independent goals rather than merely responding to parliamentary proceedings and elections. In this context Gast became connected with a group of more extreme radicals around Dr James Watson, because it was through their network that he initially encountered delegates from the Lancashire spinners, leading to the establishment of the Philanthropic Hercules in London in 1818. Gast now placed a greater emphasis on the positive contribution of skilled workers as a significant social force and urged them to unite, not only through wider trade-union links but also through campaigns for political reform. For example, in his first major public speech, at a demonstration outside Westminster Hall in September 1818, he urged them to think more respectfully of themselves and to take a greater interest in politics:

Their highest interest was the examination of the conduct of the Government of the country, which took away half of the produce of their industry. Yet they rarely attended to this important object until the distress of the country excited them to think, and compelled them to feel. The change was fortunate, for the people now considered politics, upon which they were quite as competent to judge as those who presumed to regard themselves as the highest order. But why should any man of any mind shrink from forming an opinion upon political questions? For the great Locke had observed that political knowledge was nothing but the fruit of common sense applied to public affairs. This was the language of a genuine Englishman, who felt that all rational Englishmen could and should understand their public duties.[2]

John Gast's connections with the Watsonites were to continue for many years, despite their minority position and the notorious activities of another member of the group, Arthur Thistlewood, who led the 'Cato Street Conspiracy' to assassinate the government in 1820. However, Gast's own contributions usually seem to have been an emphasis on orderly behaviour and a talent for eye-catching symbolism at public demonstrations. Thus he went on to play a significant role in the massive response of Londoners during the 'Queen Caroline Affair' of 1820, and then to become a recognized leader of trade-union opinion during the repeal of the combination laws in 1824–5 and the first step towards wider parliamentary democracy in the 'Great Reform Act' of 1832.

This brief account of one individual's involvement in early-nineteenth-century politics touches on a number of important aspects of the relationship between trade unionists and popular radicalism. Perhaps one of the most obvious points is the shift taking place, away from an eighteenth-century pattern in which working men who were interested in political issues tended to act as supporters of Whigs and in response to processes occurring within the existing political system, towards a nineteenth-century pattern in which working men began to organize independent demonstrations to set the pace for fundamental reforms of that system. The connection between this shift in behaviour and the growth in the strength and confidence of the skilled unions during the French Wars will be clear, and this also produced a more advanced programme of manhood suffrage advocated in a language of increased self-respect. In this sense it can be said that the years after 1815 saw the emergence of a new type of radicalism which was to form the mainstream of trade-union involvement in politics for the next hundred years and more.

However, it is important not to overlook the important continuities which remained from the previous centuries. In the first place this political movement was based on alliances between distinct groups. Romilly may have been replaced by Hunt and moderate reform by assertive democracy, but radicalism still required cooperation with middle- and upper-class politicians active within the existing political system. Indeed the extra-parliamentary movement was itself made up of a range of factions with different priorities and a range of individuals from widely differing social backgrounds: Gast, the skilled worker with his emphasis on the power of peaceful demonstrations, was to be found alongside Watson, the medical doctor who hoped for a confrontation with the authorities, and Thistlewood, the gambler and common informer who favoured a conspiratorial coup. Moreover, what brought all these people together was a shared commitment to a long-standing tradition dating back to the constitutional settlement of 1688 and seen as the most genuine form of patriotism: even when Gast shifted towards his post-1815 emphasis on the independence of the working classes, John Locke, the theorist of late-seventeenth-century liberalism, was still one of his main political touchstones. In this tradition social and economic problems were seen as the result of governments which promoted the interests of corrupt minorities rather than the people as a whole: the answer was therefore political reform to secure more democratic government as the key to national well-being. The cornerstone of such government would be greater personal liberty for religious observance and intellectual inquiry, and greater scope for the self-organizing tendencies of a natural society, including free trade and the freedom to organize trade unions. It would also include the enjoyment of a greater reward for one's labour, through a shift away from corruption and waste paid for by taxes on consumption, and towards open and efficient government requiring less taxation and raising what it needed from taxes on income. The experience of freedom and prosperity under such a reformed political system would lead to an increase in generous feelings and the desire to extend the same conditions to others in less favoured parts of the world, at this time above all to the enslaved Africans and the oppressed Irish.

Of the two main forms of association then prevalent among working men, trade unions and friendly societies, the former, though the less numerous, was likely to have the stronger connection with national politics. For the friendly societies had been allowed to grow up on a completely unregulated basis until the late eighteenth century, and the first statute connected with them was the enabling act of 1793. In some contrast, the craft guilds had long had a legal standing under their charters, including a widespread connection with the 'freedom' of cities and thus with votes in parliamentary elections, as well as a connection with statutory regulation since the late sixteenth century. As a result trade unionists inherited a stronger orientation towards public institutions, with an early interest in the franchise and a growing concern over labour law.

THE POST-WAR UNREST

The French Revolution of 1789 was initially a great stimulus to democratic politics in Britain and participation began to spread down the social scale from the traditional landed and gentlemanly classes. However, although able to win wider support in times of economic distress, the organizers of even the most democratic of the reform groups were still mainly professional men, shopkeepers and small masters, involving only a few skilled working men with strong personal commitments to intellectual self-improvement. Moreover, after war with France broke out in 1793 the reformers' identification with the principles of the French Revolution placed them in a very difficult situation, hemmed in as they were by the suspension of many traditional civil liberties, hostile government propaganda and widespread loyalist feeling. After the Combination Act of 1799 the trade unions were particularly careful to avoid attracting unwanted attention by publicly endorsing political reform, though some individuals remained active in both spheres. Thus only a small minority of reformers were determined enough to continue an open agitation, particularly Sir Francis Burdett, whose election as MP for Westminster in 1807 gave him a national platform for brave criticism of the conduct of the war, and Major John Cartwright, whose energetic speaking tours from 1812 made the demand for the extension of the suffrage familiar in the manufacturing districts of England and Scotland.

The end of the French Wars in 1815 was therefore important not only because it led to economic distress for some groups of skilled workers but also because it relieved political reformers of much of the wartime restriction they had had to endure. The establishment of a lasting peace led to the running down of war-related industries like iron and shipbuilding, to the re-emergence of international competition in export markets, and thus to falling wages and rising unemployment. Moreover, the government acted through the Corn Laws to protect the country's farmers by prohibiting the importation of foreign wheat until the price in the home market reached a certain level, effectively passing on the costs of this agricultural subsidy to the purchasers of bread. The focus of all these material grievances on the very high levels of taxation on consumption, and ultimately on the unreformed political system which had produced such a policy, was promoted by the establishment of cheaper, more widely circulated, radical newspapers pioneered by William Cobbett's *Political Register*, and within a few years of the end of the wars manhood suffrage was increasingly held to be the fundamental remedy for the problems of the working classes among those who were politically active.

From the autumn of 1816 the London extra-parliamentary radicals launched an open agitation through a series of large public meetings at Spa Fields, Smithfield and Covent Garden under the talented sponsorship of Henry Hunt, but failed to consolidate much of a permanent following. Their links with the London trades were limited to loose contacts with the coachmakers and shoemakers, and the association of the shipwrights' leader John Gast with the small group around Dr James Watson from 1818, and they were increasingly discredited by the illegal activities of the even smaller group around Arthur Thistlewood which favoured armed insurrection. This minority's riotous behaviour in December 1816 led to the suspension of habeas corpus for a year and the attraction of *agents provocateurs*, who were eventually able to encourage the 'Cato Street Conspiracy' into an attempted assassination of the government in February 1820, finally allowing the dispersal of the insurrectionists through four executions and five transportations for high treason.

However, the almost simultaneous succession of the already unpopular Prince Regent as George IV sparked off a period of genuine mass unrest in the capital in protest against his attempt to exclude his estranged wife Caroline from the throne. This provided a powerful symbol of the Tory government's increasingly repressive policies and a golden opportunity for reformers of all shades to undermine the monarchy and the ministers, and it led to an unprecedented alliance between parliamentary Whigs, extra-parliamentary radicals and much of the population of London. A long sequence of incidents was launched by the Queen's triumphant arrival in the capital in June 1820 and reached a peak with the public discussion of all the evidence presented at her 'trial' through the government's promotion of a divorce bill in the House of Lords the following autumn. This became the occasion for almost continuous demonstrations declaring popular support for her cause, with Gast playing a leading part in organizing the London trades into an orderly procession on 15 August 1820, wearing white favours in support of the Queen; and then in coordinating two series of processions along similar lines by each of the main trade societies in turn in September 1820 and January 1821. The government's abandonment of its case against the Queen and her acceptance of a financial settlement took the steam out of the agitation, but it revived briefly after her sudden death on 7 August 1821, in particular because of a contest between the government and the London crowds over the route of her funeral procession, during which a carpenter and a bricklayer were killed by the military escort. Their funeral in turn provided a final occasion for Gast to organize an orderly demonstration of the London trades and, despite the risks of further provocation, it was a large and impressive one.

Meanwhile, the distressed handloom weavers, stimulated by the first post-war meetings in London, had begun to organize themselves from the autumn of 1816 in pursuit of both immediate relief and radical reform. At first this took the form of a brief flurry of local Hampden Clubs, named after the seventeenth-century tax resister, stimulated by agents sent north by Burdett and Cartwright, and attracting several thousand members in the Manchester and Glasgow areas by the spring of the following year. However, the breakthrough to a more widespread following came in Lancashire after the failure of a strike for higher wages in 1818, with local organization now taking the form of a well-organized network of Union Societies with a strong emphasis on self-education, and linked up with London radicalism through the charismatic figure of 'Orator' Hunt. This produced a growing wave of well-supported petitions from towns throughout the textile districts alongside a series of increasingly large and increasingly political meetings starting in January 1819 and focused on St Peter's Fields in Manchester. Although trade unions did not parade as such, the demonstrations being organized in contingents according to the towns they had set out from, there is strong evidence that majorities of both the organizers and the crowds were handloom weavers and their families, and a survey of the material they produced shows that they had a well-articulated radical programme of manhood suffrage, vote by ballot, annual parliaments and repeal of the Corn Laws. As one of them wrote to a hostile local newspaper:

As to the present distress, you and those of your kidney, say it's all owing to bad markets, want of trade with foreigners and such like . . . The root of the evil, in my judgment . . . lies deeper by a long way . . . The Constitution's become rotten at the core – there's foul-play at head quarters – the Parliament! Sir, the Parliament! Corruption's at the very helm of the State – it sits and rules in the very House of Commons; *this* is the source, the true and the only one, of all our sufferings – And what's the remedy, then? Why, *reform* – a radical complete constitutional *Reform*; we want nothing but this . . . to mend our markets and give every poor man plenty of work and good wages for doing it.[3]

This was a more widely supported movement than that in London and it led to more nervous reactions from the local authorities, including the most serious incident of repression in this period, when the Manchester magistrates sent in the inexperienced local yeomanry to arrest Hunt at a meeting of 60,000 people at St Peter's Fields on 9 August 1819. This led to confusion, panic, 400 injuries, a quarter of them women and girls, and eleven deaths before regular troops could be moved in to restore order. The incident became notorious as the 'Peterloo Massacre', in mocking reference to the army's most recent real victory at Waterloo, and outrage about it promoted considerable unity between parliamentary Whigs and extra-parliamentary radicals, leading at a local level to a flourishing of middle-class radical journalism including the establishment of the *Manchester Guardian*. However, the Tory government stood by the Manchester magistrates, jailing Hunt and four others of the Peterloo platform party, as well as a number of national radical leaders who protested about the repression. It then went on to pass the notorious six 'Gagging Acts' at the end of the year to restrict the press and the right to call public meetings, as a form of retrospective justification to make it seem as if there really was a national crisis. To some degree this created the very thing it was supposed to prevent, precipitating the 'Cato Street Conspiracy' in London and pushing the protests against 'Peterloo' in the Scottish weaving districts into an increasingly clandestine pattern which led to a vicious spiral of arrests and further escalating protest. An openly insurrectionist proclamation was posted up throughout the west of Scotland on 2 April 1820, stimulating brief but widespread strikes in Glasgow and Paisley, said to have involved up to 60,000 people, and exciting a small group of ultra-radical weavers to clash with the 10th Hussars at the 'Battle of Bonnymuir': the result of all this was over eighty arrests, three executions, sixteen transportations and the collapse of protest in the region.

During the period of the post-war unrest, then, there was increasing support for a programme of political reform as a precondition for the relief of material grievances. However, the extra-parliamentary movement was unable to maintain any real momentum and its moments of maximum impact were a result of government blunders: the 'Peterloo Massacre' and the 'Queen Caroline Affair'. The Whigs in opposition were in no position to turn even these incidents of more widespread protest into positive legislative initiatives, with Lord John Russell even failing to secure enough parliamentary support for a moderate redistribution of seats. Moreover, as economic prosperity returned, the handloom weavers in particular experienced an Indian summer of material well-being and had much less reason to concern themselves with wider political remedies. Though by the early 1820s the main planks of the reform programme had been clarified, groups of committed activists had been set up in urban centres throughout the country, and at some particular moments they had been able to link up with wider currents of public feeling, radicalism had yet to establish enough consistent and widespread support to make it into a genuinely popular movement.

THE REPEAL OF THE
COMBINATION LAWS

As associations of workmen had grown stronger under wartime conditions in the 1790s there had been increasing government concern about their activities, which were becoming associated with intimidation and suspected by some as a cover for revolutionary conspiracy. With the last years of the 1790s seeing naval mutinies at Spithead and the Nore in 1797 and a rising in Ireland supported by a landing of French troops in 1798, it is not surprising that in 1799 the government should have taken further steps against combinations of workmen. The actual occasion for general legislation was a petition from the London engineering employers for a particular act aimed at the skilled engineers, then known as millwrights. Since this coincided with employers' complaints about the growing strength of the Lancashire weavers, the government dropped the bill drafted for the master millwrights and substituted a general bill against combinations modelled on the most recent particular act, that of 1796 aimed at the papermakers, with its provision for summary conviction by one Justice of the Peace. This became law as the Combination Act of 1799 despite strong objections from the Whig opposition, including Lord Holland's pointed analysis of the situation which had made it possible:

On the part of the workmen, they laboured under the disadvantage arising from a certain degree of dread, that pervaded all the upper ranks of mankind, lest the lower ranks should be seduced by principles, supposed to be particularly afloat at this period, and subversive of society ... Was it not possible also that the masters, conscious of this temporary advantage, had availed themselves of this period, rather than any other, to enforce their views, and render their workmen more dependent than they had hitherto been, and that in all fairness and equity they ought to be.[4]

Despite the pressures of national security in the middle of a major war, there was then an effective campaign of petitioning against the act by workmen in all the major cities of the country, in particular over its reliance on one magistrate and its restriction of the right of appeal. A special Commons committee was set up to respond to these objections and its replacement Combination Act of 1800 conceded both of the main procedural points, as well as making the legislation appear more equitable by adding the crime of combination by masters to that of combination by men, though the punishment was only a £20 fine for the former as opposed to three months in prison for the latter.

Thus in contrast to most of the other special wartime legislation, such as the Act against Unlawful Oaths of 1797 with its provision for seven years' transportation, the amended Combination Act of 1800 was very much along the lines established by the particular combination acts of peacetime in the previous century, with scrupulous procedures and relatively light penalties. Indeed the major contrast with that earlier legislation, other than the addition of a more explicit element of equitable treatment for masters and men, was the deliberate abandonment of the language of government regulation of wages and hours and the offer instead simply of arbitration between contending parties. Moreover, while special legislation was passed for Ireland at Westminster in 1803, the Irish parliament having been abolished in 1800, there was no special legislation for Scotland, which meant that the act was inoperative north of the border. As a result of all these limitations the wartime use of the Combination Act of 1800 was much less than has often been assumed. The government itself generally declined to use it in cases of ordinary industrial disputes, reserving it for outbreaks of intimidation and violence which suggested more subversive intent, such as that among the West Country shearmen in 1802. There were some cases of employers making use of it to threaten their men out of disruptive behaviour in important war-related industries, for example at Bulmer's shipyard in South Shields in 1801. However, as has been seen in the previous two chapters, this was a period remarkable for the growth of more or less open trade unionism, and there were numerous cases of industrial action in war-related industries quite unimpeded by the act. For example, there were riots in the Royal Dockyards at Plymouth and Sheerness in 1801, and strikes among the London dockers in 1810, as well as among the London engineers themselves in 1801, 1805 and 1812.

If anything the post-war years saw more interest in the potential of the Combination Act as the employers tried to claw back some of the ground they had lost in the tight wartime labour market and, as seen in the last chapter, were prone to particularly confrontational methods in the process industries. In the cotton industry, for example, the use of the act was raised during three strikes in 1818, those of the Manchester spinners, the Stockport power-loom weavers and the Lancashire handloom weavers. However, once such disputes were under way it was considerably more intimidating to use the common law of conspiracy with its much harsher punishments: it was on such a charge that John Doherty, the spinners' leader, was imprisoned for two years, so his own statement in 1828 that he had been sentenced 'under the late combination laws' needs to be interpreted with care. Similarly when Francis Place complained in his autobiography that 'any combination to settle the matter by conference would have been prosecuted . . . the law was wholly on the side of the master',[5] he was recalling a strike in 1793, and so was referring either to the common law of conspiracy or to the 1749 act against combination in the clothing industries. Thus the growing post-war sense of grievance among trade unionists and their allies was not just over the Combination Act of 1800 but over all of the then-current statute and common laws restricting industrial action.

This campaign for the repeal of all the laws restricting combination was focused on a small group of political activists in the Westminster constituency who were generally intellectual republicans, but who worked for specific practical reforms through the collection of exhaustive evidence and the presentation of rational arguments in the press and Parliament. The central figures as far as the trade-union issue was concerned were Francis Place, the ex-tailor, and Joseph Hume, the MP for the Border Burghs. Place's sympathies for the ordinary working people among whom his life had begun had led him by 1814 to a strong sense of the injustice of legal restraint on trade-union activity, especially since it only created unnecessary bitterness and antagonism, thus interfering with the more rational conduct of industrial relations according to economic realities. He began to appeal to the growing free-market consensus in a series of letters and newspaper articles arguing that, since the long-term level of wages was the result of the operation of supply and demand in the labour market, there was nothing to fear from trade-union activity: if it did on occasion manage to raise the level of wages then those wages must have been lower than the true market level. Where workers attempted inadvisedly to raise wages above the market level this could usually be traced to the irritating nature of the combination laws themselves, which encouraged them to support industrial action out of resentment against its prohibition. Last but not least, Place argued, the combination laws were unequal and unjust because they were enforced by magistrates from the same social background as the employers and because they prescribed differential penalties of imprisonment for men and only fines for masters.

However, it was not until the early 1820s that the post-war alarm over public order began to subside and the formation of Lord Liverpool's new cabinet of 1822, with its liberal approach to economic policy and its interest in the consolidation and rationalization of legal matters, allowed Place and Hume to mount effective pressure for a Select Committee of the House of Commons to review the inconsistencies and inequities of existing trade-union law. Although this process involved an element of parliamentary wire-pulling, it also had a good deal of support from trade unionists throughout the country: Place had long-standing contacts with the London compositors, hatters and carpenters, with the Manchester spinners, and with the handloom weavers in Lancashire and Scotland; and in 1824 he managed to arrange over 100 petitions with thousands of signatures. He then acted as an informal secretary to the Committee, conducting preliminary hearings of the evidence from employers and workmen and briefing Hume, who was in the chair throughout, so that he could steer the proceedings in the intended direction. Interestingly enough, the employers who gave evidence were also in favour of repeal of the Combination Act of 1800: some of them agreed that it was unjust, others felt that it merely aggravated industrial relations, and even those who wanted tough measures against trade-union activity thought that this particular act was ineffective. As a result the Committee concluded that Place was correct and that the existing legislation had proved useless and indeed aggravating by promoting distrust in industrial relations and a tendency towards secrecy and violence. Moreover, it extended this conclusion to cover the common law of conspiracy as well. After some further wire-pulling behind the scenes Place then secured the passage of the Combination Laws Repeal Act of 1824, which not only, as its title suggested, repealed a total of thirty-five existing statutes (the nine particular eighteenth-century English acts, and the rest being either older or dealing with Scotland and Ireland), but also declared that the mere act of combining should no longer be a ground for prosecution under the English common law. At the same time it embodied another recommendation of the Select Committee: to retain the summary jurisdiction of the 1800 act for persons using intimidation or violence to impose the rules of a combination.

Unfortunately for the reformers, the immediate aftermath of this new dispensation saw a sharp inflationary boom accompanied by a wave of strikes, ambitious attempts at the regulation of working conditions, especially among the London shipwrights, and some violence, especially among the Glasgow spinners. The employers in shipbuilding and cotton-spinning were then particularly active in counter-pressure on the government, and managed to secure a second Select Committee in 1825 to hear their case for the reimposition of prohibitive legislation. Although Hume was not in the chair this time, he was still present and was able to cross-examine the employers, and Place joined forces with John Gast of the London shipwrights to coordinate an impressive extra-parliamentary campaign of resistance. They set up a general committee of trade-union delegates in London to monitor the proceedings of the Select Committee, continually petitioning it to hear representatives of the trades under attack from the employers. When this was permitted Gast himself went to make an effective defence of the shipwrights; meanwhile Place wrote an equally effective pamphlet for distribution to MPs and influential journalists, and they arranged almost 100 petitions with over 100,000 signatures from all over the country. The government was then subjected to strong pressure from Hume and from the two MPs for Westminster, Sir Francis Burdett and J. C. Hobhouse, during the committee stages, with the result that the more coercive employers' proposals were defeated. Indeed the new act of 1825 re-stated the legality of strike action and its immunity to common-law prosecution for conspiracy as long as it was restricted to the regulation of the wages and hours of labour. The main differences from the previous year were increases in the sentences for intimidation and violence and the introduction of an element of confusion into the definition of such offences by adding the phrase 'molesting and obstructing'.

Though a number of trade-union leaders were active in the campaigns both for radical political reform and for trade-union law reform, for obvious reasons it was the latter which attracted the most support from trade unionists in general, particularly in response to the threatened reimposition of coercive legislation. This campaign appealed to a very wide range of occupations and regions, with the daily London meetings of the trades committee in 1825 consisting of delegates not only from the leading London craftsmen's clubs but also from the shipwrights and seamen of the north-east, from the cotton spinners of Lancashire, and from unions in Scotland, Yorkshire and the Midlands. Moreover, a weekly *Trades' Newspaper* was set up and run for several years by a committee of trade-union leaders under Gast's chairmanship to maintain this high level of cooperation beyond its most immediate goal. John Doherty was very active in Manchester during this campaign and wrote to Place, echoing the latter's basic analysis but taking it a step further in the context of this impressive trade-union response:

If they leave us to ourselves, some few outrages may be committed, but the only contention will be between the more violent and foolish, and the more intelligent and discreet part of the labouring classes; the one side is advocating, the other is deprecating all violent and improper measures, until ultimately, all shall be convinced that the line of conduct best calculated to promote their interests would be reasonableness in their demands, submission to the laws, and obedience to and respect for their employers. But if they oppress us, if they make a law that will place us under the control of our employers, they will *force* all to *unite* in one great combination, not only against our employers, but against *themselves* and they will find us more troublesome than they expect.[6]

During the long French Wars the employers had increasingly opposed trade-union attempts to revive and extend the legislative regulation of wages and hours, perhaps because of the rise of the process industries in new centres of manufacturing, perhaps because the unions were already able to secure more favourable deals from government bodies faced with the manpower requirements of a major war. Thus by the years after 1815 not only were emergency wartime restrictions no longer required, but the overall balance of the law had also become increasingly one-sided: for while there was still a ban on strike action there was now considerably less scope for sympathetic consideration of workers' grievances by public officials. The repeal of the combination laws in 1824–5 was therefore a necessary tidying-up operation, but one which gave important confirmation to the increasing influence in British policy-making in this period of Adam Smith's liberal conception of the operation of a modern commercial society. This also had important implications for popular politics. For, while the adoption of demands for political reform alongside greater state intervention was clearly possible in principle, most organized workers had experienced the first decades of the nineteenth century as a period when petitioning for government regulation failed and free collective bargaining succeeded. When this was underwritten by the repeal of the combination laws the way was cleared for a more consistently libertarian popular politics, calling for further measures of political reform to secure a largely non-interventionist state.

PART TWO

The 1820s to the 1870s

5

Financial Centralization among the Assembly Workers

'You're from the Trade Union?' said the great man abruptly, when Applegarth entered, and Applegarth said he was.

'Well,' remarked Mr Brown, 'I shall cut you short!'

'Pray don't,' was the good-humoured response, 'I'm only five-foot-two, and that's short enough.'[1]

This brief exchange in Sheffield in 1859 between John Brown, the founder of the great steel and shipbuilding company, and Robert Applegarth, soon to become the leader of the Amalgamated Society of Carpenters and Joiners, illustrates much about the new spirit among the craftsmen in the middle of the nineteenth century. Their organizations were developing from local clubs into more ambitious unions, and their long-standing willingness to negotiate with their employers was becoming more public and more fully recorded. Perhaps even more remarkable, however, was the new-found confidence of their representatives, for, even though he was only twenty-five years old and had just become the secretary of his local carpenters' society, Applegarth was prepared to step outside the usual polarity of deference/rebelliousness and to assume the right to equal treatment by insisting on it under the guise of good-humoured word play. Applegarth was remembered as a short, wiry man with a voice strong enough to carry well at large public meetings but a new way of speaking. Moving away from the passionate and declamatory style common in the early nineteenth century, he put his energy into collecting information, building up a coherent case and presenting it clearly and directly: 'he would speak with incisive, but unassuming, gesture; speak and bear himself in a way which seemed to challenge contradiction; impress his hearers with the intensity of his own conviction'.[2]

Robert Applegarth had been born in Hull in 1834 and, having finished his training as a woodworker at a time when jobs were relatively scarce, had emigrated to the United States in 1854. While there he had found employment in a railway depot near Chicago, gone on a memorable trip to St Louis to see the slave trade at first hand and been actively involved in the anti-slavery movement. He later recalled that these experiences had strengthened the radical views he had initially picked up as a teenager through reading Chartist newspapers. Because his wife was too ill to join him in America, he had returned to England in 1857, settled in Sheffield and become a leading figure in the local carpenters' society, first as president and then as secretary. He spent much of his spare time reading in the local public library and was a founding member of the Sheffield Cooperative Society. He persuaded his trade-union colleagues to move their meetings out of the traditional public house and into a reading room, and he introduced wider discussions of political and social issues after the organizational business was concluded. Then in 1861 he led the Sheffield carpenters into the newly founded Amalgamated Society of Carpenters and Joiners, and the following year, having made an impression at a delegate conference held to revise the society's rules, was elected as its national secretary. Applegarth and his wife moved to London, where they lived at the union's offices in Lambeth on a salary of 33s. a week: out of this he paid for lessons to improve his handwriting which he found also improved his spelling, and he soon began to demonstrate that he could not only sustain long passages of sophisticated prose in the union's journal, but could also maintain a clear mental picture of all the business of a complex national organization.

Applegarth's outlook was rooted in the traditions of craft unionism but went far beyond narrow sectionalism to a broad vision of social improvement for all working people. The principles of effective trade unionism were from this point of view fundamentally cooperative ones. For example, the recruitment of new members and the opening of new branches would benefit not only the previously poorly organized through improvements in wages and hours, but also the already well organized through the removal of the threat of undercutting and an increase in the overall funds of the society. Clearly grasped, these pragmatic reasons for building a national organization for one occupation naturally extended into concern for other, even less advantaged, groups of workers: particularly for the coal miners who suffered from dangerous working conditions and inadequate government inspection, and for the agricultural labourers who were repressed by the local gentry and exploited by sub-contractors. This involved a real sympathy with, and understanding for, the distinct experiences of others. For example, at a time of violent incidents in the Sheffield metal-grinding trades in the middle of the 1860s, Applegarth was keen to distance the majority of trade unionists from such illegal behaviour but also emphasized the unhealthy working conditions of these particular workers and their need for maximum unity: 'lives are cut short by the work in which the men are engaged, and it is natural that men who have subscribed to the Union should feel hurt at seeing others who have not done so reap advantages for which they do not pay'.[3] Similarly, when a local vicar urged a public meeting of agricultural labourers in the early 1870s to save more and drink less, Applegarth responded: 'if I were a labourer struggling to make ends meet on thirteen shillings a week, and I thought that, by going to the public house, I could purchase forgetfulness of my misery, then by God, I'd go and I'd spend the lot!'[4] In other words, in this case at least, the well-organized craftsmen's emphasis on law-abiding, collective self-improvement was based on their experience of its effectiveness in their own situation, not on a wish to moralize other groups about their behaviour or adopt a superior position.

Like Francis Place before him, Applegarth aimed to remove all the legal obstacles to trade unionism and expected that, given full recognition, workers would be less inclined to strike and more willing to engage in reasonable bargaining. He therefore played a leading role in presenting the union case in all the major public forums of the 1860s, and he was so convinced of the inherent justice of their demands that he urged his members to open up the details of specific disputes to the scrutiny of the general public:

If they had any grievances they should write to their employers, and if the employers refused to agree to their terms, or took no notice of the appeal, the best thing to do was, not to strike, but to lay their claims before the public; and the masters would then be compelled to state their objections or the public would pass their opinion, which might be considered the verdict of the jury. If the public agreed with the employers it was of no use for the men to press their case any further, and if public opinion was with the men it would be of no use for the masters to hold out any longer, for it was not out of the employers' pockets that the advance of wages or the reduction of hours would come. In all such cases it was the public who had to 'pay the piper'.[5]

Sometimes it was indeed possible to proceed in this way, but as often as not contemporary reality still fell considerably short of Applegarth's ideal, for the unions were still not completely unhindered by legal restraints, fully recognized by their employers or able to appeal directly to a jury of well-informed public opinion. As a result he was not opposed to striking as a matter of principle, calculating that in 1865 alone industrial action had involved around 4,000 of his own members at considerable expense but also with a benefit of £6.14s. per man in improved wages and hours. Similarly, when the Yorkshire miners failed in their approach to their employers for peaceful talks in 1869, he urged them to stand together to the bitter end in their strike; and, when the Beckton gas stokers were prosecuted for preparing to strike in 1872, he raised financial support for half a dozen of them to leave the country quietly to avoid arrest. Looking forward to a time when a reduction in the need to finance strikes would allow increasing resources to be devoted to more constructive purposes, his position was: 'never surrender the right to strike; but be careful how you use a double-edged weapon'.[6]

As if his work as a national trade-union leader was not enough to take on, Applegarth's ambitious vision of social advance for all working people led him to involvement in virtually every progressive movement of the time. He was a leading figure in the campaign for a system of national secular education, and in all the campaigns in support of movements for liberty and democracy in the rest of Europe. He played a major role in the campaigns for the extension of the parliamentary franchise and then, after the 1867 reform act, for the election of the first working-men's candidates. Indeed, he was one of the earliest labour representatives in local government himself when he sat on the Lambeth Vestry, and in 1870 he became the first working man to be appointed as a member of a Royal Commission. However, this latter unfortunately led to his resignation as secretary of the joiners' union, as a number of the London branches felt that he should focus exclusively on union business during his normal office hours, while he felt that it was just as important to represent the trade-union movement in national public life. It seems that what many of the members actually objected to was his connection with this particular Commission because it was inquiring into the Contagious Diseases Acts, which regulated prostitution, and they found its subject embarrassing. Applegarth, in contrast, was the leading voice within the Commission in favour of taking direct testimony from the prostitutes themselves as well as from other local women, and as a result he became a convinced advocate of the repeal of the acts as a serious infringement of women's civil rights. Having lost his major source of income as a trade-union officer, he set himself up in business in a small way, selling breathing apparatus for use in mine-rescue operations and later pioneering the application of electricity to lighting, while still remaining a member of his own union and an active participant in wider trade-union and cooperative affairs.

Robert Applegarth was unusually long-lived, surviving until 1924 to be hailed as one of the forerunners of the Labour Party, but in most other respects he was a typical member of his generation. There has been much discussion about whether the craftsmen's organizations in the middle of the nineteenth century deserve to be called 'new model' unions, as they drew many of their practices from earlier organizations and their methods were far from being universally adopted. Be that as it may, Applegarth and his colleagues may still be referred to as 'new model' unionists, for together they made up an important and influential group, highly intelligent, efficient and articulate, and able for the first time to carve out a central place for their organizations in British public life.

FROM LOCAL CLUBS TO
UNION BRANCHES

After the burst of energetic activity around the repeal of the combination laws in 1824–5 there had been a long period of industrial
depression and unemployment lasting into the 1840s. This had been
more severe in some years than in others: 1826–32 and 1837–42 had
been particularly bad, and even though the first signs of a long-term
recovery had become evident soon after, there had been a reversion to
slump in 1847–8. With such bad years causing complete unemployment for up to a third of the workers in the craft trades, and under-
employment for up to another third, the local craftsmen's clubs had
been subjected to severe financial and organizational pressures: they
had to make more provision for unemployment and sickness at the
same time as they were finding it hard to retain their members and
collect subscriptions. The longer-term recovery which began in the
mid-1840s was based at least in part on the widening of markets
through innovations in transport based on the steam engine, above
all the railways, and since this emergence of a national market was
accompanied by an increasingly national cycle of boom and slump,
it began to undermine the practicality of relieving local unemployment through the tramping system: with everywhere experiencing
unemployment at the same time there was little advantage in travelling
round the country in search of work. Moreover, with such high levels
of unemployment, those on the road were no longer mainly the younger
men but began to include many of the older and more settled members,
leading to more ill-health among the tramps as well as serious financial
problems and disruption of domestic life for those families left behind.
Given that in such periods of general unemployment there was simply
no work, it began to seem as if the tramping system had become little
more than a 'treadmill', or a requirement to walk in order to qualify
for unemployment benefit.

One significant response was to extend tramping even more
radically, through the encouragement of emigration. Following the
mid-1820s repeal of legislation which had attempted to prevent
the emigration of skilled workers, there was a steady increase in

the numbers leaving the country for the United States, Canada and Australia, and later also New Zealand. Although for some this had negative associations with criminal transportation and schemes of forced migration of paupers, a growing number of craftsmen's organizations began to provide financial incentives for their members to join the stream of overseas emigrants, as a way of reducing the pressure of over-supply of skilled labour in Britain. The standard schemes required a few years' membership with no subscription arrears, and then supported the cost of the long sea passages for the chosen men by providing grants of £10 to £15, a similar sum of money to that which would have been provided for a year's tramping at home: by the 1850s there were well-established schemes of this type run by the engineers, carpenters and printers among others. Although the numbers leaving the country under such schemes probably only amounted to a few thousand, skilled urban workers continued to make up around 20 per cent of British emigrants, or around 1 million men in the second half of the nineteenth century, which must have had a significant impact on the domestic labour market. For many the results were disappointing; they merely continued to tramp around by foot and rail without finding long-term employment or settling down, and perhaps as many as half of them returned home. For the other half the experience of emigration, while still not an easy one, had more worthwhile and long-lasting results: they settled in reasonably well-paid jobs and were able to save enough money to buy their own houses and small plots of land. On this basis local organizations of skilled men along familiar lines were then established in the main areas of British settlement, sometimes even closely affiliated to those back home. Like emigration itself, this was in a real sense only an extension of the old tramping system which had for many years been having similar effects in unorganized districts: by the end of the nineteenth century, for example, the engineers had eighty-two overseas branches while the joiners had sixty-seven. In most cases these then either became the basis of, or were otherwise absorbed into, independent national bodies throughout the English-speaking world which based themselves on similar principles of organization to those of British craft unionism.

As far as the development of trade unions in Britain itself was concerned, a more important response to the mid-nineteenth-century pressures on the tramping system was the shift towards the provision of unemployment benefit at home. Arrangements were usually left in place for voluntary tramping for those who still wanted to try their luck (usually no more than 10 per cent of unemployed members in the middle of the nineteenth century), and they were usually relaxed enough to allow the men to use cheap railway transport and go straight to where there was most work. Thus systematic tramping round the complete circuit of local clubs began to be replaced by reliance on regular 'trade reports' from other localities. Meanwhile the shift towards the provision of 'home donation' or 'static' unemployment benefit to most of the members made it easier to sustain the local organization of the craftsmen in each area, using the gains in membership and funds of boom periods to tide themselves over the periodic slumps and maintain a long-term upward trend. Similarly during strikes the men involved also began to receive money at home rather than being sent on the tramp, for, as rising membership and increasing employers' coordination meant that larger numbers were involved in longer disputes, it became increasingly important that these men should not be imposed on other areas throughout the country.

This shift towards a more stable local membership through the ups and downs of economic cycles and industrial disputes made it possible to maintain systematic records of individual subscriptions and benefits, and on this basis to transform the local clubs into genuine branches of fully integrated unions. The new network of cheap and speedy communications which had undermined tramping simultaneously enabled the organized craftsmen to maintain better contact throughout the country and to circulate papers and correspondence. The earlier arrangement of branches retaining their own funds, except for occasional transfers to equalize the burdens of the tramping system under the guidance of one branch acting as the headquarters, now began to be replaced by the centralization of funds under the control of increasingly professional, full-time secretaries. These men had to be literate enough to maintain the society's correspondence and numerate enough to maintain its financial ledgers, as well as committed and steady enough to keep up a consistent routine of office work without daily supervision or special incentives. Their administrative work was, however, checked by new constitutional arrangements: they were

themselves frequently subject to regular re-election; executive committees, which might still be drawn from one locality to save expenses in
travelling to regular meetings, heard all the appeals about benefit
payments even in cases of individual appeals; and periodic delegate
meetings of representatives of all the branches were called whenever
it was felt necessary to review the organization's standard rates of
subscription and benefit, or its basic constitutional structure. These
central bodies did not have the power to prohibit local strike action
but they did have the power to decide whether it should be given
support from the union's funds, and those organizations which did not
use this power wisely, or did not make sufficiently rapid adjustments of
the balance between subscriptions and benefits, would face serious
financial crises. Another important tool in building a successful union
along the new lines was a regular journal issued by the general secretary, always an annual report on the overall position of the society's
finances, increasingly also monthly reports with details of branch
activity and the condition of local labour markets. At the same time
the local branches retained vital functions. It was still at this level that
new members were admitted and subscriptions collected. It was still
at this level that initial decisions about individual entitlement to benefit
were made, on the basis of personal knowledge of the applicants'
situations regarding sickness or unemployment. It was increasingly at
this level that discussions about wider industrial and union matters
would end in votes, which might lead to the formulation of a district-
wide demand on the employers, or which might take the form of a
national referendum binding on the central executive. Finally, it was
from this level that officials of all sorts, branch, district and national,
were ultimately recruited through democratic processes.

The middle decades of the nineteenth century therefore saw an
impressive development on the institutional side of craft organization,
but the unions' key functions were still largely as benefit clubs, employment exchanges and occasional bargaining agents at the more respectable ends of their trades. They were still far from being able to recruit
all those working in their occupations, and even among their own
members perhaps as few as 10 per cent had served formal apprentice-
ships, the majority being admitted on the basis of their reputations as
capable and steady workmen. Given this lack of control over methods

of entry to the trade, there was equally little control over the number of entrants: though some unions had rules on the ratio of apprentices to journeymen, regulation of this kind was impossible to maintain in the workshops in a period of rapid industrial growth and steady migration from rural to urban areas. This basic lack of control over the labour market then made it very difficult to regulate the terms and conditions of employment. For example, most craft unions were formally opposed to piece-rates, on the grounds that they increased work loads and lowered quality, but when their members really did refuse work on this basis it was usually given to someone else. However, one area in which the development of coordinated craft unions did begin to make an impact was through the provision of information about labour markets over a wider area. This made it possible for their members to take advantage of any increased labour requirements more quickly, either by demanding more pay in their existing jobs backed up by the threat of collective industrial action, or by taking individual decisions to move to other employers who were already offering more money. Thus, though wages still basically reflected market forces, coordinated craft unionism was promoting the increasingly rapid transmission of market information to the distinct benefit of its members. This then began to produce a gradual convergence of local rates and hours of work towards minimum occupational standards, at least at a district level if not yet at a national one.

Overall, then, the craft unions in this period continued to restrict their membership to men who were skilled enough to be attractive to employers even when they insisted on union rules on rates and hours. And when their members could not find work under these conditions, they were able to provide better information on jobs elsewhere and, if necessary, more attractive forms of strike and unemployment benefit. As the leader of the ironfounders, Daniel Guile, argued before a major public inquiry in the 1860s:

Now if all men were society men, and asked a fair day's wage for a fair day's work, and all masters were willing to abide by that rule, then all the masters could go into the market on the same footing; not only that, but the union encourages a man to become proficient in his trade. He knows that if he would be a respected member of society he must be at least above the common rank, and it gives him a stimulus; and another thing is, that it enables the working man, who is looking on with some degree of anxiety 40 or 50 years, to see that there will be something at the end of that time to rely on; superannuation money, sick pay, accident money, and all those things are in his favour, and make him a provident man.[7]

Thus the growth of the local trade clubs into national trade unions was accompanied by a consolidation of the wider culture of the craftsmen. Thrift had long been established as the very basis of their organization, but it now evolved into a more systematically recorded and more publicly visible form, with the annual reports of the engineers and carpenters, for example, being regularly reviewed in the middle-class press. The reduction of alcohol consumption was a slower matter for, while increasing numbers of trade-union leaders were advocates of temperance and there is some indication of a decline in workplace drinking customs, many of the men were still carrying out heavy physical tasks over long working days and they continued to rely on more or less heavy drinking as the basis of much of their recreation. Thus, though a minority campaigned for the removal of meetings from their traditional location in public houses, only a handful of unions had done so by the end of the 1860s, and even by the end of the century almost three-quarters of labour organizations continued to meet in pubs. It should, however, be noted that this was also due to the continuing function of public houses as local labour exchanges and ports of call for the voluntary tramps, and that in any case few working-class districts contained suitable alternative rooms for meetings. Meanwhile, spreading literacy was reflected not only in the individual union journals but also in the spread of a weekly press aimed at working-class readers and favourable to trade unionism. This flourished first in particular industrial districts, for example the *Potteries Examiner* (1843) and the *Glasgow Sentinel* (1850), spreading from there to the national level with the rather sensationalist *Reynolds' Newspaper* (1850) and the more sophisticated *Bee-Hive* (1861), edited by a young carpenter, George Potter. Meanwhile, it was not unknown for the newly prosperous unions to use some of their funds to establish libraries, for example in the cases of the printers and bookbinders, as well as the Scottish masons; and there was an even more widespread movement in support of the establishment of free local public libraries. In addition there was a greater availability of, and participation in, a wide range of evening classes provided by labour organizations covering such subjects as the sciences and modern languages, as well as more obviously useful matters such as economic theory. On this basis the craftsmen were increasingly able to produce not only efficient administrators but also effective publicists who could take on the ideas of anti-union thinkers in their own terms, for example Thomas Dunning of the London bookbinders, whose *Trades' Unions and Strikes. Their Philosophy and Intention* (1860) was the first extended argument by a trade unionist to be published as a book.

The growth in organizational stability, financial reserves, and professional administration, accompanied by an impressive number of articulate speakers and writers, led to a significant shift in frequently hostile educated public opinion. As had always been the case, trade unionism in this period had a number of particularly active supporters among the middle and upper classes. First, there was a group of socially concerned young barristers influenced by the chaplain of Lincoln's Inn, F. D. Maurice. They developed a distinctive form of Christian Socialism which emphasized cooperative production, with J. M. Ludlow and Thomas Hughes becoming increasingly concerned with trade-union issues following a national engineering dispute in 1852, when they deplored the employers' refusal to accept arbitration and established close links with the leaders of the engineering craftsmen. Secondly, there was a group of intellectually progressive young academics influenced by Richard Congreve of Wadham College, Oxford. They developed a distinctively English form of Positivism which looked for practical and democratic social improvement among the working classes and quite naturally took up the cause of trade unionism during a London building dispute in 1859, with Frederic Harrison and E. S. Beesly going on to establish strong links with Robert Applegarth of the carpenters. With the help of these particular friends, above all through their influence on the highly favourable report on *Trades' Societies and Strikes* of the National Association for the Promotion of Social Science in 1860, craft unionism was able to win the approval of important authorities of mainstream liberalism. In the 1862 edition of his *Principles of Political Economy*, John Stuart Mill accepted that collective bargaining had a role to play in the adjustment of the labour market, and by the end of the 1860s even *The Times* had come round to acknowledging that the bulk of trade-union activities were entirely beneficial. Thus in the second half of the nineteenth century the unions were always able to call on a large group of sympathetic radical MPs whenever they felt it necessary, and sizeable delegations to meet the relevant ministers, or even the Prime Minister, became an accepted part of the business of parliamentary government.

LONDON AS A CENTRE OF NATIONAL ORGANIZATION

A review of these processes in operation in particular unions and industrial disputes may well begin in the early 1830s, when a short period of prosperity after almost ten years of falling wages and organizational weakness led the London tailors, shoemakers and building craftsmen to become active and assertive again, with a particular emphasis on tackling the chronic surplus of labour in their trades. The tailors and shoemakers attempted to restrict the influx of newcomers and to limit the hours of work through a Grand Lodge of Operative Tailors of London and a Grand Lodge of Operative Cordwainers in 1833. Meanwhile, the building trades set up a national federation known as the Operative Builders' Union, a network of local lodges linked through an annual conference known as the Builders' Parliament which had up to 300 delegates, representing perhaps as many as 30,000 men. Then in the winter of 1833–4 a number of trades, most importantly the silk weavers, became involved in a dispute in Derby during which the employers threatened not to take back any men who had been involved in the unions, and the London tailors responded to the men's call for assistance by initiating a Grand National Consolidated Trades Union. This support fund was organized along lines which had become familiar during the previous decades, but with far more participants: about 16,000 workers, mainly among the London tailors, shoemakers, and other traditional consumer crafts. However, any vestiges of national coordination began to fade away as the Derby dispute came to an unsuccessful end. There was considerable rivalry between the London tailors, who managed to secure some financial backing for an unsuccessful strike in April 1834, and the London shoemakers, who felt they had a prior claim: the ambitious federation began to fall apart amid accusations of embezzlement of funds by its officers. Meanwhile the employers began to move against the Operative Builders' Union by imposing an anti-union pledge known as the 'document' and, though at first this seems to have stiffened resistance, the builders' national organization was decisively defeated in September 1834 and had disappeared by 1835.

Apart from the appeal of its title, the prominence of the Grand National Consolidated Trades Union was largely due to its role as the organizing body for a great meeting of perhaps as many as 30,000 people at Copenhagen Fields in London in April 1834, to protest against the harsh sentencing of six Dorchester labourers who became known as the 'Tolpuddle Martyrs'. These men, led by George and James Loveless, had organized a society to resist the reduction of their wages from 7s. to 6s. a week but, before they had undertaken any kind of activity, had been prosecuted under the old Act of 1797 against seditious oaths and received the maximum sentence of seven years' transportation to Australia. This conviction was the result of the unusual zeal of a particular group of local magistrates being uncharacteristically backed up by central government because one of them happened to have the Home Secretary for a brother-in-law. The campaign over this notorious case became increasingly well organized for a long haul by the Dorchester Labourers' Committee, which maintained pressure inside and outside Parliament, mobilized a great deal of sympathy among trade unionists throughout the country and provided financial support for the transported men's families. All this was eventually successful under a new Home Secretary: the Dorchester men's sentences were remitted in 1836 and they were allowed to return home in 1838.

However, despite such occasional victories, these bodies of the 1830s were desperate attempts to mitigate the effects of long-term depression and unemployment, formed against a background of organizational weakness. Their main claim to being 'national' was that they were based in London, and they were premature in trying to build general unions or industrial federations when the component parts of such movements were too weak to regulate their own affairs. If anything was learned from these movements it was that among the assembly workers ambitious forms of wider organization were not the solution to major problems, indeed they could only succeed on the basis of strong and effective occupational trade unionism. It was the relatively new trade of engineers which was to show the way forward on the basis of the wider networks which had already been built up within occupations around the tramping system.

While the growth of industries like coal and cotton was largely in the north, the building of machinery for them and for other uses led to the emergence of new engineering firms in London and the older urban centres of the craft clubs. The modern trade of engineering grew out of a number of traditional occupations: the smiths, who had originally been part of the hammermen's guilds and who had gradually absorbed the gunsmiths; the clockmakers, who had resisted absorption by the smiths; and various woodworking trades, such as carpenters and wood turners, whose skills could be transferred to metal. Techniques borrowed from these long-standing occupations gradually merged in the course of the eighteenth century to produce the highly skilled trade of the millwrights, who used a combination of metalworking and woodworking skills in the construction of machines and engines for the textile and coal industries. Their high levels of skill and independence frequently enabled them to take leading roles in disputes in the eighteenth century, and their associations became more publicly visible after the repeal of the combination laws. Initially they still catered for specific occupations in specific localities as the older craft clubs had done, with particular centres of activity in the 1830s in London, Manchester and Yorkshire, then they slowly and cautiously began to establish tighter national links. For example, the Manchester-based Friendly Society of Mechanics (1826) renamed itself the Journeymen Steam Engine and Machine Makers' Society in 1838 when it absorbed a parallel Yorkshire society; it then adopted both the new benefit of 'home donation' and the principle of financial centralization, and in 1843 it appointed its first full-time secretary and its first elected executive council.

By the late 1840s it was becoming clear that an even more all-embracing organization was needed in the industry to unite all the engineering trades into one union, so that if any specific group was involved in a dispute all the other skilled workers in that shop could be brought out in support. Eventually in 1850–51 two members of the Journeymen Steam Engine Makers, its secretary William Allan, a Scotsman working in Crewe, and William Newton of London, led the way through a series of negotiations between local societies towards their fusion into the Amalgamated Society of Engineers, Machinists, Smiths, Millwrights, and Patternmakers, usually known by the shorter title of the Amalgamated Society of Engineers, with 12,000 members by the end of 1851. This ambitious union required a high rate of contributions from its members (1s. a week instead of the usual 1d. or 2d.) and aimed to provide a generous scale of sickness, retirement, funeral and 'static' unemployment benefits (the latter set at 10s. a week for full members). The bulk of the funds was handled at a central office in London by a full-time general secretary, who was supervised by an executive council of delegates elected by the branches in the metropolitan area. William Allan became the first of the general secretaries, and his cautious and efficient approach to administration and the gradual accumulation of financial reserves was the bedrock on which the society was to prosper.

While the new union drew many of its practices from the Journeymen Steam Engine Makers out of which it had emerged, it also had some genuinely novel features with its prominent national headquarters and its rapidly growing membership and financial strength. The employers mounted an immediate counter-attack, coordinating pressure for an increase in the numbers of unskilled men in workshops in London and Lancashire simultaneously, and locking out those tradesmen who refused to accept it. The union had to raise a special levy of £12,000 from those still at work, and as much again from other societies, but with the press, especially *The Times*, against it and the employers well organized, the union was defeated and its members forced to sign the 'document' on returning to work. Naturally in the immediate aftermath of the dispute its membership slumped badly, and it turned back for a while to the idea of sponsoring cooperative workshops in association with the Christian Socialists. However, over the next ten years of industrial prosperity skilled engineering workers consolidated their position in the division of labour, membership more than recovered and the employers began to recognize the union and to reach compromise agreements with it over wages and working conditions for its members on a district-by-district basis. By the mid-1860s the Amalgamated Society of Engineers was established as a genuinely national trade union with over 30,000 members in over 300 branches (perhaps around 75 per cent of the skilled men), an annual income of over £80,000 and reserves of around £140,000. Indeed by the early 1870s it was in a strong enough position to impose improved conditions unilaterally on reluctant employers during a district-based campaign for a nine-hour day initiated on Tyneside under the leadership of John Burnett, who went on to succeed Allan as the union's general secretary in 1874.

This type of centrally coordinated society, with high rates of subscription, high benefits paid at home, and the capacity in periods of exceptional prosperity to gain favourable terms from the employers, was found in a fairly pure form among other highly skilled metalworkers. For example, the Friendly Society of Ironfounders had long been a pioneer in the field of benefit provision, and became even more effective under Daniel Guile, its secretary from 1863. Meanwhile, the United Society of Boilermakers had also been moving independently in this direction with full financial centralization in 1856, and it rose to a position of enormous influence after it appointed Robert Knight as its secretary in 1871, with its members going on to become the main structural-steel workers in the rapidly expanding shipbuilding industry.

The 'amalgamated principles' also found a receptive audience among some of the highly skilled woodworkers, once again involving a major dispute in the national capital. Despite the serious defeats of the more ambitious building workers' movements of the mid-1830s, the organizations within each occupation had continued to exist and at times even to grow. Then in the late 1850s the London building workers began to feel strong enough again to coordinate requests for a reduction in hours from ten to nine a day under the leadership of George Potter, the secretary of one of the capital's many small woodworkers' societies. A strike of masons at Trollopes of Pimlico in 1859, over the dismissal of a trade unionist who had submitted one of these requests, spread to other firms and eventually led to a six-month-long metropolitan lock-out of 24,000 masons, bricklayers, joiners and labourers. The employers, supported again by *The Times*, insisted on the 'document' and the men were supported again by contributions from other societies, above all the engineers, who were able to provide three successive payments of £1,000. On the basis of this outside support, the London building workers were able to end their dispute with an honourable compromise in February 1860: they dropped the nine-hours' demand, and the employers dropped the 'document'. The General Union of Carpenters, founded in 1827, had continued to open up branches throughout the country and struggled to establish standard rates, at one stage even managing to absorb a Scottish rival. However, impressed during the 1859–60 dispute both by the effectiveness of their employers' response and by the financial strength of the amalgamated engineers, the more advanced London woodworkers now set themselves up as the nucleus of a new national body called the Amalgamated Society of Carpenters and Joiners in 1860, and in 1862 found themselves a 'new-model' secretary in the person of Robert Applegarth. This new union followed the engineers in providing 'static' unemployment pay at the rate of 10s. a week, financed through a high subscription of 1s. a week when in work. By the mid-1860s it had 8,000 members in 190 branches, and an annual income of over £10,000, and a decade later all of these figures had just about doubled again. Thus at a major public inquiry in the late 1860s, Applegarth answered charges that union finances were not actuarially sound with an optimistic vision of the resources available in the pockets of current members to support any new levies which might become necessary:

We had the advantage of the experience of the Engineers' Society, a society which was formed by amalgamating a lot of local societies containing very many old members. They started, from their very formation, to pay all the benefits which we pay, including superannuation, and had been in existence something like ten years when we started, and we naturally thought that if, having started with a few thousand members, and a very few thousand pounds, they had got up to something like £80,000 or £90,000, there was something more than speculation about that; we believed that a shilling would purchase just as much for a carpenter and joiner as it would for an engineer, and that we have taken to be the result of experience, and we have, right or wrong, attached more importance to the experience of the past than we have to actuarial calculations.[8]

THE PERSISTENCE OF
REGIONAL IDENTITIES

However, the joiners took much longer to bring about full national integration than the engineers had done, with their amalgamated society being unable to recruit more than 10 per cent of the skilled men until after 1890, in large part because of the survival of rival organizations. Thus the General Union of Carpenters retained a strong base in Manchester with around 10,000 members in the north of England in the mid-1870s and, by adopting some of the amalgamated methods, managed to resist fierce poaching of its members by the new London-based society until finally being absorbed at the end of the century. Meanwhile in Scotland, where there had been local woodworkers' clubs throughout the 1840s and 1850s, often focused around tool insurance, a strike in Edinburgh in 1861 led to the formation of another rival, the Associated Carpenters' and Joiners' Society. This union was much less influenced by the model of the engineers: it set lower rates of individual subscriptions and exercised less influence over local strikes, but it did not confine its ambitions to the territory north of the border. By the mid-1870s the associated society had around 7,000 members and continued to compete with the amalgamated society for members until their eventual fusion in 1911.

A similar persistence of regional identities was to be found in the other building trades. The Operative Stonemasons' Friendly Society, for example, which had been formed in 1833, carried on recruiting members in new districts after the defeats of the mid-1830s and by the middle of the 1870s had the largest membership of the building trade unions at 25,000, focused mainly around Manchester, Birmingham and Bristol. However, while it modernized to the extent of giving up its traditional regalia, initiation and pass words in 1838, its subscriptions remained at only half the level of the amalgamated societies. Thus Henry Broadhurst recalled tramping around the south of England throughout the 1850s, and when he began to push for amalgamated methods within the society in the late 1860s he encountered significant opposition. He was successful in persuading the members to establish retirement benefit, a national executive committee and regular delegate meetings, but was unable to convince them of the value of 'static' unemployment benefit and encountered deep hostility when he struggled to bring local strike movements within some national coordination, particularly in the Bristol district. On one occasion he recalled:

A strike had been proceeding for six weeks when I, with other members of the Central Committee, went down to try to bring the dispute to a close. When we arrived in the neighbourhood we found among the men a widespread spirit of antagonism to our mission. To such an extent did this spirit exist that threats of violence if we dared to visit the works were freely indulged in. On the principle that threatened men live long, we paid little heed to these menaces and proceeded with our task. But the stubbornness of the men baffled all our efforts at conciliation.[9]

Meanwhile, the Scottish masons had been able to maintain a skeleton organization throughout the 1840s, particularly in Glasgow where they had struck for higher wages in 1848 and set up workers' education classes. In 1852 they began to operate on a Scotland-wide basis again in the form of the United Association of Operative Masons, pressing for payment by the hour rather than by fortnightly reckonings, and also for a reduction in the length of the working day. The union achieved a breakthrough over its nine hours' demand in Edinburgh after a three-month strike in 1861 and then managed to extend this throughout Scotland over the next few years: by the mid-1870s it had nearly 14,000 members in over eighty branches. Similarly, the bricklayers survived throughout the 1830s and 1840s, but provided few benefits and were divided after 1847 between two rival Orders based in London and Manchester: the northern one was initially the larger of the two, but the southern one adopted some of the 'amalgamated principles' and became aggressively expansionist through intrusive tramping and the active poaching of members.

Although the printers had long been a highly skilled and strongly organized trade, they too found the process of modernization a slow and difficult one. The pressures of unemployment during the long depression from the mid-1820s had led to attempts at the equalization of funds between local societies linked by the tramping system, through the formation first of a Northern Typographical Union in 1830, then of a National Typographical Association in 1844. However, the London societies felt that they were being required both to subsidize northern disputes during periods of prosperity and to accommodate northern tramps during periods of depression, so in 1848 the national federation split into three: the Provincial Typographical Association, based in Manchester, with differing local branch arrangements for subscriptions and benefits; the London Society of Compositors, with very limited benefit provision; and the Scottish Typographical Association. This failure to establish a single national body was paralleled by a failure to sustain attempts at the establishment of 'home donation', so tramping remained the basis of unemployment relief among the printers for another generation.

In Ireland the amalgamated societies were successful in penetrating into the Belfast area, where the relative scarcity of skilled labour and the accommodating attitude of the main engineering and ship-building employers made for favourable bargaining conditions. However, matters were very different in the south, where societies of the old local type continued to hang on. The traditional consumer crafts had achieved a high level of organization and inter-trade cooperation in Dublin in the 1820s, even if the employers' accusations of a conspiracy of coercion and intimidation headed by 'The Board of Green Cloth' were probably exaggerated. However, the Irish capital, while remaining a growing city on the basis of food processing and government administration, was in terms of general prosperity a city in decline from its late-eighteenth-century peak as free trade led to the increasing penetration of Irish markets by British manufactures. Dublin's craft organizations became rather stagnant and backward-looking, even without taking into consideration the growth of popular nationalism, which tended to weaken trade unionism as a result of a combination of nationalist hostility towards separate workers' organizations and Irish workers' own hostility towards mainland-based organizations, even when they were the best hope of improving their economic bargaining power. Within the building trades, for example, both the Dublin and Cork woodworkers rebuffed advances from the amalgamated joiners until the 1890s; and even when branches of mainland amalgamated unions were established they usually caused serious administrative problems for their headquarters by continuing to function as local craft clubs.

Thus the new 'amalgamated principles' of organization spread slowly through the more traditional crafts, in which there was a long persistence of low levels of subscription and benefit, of uncoordinated local wage strikes and above all of rival organizations based in London, Manchester, Glasgow and Dublin. Indeed the transition from loose networks of local clubs to more integrated unions with ambitions to wider coverage began to produce a significant degree of direct competition between these rival centres over members and territory. In some occupations this regionalism was connected with variations in working conditions and the strength of craft regulation, but in general the rivalries were due less to the pursuit of radically different principles on either welfare or industrial issues than to a preference for decision-making at a local level rather than the adoption of the new forms of national, representative democracy. Indeed such local feeling was frequently also evident in hostility towards the influxes of outsiders migrating from depressed areas, especially when they were easily identifiable by their accents, as in the case of periodic arrivals of large numbers of Scottish craftsmen in London.

However, the other side of the coin of this persistence of regional identities was the emergence of cooperation across occupations within the same area. Of course solidarity within the major towns had long been in evidence on a sporadic basis, in the form of support funds for trades involved in particularly serious disputes or of *ad hoc* committees to petition for specific pieces of industrial legislation. In 1843, inspired by the political movement of Chartism, a more ambitious body was set up to promote permanent cooperation of this type among the Sheffield trades, and in 1845 it called a national conference to encourage parallel bodies in other towns under the loose federation of the National Association of United Trades for the Protection of Labour. For a short while this body managed to support three full-time officials in London for lobbying purposes and to gain important parliamentary support from Thomas Slingsby Duncome, the radical MP for Finsbury. However, it became entangled in a costly legal dispute arising out of a strike among the Wolverhampton tin-plate workers in 1850, and its resources were fatally depleted. A few of the parallel bodies established at this time did, however, manage to survive, for example the Liverpool Trades Guardians' Association of 1848 and, as the prosperity of the following decade led to larger industrial disputes and greater political confidence, their meetings became more frequent and more ambitious.

From 1858 these local movements began to take firmer shape as permanent Trades Councils, the first two being in Glasgow and in Sheffield, where the young Robert Applegarth sat on the executive committee. In London a network of trade unionists had been meeting frequently during the 1850s at the Bell Inn near the Old Bailey to organize support funds for disputes both in the capital and elsewhere. Eventually, as a result of the major London building dispute and at the prompting of William Allan of the engineers, it gave itself a regular form as the London Trades Council: from 1861 it had fifteen elected members and George Howell of the bricklayers as its energetic secretary. In the course of the 1860s similar bodies were set up in urban areas throughout the country, either in conscious imitation of the pioneers or as a result of major local industrial disputes, and they achieved permanence in around twenty of the larger cities and towns. In Ireland they were established significantly later: not until 1881 in Belfast, where cooperation between groups of workers tended to be undermined by sectarian religious rivalry; not until 1886 in Dublin, where the sense of a separate labour interest tended to be overwhelmed by nationalist sentiment. However, despite this later start, these two Irish bodies were to play more important roles than their counterparts elsewhere in Britain, precisely because of the local barriers to even more ambitious forms of independent labour politics.

The trades councils were in principle open to all organized workers in their area but in practice became dominated by the smaller and more traditional craft unions. For the larger amalgamated societies became reluctant to waste their time in meetings where they could be out-voted by unions they tended to regard as irresponsible, and in any case they had much less need of external support. Thus the trades councils came to function largely as local forums for the discussion of industrial and political issues. They could offer advice and assistance during local industrial disputes, lead wider campaigns over local hours and conditions, and act as a stimulus to the extension of organization among the less skilled occupations and among women. They could also press for local and national legislation to protect weaker groups such as the sweated trades, and would frequently sponsor candidates for elections to local councils and school boards, as well as occasionally putting up candidates for Parliament. Thus, though the trades councils remained rather weak organizations which were vulnerable to the undermining of their financial resources during economic depressions, their local activities contributed significantly to the cultivation of the sense of a distinctive labour agenda.

6

State Intervention among the Process Workers

The Coal and Iron Miners of Lanarkshire have just passed through another ordeal. They solicited, several months since, the Masters to give a rise of wages such as they thought the trade could yield. The petitions were unheeded – the demands unanswered. Knowing that our cause was just, we struck work; and after, in some instances, a protracted, in others a brief struggle, our masters yielded and we are now about to enjoy the fruits of our perseverance and patience. During the time of our cessation from work our sentiments were fully interchanged. We saw that our divided condition served well the masters if they were, in any instances, wishing to resist a just demand. We accordingly agreed that in order to obviate this state of matters, our own anarchy should be overthrown, and that we should again lay, if possible, a basis whereby all the Coal and Iron Miners in Scotland might unite to save themselves from either being treated unjustly or oppressively.[1]

This was the bulk of an address to the miners of Scotland published in the *Glasgow Sentinel* in October 1855 which, after a couple of delegate meetings, had been drawn up for wider circulation by Alexander McDonald of the Holytown miners, and it illustrates well a number of features of the process industries and their unions in the middle of the nineteenth century. They clearly still had considerable difficulty in persuading their employers to accept the legitimacy of their existence and the value to both sides of collective bargaining, and the basis of their organization was still very much at the local level. While they were occasionally successful in pressing their demands for wage increases on their employers in periods when trade was good and prices were rising, they were rarely able to resist wage reductions when trade was poor, which led to considerable suffering for the men and their families.

Trade unionism was spasmodic, with widespread wage movements erupting from time to time, but the continuity of organization being dependent on tight networks of activists in specific districts. In the case of the Scottish coal miners there was a long tradition of able leadership coming from the rural pit villages around Airdrie in Lanarkshire: William Cloughan, an Irish immigrant to the district, had been one of the mainstays of local trade unionism in the 1840s, and James Keir Hardie was to be born there in 1856, becoming secretary of the Scottish miners in 1879 and one of the founders of the Labour Party in 1900. Meanwhile in the middle of the nineteenth century, the district's miners had clearly found an exceptionally articulate leader in Alexander McDonald, who was to become the recognized spokesman of the British miners as a whole during the 1860s.

Alexander McDonald had been born in 1821 on a farm just north of Airdrie, where his father had been working as an itinerant labourer, and when the latter shifted into underground work in the local iron-mining industry, young Alexander had gone down the pit at the age of nine to assist him as a 'drawer', hauling the tubs from the face to the bottom of the shaft. Almost forty years later, in his evidence to a major public inquiry, McDonald still vividly recalled the appalling working conditions he had experienced:

In the mines at that time the state of ventilation was frightful . . . The gases pervading the mines at that time in Scotland were, for the most part carbonic acid gas, not carburetted hydrogen; and I remember well often having three or four lamps put together for the purpose of keeping so much light as to enable us to see by. A very great deal of our drawing as we call it was performed in the dark in consequence of the want of ventilation in the mines . . . I may say incidentally here that in the first ironstone mine that I was in there were some twenty or more boys beside myself, and I am not aware at this moment that one is alive excepting myself . . . They died as miners . . . Their deaths were caused, I am satisfied, from the noxious gas, carbonic acid gas, that we then worked in, and the degrading kind of labour which we were subject to, and the long hours, 16 to 17 hours every day.[2]

As McDonald had grown older he had gradually worked his way up to the position of hewer, and had then deliberately sought out the more demanding and better-paid jobs so that he could save some money after making his contribution to the family's household income. For, having enjoyed a few years at the parish school where he had acquired an unusual passion for learning, he had continued to attend evening classes in Latin and Greek while working down the pit and after sixteen years had saved enough to study at Glasgow University for three years, still returning to work in the mines during the long summer vacations. McDonald had taken university classes in Latin, Greek, philosophy and mathematics, an intensive training in thinking and discussion which was to leave its mark in a sophisticated rhetorical style in his maturity, and which had eventually allowed him to return to Airdrie to work as a secondary-school teacher, while continuing to use his university contacts to build up a successful portfolio of industrial investments. However, as someone who had been an active trade unionist during his own time down the pit, living once again in the middle of a mining community surrounded by relatives and friends who still suffered from the industry's appalling working conditions, it had been impossible for McDonald to stand aside. Within a few years a local committee to campaign against the compulsory purchase of foodstuffs from the mine owners' 'truck' shops had begun meeting in his schoolroom. Then in 1855, largely on the basis of his private income from investments, he had taken on both the full-time secretaryship of the Holytown miners' union and the full-time secretaryship of the newly founded Coal and Iron Miners' Association of Scotland.

As a young man with personal experience of the benefits of self-improvement, education and small-scale business success, McDonald was impressed by the values and practices of the assembly workers in the local towns and cities. Indeed, in his early years as a miners' leader he attempted to introduce a number of the methods of the well-organized craft societies: welfare benefits, a financial interest in the *Glasgow Sentinel* newspaper, membership of the Glasgow Trades Council and later an emigration scheme. However, none of these attempts had any lasting success in the quite different circumstances of the miners, whose scattered semi-rural workplaces and vulnerability to substitute labour seemed to pose intractable problems of organization. Thus in 1856, immediately after McDonald's appointment as secretary of the Scottish association, their largest strike to date involved around 30,000 men over three months but failed to prevent the imposition of a wage reduction by the employers. McDonald himself preferred restriction of output and selective strikes supported by those still at work in other pits, but did what he could to support the widespread withdrawal of labour once it had broken out. The Scottish Miners' Association set up speaking tours and mass meetings, but there were no accumulated funds to support the men on strike and there was no attempt to extend the basis of organization beyond the hewers. There was more continuity of activity at the district level than there had been in the early years of the century and more energy, largely McDonald's, was put into maintaining communications between the district headquarters. However, the Scottish association was really only a loose federation for the purposes of public relations and parliamentary petitioning, and even the districts were still largely federations of individual pit societies which retained a great deal of autonomy over financial and industrial matters. In effect the miners' conception of wider trade unionism was still that of temporary combinations around specific wage demands, and as late as the middle of the 1860s the membership of the Scottish association was only around 6,000, or 15 per cent of the workforce.

McDonald, however, as a university-educated ex-miner, was well placed to make an already long-standing element of the miners' activity into a centre piece of trade-union strategy. For, when he began to appreciate that the best hope for progress was through the local law courts and the national parliament, he found that his personal experience of conditions in the industry combined with his ability to use the professional language of the day to make him into an extremely effective public advocate. Initially he focused on taking cases against Scottish employers under the existing anti-truck act and pressurizing Parliament for favourable amendments to it, but he soon moved on to tackle the whole range of working conditions in the industry. After his first visit to London in 1856, and the courtesy and encouragement he received from the Whig Home Secretary Sir George Grey over the issues of unjust weighing and excessive fines, McDonald wrote to his members through the *Glasgow Sentinel*:

From the little experience I have now had of the lobby of the House of Commons I believe that there is not a wrong that you now labour under that would not be redressed if you were now united to one another.[3]

In effect, faced with the problems of organizing the miners on a purely economic basis, McDonald was beginning to urge them to concentrate more on the industry-wide benefits of parliamentary legislation. He soon became a leading figure in a series of talks between representatives of mining districts throughout the whole of Britain which culminated in the formation in 1863 of the Miners' National Association, to mount pressure over such key issues as fair weighing, improved inspection and shorter working hours, and over the next ten years this body was able to achieve several notable pieces of state intervention.

Following this long and successful experience of political lobbying, it was McDonald who persuaded the Trades Union Congress to make its Parliamentary Committee into a permanent watchdog over Westminster affairs and he was elected to serve as its first chairman from 1872 to 1874. Then, after a false start at Kilmarnock Burghs in 1868, he became one of the first two trade unionists to be elected to Parliament under the auspices of the Labour Representation League when he became the 'Liberal and Labour' MP for Stafford in 1874, with his expenses covered by the Scottish miners. He held the seat until his death in 1881 and was a frequent speaker on working conditions and social legislation, especially accidents in the coal mines and employers' liability for industrial injury; as well as on such wider issues as free elementary education, Home Rule for Ireland and the excessive cost to the taxpayer of the royal family. Indeed, such was the contrast between the rhetorical style and intellectual confidence he had gained from his time at Glasgow University and the more modest and unassuming manner of his fellow miner MP Thomas Burt, that McDonald became something of a butt of journalistic sarcasm for having risen too far above his station in life.

Alexander McDonald was clearly an unusually gifted man, whose individual contribution may well have changed the course of labour history; certainly he was held in almost religious awe by the young Keir Hardie, who introduced him to a mass meeting of the Lanarkshire miners in 1879 with the following words:

There had often arisen great crises in history which required some great man to lead his fellows. They saw that in the case of Moses and children of Israel, Luther at the rise of Protestantism – and when they, the miners of Lanarkshire were crouching in a state of slavery they had found a McDonald with his high and lofty purpose, his strong will and his one-ness of aim, to place them on a level with other trades.[4]

Meanwhile, alongside McDonald's own formidable determination, the methods he pursued were beginning to emerge as typical of the seniority unions in general: campaigning for state intervention to protect standard hours and conditions of work as the only viable focus of unity in highly fragmented industries.

COTTON WORKERS

The cotton industry retained its predominance among the country's export sectors into the second half of the nineteenth century, at least as far as the size of its workforce was concerned: at almost 500,000 it was by far the largest in manufacturing, all the more impressive because of its concentration in Lancashire. However, despite the opportunity this would seem to have presented for trade unionism, the cotton workers still faced serious problems of organization as the continued expansion of the industry depended on increasing specialization between its branches. For example, there was a long-term movement away from combined weaving and spinning firms, with the former increasingly concentrated in the north and the latter in the south of Lancashire. Although more weavers tended to be organized than spinners, they were only a minority within their occupation, for even after the shift from outworking into factories they were still faced with smaller workplaces and larger numbers of female workers. The spinners were in a more advantaged position, but this was built on restriction of entry to the trade which had its cost in a tendency towards exclusive organization, initially leaving out even the piecer-assistants, not to mention the rest of the factory workforce. Moreover, even among the skilled and better-organized spinners themselves there was a broad distinction between the fine and coarse branches. Fine spinning produced more for the home market and was usually less affected by trade depressions. Production was concentrated in Glasgow and then increasingly in Manchester and Bolton, where the employers were introducing longer mules accompanied by discounts from the normal piece-rates for thread produced by the additional spindles, though once these were established and running at higher speeds the men usually found that their overall wages were not reduced. Coarse spinning produced more for export and was usually more severely affected by trade depressions. Production was concentrated to some extent in Oldham but was also more widely dispersed, with the low wages paid in the country posing a threat to the better-organized workers in the larger towns and the gradual introduction of self-acting mules creating a new occupation of semi-skilled minders, who became increasingly keen to form their own organizations.

Throughout the industry there was also still a good deal of local rivalry between regions and towns, which made united action difficult even among the men in one branch. For example, the spinners in the west of Scotland began the period better organized and tended to stand aloof from wider movements originating in Lancashire, while even within Lancashire the dominant position of the Manchester union was resented in some of the other large towns. Meanwhile, the smaller cotton towns in Lancashire were much affected by the increasing immigration of Irish Catholics after the potato famine of the 1840s, whose availability as substitute labour during disputes combined with their ethnic and religious distinctiveness to provoke significant outbursts of popular anti-Irish prejudice. While the cotton workers were therefore struggling to adapt to the continuously changing conditions within their own specialities and towns, the employers found it easier to establish a degree of coordination and soon learned to time their major confrontations to ensure that the unions were financially overstretched.

One answer to these problems of organization lay in the development of a particular kind of business ethos among the cotton workers. The wage-earning opportunities for several family members combined with the intense concentration of the industry to create strong occupational and local identities. Spinners were frequently assisted by their sons as piecers, while their wives and daughters might have been working in the preparatory carding department. The lower-paid weavers were even more dependent on the earnings of the whole family, with husbands and wives frequently working side by side in an unusually cooperative relationship. This sustained a strong sense of the household economy as well as strong links of mutuality between neighbours in the same position. The Lancashire cotton workers thus became renowned for their voluntary associations for economic purposes: friendly societies for savers, building societies for home-owners, going-off clubs for holidaymakers and above all cooperative societies for consumers. Indeed, the more pragmatic version of cooperation which spread rapidly outwards from Manchester in the 1850s promoted a particularly businesslike approach to household finances. For by refusing credit it encouraged tight budgeting, while by offering shares and dividing profits among shareholding members it encouraged both loyalty and an opportunistic approach to saving. On the basis of these practices it is less surprising to find the cotton workers keen to purchase shares in their own industry as they became increasingly available from the 1870s, but this should not obscure the deeply democratic nature of the voluntary organizations or their close connection with powerful drives towards self-education and self-assertion. As one experienced local observer wrote during the 'Cotton Famine' of 1866, when the drying up of raw-cotton imports due to the Civil War in the United States led to a short period of high unemployment, but surprisingly little social unrest:

The discipline of the cotton mill has spread its influences beyond the workshop, and regularity and punctuality have become essential parts of Lancashire life ... the effects of manufacturing discipline have not been less upon the workpeople than upon their employers. The habit of working together has taught them to associate for other purposes, and the necessity of submission to strict rules within the mill has led them to make rules for their own guidance in matters which seem to concern themselves more immediately ... [they show] an amount of prudent forethought and practical frugality for which few people give the working classes credit; and which must be productive of important results.[5]

These dense networks of mutual self-help may have encouraged an inward-looking localism as well as reducing the cotton workers' need for trade unionism, but they also provided them with important organizational resources. For example, most of the early union leaders supported themselves through small business ventures: John Doherty had become a printer and bookseller in the 1830s; Thomas Mawdsley, the long-serving secretary of the Lancashire short-time committee, was a provisions dealer; and John Fair, the secretary of the Manchester fine spinners, ran the Woodman's Hut Tavern in Manchester. As trade improved from the late 1840s the cotton workers tended to give up their early attempts to form grandiose federations and settled instead for solid local unions and hard-headed bargaining with their employers over the details of wage rates. When they began to give financial support to full-time officials the main function of these men was to work out the implications of particular wage offers, taking into account the size of the machinery, the speed of its operation and the thickness of the thread: for this they needed to have a good familiarity with the industrial processes involved alongside a high level of arithmetical expertise, and it eventually became customary to appoint those who came top in examinations in these skills. This business ethos was also reflected in the strategy of the cotton workers' pressure groups, with the factory movement continually resorting to calculated appeals to public sympathy for women and children as a device to secure a shorter working day for the adult men. Moreover, the very length of such agitation drilled them thoroughly in the business of petitioning Parliament, canvassing MPs and intervening in constituency election campaigns. Thus, even after the extension of the vote in 1867 gave the large concentrations of cotton workers in particular areas a decisive influence, they engaged in a more or less open bartering of votes for favourable legislation, especially in those Lancashire seats where there was no clear dominance of either of the two main parties.

Reviewing the course of events in the industry may begin in the late 1820s, when the mill owners became keen to challenge the position of relative advantage the spinners had gained during the long Napoleonic wars and maintained to some extent into the early 1820s, an impulse strengthened by the repeal of the combination laws in 1824 and the burst of strikes in its immediate aftermath. As a result the employers seized the initiative from the middle of the 1820s to the middle of the 1840s, managing to establish a downward trend in wage rates by engaging in fierce industrial disputes accompanied by the extensive use of substitute labour and the harsh victimization of union organizers.

In Lancashire reduced wages were imposed quickly on the spinners following strike defeats in 1826–7 in Ashton and Oldham, and then in 1829 in Stockport and in Manchester where the men were unusually well organized, paying high subscriptions in return for generous strike pay. Thus the defeats of 1829 were particularly bitter: violence against substitute labour in Stockport led to the deployment of troops, one hanging and three transportations; and a similar pattern was only avoided in Manchester by the district committee fudging the figures in favour of a return to work in a very narrow ballot result. Despite this tactical retreat the Manchester spinners were determined not to give up their position of relative strength without a struggle and, once again under the experienced leadership of John Doherty, they began to construct wider networks of financial support. First they set up the Grand General Union of Cotton Spinners throughout the United Kingdom, with the aim of providing strike pay of 10s. a week for district disputes approved by a national committee. Secondly, and even more ambitiously, they set up the National Association for the Protection of Labour as a general combination to provide a similar service across occupations: at its peak it claimed 100,000 members, though only 10–20,000 actually paid subscriptions regularly and they were mostly from the Lancashire textile trades. Doherty now became even more prominent as secretary of the Grand General Union and editor of the National Association's newspaper, initially called the *United Trades' Co-operative Journal* and later renamed *The Voice of the People*. However, these ambitious networks failed their first serious test at the end of 1830, when wage reductions were imposed in the coarse-spinning district around Ashton and 2,000 men came out in a dispute marked by serious incidents of violence, including the murder of the son of one of the employers. Despite the commitment of the Grand General Union to solidarity action as well as financial support, very little of either was forthcoming: the strike call was largely ignored by spinners elsewhere, the strike pay was only half what had been promised and it was all raised locally. As a result the house of cards constructed by the Manchester spinners collapsed rapidly in the course of 1831. The Ashton men returned to work in February and the Grand General Union dissolved in March; wage cuts were then imposed throughout Lancashire and the Manchester spinners' union itself disintegrated; this seriously weakened the National Association, which had already been undermined by its secretary's embezzlement of funds, and it effectively ceased to function in September. Despite an outburst of protest in Oldham in 1834 against the arrest of trade unionists, and temporary wage gains in Bolton and Preston in 1835–6, the employers retained the upper hand in Lancashire, especially during the trade depression of the late 1830s and early 1840s: even the strongest town unions involved only 30 per cent of the local spinners and there was no effective regional federation. Another association was attempted in the middle of the 1840s to press for wage increases, but this was undermined by the coordinated activity of the employers, the continued weakness of factory organization and the spinners' inability to back up their rhetoric about a region-wide strike with effective action.

In the west of Scotland the spinners retained their position of relative advantage for somewhat longer, feeling strong enough to keep their distance from the Manchester attempts at federation in 1829–30. Although further progress had been held back after bitter disputes in the 1820s, the Glasgow masters did recognize a standard rate throughout the area and the men continued to be able to make significant wage gains in years of trade recovery. Even into the 1830s the Glasgow union was able to maintain a solid regional organization with a reasonably stable membership of around 1,000, sustaining a reserve fund of £2,000 and a network of shop and delegate meetings. However, here too the spinners eventually experienced a major defeat when the employers coordinated a general reduction of wages to the Lancashire levels during a thirteen-week dispute in 1837. As usual the introduction of substitute labour provoked some attacks, including one fatal shooting, and this was used as an excuse for the prosecution of the union's officials in a major murder and conspiracy trial, extended to implicate them in a wide range of local incidents which had occurred since the 1820s. In the end only relatively minor charges of intimidation and molestation were sustained, but the prosecution's lurid picture was used to justify the transportation of five of the spinners' leaders. The tarnished image of Glasgow trade unionists inhibited the ensuing campaign of support, but persistent petitioning was eventually successful in securing their pardon and release from the hulks at Woolwich in June 1840 following the intervention of Lord Brougham, an independent Whig, and Thomas Wakley, Radical MP for Finsbury. The union managed to survive but in a much weakened form: a local wage list was established once again in 1840, but the employers were able to introduce female minders on some self-acting mules and in any case cotton spinning and weaving in the west of Scotland soon began a terminal decline in the face of Lancashire's overwhelming competitiveness.

It was not until the revival of trade after 1849 that the Lancashire cotton workers began to rebuild their organizations on a permanent basis and a long-term upward trend in wage rates was restored. Despite the gradual spread of the self-acting mule, the adult male spinners and minders were generally able to maintain their skilled status in the industry and their control over the employment and promotion of their assistants, involving the exclusion of women from work both on the smaller mules and on piecing. In sharp contrast the weavers achieved an improved bargaining position by the successful inclusion of women, many of whom were closely related to existing male members. Industrial disputes in cotton were generally conducted with less violence than they had been earlier in the century, although there did remain some mild intimidation of workers who refused to strike or would not make contributions to the strike funds. Instead the unions became increasingly realistic and prepared to compromise. It had become apparent that the industry would continue its long-term expansion despite periods of difficulty and that workers and employers had a common interest in maintaining their dominance of export markets: this would be the basis for wage advances but would also sometimes require wage reductions.

The spinners now began to make lasting progress in building up stronger district bodies, initially around Bolton, Oldham, Ashton, Stockport and Manchester. It had long been one of their tactics to focus their pressure on firms which paid less than the local average and hope for support or at least inaction from the rest, and this became increasingly formalized as unions and employers began to reach jointly agreed district piece-rate lists, beginning in Blackburn in 1852–3. The trend was briefly interrupted by the impact of a vigorous region-wide movement for a 10 per cent wage increase among the weavers, which drew in the more cautious spinners and met with initial success in Stockport, but was halted when the Preston employers stood firm in a thirty-eight-week lock-out of the whole local cotton industry in 1853–4. This dispute ended in another defeat for the cotton workers but it also revealed that in a prosperous period, with extensive financial support from other districts and other occupations, they were evenly enough matched against their employers' use of substitute labour not to need to resort to violence. What gave the final victory to the employers was the overstretching of the resources available to the Preston strikers by the outbreak of simultaneous disputes in Stockport and Blackburn. Although the wider wage movement then dissolved and the spinners returned to building up their separate district bodies, the huge expense and largely peaceful nature of the Preston dispute seems to have had the positive effect of encouraging more of their employers to recognize trade unionism and engage in detailed local collective bargaining. Meanwhile, the wage movement had been accompanied by a renewed federation and this eventually evolved into the permanent Amalgamated Association of Operative Cotton Spinners in 1870 with over 10,000 members, soon further strengthened by the affiliation of the large Oldham and Bolton districts which had initially held aloof. However, despite the gesture towards 'amalgamated principles' in this new body's title, disputes continued to be initiated at the district level, with the association's own monthly subscription set at only 2d. in contrast to an average of 24d. to its constituent bodies.

There were parallel developments among the weavers in the aftermath of the Preston dispute with the development of stronger organization at the district level, not only in Preston itself but also in Blackburn, Padiham, Darwen and Accrington. However, trade unionism among the cotton weavers had two distinctive features. First, there was a stronger tendency towards wider federation, with a power-loom weavers' association of 1858 developing into the North-East Lancashire Weavers' Amalgamation of 1878, which had 16,000 members. The power-loom weavers' district unions did retain considerable autonomy in the conduct of industrial disputes, but their county bodies were well enough financed to provide a group of specialized officials able to assist in calculating the effects of changes in complex district piece-rate lists. Second, the establishment of the first of these local piece-work lists had been the result of joint action by male and female workers, and by specifying the rates for each job they embodied the principle of equal pay. In practice the women were usually restricted to the smaller looms and lighter products and therefore remained on lower overall earnings, but this strategy of mixed membership and equal wage rates encouraged unusually high levels of participation among female workers and soon over half of the members of the weavers' organizations were women.

Throughout the difficult years from the middle of the 1820s to the late 1840s, the cotton workers led by the Manchester spinners had continued their pressure for state intervention to limit the hours of work in factories, aiming at a general ten-hour day. In the course of all his other activities John Doherty had set up a Society for the Protection of Children Employed in Cotton Factories in 1828, initially taking legal actions against employers under the 1819 and 1825 acts, but then turning it into a revived Manchester Short-Time Committee petitioning for new legislation. However, the initiative had passed across the Pennines after Richard Oastler's emotive 'Yorkshire Slavery' letter to the *Leeds Mercury* in September 1830, and the popular campaign for a ten-hour day for juveniles had come to be actively supported by many prominent Anglican paternalists for, although usually conservative in their politics, they felt responsible for the maintenance of basic social conditions. This led to unsuccessful Ten-Hour Bills proposed by the Tory MPs Michael Sadler (Leeds) and Lord Ashley (Dorset) and eventually, after delays for a parliamentary committee and a royal commission, to partial success in the Whig government's own 1833 Factory Act. This prohibited the employment of children under nine years old, limited the hours of work of those under eighteen and established a factory inspectorate to enforce all the existing legislation. In the face of these significant concessions it proved difficult to sustain the short-time movement, though there was continued pressure with further small peaks of agitation in 1836, 1837 and 1840–41. Local short-time committees revived as a stronger movement from 1844, coordinated this time by the Lancashire Central Short-Time Committee, with the organized spinners providing the bulk of its finances and leadership. This secured the passing of further restrictions on children's hours in 1844, and finally an apparent victory in 1847 with the passing of a Ten-Hour Act for women and young persons proposed by the radical MP John Fielden (Oldham). The employers, however, were able to evade the law by running staggered relays of protected workers alongside the same single shift of adult men: this kept the women and children at the factory for a long day even if they were not actually working all the time, and it simultaneously frustrated the expectation that protective legislation would have beneficial implications for the hours of the adult men. Despite the Short-Time Committee's futile call for a regional general strike, the spinners were in practice unable to do anything about it.

Once again it was through well-organized pressure on Parliament that progress was made: further measures in 1850 and 1853 established a normal working day of ten and a half hours, with a shorter Saturday for all protected workers, and thus also for those men dependent on their labour as assistants. In 1858 the Central Short-Time Committee was revived during a campaign to extend the factory acts to bleaching works, eventually successful in 1860, and over the next five years the benefits of the legislation were further extended to cover women and young people in lacemaking, the potteries, match-making, cartridge manufacturing and paper staining. In the early 1870s the short-hours movement revived once again in pursuit of a proper half-day Saturday, encouraged by the prosperity of trade and the strength of the district unions, initially through local collective bargaining. However, signs of coordinated resistance by the employers, especially in Oldham, made it clear that this could involve huge amounts of strike pay, and the spinners turned back again to their established method of pressurizing Parliament over women and children to win public sympathy. In 1872 the spinners and weavers joined together to form the Factory Acts Reform Association, organizing a mass petition with 200,000 signatures, coordinating the evidence presented to a select committee and closely questioning candidates during the 1874 general election. As usual this resulted in partial success, in the form of the new Conservative government's 1874 Factory Act reducing the working week to fifty-six and a half hours.

Despite their increasing concentration in one region and their prominence as initiators of 'general unions' in the early nineteenth century, the cotton workers had been unable to organize effective 'general strikes'. Indeed it had become increasingly clear that the main purpose of a Lancashire federation should be to prevent widespread industrial action and focus resources in support of a single local dispute, and it was the inability to enforce such discipline in a highly fragmented labour market which continually undermined the effectiveness of the spinners' wider associations. Thus it was the campaigns mobilized to press for state intervention over the hours of work which formed the most significant wider organizations among the spinners and the weavers, and which achieved the most significant general advances for employees throughout the industry. Moreover, with the achievement of a significantly shorter day by the early 1850s, the cotton workers had won themselves the free time in which to consolidate and extend the local networks of economic self-help which were to lie at the basis of subsequent trade-union expansion.

COAL MINERS

Steam-powered railways and steamships opened up new parts of Britain for mining, created wider markets for the product and were themselves dependent on readily available supplies of fuel: as a result the output of coal grew continuously from the middle of the nineteenth century. However, as new mines were opened up and the workforce grew to over 200,000 it became if anything more difficult to organize, for there were increasingly wide divergences of conditions between the coalfields and even between the localities within them. One of the most important divergences which began to emerge between the fields was that between those on the east coast exporting to European markets and those in the west selling in the home market. In the export fields, such as Northumberland, Durham and Fife, the companies were less able to resist downward pressure on prices from overseas competitors, the miners began to recognize that they had an interest in common with their employers in maintaining market supremacy, and they began to accept that wages would have to be reduced from time to time to achieve this. In the home-market fields, such as Yorkshire, Lancashire and the Midlands, the companies could hope to maintain coal prices more easily, the miners retained an attitude of greater assertiveness over their own share of the revenues, and they began to develop a more ambitious set of demands around minimum wages and maximum hours. Indeed such variations in types of coal and management strategies could also lead to divergences of bargaining conditions between the localities within each field. For example, while the Lanarkshire field in the west of Scotland was producing largely for the home market, the pits south of the Clyde sold coal for domestic use while the pits north of the Clyde were frequently owned by expanding iron companies. As a result the sort of divergence noted between fields was also found within this field: the southern firms could pass on the cost of wage increases more easily to the consumer and tended to allow the emergence of more independently organized workforces; but the northern firms were less prepared to absorb wage increases in the cost of the coal they were going to use themselves and were active in promoting more subservient workforces.

Meanwhile, the rapid expansion of the industry and its demand for labour was leading to the equally rapid establishment of residential settlements and a legacy of significant divisions within them. For waves of migration could lead to conflict between local workers and newcomers, particularly in the western coalfields where the arrival of large numbers of Irish workers after the famine years of the 1840s was compounded by the historic bitterness between Protestants and Catholics. In the west of Scotland, for example, a society of mainly local workers emerged in the 1860s known as the Free Colliers: with close parallels to the Freemasons and the Orange Order, it had a policy of excluding Irish Catholics, and, while it devoted most of its energies to social functions, it also operated as a distinct faction within the Scottish miners' association. Even in the eastern coalfields, where there was less ethnic tension, there were still important differences between underground and surface workers, and between male wage earners and female household managers, each of whom tended to form separate networks, each with its own distinct sense of the interests of their community. Thus, while there were powerful elements of spontaneous feeling arising from the common experience of dirty and dangerous work and the compact structure of the residential settlements, the renowned industrial solidarity of the miners still had to be consciously constructed.

The core groups of activists committed to this task in the early years were usually members of evangelical religious sects, above all the

Primitive Methodists. This provided them with the energy and group discipline needed to persevere in a hostile environment; it gave them a vivid biblical language of slavery, trials and the promised land to make sense of their harsh experiences; and it trained them in such basic techniques of organization as reading, writing and public speaking. Thus in contrast to the city craftsmen's long-standing connections with the public house, trade unionism in coal mining became intimately bound up with the chapel, and it spread into less well-organized districts through continuous speaking tours and mass meetings in which the tradition of the tramping artisan was paralleled by that of the evangelical lay preacher. Once a degree of support had been gained at the local level, the activists consolidated it through the use of powerful symbols, above all lodge banners which combined highly coloured images of brotherhood and carefully chosen mottoes imbued with the outlook of religious nonconformity. Thus among the earliest phrases on the Durham miners' banners were: 'We live for the well being of our fellowmen in order that they may live for ours,' and 'May we ever be united, let us love one another.'[6] These banners were regularly paraded, accompanied by local brass bands, not only within each settlement but also at the county level during the annual 'galas' held at the height of summer, a combination of family outing and ritual occasion which had a powerful emotional impact on all who attended. According to the local press, the first Durham Miners' Gala in 1871 was attended by 25,000 of the union's members:

In addition . . . not less than from 40–50,000 men, women and children were present, making a total of between 70 and 80,000. Each of the lodges and its accompanying friends marched in procession through the town from the railway stations at Shincliffe and North Road to the meeting place, and a great feature was the banners they carried . . . [the president said] their object in meeting was to have a day's pleasure and enjoyment, to congratulate each other on their past success, to bond themselves more closely, if they possibly could, in the bond of brotherhood, and to show the country at large that the Durham Miners' Association was not a myth or a creature of the imagination, but a stupendous fact.[7]

On this basis of the intimate social network around the local chapel and the regular mass celebration of the county gala, the activists were increasingly able to build lasting cooperation in county unions and, after the 1867 Reform Act extended the vote to more working men, to secure the election of favourable MPs in the parliamentary constituencies where the mining population was predominant.

Reviewing the course of events in the industry reveals that, as in cotton, the relative prosperity and success of local trade unionism in the first two decades of the nineteenth century was followed by a long period of less secure employment, wage reductions and outbreaks of violence during disputes in which the men were usually defeated. The miners in the Northumberland and Durham coalfields continued to produce the most ambitious attempts at trade-union organization, for here there were already fifty pits employing around 200 men each in the 1830s, when the national average was nearer fifty men per pit. In 1831 the Primitive Methodist hewer Tommy Hepburn emerged as the leading figure in a union bridging the two counties which held together during a two-and-a-half-month strike of 17,000 men in pursuit of wage increases and other concessions: it was successful in winning shorter hours for juveniles and was even able to provide Hepburn with a salary as a full-time organizer. Hepburn was strongly opposed to the use of physical coercion but in 1832 the employers mounted a determined counter-attack by introducing a non-union oath and substitute labour from other regions, provoking more violent incidents than during the successful strike of the previous year and eventually breaking up the union. Meanwhile in the Scottish coalfields the aftermath of the unsuccessful strike wave of 1825–6 had reduced the miners to bitter struggles at individual pits to maintain some control of the relationship between their output and earnings, involving ejections, beatings and even ear-cuttings of those who refused to take part. There was then a wider movement for wage increases during a short boom in coal and iron prices in 1835–6 and the re-establishment of a General Union of Operative Colliers throughout Scotland, but when prices began to fall again the mine owners were able to cut wages by bringing in substitute labour whenever necessary and the union had collapsed by October 1837. Throughout these years it remained common for striking miners in Scotland to take the crops from local farmers' fields to support themselves and their families during disputes, and this led to large counter-mobilizations of yeomanry and special police.

Meanwhile, the level of unrest in south Wales was even more serious, for here the coal mines were closely connected with the local iron works, and the workforces of both suffered from particularly aggressive wage cuts and high levels of indebtedness. A sequence of riots in Merthyr during the parliamentary proceedings of Grey's Reform Bill came to a dramatic climax on 3 June 1831. A tussle between a crowd and soldiers from a Highland regiment resulted in the shooting of at least sixteen people including some innocent bystanders. Unusually, the crowd did not disperse but rather kept control of the town for the next three days; however, this only resulted in three transportations and the hanging of one young miner, Richard Lewis (Dic Penderyn), as a scapegoat. Similarly, in the Monmouthshire coalfield physical coercion by the miners was endemic, and 1832–4 saw the peak of the 'Scotch Cattle' movement, which used the long-standing rural tradition of 'ceffyl pren' (mock trial) as the basis for night-time meetings, anonymous letters, attacks on pit-head equipment and the intimidation of substitute workers, who were frequently English immigrants. This too was ultimately suppressed by stiff action and the hanging of one more miner, Edward Morgan, as a scapegoat in 1835.

In 1842–3 links were established between activists in Yorkshire and Durham resulting in the ambitiously titled Miners' Association of Great Britain and Ireland, under the influence of Tommy Hepburn and the leadership of David Swallow, a Yorkshire miner, W. P. Roberts, a solicitor from Bath, and Martin Jude, an ex-miner and Newcastle publican. All of these men were active in the political movement of Chartism at this time, which gave them access to skilled organizers and journalists from outside the industry as well as a ready-made network of national links. At its peak in 1844 the organization claimed to represent 70,000 miners, around 30 per cent of the industry's workforce, but its support was still predominantly in the north-east of England, where it took the customary form of a temporary movement against wage reductions in a trade depression, doomed to fail and to have its national pretensions rapidly exposed as a hollow shell. The association had a full-time general secretary, a national executive and a regular delegate conference, as well as its own newspaper, the *Miners' Advocate*. It also had a clear strategy, favouring restriction of output to raise coal prices and wages, and only being prepared to consider striking if it took the form of industry-wide action. However, it was unable to centralize its affairs fully, for at least half of the subscriptions remained in the hands of the districts and the full-time travelling lecturers had considerable scope for independent action. Even at the national level W. P. Roberts became increasingly wild: having established his popularity in Northumberland and Durham after winning legal cases against employers' oppressive use of the yearly contracts or 'bonds', he began to encourage local disputes against the policy of both the executive and the conference. This led to a major four-month strike in the north-east in 1844, which was defeated by the usual methods of importing substitute labour and victimizing union activists, after which organization in this key region collapsed and with it the ambition to maintain a genuinely national union. The title of the Miners' Association of Great Britain and Ireland survived for another four years, but after 1844 it was a loose federation of districts, mainly in Lancashire, engaged in frequent local strikes and conflicts with substitute labour: its final demise was signalled by the imprisonment of its remaining activists for their involvement with a Chartist revival in the summer of 1848.

From the late 1840s the coal industry began to grow more rapidly again, with the output of coal remaining on a long-term upward trend throughout the second half of the century. Coal miners' organizations having survived at the pit and district level, stronger county federations now began to emerge and disputes in the industry tended to become less violent, due partly to generally improving conditions and partly to the law-abiding advice of their leaders. Alexander McDonald emerged as the leading figure in a Scottish association as early as 1855, but its district components were both weaker and less cooperative than those in the major English coalfields. Partly for this reason McDonald spent a great deal of energy building Anglo-Scottish links particularly with the Northumberland and Durham activists, culminating in the Miners' National Association of 1863, which claimed over 120,000 members in 1873. However, despite the awesome potential of such an enormous national organization (four times the size of the powerful engineers' union), this was a very different kind of occupational body from the amalgamated craft unions of the period, for it levied only 1d. per member per month (in contrast to the 4s. of the engineers and the joiners), and it used this money to press for parliamentary intervention rather than its own independent welfare and strike funds. At the same time, its existence does seem to have increased the miners' confidence to build up organizations for these other purposes. A Northumberland Miners' Mutual Confident Association was formed in 1862, with the highly effective Thomas Burt as secretary from 1865; a parallel Durham Miners' Association followed in 1869 with William Crawford as secretary from 1872, introducing an unusual degree of central coordination. The West and South Yorkshire Miners' Associations were both initially formed during strikes in 1858, South Yorkshire with John Normansell as secretary after 1864 becoming one of the best-organized coalfields. These county unions began to adapt more pragmatically to market conditions, as they learned from repeated experience that strikes for higher wages in periods of rising prices were likely to succeed, while strikes against wage cuts in periods of falling prices were likely to fail. At the same time the pits and districts still retained a great deal of control over funds and local bargaining, so it was not always easy for the county leaderships to maintain common policies or coordinate industrial actions.

Indeed, the persistently divided nature of miners' trade unionism was further underlined by the emergence of a rival federal body, the Amalgamated Association of Miners, founded in 1869, with its base in Lancashire but extending its influence into the neighbouring districts of the Midlands and south Wales. Under the influence of Thomas Halliday this organization adopted 'amalgamated principles' at least as far as the establishment of a centralized strike fund under the control of a representative executive committee, but it cooperated with McDonald's National Association over pressure for parliamentary legislation. It claimed almost 100,000 members in 1873; however, as coal prices fell from 1874 onwards, it collapsed during an uncoordinated wave of local strikes against wage reductions, leaving in its wake the long-established patchwork of pit and district bodies, and merging what was left of its central organization with McDonald's association to form the Miners' National Union in 1875.

McDonald's emphasis on the formation of a political pressure group achieved more long-term success due in part to increasing public recognition of the exceptional danger of underground work in the industry. Already in 1860 a national movement of districts under his leadership had been able to secure favourable amendments to the government's Mines Inspection Act, with the parliamentary assistance of the Whig MP Arthur Kinaird (Perth). These improved the inspection of pit safety arrangements and enforced the practice of 'checkweighmen' to ensure that the miners were not cheated during the weighing of coal and the calculation of their piece-rate payments. Then, as first president of the Miners' National Association from 1863, McDonald found another parliamentary ally in Lord Elcho, the liberal-minded Conservative MP for Haddingtonshire, who helped to secure favourable amendments to the Master and Servant Acts in 1867 and a further Mines Regulation Act in 1872. This controlled the hours and conditions of work of boys and further strengthened the powers of both the mine inspectors and the checkweighmen. With the onset of industrial depression in the mid-1870s the Miners' National Association also suffered defeats in local strikes against wage reductions and was gradually pushed back into its heartlands of county organization: in England mainly Northumberland and Durham, in Scotland largely restricted to Fife.

McDonald's further ambitions for an eight-hour working day in the mines and the statutory enforcement of employers' liability for industrial accidents therefore remained unfulfilled. However, his strategy had not only achieved a number of immediate improvements for working miners but had also introduced an important basis of organization in the checkweighmen, who gradually evolved into a vital layer of full-time union officials with statutory protection. For they were elected by ballot and paid by the miners in the pit, they could be chosen from outside the immediate workforce and they had legal rights of inspection and representation. The miners still faced a major struggle to build an inclusive federation for the coal industry but the interdependence of their trade unionism with state intervention was firmly established: favourable legislation was not only their national goal but also lay at the basis of their local organization.

7

Trade Unionists and Popular Liberalism

I seek your suffrages to defend a right, the right of *the great mass of the people* to a voice in the making of our laws; to support a policy – the policy of the Liberal Party, whose recognized leader is Mr Gladstone; and to promote a principle – the principle that other interests in the State, besides land and capital, should have their representatives in the British Parliament – the interest of the Wage-receiving classes, and of the entire industry of the Nation, whether Agricultural or Manufacturing.[1]

This was part of the election address of the trade unionist George Howell when he first stood as a parliamentary candidate in 1868 for the rural borough of Aylesbury in order to test opinion in the agricultural community following a significant extension of the franchise. The Liberal leader William Gladstone had already made considerable headway in reducing the burdens of government spending and indirect taxation during his career as Chancellor. Now an increasingly broad alliance of reforming candidates, particularly such 'advanced Liberals' as Howell, promised to provide legislative relief across the whole range of long-standing radical grievances: further measures of political reform, church disestablishment, land reform, education provision, industrial arbitration, and the equalization of the poor rates. Though supported by the leading radical MP John Stuart Mill, Howell's lack of a local connection, along with the bribery and coercion usual in such constituencies, guaranteed a victory for his Tory opponent. However, undeterred by this initial failure, he continued to fight elections and by-elections until finally successful for the more suitable London borough of Bethnal Green in 1885, following yet another extension of the franchise and a redistribution of seats. As a 'Liberal-

Labour' MP Howell remained a champion of radical reform until he retired from politics ten years later: presenting regular bills for manhood suffrage, triennial parliaments and the public payment of election expenses; pursuing cases of business and public corruption; and being chosen by Samuel Plimsoll as the main parliamentary spokesman for the agitation over improved safety at sea.

George Howell had been born in 1833 in Wrington, Somerset, by a coincidence also the birthplace of the liberal philosopher John Locke almost exactly 200 years earlier. For his part, Howell had little formal schooling and began working long hours on building sites with his father from the age of twelve, but after two years escaped to begin an apprenticeship with a local shoemaker. This was a turning-point in his life: he had been brought up in a fairly conventional Anglican environment but was now introduced to the world of workshop debate, the Chartist press and religious nonconformity, through which he began an energetic pursuit of self-education. In the course of wide reading, seventeenth-century republicanism soon emerged as a central point of reference, with John Milton later remembered as his teacher and Oliver Cromwell as his hero. Howell returned to work for his father for a while, picking up the skills of bricklaying, and then moved to London in 1855 with the ambition of pursuing a political career:

My ideals were scarcely those of the class of workmen with whom I was to come into contact. The book world was my ideal, but I had no fitting preliminary training for the use of my pen as a mode of even assisting me to get a crust. In character I was almost puritanical, a total abstainer, which in itself was scarcely a recommendation in the building trades at that date. I was strongly imbued with religious convictions, which I can only describe as puritanical protestantism. I was modest, even to shyness, and yet there was a firm self-reliance, natural to my character. I do not think that the idea of not succeeding ever entered into my head.[2]

Of course it took him longer to make his way in the world than he anticipated, but by 1859 he had become a deputy foreman, had acquired a treasured reader's ticket to the British Library, and had relaxed his religious principles enough to become deeply involved in the more secular world of the capital's radical clubs. Howell then became very active during the London building dispute of 1859 and subsequent trade movements involving the bricklayers, and in 1861 was elected as his union's delegate to the executive committee of the London Trades Council. Here he collaborated closely with Robert Applegarth of the joiners and George Odger of the shoemakers to persuade trade unionists of the value of political action. This took some time and the additional stimulus of overseas events, but they eventually succeeded in establishing the National Reform League in 1865, with Howell securing the post of paid secretary as well as lodgings for his family in the back room of the office. This required the same administrative skills as running a national trade union: there were minutes to take, financial records to keep, a massive correspondence to maintain and public meetings to arrange and address, and Howell proved not only adept at all of them but able to sustain very long hours of office work. As a result he established himself as the first full-time political organizer in the trade-union world and was then the natural choice to become the first secretary of the Trades Union Congress's Parliamentary Committee in 1871, in which post he developed outstanding lobbying skills around the issue of the reform of labour law. Thereafter Howell continued to use his experience and skills to put together an income from journalism and organizing work, including securing the election of working men to the London School Board and raising the parliamentary profile of the National Union of Women's Suffrage Societies, before finally achieving his real ambition of election to Parliament as one of the early group of trade-union MPs.

While the National Reform League was financially dependent on its middle-class sympathizers and tailored its strategy to support its parliamentary allies, and Howell himself had a quiet, almost scholarly, temperament, there was never any sense of hesitation or deference in his manner. Already in October 1865, at the beginning of what was to become a successful national campaign for the extension of the franchise, he was urging the radical leader John Bright:

... no time should be lost by the Liberal Party in arranging their tactics, and organizing their forces, for a determined parliamentary campaign for Electoral Reform during the coming session ... If the Liberal Party through procrastination or supineness, or by apathy or indecision, neglect to take their stand upon the present vantage ground, as the representatives of the liberal and progressive spirit of the nation, they will properly forfeit the confidence and support of the toiling masses of their countrymen, and instead of occupying the foremost place in the councils of the nation, will sink into deserved insignificance and obscurity.[3]

For Howell in other words the dependence was mutual: the middle-class politicians would have to respond to the mounting tide of popular opinion as embodied in the trade-union movement or be swept aside. Indeed, after the success of the franchise campaign, when the League decided to support existing Liberal candidates fighting under the new electoral arrangements, the influence of his exposure to Chartism as a teenager was still evident in Howell's indication of the conditions required for their approval:

We must go in for the best men we can get to come forward, but better have *new* liberals than old Whigs. *I hate the Whigs*. They have been our enemies and are now . . . we must tell the professing Liberals that their programme must be a good and bold one and their pledges must be kept or they will not do for us.[4]

Similarly, while the Trades Union Congress was dependent on its close allies among the radical MPs for their parliamentary interventions during the campaign to reform trade-union law, it was clear where the real pressure for the repeal of the offensive legislation was coming from. As the TUC resolved in 1874:

. . . every delegate present pledges himself to assist in holding public meetings, arranging demonstrations, and making such other efforts as are in his power to remove this obnoxious piece of class legislation. If the Act is not repealed during the ensuing session of Parliament, it will be the duty of working men to oppose all candidates at the next General Election who uphold the Act.[5]

As a result, while urging these popular campaigns to aim for moderate and realistic demands, Howell was rarely reluctant to embark on public demonstrations of mass support. During the franchise campaign he was the main organizer of the rally which came to be regarded as a highly threatening riot in Hyde Park in July 1866, and then of a further, though this time orderly, defiance of a government ban on assembling there in May 1867. During the labour laws campaign he and Alexander McDonald launched strongly worded criticisms on the Liberal government from platforms at large demonstrations held in the major cities and throughout the mining districts in the spring and summer of 1873. Finally, when in his retirement Howell put together his own recollections with detailed research to produce a survey of *Labour Legislation, Labour Movements and Labour Leaders* (1902), it was published in *The Reformer's Bookshelf* series alongside the life stories of Samuel Bamford, the veteran of 'Peterloo', George Jacob Holyoake, the pioneer of Cooperation, Richard Cobden of the Anti-Corn-Law League and Charles Bradlaugh, the leading secularist agitator. As the main organizer of two of labour's most important political successes in the course of the nineteenth century, the parliamentary reform of 1867 and the trade-union law settlement of 1871/5, George Howell fully deserved his place in this radical pantheon. And he made it clear in his Preface that he saw himself as part of a long tradition of assertive campaigning:

The story of Labour's struggles, its victories and defeats; the fierce contests which for centuries were waged against it to keep it in subjection; and its resistance from time to time, involving suffering, privation, prosecution, and persecution required to be told, for it finds no place in the so-called 'Histories of England'. For half a century my lot has been cast amid those struggles; and I have, as best I could, contributed to the amelioration of the hard conditions under which working men still suffered fifty years ago, to emancipate themselves from which they fought and strove against the oppressive forces opposed to them.[6]

George Howell's career thus illustrates a number of important developments in the mid-nineteenth-century world of labour. While he emerged on the public scene as a result of the dispute in the London building trades, he came from the Bristol area and brought with him a personal experience of the attitudes and outlook of religious nonconformity, which had become increasingly important in the rest of the country. Moreover, the London-based campaigns for which he went on to work as a paid organizer were the first well-coordinated national political movements of labour, and most of his close collaborators in them were full-time officials of the first unions with a genuinely national coverage. On the basis of this improved mobilization of trade unionists as a recognized interest group, and of the extension of the franchise which they played a major part in securing, it then became possible for ordinary working men to enter Parliament for the first time. This was soon taken for granted, but initially it was seen on all sides as an almost revolutionary development, brought about by strenuous agitation on the part of those previously excluded from political participation and regarded with deep misgivings by many of those still ignorant of the real opinions of the people.

RADICALISM AND CHARTISM

Earlier in the century the London radicals had managed to keep their networks alive despite the weakening of trade unionism in the second half of the 1820s, with Francis Place continuing to provide guidance over petitioning and parliamentary procedure and John Gast still tirelessly appealing for wider alliances between the local craftsmen's clubs. Their main campaigns, both of which met with some success, had been for the repeal of the Corn Laws, seen as an unjust tax on the productive community to benefit the parasitic landed classes; and against government regulation of benefit societies, seen as an unwarranted interference in democratic organizations which had ominous implications for trade unions. Though they disagreed in their interpretation of the emerging economic ideas of the time, they all began to accept the existence of a market and looked to improve their position within it. The parliamentary radicals tended to accept the more orthodox version of 'political economy' and to argue that birth control and emigration would reduce the supply of labour and lead to higher wages. Meanwhile, the trade unionists tended to look from the other end of the chain and to argue that higher wages would increase consumer spending, stimulate production and promote full employment.

In Manchester John Doherty had continued to act as a point of contact after the middle of the 1820s, particularly over the campaign for the repeal of the Corn Laws, but the process workers were increasingly pursuing a distinct agenda of state intervention to deal with problems they were unable to resolve on their own. Thus the spinners were reviving their Short-Time Committees to press for legislative reduction of the factory working day, the handloom weavers were pressing for local 'boards of trade' to enforce standard wage rates, and the miners were complaining about the lack of regulation of the company 'truck' shops. As has already been mentioned in the previous chapter, these campaigns tended to attract more support from paternalistic Tories than from liberal Whigs, who were more concerned to remove the old system of state regulation and to extend the freedom of trade. In addition, the consistently bitter nature of industrial disputes in the coal and textile industries fuelled a tendency for these workers to use violent anti-employer rhetoric even when they were only struggling for basic trade-union rights. Despite significant points of contact, then, there were also important differences and potential misunderstandings between the assembly workers in the major cities and the process workers in the northern industrial districts.

These years of depressed trade and weaker trade unionism had also seen a wave of interest in various forms of cooperation, mostly based on long-standing popular practices. Thus the device of setting up cooperative workshops to support strikers during industrial disputes was extended in the late 1820s to support craftsmen suffering from unemployment particularly in the building, clothing and metalworking trades in London and Glasgow. Simultaneously, cooperative bulk buying and food processing, long in evidence among the Scottish weavers and the London shipwrights, became more formalized in retail stores along the lines of a model project set up in Brighton in 1828. More ambitiously, these schemes were brought together in the early 1830s in Labour Exchanges in most of the larger cities, offering to buy workers' products for 'labour notes' which could be redeemed for other goods in stock. However, these quickly proved vulnerable to the tendency to make over-generous allowances for labour in a period of falling wages, while the goods in stock were not only more limited in range but also more expensive than those available in ordinary shops.

Some of those involved in this widespread movement had already been inspired by the ideas of Robert Owen, the enlightened manager of a cotton mill at New Lanark in the west of Scotland, where he had also provided housing, shops and a school, and developed his own distinctive vision of alternative communities as the basis of social change. Owen had just returned from a failed attempt to set up 'New

Harmony' in North America and began to urge his followers to use the devices of popular cooperation in order to raise money to buy land for a new moral community in Britain. He was a persuasive lecturer and attracted a number of significant figures in radical circles, for example William Lovett, a cabinetmaker who served for a time as the storekeeper of the Owenite society in London, and Alexander Campbell, a joiner who became an influential newspaper editor in Glasgow. However, both Owen's paternalism and his anti-Christianity were obstacles in the way of securing a wider following and his links with trade unionism should not be exaggerated. At the height of the building workers' ambitions in 1833, Owen encouraged them to set up a cooperative initiative known as the Grand National Guild of Builders with himself as president, which was to provide employment for those thrown out of work, particularly on an ambitious Guildhall in Birmingham: however, the financing of this project quickly ran into serious trouble and the Guild as a whole had disappeared by 1835. Similarly, during the activity around the Grand National Consolidated Trades Union, Owen encouraged the London craftsmen to acquire cooperative workshops and he appeared at the front of their demonstration over the Tolpuddle martyrs: however, by the end of 1835 this had all fizzled out along with the Grand National itself. Moreover, in both these cases there was a significant tension between the trade-union tradition of running temporary workshops to subsidize industrial conflict with the employers, and Owen's aim of promoting social harmony through paternalistic guidance of permanent communities, and his closest followers' energies turned increasingly towards a particular brand of secularist education.

The political vision of the mainstream of organized labour continued to revolve around the reform of Parliament to remove the burden of the parasitic classes, with activity reviving during the 1830 election which followed the death of George IV and being further stirred up by news of the overthrow of the reactionary monarchy in France. The Duke of Wellington's unpopular Tory government fell in November 1830 and the following spring the Whigs introduced an ambitious reform bill to extend the borough franchise and redistribute seats towards the manufacturing districts. However, this was repeatedly held up by the House of Lords, provoking a series of massive demonstrations which were accompanied by particularly violent incidents in Bristol, Nottingham and Derby in the autumn of 1831, and by a threat of a run on gold at the Bank of England in the spring of 1832: the Lords were forced to give way and the 'Great Reform Act' was passed at the third attempt in June 1832. There was a good deal of popular interest in this agitation for parliamentary reform, particularly among the assembly workers in the cities: a large number of craft unionists were undoubtedly active as individuals, and craft-union contingents were in evidence at demonstrations to protest against the Lords' obstruction and to celebrate their giving way. Under the influence of Place the strategy of cooperation with the middle classes in local Political Unions to support the Whig measures, as a first step in the right direction, remained the dominant one in London, Birmingham and Glasgow. A rival National Union of the Working Classes, with Gast and Lovett among its leaders, did not secure much of a following for its opposition to the reform bill, which it condemned as a consolidation of the establishment through the inclusion of the middle classes, though it did have links with the followers of Henry Hunt in Manchester and with some of the more plebeian Political Unions in the handloom-weaving districts.

In the aftermath of 1832 the Whigs became keen to distance themselves from extra-parliamentary unrest and, though there were more radicals in Parliament as a result of the new electoral arrangements, they were too divided among themselves to act as a coherent pressure group for more democratic measures. As a result Whig governments were constantly prosecuting and imprisoning the radical editors of the 'unstamped' press, who were determined to keep their publications affordable by refusing to pay the required duty. They were equally repressive towards trade unionists, above all in the cases of the 'Tol-puddle Martyrs' in 1834 and the Glasgow cotton spinners in 1837, leading to the establishment of a London Combination Committee to keep a vigilant eye on the government's broader intentions. Moreover, the Whigs did nothing to improve conditions for adult textile workers, as their 1833 Factory Act only covered those under eighteen years old. Above all their major piece of social innovation, the New Poor Law of 1834, became highly unpopular for its withdrawal of outdoor relief and its establishment of the deterrent effect of the segregated workhouse, a particularly unsuitable way of dealing with local cyclical unemployment in the textile-factory districts. Consequently the Lancashire cotton workers' Short-Time Committees transformed themselves into Anti-Poor Law organizations and mounted a massive protest campaign, effectively maintaining the payment of outdoor relief in the north and sometimes even electing their own representatives on to the Boards of Guardians.

This widespread disillusionment with the results of 1832 provoked three waves of protest centred on the demands of the 'People's Charter', which marked the emergence of radicalism as a genuinely popular movement. The Charter itself was a product of the familiar London leaders, with their decades of experience of campaigning for greater democracy in local and national government: drafted by Place and Lovett in 1837–8, the famous 'Six Points' were for annual parliaments, equal electoral districts, universal male suffrage, vote by ballot, the abolition of property qualifications for candidates, and the payment of MPs. The long-established practice of pursuing these demands in cooperation with middle-class radicals and parliamentarians was continued by the London Working Men's Association, the revived Birmingham Political Union and the Glasgow Universal Suffrage Association, the latter including ministers of the Church of Scotland among its leading figures as well as inspiring the formation of new 'Chartist Churches'. However, the first breakthrough to wider popular support came in the Lancashire and Yorkshire textile districts where, in speaking tours from 1835 and as editor of the highly influential *Northern Star* from 1837, the charismatic Irish former MP Feargus O'Connor was able to step into Hunt's shoes as the gentlemanly hero of radicalism and at the same time to capitalize on the massive regional protests against the New Poor Law by turning his oratory into sharp attacks on the Whigs. This campaign had elements of violent rhetoric and Tory paternalism which tended to alienate the London radicals, but in 1838–9 it culminated in a major wave of outdoor meetings throughout the north of England, at the largest of which hundreds of thousands of protesters, many of them marching behind trade-union banners, signed petitions for the Six Points and seemed prepared to defend themselves against the kind of state-sanctioned violence which had taken place at 'Peterloo'. The Newcastle tailor and Chartist agitator Robert Lowery left a vivid impression of one of these massive meetings on Kersal Moor outside Manchester:

When we got out of the streets it was an exciting sight to see the processions arriving on the Moor from different places, with their flags flying and the music of the bands swelling in the air, ever and anon over-topped by a loud cheer which ran along the different lines. On ascending the hustings a still more exciting sight awaited us. The *Times* estimated the meeting at about 300,000. One dense mass of faces beaming with earnestness – as far as you could distinguish faces – then beyond still an immense crowd, but with indistinct countenances. There is something in the appearance of such multi-tudes, – permeated with one thought or feeling, – whom no building made with human hands could hold, met beneath the mighty dome of God's sublime and beautiful creation, and appealing to Him for a cause which they believe to be right and just, – something which, for the moment, seems to realize the truths of the ancient saying – 'The voice of the people is as the voice of God'.[7]

However, Parliament disappointed the moderates by rejecting the massive petition and the government simultaneously frustrated the extremists by avoiding clumsy repression, limiting itself instead to a series of arrests of local leaders. There were some outbreaks of violence, especially notoriously the exchange of fire at Newport in south Wales in November 1839 when twenty demonstrators among a crowd of 5,000 were killed by a small group of soldiers stationed in a local hotel. However, this was largely the result of the strong traditions of intimidation in the region's coalfield, which had produced both the Merthyr riots of 1831 and the endemic 'Scotch Cattle' movement: the leading local Chartist, John Frost, played an ambiguous role and the evidence for links with other centres of ultra-radicalism is unclear. In any case, with the government holding back from executions of the Newport men but confining over 500 other Chartist leaders in prison throughout the country, the main wave of mass support began to fall away and never really recovered.

Three years later, after Parliament's rejection of a second Chartist petition, there was a brief wave of industrial action in the north of England in the summer of 1842, usually referred to as the 'Plug Plot' riots and considered to have had significant political overtones. Deepening industrial depression was leading to further rounds of wage cuts in the coal and textile industries and widespread resistance in Staffordshire and Lancashire, which spread across the Pennines to Yorkshire. The main protests were therefore over economic issues: wage reductions and the truck issue in the Staffordshire coalfield, wage reductions and the Ten Hour Bill in the Lancashire cotton mills. They received their name from a new form of coercion when activists not only used the intimidation of numbers but also took the plugs out of steam boilers and thus enforced a total stoppage of workplaces: it is therefore difficult to be sure how much support the movement had, as many of those involved were simply forced to stop work, but eventually there were over 1,500 arrests and seventy-nine transportations. The national Chartist leadership was keen to keep its distance, but groups of activists, inspired and brought together by the wave of Chartist meetings three years earlier, emerged as the leaders of the industrial protest in most of the areas affected and were able to persuade a number of local and regional delegate meetings to adopt the 'Six Points' as one of their demands. However, they were unsuccessful in persuading the strikers themselves to stay out for political goals and, in a period of weak trade-union organization, even the determination to resist wage reductions was soon worn down. Once again the government was careful to minimize political provocation: though in the initial panic there were arrests of national Chartist leaders, their trial eventually petered out without sentencing.

In the years that followed there were increasing signs of a realignment of Chartist activists with middle-class radicals in the north of England, especially as they were now able to join in attacking a Tory government. Initially the Chartists had bitterly opposed the Anti-Corn Law League led by the Lancashire businessmen Richard Cobden and John Bright, harassing its meetings so much that they often had to be restricted to ticket holders. This was partly because they saw the issue as a diversion from further parliamentary reform, partly because many of them were still unsure about the principles of free trade, and partly because Cobden and Bright were opposed to the Factory Acts. However, the League's highly professional publicity, including the foundation of the *Economist* magazine in 1843, made its mark over what was after all a long-standing radical issue with immediate consequences for working people. The total abolition of the Corn Laws was increasingly seen as a strategic assault on the privilege of the landed aristocracy; the parliamentary leaders of the Irish movement and leading figures among the nonconformists were won over; O'Connor was bested by Cobden in a public debate in 1844; and eventual repeal under the additional pressure of the Irish Famine was widely and enthusiastically welcomed in 1846. A number of attempts to start a new joint campaign for national political reform came to nothing, but radical craftsmen in the larger urban centres, particularly Leeds and Sheffield, were achieving significant successes as Chartist candidates in elections to local government bodies, where they began to cooperate with the more advanced elements in the local Liberal parties.

Meanwhile the London assembly workers were continuing with their traditional forms of self-organization under the broad label of Chartism. The London Working Men's Association had always been predominantly a debating club and William Lovett in particular began to emphasize educational projects. The lasting influence of Owenism was also evident in the widespread appeal of plans for buying land and establishing new settlements. The London radicals remained highly sensitive to events overseas, especially in Poland and Ireland, and maintained strong links with liberal and republican exiles from the more repressive states of continental Europe. Thus the third and final wave of Chartist activity which came in the aftermath of the overthrow of the French monarchy in February 1848 saw particular excitement in London, especially as it coincided with a brief period of severe unemployment in the capital's skilled trades. O'Connor's National Charter Association organized another mass petition and a rally which attracted perhaps as many as 150,000 demonstrators at Kennington Common in April, matched by equal numbers of policemen, soldiers and special constables, as the authorities too had been stirred up by the events in France. On being told that it would be barred from marching to Westminster the crowd broke up peacefully; however, with continued rumours of ultra-radical conspiracy and riots in the East End over the summer, the government was taking no chances: by the end of the year 300 leading Chartists were once again in prison.

Chartism is rightly remembered both as the moment of entry of really large numbers of ordinary working people into the political arena and as a demonstration of the centrality of constitutional reform at the heart of their concerns. The 'Six Points' had a genuine appeal in factories, mines and workshops, in the north and in the south; they secured a considerable degree of formal support at trade-union meetings; and they directly influenced labour politics up to the First World War with significant echoes even down to the present day. However, Chartism was also deeply marked by its historical context, which was one of economic depression, organizational disarray and political division: its goals may have been shared by a wide variety of working people, but they were not pursued at the same time or by the same methods. The core of mass support came from the textile districts in the north of England, where concessions over the operation of the New Poor Law, further instalments of factory legislation and the repeal of the Corn Laws took much of the heat out of the protest. The use of 'physical force' was always controversial, with only small groups of ultra-radicals keen to pursue the French revolutionary model and only attracting supporters in districts where violent methods in pursuit of moderate goals had long been prevalent in industrial relations. Elsewhere the tradition was one of 'moral force': intimidation by sheer numbers, which might spill over into violent incidents but could generally be contained by careful police action. Even at the height of the Chartist movement there was no evidence of any widespread popular will for political insurrection, and most of those imprisoned for their involvement in violent incidents emerged from the whole experience convinced that in future it was only worthwhile pursuing peaceful methods, and that these were more likely to succeed if supported by the broadest possible alliance of reformers.

LABOUR AND LIBERALISM

While the 1850s marked something of a lull in mass political mobilization between the bitter protest of the 1840s and the more confident assertiveness which was to emerge in the 1860s, the groups of committed radicals remained just as active as they had been ever since the end of the Napoleonic Wars. With around eighty radical MPs associated with the Whigs in Parliament there was a constant stream of reform bills, none of which came to anything because of the lack of public interest combined with divisions among the reformers themselves. Meanwhile, the aged Francis Place was still a figurehead for such extra-parliamentary agitations as the National Parliamentary and Financial Reform Association and the more focused Association for the Repeal of the Taxes on Knowledge, which, by gradually removing all duties from newspapers, eventually achieved a victory for the old agenda of the unstamped press. There was also still a lively interest in the struggles of liberals and republicans in the rest of Europe, especially in Poland, Hungary and Italy, with Tsarist Russia emerging as something of a bugbear during the Crimean War, which once again highlighted the corruption of the aristocratic establishment at home. Among the London craftsmen William Newton, a skilled engineer and former Chartist, had emerged as a successor to John Gast in coordinating joint activity through the Metropolitan Trades Committee: he was editor of the *Operative* and a succession of other labour papers, a leader of the newly founded Amalgamated Society of Engineers in its national dispute in 1851, the first trade-union parliamentary candidate when he stood for Tower Hamlets in the general election of 1852, and a prominent spokesman for the union case during the London building dispute in 1859. In the course of the 1850s he also played an important role in an unsuccessful campaign over the master and servant law as well as in a successful one for the extension of friendly-society legislation to protect trade unions, both of which received some radical parliamentary support.

By the early 1860s the unions had established themselves as a significant national pressure group centred on the London Trades Council, which had emerged out of the 1859 building dispute. The leading figures were increasingly drawn from among the national officials of craft unions which had their headquarters in London: William Allan of the engineers, Robert Applegarth of the joiners, Edwin Coulson of the bricklayers and George Odger of the shoemakers. These men were the 'new model' secretaries, renowned for their caution over the use of strikes and their efficient administration of welfare benefits but also committed to political action, both as a first step towards the reform of trade-union law and also as a matter of principle, influenced by their youthful exposure to Chartist ideas. In 1862 they set up the Manhood Suffrage and Vote by Ballot Association, announcing that 'hitherto, our efforts have been directed to the removal of one evil only, forgetting, or only partially remembering, that all the evils under which we suffer have a common origin – namely, an excess of political power in the hands of those holding a higher social position'.[8] By this stage public expressions of the views of non-voters had become a recognized feature of election campaigns in the manufacturing districts and it was widely accepted that it was only a matter of time before there was another major instalment of constitutional reform. John Bright, now an MP for Birmingham, had launched an extra-parliamentary campaign against aristocratic government, focusing on household suffrage, the secret ballot and a further redistribution of seats, which evolved into the National Reform Union. And Ernest Jones, a former Chartist, had launched a parallel campaign for political rights, focusing on manhood suffrage, the secret ballot and the abolition of property qualifications for MPs, but pre-pared to cooperate with any realistic move towards reform even if it fell short of this programme.

Two international catalysts then fused these groups of radicals into the leadership of a new mass movement. First the American Civil War, which, especially after President Lincoln's Emancipation Act of 1863, united reformers of all ages and shades under Bright's leadership in support of the democratic North against the aristocratic and slave-holding South. And second, the visit of the Italian radical leader Garibaldi in 1864, which produced a huge trade-union procession to escort him through the streets of London and subsequently a campaign of protest, alongside middle-class radicals, against the government's termination of his stay before he had toured the provinces. This sense of participation in a broad international struggle for democracy led to the London Trades Council's leading role in the foundation of the International Working Men's Association, which increasingly fell under the influence of its more revolutionary elements. It also led to a wider popular interest in a further instalment of constitutional reform at home and the setting up of the National Reform League to campaign for manhood suffrage, with George Howell as its secretary and the affiliation of craft unions and trades councils throughout the country. The League's first success was in coordinating trade-union resources during the general election of 1865 to secure the victories of such important pro-union Liberals as Thomas Hughes at Lambeth, John Stuart Mill at Westminster and Joseph Cowen at Newcastle. Then the death of Lord Palmerston later that year removed a major conservative force from the leadership of the Liberal Party and the radical movement emerged in full force: despite the difference in their ultimate goals the trade unionists' Reform League began to work closely with Bright's Reform Union, functioning as the popular wing of a sometimes uneasy but nevertheless effective alliance.

The wider public response grew stronger with every obstacle placed in the way of a further extension of the franchise, especially after the defeat of the Liberal Chancellor William Gladstone's moderate reform bill of 1866, the formation of a Conservative government initially opposed to any change, and an escalating crisis over the legal status of trade unionism described in more detail below. There was a rising wave of Reform League protests which began to include the additional issue of the prohibition of political meetings in public parks, leading to a notorious incident in London when a huge crowd pressed so strongly against the railings of Hyde Park that they were pushed over and the park was occupied for several days in July in defiance of the police and several companies of troops. However, the League's leaders carefully avoided any violent provocation and continued to build the momentum of peaceful meetings throughout the country. The largest of these were in the traditional centres of extra-parliamentary radicalism, Birmingham, Glasgow, Manchester and the West Riding of Yorkshire: there were huge trade-union processions and the reappearance of Chartist colours and emblems as hundreds of thousands gathered to hear celebrated orators, including John Bright and Ernest Jones. When the Conservative Chancellor, Benjamin Disraeli, brought in a reform bill based in principle on the household suffrage but so qualified with propertied safeguards that there would be little real extension of the franchise, the Reform League constituted itself as the head of a permanent and genuinely national movement, with fortnightly delegate meetings in London, weekly demonstrations in Trafalgar Square and another massive rally in Hyde Park in May 1867. The initiative was then taken by the parliamentary radicals: during the committee stages of his bill Disraeli, hoping both to defuse the extra-parliamentary agitation and undermine Gladstone's leadership of the

Liberal party, accepted a stream of radical amendments resulting in a genuine household suffrage act with even the inclusion of some lodgers. Overall this gave the vote to about 30 per cent of working men, amounting to a majority in some urban constituencies, the significance of which was later consolidated by the Liberals' introduction of the secret ballot in 1872. Full democracy may still have been some way off but, especially on the eve of the first general election under the new franchise, it seemed that something very significant had been achieved after fifty years of struggle. In the words of the leading radical newspaper in the north of England:

We are 'recurring to the ancient principle of the Constitution' – returning to the 'wisdom of our ancestors'. The inhabitant-householders have recovered their long-lost rights; and wherever there is a contested election, they will exercise them today at the poll . . . the People's Parliament is coming into life. The principle of the old Reformers are triumphant. The franchise for which they contended amid obloquy and proscription, is now in the hands of the people . . .[9]

Thus began a real if slow process of change in the political system: the aristocratic establishment may not have been abolished overnight, but the larger urban electorate called for more professionally organized political parties, over which ordinary working people were increasingly able to exercise an influence. This was especially the case with the Liberal Party, which was becoming radicalized under Gladstone's leadership and acquiring considerable credit for its role in promoting all of the measures which concerned trade unionists in the period. In addition to the extension of the parliamentary franchise itself, another important democratic measure was the Liberal Education Act of 1870: initially welcomed for its introduction of publicly funded primary schools, it became enthusiastically regarded after pressure from the union-backed National Education League brought about the establishment of local school boards directly elected by all ratepayers with no propertied or gender qualifications. Then in 1875, over the most contentious issues of trade-union law, the pattern of 1867 was repeated when a promising Conservative bill was transformed into a 'final settlement' through a series of Liberal amendments. Meanwhile the issue of government intervention to regulate working conditions in factories and mines, which had earlier divided radicals, was now so well established as to be taken for granted as a bi-partisan and largely technical matter. Within this context of substantial legislative concessions, Gladstone himself was beginning to emerge as a unifying focus for the diverse currents of radicalism. A long series of appointments as Chancellor had given him an unrivalled appeal as a champion of free trade, reduced government expenditure and lower indirect taxation, closely connected with a broader liberal concern for educational and moral improvement. A celebrated speech in 1864, accepting the broad principle of the moral qualification of responsible adult men to have the vote, had become a standard point of reference in the popular liberal press. And almost simultaneously, in 1865, he had made clear his support for religious liberty and his willingness to begin the disestablishment of the Anglican church, building a bridge towards militant nonconformity. In this way the basis was laid for an important transition from popular enthusiasm for outstanding heroes of extra-parliamentary pressure, in the tradition of Hunt, O'Connor and Bright, to popular enthusiasm for outstanding heroes of statesmanlike reform, with Gladstone eventually taking on the role of the 'Grand Old Man' of the new tradition.

Moreover, a similar pattern was repeated at the level of the constituencies, where the electors favoured well-known local figures with proven track records on radical issues. In the coalfields the miners' unions tended to become the grass-roots organization of the Liberal Party and their local leaders emerged as natural candidates and often as successful Liberal MPs. Elsewhere, however, trade unionists had a hard time pursuing parliamentary careers: they had no money to pay for their election campaigns or their expenses as MPs, and when national trade-union bodies attempted to resolve this problem it usually involved introducing candidates without any local connections. In the 1868 general election the Reform League simply campaigned for existing advanced Liberal candidates and, even after its evolution the following year into the Labour Representation League to support trade-union candidates, it was unable to make much headway. Indeed the very success of the miners' independent political organization led to a significant divergence in trade unionists' perceptions of the need for a coordinated initiative. Thus, despite the distinctive contribution of Alexander McDonald, the leading parliamentary figures of popular liberalism still tended to be drawn from among the business and professional middle classes: statesmen such as A. J. Mundella, who played a key role in the reform of trade-union law; thorns in the side of the establishment such as the secularist Charles Bradlaugh and the independent Joseph Cowen; and, increasingly acting as the informal leader of the trade-union group of MPs, the republican radical Sir Charles Dilke.

The contrast between the failure of Chartism and the success of the Reform League was the result of a number of factors. The simple passage of time allowed the innovations of 1832 to become familiar, making it easier for the nation's rulers to consider a further step towards democracy. Meanwhile on the part of the reformers there was a greater willingness to settle for demands which had a chance of being met, a more effective alliance between the popular and the middle-class wings of radicalism, and better links between the extra-parliamentary movement and sympathetic MPs. However, the most important difference between the 1840s and the 1860s was the emergence of a really strong and nationally coordinated trade-union movement, able to impress the urgency of its demands and the seriousness of its intent on the minds of the governing classes. A more detailed consideration of its policy ambitions and the organizational constraints of the period then clarifies what might otherwise seem paradoxical from the standpoint of the twentieth century: why such a democratic triumph for organized labour should not have been quickly followed by the emergence of a separate Labour party. Indeed, from the standpoint of the nineteenth century the mystery would rather seem to be the other way around: why such a separate Labour party should eventually have been felt to be necessary at all.

THE STRUGGLE FOR
LEGAL ACCEPTANCE

Despite the success of the campaigns of the 1820s in repealing all the laws against combination and in providing immunity against criminal conspiracy for actions over wages and hours, the legal status of strikes remained ambiguous into the second half of the nineteenth century. This was partly because the 1825 act had also introduced the new offences of 'molesting and obstructing' during industrial disputes without adequately defining the meaning of these terms. While some judges interpreted them narrowly as applying to threats of physical violence by pickets, others began to interpret them much more broadly as applying to any interference with the conduct of an employer's business, thus setting precedents for regarding the act of striking itself as illegal once again (*Regina v. Duffield* and *v. Rowlands*, 1851). Sustained pressure from the National Association of United Trades for the Protection of Labour, which had suffered from this latter interpretation, led to the 1859 Molestation of Workmen Act, which clarified the meaning of the 1825 act by permitting 'peaceable and reasonable' forms of persuasion of other workmen during industrial disputes. However, some judges quickly began to undermine this through the application of the law of threats to cover the threat of economic harm to an employer (*Walsby v. Anley*, 1861). Then, as the tide of trade unionism rose increasingly rapidly in the 1860s, judges of an individualist turn of mind tried to resist it through broad reflections on liberty (*Regina v. Druitt*, 1867), and particularly through the application to industrial relations of the concept of 'restraint of trade', which had originally concerned promises by sellers of business property not to compete with the buyers. Thus, despite the earlier success of the Metropolitan Trades Committee's pressure in achieving protection for trade-union funds under the 1855 Friendly Societies' Act, some judges began to rule that unions were not entitled to use the courts to take actions for fraud against their own officials because they were inherently in restraint of trade and therefore illegal bodies (*Hornby v. Close*, 1867).

While there were still pockets of genuine coercion among the shoemakers and the brickmakers, matters had been brought to a head by the 'Sheffield Outrages' of 1866. These were the product of local conditions in the small workshops of the cutlery trades, in which trade unionists had long practised acts of sabotage against uncooperative workers, including 'rattening' or removing the power belts from tools, and now engaged in acts of violence, including the blowing up of one workman's house. Trade unionists more generally realized that they

would have to take urgent steps to clear their reputation: the other
Sheffield unions supported the town council and local employers in
calling for a government inquiry, and Robert Applegarth went to see
the Home Secretary. A body of Examiners was indeed set up to inquire
into the issue of intimidation in Sheffield and elsewhere, but the resistance of much establishment opinion to rising trade-union strength also
led to the setting up of a more wide-ranging Royal Commission in
February 1867. The leaders of the amalgamated crafts realized that
this situation needed concerted handling if the whole legal status
of trade unionism was not to be permanently undermined: Allan,
Applegarth, Coulson, Odger and Daniel Guile of the ironfounders set
themselves up as the Conference of Amalgamated Trades to meet
weekly with professional advisers and coordinate their response. They
were unsuccessful in their first request for two trade unionists to be
appointed to the Royal Commission, but did secure the nomination of
one member who was friendly to their case, for which they chose
Frederic Harrison, and the attendance at hearings of one expert trade
unionist, for which they chose Applegarth, with Thomas Hughes
already being a member as an interested MP.

The strategy then pursued was to focus the Commission's attention
on the amalgamated societies, with Applegarth appearing as the first
witness to give evidence on his own union, followed later by Allan,
Coulson and Howell. The picture they presented of their organizations
was partly as friendly societies providing welfare insurance, partly as
craft organizations exclusively concerned with wages and hours: they
played down anything which might be interpreted as restraint of trade
and anything which went beyond peaceful persuasion. Moreover when
J. A. Roebuck, the strongly anti-union MP for Sheffield, challenged
the actuarial soundness of the friendly-society side of their activities,
Applegarth and Allan were only too happy to engage in a detailed
discussion of financial matters. Finally, when evidence on the building
and cutlery trades brought to light clear cases of intimidation, the
friends of the unions were reassured by the evidence of the Nottingham
hosiery manufacturer A. J. Mundella, who strongly supported trade
unionism and presented evidence on his own system of collective
bargaining. The Commission remained fairly evenly divided but, in
order to get an agreed report, the anti-union judge in the chair made

concessions to Harrison's whittling away at an initial draft until the overall tone was entirely altered. As a result the first comprehensive Royal Commission on the subject came out broadly in favour of collective bargaining, recommending the separation of strike and welfare funds and the protection of the latter under the friendly societies' legislation, which was indeed immediately reinstated by a special act in 1869. Harrison and Hughes put forward their own Minority Report, calling in addition for protection from the doctrine of restraint of trade and the restoration of immunity from charges of criminal conspiracy. Along with Mundella, who had just defeated Roebuck during the first general election under the new franchise, they worked on a private member's bill along these lines but withdrew it on the promise of further comprehensive government legislation.

Meanwhile, steps had been afoot to establish a permanent national forum for trade unionists. Ever since the favourable attention to the unions at the 1860 conference of the National Association for the Promotion of Social Science, a number of self-educated printing workers had participated in that body, and when it had taken an anti-union stance after the Sheffield Outrages they had responded with independent initiatives of their own. In 1868 Sam Nicholson, then president of the Manchester and Salford Trades Council, organized a conference where thirty-four delegates from other provincial trades councils discussed papers on issues of common concern and also pledged their support to the amalgamated craft leaders in their activities around the Royal Commission. A follow-up conference in Birmingham in 1869 then saw greater coordination of the provincial and the London activists when forty delegates met and agreed to publicize the union case and lobby MPs in support of the Minority Report. It is worth noting that this increasing national unity had been preceded by greater unity among the London assembly workers themselves. For George Potter, a young carpenter who was a member of an independent local society in London and had played a leading role in the 1859 building dispute, had for some time been critical of the national officials of the amalgamated craft unions who had become so influential on the London Trades Council. He had favoured more independent decisions about local strike action, propagated his case through his editorship of the *Bee-Hive* newspaper, and even attempted to secure separate representation at the hearings of the Royal Commission. However, his failure to achieve this, along with declining sales of his newspaper, led to a rapprochement with the leaders of the amalgamated crafts after the general election of 1868: Potter agreed to support the Minority Report and Applegarth, Coulson and Odger joined the managing committee of the *Bee-Hive*.

This increasing unity of the various centres of labour organization around the radical programme of the Minority Report contributed significantly to the passing of the Liberals' two trade-union acts. In 1871 the third national conference in London of what was now known as the Trades Union Congress (TUC) successfully lobbied to have the clarification of the contentious issues of 'molesting and obstructing' dealt with separately, so that the legislation on strike action could be further amended in due course without reopening basic questions about the status of trade unions. Thus the 1871 Trade Union Act gave permanent protection to union funds under the friendly societies' legislation as well as relieving unions of the legal consequences of restraint of trade. Meanwhile the 1871 Criminal Law Amendment Act made it clear that the form of threat or intimidation at issue was indeed that to persons but, amended by the House of Lords under the impact of the Paris Commune, added new categories of offence including 'watching and besetting'.

Although pleased with the progress that had been made, the TUC maintained its campaign of pressure for completely equal treatment under the law, not only reaffirming the permanence of its Parliamentary Committee with George Howell as its secretary, but significantly broadening its basis by electing Alexander McDonald as its chairman. Previously the geographical separation of the coalfields from urban manufacturing centres and the miners' willingness to make use of Conservative parliamentary support to secure state intervention over their working conditions had distanced them from the radical-liberal movement for parliamentary reform. Thus when McDonald had lent his weight to the Glasgow Trades Council's campaign against the particularly harsh application of the 1823 Master and Servant Act in cases of workers' alleged breaches of contract in Scotland, he had brought success through his close links with the chairman of the relevant Select Committee, the Conservative MP Lord Elcho. A special act of 1867 had subsequently removed the provision for immediate arrest and replaced sentences of up to three months' hard labour with fines of £20 as the maximum punishment in normal cases. Then, when McDonald had first begun to show an interest in broader issues of labour law, he had initially aligned himself with Potter against the London Trades Council. However, from 1872 the forum of the Parliamentary Committee united the most experienced labour parliamentary lobbyists, and McDonald established a particularly close partnership with Howell.

While there were a number of bills of particular interest to the miners to monitor, the main focus remained the more general issues of labour law, for some judges continued to act as if the legislation of 1867 and 1871 had not been passed. In the case of the London Gas Stokers in December 1872, unusually severe sentences of twelve months' hard labour were handed out to six of their leaders for criminal conspiracy to organize a breach of contract and to interfere with their employer's liberty. And in 1873 sixteen agricultural labourers' wives from Chipping Norton were sentenced to several days' hard labour for the intimidation of substitute labour through shouting. Through pressure on the government the TUC secured a reduction in the gas stokers' sentences and then, through careful lobbying and a particularly impressive demonstration in Edinburgh, the agreement of the new Home Secretary, Robert Lowe, to the repeal of the Liberals' own Criminal Law Amendment Act. However, the TUC was still not taking any chances and drafted detailed questions on labour law to be put to candidates of both parties during the snap 1874 general election, urging trade unionists to withhold their support from candidates who did not give satisfactory replies. Meanwhile the Labour Representation League put forward a group of trade-union candidates and managed to get two members of the Parliamentary Committee elected with local Liberal support: McDonald himself for the shoemaking town of Stafford and Thomas Burt for the mining constituency of Morpeth.

Although it was the Conservatives who won the election, the extraparliamentary campaign had been successful in securing a measure of bi-partisan agreement. Matters were delayed by the setting up of another Royal Commission, but the Conservative Home Secretary R. A. Cross showed his willingness to move in the trade-union direction in his Conspiracy and Protection of Property Bill. Then, faced with tireless lobbying by Howell and unusually high turnouts of Liberal MPs, Cross accepted a number of key amendments from Lowe and Mundella. These effectively enacted the programme of the original Minority Report by excluding the charge of criminal conspiracy from industrial disputes unless the action itself was criminal, and permitting the communication of information as an exception to the offences of 'watching and besetting'. At the same time the 1875 Employers and Workmen Act completed the amendment of the master and servant law by putting workmen's breaches of contract on the same purely civil footing as those of employers.

As in the case of the extension of the franchise, then, the trade-union struggle for legal acceptance gathered strength from popular outrage over conservative resistance to what were widely seen as morally justified demands. This gave trade unionists a good deal in common with religious nonconformists and, when their case was presented in the form of a right to equal treatment under the law, an irresistible claim to the support even of moderate Liberals. Moreover, in the case of labour law the rights being pursued could plausibly be seen as having already been established in the early nineteenth century, then re-stated and extended in the 1850s, and only under discussion once again because of the stubborn and ingenious rulings of hostile common-law judges. If the constant enemies of trade unionism were obvious, so were its constant friends, and ten years later one of the Durham miners' leaders was still commenting:

If anyone looks through the discussions of these measures they will see that the best portions of the acts . . . were amendments prepared by the Liberals, and incorporated into the acts as a result of their labours. With these facts before me . . . I cannot see any inducement to make working men endorse Conservative politics, but on the other hand, there is much to make them . . . have some respect for Liberals and Liberalism.[10]

PART THREE

The 1870s to the 1920s

8

National Bargaining among the Assembly Workers

They knew that in Germany and in Russia it was the intention of the rulers to get the better of Trade Unionists and to forget the rising tide of democracy in those countries. They knew that that was part of their war scheme. Were they quite sure that there was no such original intention on the part of the rulers of this country? They found that the longer the war went on, the more their liberties as Trade Unionists were curtailed ... Why should they always have the necessity of going to the Government on their questions? Did the financiers of the country require to go to the Government to make sure that their investments would be returned to them? ... The Trade Unions' fault had always been their modesty. They had never asked and demanded enough, and he hoped that now they were going to take the Prime Minister's advice when he said to them some months ago that what the workers of this country wanted was 'Audacity, audacity, audacity'.[1]

These are extracts from a speech on the restoration of trade-union conditions given by John Hill, the secretary of the boilermakers' society, at the Labour Party conference of 1918 when the party was laying out its first comprehensive programme as a fully independent alternative to the Liberals. Hill had been chosen to propose the official resolution on these matters because he was widely regarded as one of the most influential union leaders of the time, and his remarks therefore indicate a number of important features of trade unionism among the assembly workers in this period. The first thing which is striking is his confidence as a player on the national stage, now prepared to approach on equal terms not just the employers but even the government. Indeed, as Applegarth had done fifty years earlier, Hill expressed this assertiveness through a cheeky response to a traditional authority figure:

taking the Prime Minister's earlier words out of context and using them as an appeal to the unions to challenge the government. The second thing which is striking in Hill's remarks is the persistence of long-standing concerns over democracy, liberty and equal treatment. He expected a growing popular movement to be given a fair hearing by the government, but his underlying aim was to secure the widest possible scope for self-organization, contrasted sharply with the dangers of state intervention which could be seen elsewhere in Europe. Thus Hill and the Labour Party were calling on the British government to move quickly over its promised withdrawal from wartime involvement in employment relations in the munitions industries, involving the complete restoration of pre-war custom and practice, the removal of emergency restrictions on the right to strike, and full consultation with the unions over all proposals for future changes in wages, hours and working conditions.

John Hill had been born in Govan on the Clyde in 1862, and after serving an apprenticeship as a plater in a local shipyard had continued to work in the industry locally, as well as becoming actively involved in his branch of the boilermakers' society. In his early forties he had emerged on to a larger stage as one of the union's full-time officials for Clydeside, gaining a reputation for being unusually assertive and effective in pursuit of his members' interests, both through peaceful negotiations and through industrial action. As a result, in 1909 he became the boilermakers' national secretary, with the task of re-building the union's financial and industrial position after a brief period of rather ineffective leadership by his predecessor. Hill moved to live in the headquarters building in Newcastle, and his strenuous efforts on behalf of the society fully justified his repeated re-election over the next thirty years. During the earlier part of his career, he had also been a keen participant in a wide range of local organizations in the lively and democratic burgh of Govan: in the Cooperative Society and the Independent Labour Party, as a parish councillor and above all in the Congregational church, which had a profound influence in shaping his wider political vision. Thus, while he came to be widely seen as one of the most significant figures in a rising generation of socialist trade-union leaders, Hill's concerns remained deeply rooted in the traditions of local self-government which had formed the outlook of craft unionists throughout the nineteenth century.

For example, Hill frequently paid lip-service to the idea of national legislation for an eight-hour working day, which had been one of the central socialist demands since the late 1880s. But in practice he preferred to achieve shorter hours through collective bargaining on an industry-by-industry basis:

There is nothing binding us to work a week of 51, 48, or any other number of hours, and if the workers of this country are agreed that a shorter working week is an advantage to them there is no reason why they should not put those hours into operation. There is no law of the land against them. I am opposed to too much legislation for the fixing of hours. It is a policy which will have a reactionary effect upon you, because the men will think they are bound to work the number of hours which the Act lays down. I find that local action is most effective in bringing these reforms about.[2]

Similarly, Hill frequently referred to the principle of public ownership, which was after all at the heart of the socialist programme. But he applied it most frequently in the area of land reform, to improve the supply of food and housing, continuing a long radical tradition of concern over the 'price of the poor man's loaf'. Indeed, in relation to industrial affairs, Hill's passionate attacks on 'capitalism' turn out on closer examination to have been attacks not on private ownership, but rather on the severity of cyclical unemployment, which he blamed on narrow profit-seeking by financiers. Thus his enemies were the familiar ones of landlords and 'money lords', and even in the depths of the inter-war depression his solution was not the public ownership of the shipbuilding industry, but rather a government subsidy to scrap and rebuild shipping, based on a long radical tradition of public works to relieve unemployment:

This resolution does not attack capitalism, nor does it seek to abolish it. We simply say to the capitalist employers, take the labour which you need and the nation will organize the employment of the surplus. On one hand this problem of unemployment is talked of as if it were insoluble, and on the other hand, some of our own people talk of it as if it could be cured by revolution. The fact is that whatever economic system we have, we shall have unemployment and casual employment unless we organize the work of the nation for the production and equitable distribution of wealth.[3]

If John Hill's conception of socialism stopped short of the nationalization of industry, that was largely because his outlook as a craft-union leader was dominated by a concern to minimize government interference in his own members' affairs. Thus, while he pressed consistently for regulation of the labour market in the public interest, he was just as consistently suspicious of the bureaucracy involved in central state administration. For example, when the Liberals introduced labour exchanges before the First World War, Hill insisted on trade-union representation on the local boards of management; and when they introduced a national insurance scheme, he insisted that the unemployment benefits for craft unionists continue to be paid out through their own local union branches. Not surprisingly, then, after the outbreak of hostilities in 1914 Hill became one of the most vigilant and outspoken opponents of military conscription and industrial compulsion. Indeed, he had a very clear grasp of the long-standing libertarian criticism of the connection between war abroad and authoritarianism at home:

It will go on not indeed to the last man and the last shilling, but until every trade union rule and custom is given up; until every citizen right is lost; and until military authority and capitalist exploitation shall jointly control your lives either in peace or war. God grant that it may not be so ... I trust we shall continue to strive together, not only for trade conditions but for a fuller and freer citizenship to all the sons of toil.[4]

For Hill, as for his predecessors, fuller citizenship involved not only more liberty but also more democracy. As a result, he became one of the major trade-union proponents of further measures of political reform, including votes for women, and the organization of a more effective parliamentary Labour Party. In a powerful presidential address to the TUC in September 1917 he denied that the First World War should be seen as an inter-imperialist conflict and insisted that it had, initially at least, been a legitimate defence of democratic principles against the threat of Prussian militarism. But the longer the conflict dragged on the clearer it became that democracy could not be spread by state action from above, but only by popular pressure from below:

Who brought democracy to this country, to France, to America, and to Russia? The leaders of common men in these countries, aided by the common men who struggled, and preached, and practised these principles in all countries of the world. Democracy is not the gift of kings or Governments. It can never be achieved by military effort alone. In this war, as in all wars, we kill a hundred democrats for every one autocrat.

And in a remarkably prescient remark he simultaneously opposed another form of violence which was finding increasing numbers of supporters at the time:

This cannot be accomplished by revolution. By revolution we may only replace one set of autocrats for another, unless we have also an intelligent people who are moved by reason and not by passion. We must therefore agitate, educate, and organize.[5]

John Hill never became a national political figure, despite standing for parliament in 1906, 1907 and 1918, but he probably had just as much influence as a trade-union leader as he would have had as a Labour MP in those years. For he not only turned around the boilermakers' society in the 1900s and kept it afloat during the long inter-war depression, he also played a major role in the development of national politics through his prominent position within the TUC and his less visible part behind the scenes at the Labour Party conference. He was active in a period of significant growth in central government, initially in response to the welfare needs of peacetime, but greatly accelerated by the military pressures of the First World War. As a socialist Hill was prepared to welcome this expansion of the public sector, but he was also passionately concerned about his members' scope for self-government and political participation. As a result he struggled to maximize the trade-union influence on the regulation of working hours and unemployment, as well as on broader domestic and foreign policy. At the same time as lending his weight to the emergence of an independent Labour Party, Hill was also increasingly proud of the achievements of previous generations within his own union, which could trace its origins back to the period of the 'Great Reform Act' and the 'Tolpuddle Martyrs'. At least in the case of the craft unions then, to understand the real significance of the rise of socialism it is vital not to exaggerate the decline of liberalism.

THE EMERGENCE OF
INDUSTRY-WIDE BARGAINING

The economic boom of the early 1870s, which had produced virtually full employment among the assembly workers and significantly strengthened their bargaining power at the district level, had been followed by a long period of instability. As a result, the later 1870s had seen the employers clawing back much of the ground they had lost during the previous period of trade-union strength. For example, a massive strike led by the shipwrights on the Clyde in 1877 involved 25,000 men for six months and ended in defeat. Similarly the General Union of Carpenters was defeated in a strike in Manchester in 1877–8, and then lost half of its membership to fierce poaching from its London-based amalgamated rival. Meanwhile John Burnett of the engineers spent the second half of the 1870s successfully defending the achievement of the nine-hour day, but only by paying out more strike benefit in the one year of 1879 than in the whole previous history of the union. Thus even the most effective of the craft unions spent much of the next two decades fighting to maintain their position during a long period of industrial depression and high unemployment, while the smaller and more traditional societies struggled for their very survival. However, the organizations based on 'amalgamated principles' did continue their long-term growth and then experienced a rapid revival as trade recovered from the late 1880s, maintaining their leading position within the wider trade-union movement.

All of this was closely connected with major innovations in steam and steel shipbuilding, which were giving rise from the 1870s to new metalworking districts on the banks of northern rivers, above all the Clyde and the Tyne. Other heavy engineering firms were also developing to produce textile machinery and railway engines, sometimes attracted to the same industrial districts by the supplies of labour and components, sometimes attracted elsewhere to be closer to their customers, as in Manchester and Crewe. These rapidly expanding metalworking centres required influxes of large numbers of highly skilled men, and the sectoral and regional shift towards them was accompanied by new pressures on their unions. For the shipyards and engineering works were owned by independent-minded, self-made businessmen who preferred to run their firms without any outside interference. Moreover their workforces were unusually large, ranging from several hundred up to several thousand people, and the complexity of their products required the participation of so many occupations that by the 1880s there were as many as a hundred different craft bodies struggling for a foothold. Even once they were established these new firms were much more involved in exporting than the traditional building and consumer trades, considerably more exposed to fluctuations in world markets and consequently subject to regular cycles of industrial activity. This resulted in frequent adjustments of wage rates and almost continuous local disputes which threatened to become a huge drain on union funds.

Moreover, the individual employers were prepared to sacrifice some of their own autonomy for the benefits of local and then industry-wide associations, with the aim of undermining trade-union intervention in individual firms by locking-out their members throughout a wider area. Under these new conditions the men in each workplace had a greater need to call on the support of their wider societies and the craft-union leaders were pushed towards a growing appreciation of the weakening effects of their division into such a large number of distinct bodies. They responded in a range of ways: amalgamation between neighbouring craft societies, the extension of recruitment to include the semi-skilled grades and the formation of wider federations, which could at least reduce the impact of competition between rival unions and were sometimes able to coordinate common demands. This trend towards forms of industry-wide organization eventually resulted in a fairly even balance of forces between the main craft unions and the employers' associations, and the latter consequently shifted their emphasis away from direct confrontation and towards the imposition of formal procedures to restrict local industrial action.

This growing acceptance of powerful craft unions by the employers was partly a consequence of their own broader employment strategies. For at the most basic level their normal response to reduced profits was to cut the size of their workforces and their rates of pay: this required flexible, short-term employment contracts, and these in turn depended on the skilled workers taking care of most of their own training and welfare needs. In addition, the long-term commitment of most of the firms to specialized products limited the application of repetition work and automatic machinery, so the effective control of production processes remained largely in the hands of independent skilled labour. The emergence of strong, industry-wide craft unions then tended to highlight the internal diversification of the employers' side into a wide range of firms and products, which meant that it was only in exceptional circumstances that they were able to achieve effective unity in industrial action. As the chairman of the Engineering Employers' Federation observed in 1906:

It would be a very difficult thing to get the Federation lined up against the Amalgamated Society of Engineers . . . I think we should do everything we possibly can to avoid lining up the Federation, because we might be disappointed to find what the lining up was when the flag was raised. We need a very strong case to put before the Federation before we will get them to be as prepared to go into the sacrifice as they did on the previous occasion.[6]

Even the existence of employers' associations, then, was no guarantee of internal agreement over industrial relations issues, for each firm was concerned as much, or more, about its immediate commercial rivals as it was about the longer-term impact of trade unionism.

Moreover, the employers were subject to increasing government pressure towards union recognition and permanent collective bargaining arrangements, particularly when the Liberals were in office. One of the main channels for this pressure was the Labour Department of the Board of Trade, based on an earlier statistical bureau which had been headed by John Burnett, the former leader of the engineers, and established in 1893 under the influence of A. J. Mundella, the old champion of trade-union rights, and Thomas Burt, the veteran miners' MP. The Labour Department began by simply collecting and publishing statistical information more systematically, but its own emerging agenda was embodied in the Conciliation Act of 1896, which gave it new powers to offer the services of expert negotiators and arbitrators. This allowed the department to combine its two functions by pressing for the use of its advisers in cases of prolonged industrial disputes through the publication of information on the relative merits of each side. By 1904 it had assisted in the creation of 162 joint negotiating boards, often in the face of employers' reluctance, and, following a Liberal landslide in the general election of 1906, there was a marked increase in the number of ex-trade unionists serving among its officials. Right-wing characterizations of the Labour Department as the thin end of a socialist wedge were clearly wide of the mark, but its activities did constitute a further pressure on employers to reach their own accommodations with craft unions over which they could then retain a degree of immediate influence. As the secretary of the Shipbuilding Employers' Federation wrote to his engineering counterpart in 1911:

Within recent years, this Federation, and over a longer period both your Federation and this Federation have had difficulty in preventing the Board of Trade coming into questions at issue with their workmen under conditions which, it was considered, would have imperilled, if not sacrificed, the interests of the employers.[7]

At the same time, the financial resources of the craft unions had to be managed carefully in order to cope with the severity of industrial fluctuations in the new sectors. For if existing members were to be retained it was vital that the unions be able to pay out their promised welfare benefits, and if new members were to be attracted it was desirable that the unions have large enough financial balances to engage in effective industrial action. A major priority was keeping strict control over the payment of strike benefits, usually refusing to use national funds to support local strikes against wage cuts in periods of slack trade and rising unemployment, for it was expected that such disputes would be unsuccessful and that wage rates would rise again anyway during the next economic recovery. As this kind of prudence was not usually popular with the members immediately affected, and regional identities and local pride remained strong, long-term organizational growth called for firm national leadership. The officials of the craft unions also began to develop an approach to collective bargaining which traded some union restraint over increases in the upswing for some employer restraint over reductions in the downswing, each side being prepared to make smaller and less frequent demands. It then became necessary for the head offices not just to exercise control over the payment of strike benefits, but also to restrain the outbreak of local strikes as such, trying to persuade their members to enter negotiations with the employers rather than rushing into unilateral action.

Part-time executive committees drawn from the area near the head-quarters were still capable of checking matters of financial adminis-tration, but they no longer seemed adequate once their secretaries were involved in important local and national negotiations with the employers. A new balance between local autonomy and central control was therefore constructed through the election of full-time delegates to coordinate bargaining in each district in close contact with the members involved, alongside full-time executive committees to rep-resent the members of every district in the development of national policies. On the basis of these trends towards large financial balances and disciplined collective bargaining in the hands of a larger staff of full-time local and national officials, it then became increasingly feas-ible for the craft unions to aim at the regulation of conditions through-out their occupations. Their first priority was to secure some control over recruitment and training, above all by setting the ratio of appren-tices to skilled adults at as low a level as possible. With or without this foundation they also aimed to improve the conditions of work of the skilled men: by controlling the manning of machinery, by deciding whether or not to work for piece-rates and by reducing the length of the working day.

The emergence of an increasingly formal system of industrial relations, involving employers' associations, government depart-ments and national trade unions, therefore introduced a major new element alongside the assembly workers' long traditions of local self-government. For some this was a difficult adjustment, but having been made it was found to have many advantages. Indeed, the craft unions became strong enough not only to control their own conditions of employment more effectively, but also to see this as an influence on wider economic relationships, so that day-to-day craft regulation became the basis of a broader vision of society. From this perspective, restrictions on the supply of labour and the promotion of disciplined collective bargaining could be seen as ways of influencing the intensity of economic fluctuations. For if the supply of skilled labour could be limited by restricting the ratio of apprentices to journeymen and reducing the hours of work, it might also regulate excessive booms in production. And if disciplined collective bargaining could restrain downward pressure on wages, it might also regulate the employers' competitive behaviour during slumps. Taken together, this dual pressure might therefore promote steadier employment for the whole labour force. Then, if the actual level of wages could also be maintained, this might have a further beneficial effect on the whole economy by stimulating demand for consumer goods throughout the working population. Moreover, among the assembly workers these economic ideas were still frequently associated with broader commitments to the democratic traditions of religious nonconformity and the libertarian traditions of popular radicalism. This combination therefore began to produce a dynamic vision of full employment, higher standards of living and the redistribution of wealth, achieved without the direct intervention of central government, through the spread of powerful new forms of collective self-organization.

THE EXTENSION OF CRAFT REGULATION

Despite the employers' successful counter-pressure to extend working hours and cut wages from the late 1870s, the Amalgamated Society of Engineers had managed to remain one of the largest and wealthiest unions in the country, going on to increase its membership from 54,000 in 1888 to 170,000 in 1914. For the skilled engineers had consolidated a powerful position in the workshops as 'turners', producing components on multi-purpose lathes which they generally set up and maintained themselves; and 'fitters', refining and assembling components on the basis of technical plans and familiarity with the final products. Moreover, from its foundation in 1851 their union had brought together a wide range of neighbouring skilled groups and it continued to expand its territory into that of the highly technical patternmakers and, in the case of shipyard outfitting, into that of the plumbers. However, while this position was almost unassailable in the heavy engineering sectors, the last decades of the century saw considerable diversification, including more repetition work in armaments and in newer light engineering branches such as the Midlands bicycle trade. As a result the skilled turners and fitters were faced in some districts with growing numbers of semi-skilled production workers who were difficult to include within the union and who began to make up a threatening pool of substitute labour.

In the early 1890s the skilled men began not only to re-assert their position over the ground lost in the preceding years of depression but also to tackle some of their more fundamental problems of organization. A broadly based 'progressive' movement within the union only narrowly failed in its attempt to get the well-known socialist agitator Tom Mann elected as national secretary in 1891, but the following year secured the election as deputy of one of his associates, George Barnes, who eventually succeeded to the national leadership in 1896. Simultaneously a series of constitutional changes were agreed: appointing full-time district delegates, electing a full-time national executive and recognizing the desirability in principle of recruiting semi-skilled workers. The union then embarked on an initially successful industrial campaign to secure an eight-hour day, but soon began to face co-ordinated resistance from the employers. In 1895–6 it was frustrated in a Belfast wage demand through a parallel lock-out of its members by the employers on the Clyde; this example led to the formation of an Engineering Employers' Federation throughout the shipbuilding districts, and the potential of new American machines to displace skilled workers rallied employers in other areas who were keen to secure the upper hand in their workshops. Then, when the eight-hours campaign spread to London in the summer of 1897, the employers' federation initiated what was to become a six-month-long national lock-out of 45,000 skilled men. Though many other unions contributed a significant amount of financial support, the legacy of demarcation disputes between the engineers and neighbouring occupations led to their industrial isolation, and the growing numbers of semi-skilled workers were used temporarily as substitute labour in many districts. The costs of such a long national dispute could not be sustained even by the engineers, and in January 1898 they had to agree to the employers' 'Terms of Settlement'. While marking a significant advance on the middle of the nineteenth century by not insisting on an anti-union pledge and by recognizing collective bargaining over wages, these still required the union to drop its eight-hours campaign,

accept managerial prerogatives on machine manning, and follow procedural rules prohibiting local strikes before national negotiations had
been held.

As in the case of earlier industrial disputes affecting the capital, this
lock-out received a good deal of public attention, with the press
generally critical of the engineers for interfering with the liberty of their
employers, and the humiliating defeat of such a powerful organization
sending shock waves throughout the trade-union world. However,
the outcome for the skilled men themselves was not as disastrous as
the contemporary public reaction might suggest, largely because there
were few opportunities for repetition production in the heavy engineering and shipbuilding districts, and the scope for the application of
automatic machinery therefore remained quite limited. As a result, the
long period of prosperity in the first decades of the new century led to
a growth in union membership and the successful re-assertion of the
skilled men's position. This was partly achieved within the terms of
the new national procedures, which had to involve some concessions
to the union side if they were to remain credible, and were revised
accordingly in 1907. But above all it was achieved at the district level,
where the employment of semi-skilled labour and the spread of new
forms of piece-rates was contained, and the wage cuts were resisted
through local strikes outside the national procedures, particularly on
Clydeside in 1903 and the north-east coast in 1908. This re-assertion
of craft regulation in the heavy engineering districts created serious
problems for the union's leadership, which had been trying to adapt
to the conditions in the newer sectors of the industry and improve its
members' position within the 'Terms of Settlement': Barnes resigned
as secretary in 1908, and the whole of the national executive was
forced out in 1912 before the completion of its normal period of office.
The new leadership then followed the line of the heavy engineering
districts by withdrawing unilaterally from the employer-imposed
national procedures in 1913, re-launching the union's campaign for
the eight-hour day and pressing for more control over apprenticeship.

The growth of the shipbuilding districts had also seen the emergence
of the United Society of Boilermakers as one of the country's strongest
craft unions, as its members had shifted from the literal making of
boilers to the application of their skills in plate shaping and joining to

a wide range of structural steelwork: its numbers rose from 27,000 in 1888 to 67,000 in 1914. Boilermakers used a variety of powered tools but, far from being slaves to the machine or to management, many of them had to read and interpret complex plans and all of them continued to work as independent sub-contractors without any direct supervision. As John Hill, their national secretary from 1909 to 1936, put it:

They are not only highly skilled craftsmen, but they have that other qualification of being capable organizers of squads. They take the whole care and responsibility from the management and staff very largely. It is simply a matter, when the job comes along, of the foreman saying to Mr So-and-so, 'Here you are; these are plans of that job: get along with it' and there is no need to look after them and watch them and see if they are doing it right, or to hurry them on with the job. The whole work is taken and managed so successfully that it is not so much the price as the skill and organization of the squad that tells in the long run.[8]

In addition to their undoubted skills and independence, the strength of their union was also based on its willingness to incorporate neighbouring groups of less skilled workers so as to secure an effective monopoly of this whole sphere of production. The caulkers who closed the seams between the plates were admitted in 1877, the holders-on who assisted the riveters in joining the plates were admitted in 1882, and by the 1890s the union had secured a virtual closed shop for all its sections. This occupational territory was also defended and extended through vigorous demarcation disputes with other skilled trades, above all to keep out rival metalworkers among the engineers and to take over from traditional woodworkers among the shipwrights.

Under the leadership of the outstanding organizer Robert Knight, the national secretary between 1871 and 1899, the boilermakers went on to pioneer the imposition of national agreements on the employers. In 1890 Knight led the way in setting up the Federation of Engineering and Shipbuilding Trades, initially to resolve demarcation disputes between the skilled bodies, but eventually broadening its membership to include the general workers' unions and broadening its aims to include collective bargaining over wages and hours. Then, in the absence of a national employers' association until the end of the 1890s, it was largely pressure from Knight which led to a number of important agreements, including the limitation of the ratio of apprentices to craftsmen in 1893, and the regulation of conditions in ship repairing in 1894. As a consequence of this trend, there was also a movement for a full-time national executive representative of all the districts and, though Knight himself initially opposed this on grounds of the expense involved, it won the support of the members in 1895. The union had already had full-time district delegates for some time and the districts remained a major focus of negotiation, because the large numbers of skilled workers concentrated in areas like Clydeside and Tyneside gave them formidable industrial strength and awareness of this had become a central element in their sense of regional identity. Thus the local members were initially reluctant to accept the new bargaining procedures into which Knight drew the employers on Tyneside in 1894 and on Clydeside in 1898. However, in return for a more disciplined approach to local strike action, they were able to call on the financial resources of the national union to undertake longer strikes when necessary, and this then became a vital part of the formidable district strength of the boilermakers.

This position was somewhat eroded after Knight's retirement, as his immediate successor turned out to be less firm both in negotiations with the employers and in managing the balance between benefits and subscriptions within the union's own finances. The Shipbuilding Employers' Federation, keen to follow the recent example of its counterpart in engineering, then took advantage of this weakness to impose a national agreement in 1907, clawing back a good deal of ground over such substantive issues as apprenticeship as well as laying down elaborate national procedures before district strikes were permitted. However, the boilermakers responded rapidly, giving the post of secretary to one of their most assertive Clydeside district officials, John Hill, and re-establishing their position by undertaking a long national dispute in support of district wage strikes in 1910, not only resulting in increases but also weakening the procedural restrictions on local action. Under conditions of virtually full employment the union then began to take an increasingly independent line, tackling the question of training by establishing a special apprentice section in 1912, and withdrawing unilaterally from the employer-imposed national procedures in 1913.

Production had hardly been concentrated at all in the house-building industry, which remained fluid and dispersed, with trade-union networks continually having to be re-established on the opening of each new construction site. As a result, the skilled men's organizations had retained much of their quality of autonomous local societies, with many of them still not even paying 'static' unemployment benefit. However, here too the unions rapidly recovered after 1888 from the preceding long period of depression and doubled their membership in the years up to the First World War, with a particular spurt during the busier years up to 1900, during which the joiners grew from 25,000 to 65,000, the stonemasons from 10,000 to 19,000, the bricklayers from 7,000 to 39,000, and the smaller trades by equivalent amounts. The building trades were virtually unaffected by economic or technical change: they remained highly fragmented into small firms based largely on traditional methods, with the major exception of the increasing replacement of stonemasonry by bricklaying. Thus there was less pressure for change in the form of union organization, and the reassertion of the skilled men's position from the late 1880s was limited to the better end of each trade and carried out largely at the local level.

Even here, though, there was a movement towards industry-wide organization within each district, with union federations established first in Leicester and Nottingham, then spreading to London in the aftermath of a major dispute in 1891 in which the joiners had been disappointed to achieve only limited success by independent action. This increased coordination resulted in improvements in wages and hours and frequently also in local bargaining procedures, involving union recognition and the employers' acceptance of working rules for each trade, covering the materials that might be used, the number of apprentices and in some cases even the closed shop. In the aftermath of the 1897 engineering lock-out, the National Association of Master Builders began to attract increasing support and attempted to emulate the engineering employers by spreading a London dispute with the plasterers into a national lock-out of the whole industry in 1899. However, the response of the employers in other districts was poor and no real headway was made either in undermining craft controls or, with the exception of the plasterers themselves, in establishing national procedures. Then after 1900 the building industry entered a decade-long depression, with the unions losing up to half their members and the number of local strikes declining significantly. The employers in the north and the Midlands took advantage of this situation to impose centralized bargaining procedures, but only pressed for small reductions in wage rates and mounted no challenges to the core of the skilled men's position. When the industry and its unions began to recover after 1910 there was therefore a strong re-assertion of craft regulation, focusing on a struggle to re-establish effective local organization by refusing to work alongside non-union labour. A major dispute among the London building trades in 1913–14 was only brought to an end by the employers' threat of a national lock-out, but the resulting terms made significant concessions on the exclusion of non-union labour and the imposition of unfavourable bargaining procedures was only temporary.

In the case of the printing industry, the success of the radical campaigns to repeal the 'taxes on knowledge' and improve educational provision had had a major impact, leading to a massive growth in demand for newspapers in particular. The employers' first response had involved faster presses and larger workforces, so the traditional methods of the hand compositors remained central in setting up the actual pages of print. These skilled men's position was then somewhat eroded in the depressed years from the middle of the 1870s by the spread of piece-rates, an increase in the ratio of apprentices to adults and, particularly in Scotland, the employment of women on lower pay. However, from the end of the 1880s the regionally based compositors' unions began to tighten up their controls on recruitment and training, particularly in the newspaper branch where the employers were hampered by intense rivalries and their extreme vulnerability to stoppages, and the combined membership of the three skilled men's organizations grew from 17,000 in 1888 to 41,000 in 1914. They were therefore in a strong position to take control of the American linotype machines introduced during the 1890s, even though these reduced the skills required in composing and were much faster than hand labour. The provincial Typographical Association secured a general agreement in 1898 giving its members a monopoly of the new machines, a strict apprenticeship ratio and an eight-hour working day. The more concentrated London Society of Compositors had already achieved an even more favourable settlement in 1896, and the relatively decentralized Scottish Typographical Association also went on to secure a general improvement in its members' position. Moreover, when the employers in the less competitive book branch pressed for lower wages and female labour, prompt industrial action in London and Edinburgh won favourable terms for the skilled men. Indeed the compositors' position became so secure that they felt able to cooperate with semi-skilled men and women in a number of all-grades movements, including the formation of the National Printing and Kindred Trades Federation in 1901, with the result that a shorter working week was established throughout the industry alongside disputes procedures largely favourable to the unions.

The consumer trades had continued to thrive in the older urban centres. However, this was increasingly on the basis either of mass production in mechanized factories or of highly subdivided workshops and the spread of home working, so the skilled men tended to be swamped where they remained fragmented into small groups of rival specialists, as in the potteries. However, where they were already organized into larger bodies they managed to preserve their territory at the higher-quality end of their trades and to improve their bargaining positions. Thus the Amalgamated Society of Tailors, with 17,000 members, was able to retain local bargaining in defiance of a poorly organized employers' lock-out in 1891, then go on to recruit semi-skilled men and women, and even secure improved conditions for outworkers in London for a short period after a large strike in 1906. Meanwhile, the National Union of Boot and Shoe Operatives, with 43,000 members, was able to impose a national agreement on the employers in 1892, including the limitation of apprentices and procedures favourable to the union. This provoked the employers to fight back through a lock-out in 1895, successfully gaining a free hand over machine manning and the abolition of the disputes procedures. However, like the engineers, the shoemakers were gradually able to re-assert their control at the local level, regulating the quantity of work done by machinists and establishing a minimum wage, then, as the industry recovered after 1907, re-imposing national negotiations and winning substantial concessions particularly over reduced working hours.

Overall, then, this period saw a shift in the centre of gravity of craft unionism away from the traditional building and consumer trades towards the newer metalworking trades, in which craft regulation tended to become stronger through national bargaining. The boiler-makers, and in printing the compositors, were particularly successful, as compact bodies of skilled men, facing fairly uniform conditions in their respective industries and able to find ways of cooperating with less-skilled workers. The engineers were also reasonably successful but, with a much more numerous membership working in more diverse conditions, found themselves unable to cooperate with less-skilled workers and consequently more vulnerable to employer attacks in the short term. The strongest bodies could sometimes impose national agreements on the employers, but the more normal trend was for the employers to lay down national procedures to restrain local union action. The ever-looming threat of a major lock-out initially made union leaders more cautious in periods of uncertain trade, but it had less effect among their members. As a result there were recurrent district disputes outside the imposed procedures which, especially in the more prosperous years after 1910, pulled the union leaders into official support for assertive industrial action and the repudiation of unfavourable national agreements.

THE IMPACT OF THE FIRST
WORLD WAR

When war in Europe broke out in August 1914, a relatively short and mobile campaign was anticipated and nothing was done to control volunteering for the army: within a year nearly a fifth of the country's skilled engineers and a quarter of its skilled explosives workers had joined up, leaving a smaller workforce to cope with rapidly rising demand. The employers began to press their remaining skilled workers to relax established craft regulation, especially their unwillingness to work alongside less-skilled men, and there is evidence that some of them thought of using the war to strike a decisive blow against the pre-war revival of the craftsmen's bargaining position as a whole. The union leaders were therefore concerned about making any concessions at all without guarantees of an eventual return to pre-war practices, along with some gesture towards an equivalent sacrifice from those businessmen making high profits from wartime conditions, particularly those involved in transport and distribution in a period of rapidly rising food prices. As a result, it soon became clear that voluntary negotiations between the two sides in British manufacturing had reached a stalemate and, given the seriousness of the situation, the government quickly overcame its traditional inhibitions about direct intervention in industrial relations in the assembly sectors.

The problem was most acute in engineering and shipbuilding, which supplied the most vital weapons and munitions. Sir George Askwith was put in charge of a Treasury Committee on Production which quickly produced a 'Shells and Fuses Agreement' for the engineering industry in March 1915, under which the unions accepted the principle of less-skilled labour doing some skilled tasks in return for a government guarantee of a post-war return to normality. The question of whether the local members would go along with such agreements signed by their national leaders had already been raised by an unofficial wage strike among Clydeside engineers earlier in the month, responding to the tight wartime labour market by demanding a 2d. an hour increase on the expiry of their existing three-year agreement, and returning to work for a compromise of 1d. an hour. However, the government pressed ahead with its national approach through a high-level conference resulting in the 'Treasury Agreement' later in March, under which the leaders of the main unions agreed to a general relaxation of craft practices and suspension of strike action for the duration of the war. The sense of crisis then intensified with the revelation of a very serious shortage of shells for the western front, leading to the formation of the Ministry of Munitions under David Lloyd George in July 1915, based on the transformation of the 'Treasury Agreement' into the Munitions of War Act. This gave the new ministry the power to enforce the suspension of trade practices and the compulsory arbitration of disputes, in return for a limit on profits at 20 per cent above pre-war rates.

However, the inability of the government to prevent mass industrial action in practice was immediately illustrated by the south Wales miners' rejection of a Committee on Production wage award followed by a strike of up to 200,000 men, which Lloyd George had to settle by conceding most of their demands. Even if the government had had the legal powers to do so, locking up this number of key workers would clearly have been counter-productive for the war effort, and using the powers it did have to deport leading organizers would only have been likely to stiffen the strikers' determination. The most troublesome aspect of the new legislation then turned out to be the apparently rather technical Section 7, which required a munitions worker seeking employment to present a certificate from his previous employer confirming satisfactory completion of his contract. This had been intended to reduce the problems of unfinished work and excessive mobility in a very tight wartime labour market, but it was being used by employers, especially in the Clydeside shipbuilding industry, to increase discipline in the workplace and hold on to skilled men by threats of dismissal without a certificate, which would have been followed by at least six weeks of unemployment. The result was a wave of unrest on the Clyde in the autumn of 1915, with recurrent threats of a general strike throughout the region's shipbuilding industry which, despite their illegality, were issued by prominent district officials of the unions concerned with the tacit support of the national leaderships. Once again Lloyd George had to give in, setting up a high-profile public inquiry into the union complaints, followed by extensive revisions to the offending sections of the Munitions Act.

However, this did not immediately remove local suspicions and, during the preparations for military conscription, the introduction of 'dilution' with female labour to the Clydeside engineering industry was also accompanied by an initial flurry of resistance. Though this turned out to be on a much more limited scale than the shipbuilding unrest of the previous autumn, the region had now acquired a sinister reputation in Lloyd George's mind. Following his rowdy reception at a mass meeting in Glasgow on Christmas Day 1915, he took the unusual step of suppressing the local Independent Labour Party newspaper *Forward* for a month for reporting the meeting accurately in defiance of an official press release. Then, in the immediate aftermath of the Dublin rising of Easter 1916, some of his over-excited officials deported nine engineers' shop stewards from Glasgow and began collecting wild rumours about German agents in the area. However, behind the scenes, the actual concerns of the local engineers were being relieved by careful and sympathetic negotiations in each shop, and an early agreement with the skilled men at Beardmore's Parkhead Forge became the model for the district. This confirmed the government's intention, following extensive consultation with national union officials, that established male wages should provide a benchmark for all female labour introduced on to skilled work and that workshop representatives should be consulted over the details of the allocation of tasks and the appropriate rates of pay. In combination with the reluctance of most employers to undertake the extra expenses involved in the introduction of female labour, as well as the risk of losing their skilled men to other firms or the armed forces, this effectively inhibited any dilution of the core skilled tasks. The solution to the problem of munitions production then turned out to be found, as the union leaders had argued all along, not in the undermining of craft regulation but rather in an increase in the productive capacity of the munitions industry, both by issuing government contracts to a wider range of private firms and by building new national factories.

The role of insurrectionist and anti-war elements in these events was exaggerated out of all proportion by Lloyd George and his civil servants during parliamentary debates, in embarrassed attempts to justify their periodic over-reactions. There was widespread sympathy in the Glasgow area for the situation of the deported shop stewards, extending even to a number of imprisoned anti-war agitators, but the industrial weakness of the revolutionary Socialist Labour Party was evident in the failure of the self-appointed 'Clyde Workers' Committee' to influence the dilution negotiations in its own region, let alone to achieve coordinated action with other parts of the country. This was partly because unrest in the other munitions districts revolved not around increases in workplace discipline but rather around the intro-duction of military conscription, highly unpopular in principle and accompanied by poorly designed exemptions for essential workers. And it was partly because over this issue too, the local and national officials of the unions were much more representative of their members than the revolutionary agitators alleged, both at the time and in their later reminiscences. Thus, when towards the end of 1916 Sheffield in particular became a centre of agitation against conscription, district officials and shop stewards acted together to provide the necessary threats to back up the national leaders of the engineers in their negotiations with the government. As a result, the privileged position of the craftsmen was consolidated under the union-run 'Trade Card Agreement' of November 1916, and still reaffirmed under the government-run Schedule of Protected Occupations worked out during extensive consultation with the unions in the spring of 1917. The success of such outbreaks of industrial unrest in securing major concessions from the government undoubtedly led to the politicization of significant numbers of skilled men, but usually within more mainstream organizations such as the Independent Labour Party (ILP). While there were enough on the revolutionary fringes to begin gathering at conferences during 1917, even the most serious attempt to set up a national 'Workers' Committee' movement for the engineering industry at Manchester that August remained a rather empty gesture. For the delegates were opposed to any form of central authority even within their own organization, and the more clear-headed among them were well aware that their support was confined to a few small pockets scattered around the country.

Already during the first two years of the war other issues had added fuel to the more widespread grievances of the assembly workers. Rents had risen by 10–20 per cent in the main munitions centres, which were receiving substantial influxes of labour without any addition to the restricted and often poor-quality housing stock. In Glasgow the stormy autumn of 1915 had also seen a remarkably well-organized campaign of non-payment of rents led by the ILP, involving hundreds of tenants in the inner-city shipbuilding districts of Govan and Partick, with the threat of escalating industrial action in support of those prosecuted leading to the rapid passing of a Rent Restriction Act. While this aimed to fix rents at pre-war levels, it did nothing to provide more accommodation or security of tenure, and local rent strikes continued to flare up throughout the country. Meanwhile, food prices had doubled and, though a long campaign by the TUC was eventually successful in achieving the appointment of a Food Controller during the formation of Lloyd George's coalition government at the end of 1916, the post was largely ineffective until the introduction of rationing a year later. Thus, despite recurrent local strikes and Committee on

Production pay concessions, real wage rates had fallen by about 15 per cent and incomes were only being maintained by more continuous working and longer hours. The resulting weariness and uncertainty provided the background to a major wave of spontaneous strikes by engineers throughout the country in May 1917, perhaps fuelled by excitement over the February Revolution in Russia, and certainly calmed down by better publicity of the extent to which their own national leaders were already being consulted over the whole range of wartime labour administration. The following year saw the government addressing one particular aspect of lagging wage rates by awarding a 12.5 per cent bonus to skilled timeworkers in engineering and then, urged on by George Barnes, the former leader of the engineers who had become a special labour adviser to the War Cabinet, eventually extending the award to all those other groups which made a fuss, including a 7.5 per cent bonus for less well paid piece-workers. Those to benefit included not only the skilled men in the foundries and shipyards, but also those outside the essential war industries: in textile machine-making, electricity supply and contracting, building, printing, furniture-making and footwear.

Overall, then, the main impact of the First World War was to shift the advantage in national agreements further in favour of the assembly workers. The craft unions' bargaining power was strengthened by full employment and rapidly rising union membership, and their influence on national policy was increased by the need to retain their consent through a long series of military crises. As a result they were able to prevent industrial compulsion through their influence on the 'Treasury Conference', the revision of the Munitions of War Act and the drafting of schemes of military exemption. They were simultaneously able to extend the state provision of social safety nets through the introduction of rent restriction and food rationing. Meanwhile the employers' associations fell into some disarray as firms competed more intensely than ever for skilled workers, and local organizations protested against their national headquarters' collaboration with government departments seen as excessively favourable to labour. Lloyd George recalled the reaction of one of his Conservative counterparts on encountering such figures as John Hill and Arthur Henderson at the landmark conference in the Treasury boardroom in 1915:

He was surprised to find the workmen's representatives talked so well. They put their points clearly and succinctly, wasting neither time nor words. On the other hand, there was just a note of aggressiveness in manner and tone to which he was not quite accustomed from such quarters. For the moment it almost quelled him, and he was silent throughout . . . He saw those stalwart artisans leaning against and sitting on the steps of the throne of the dead queen, and on equal terms negotiating with the Government of the day upon a question vitally affecting the conduct of a great war . . . I had watched his mood for years from an opposing bench. In looking at him now I felt that his detached and inquiring mind was bewildered by this sudden revelation of a new power and that he must take time to assimilate the experience.[9]

Indeed, by the end of the war there were indications that a more cooperative system of industrial relations might be about to emerge. Membership growth, amalgamation and federation were making the unions even more representative and negotiations even more manageable. In 1918, for example, federal bodies were established in both the building and the foundry trades and the following years saw the engineers merging with smaller sectional societies to form the Amalgamated Engineering Union (1920) and the rival joiners' societies merging into the Amalgamated Society of Woodworkers (1921). Pragmatic figures among the employers seemed increasingly willing to accept the unions' new position of strength: the Engineering Employers' Federation, for example, was prepared to grant not only shorter hours and a minimum wage, but also shop-steward recognition and a degree of joint regulation, as a new basis for viable industry-wide bargaining. Meanwhile, the government not only honoured its pledges of a return to pre-war practices but also, under the supervision of the Ministry of Labour, established a permanent Industrial Court for the arbitration of disputes and encouraged joint regulation of a wide range of employment issues through the setting up of national and local Whitley Councils.

However, there was no guarantee that all local members of the unions would be satisfied with what was gained on their behalf in national negotiations. Indeed, assisted by a rather unexpected post-war reconstruction boom, engineering and shipbuilding saw a number of district campaigns in pursuit of a further reduction in the working week beyond the forty-seven hours which had been agreed and ratified in national membership ballots. Simultaneously, local groups of employers began to rally their forces to claw back lost ground at the earliest opportunity. Indeed, in 1919 a National Confederation of Employers' Organisations was established to coordinate action across industries in resistance to union demands for increased wages and what its more hard-line members saw as spineless government concessions. And of course the government itself had now much less reason to intervene to resolve industrial disputes. Indeed the post-war Coalition was clearly dominated by the Conservatives and began to take an increasingly tough line on trade-union disruption, seen for example in its suppression of the police strikes of 1918–19, and in its passing of an Emergency Powers Act in 1920 to allow it to intervene to maintain essential services in the event of major unrest.

Just as the mood of wartime industrial relations had been launched on the Clyde in the autumn of 1915, its disappearance without trace was signalled there in January 1919 when the Scottish Trades Union Congress and the Glasgow Trades Council initiated a strike for a forty-hour week. Their strategy seems to have been a continuation of the wartime approach of mounting a general strike in local shipbuilding and engineering with as much support as possible from the rest of the community, in the expectation that the state would press the employers to make major concessions. The government, however, approached the dispute primarily as a matter of public order, mobilizing troops to maintain essential services and declaring sympathetic action by electricity workers illegal. A demonstration of up to 30,000 people in Glasgow's George Square on 31 January became notorious as a result of ill-judged police baton charges, followed by arrests of strike leaders who had been urging the crowd to stay calm, and the arrival by rail of six army tanks as a gesture to those disturbed by fantasies of Bolshevism. Despite a parallel movement for forty-four hours in Belfast and the beginnings of solidarity action in London, the employers were able to stand firm and insist that the union leaders enforce the national agreement: the Glasgow and Belfast district committees of the engineers were suspended, instructions for an immediate return to work were issued, and both strikes collapsed within a week. Similarly, in the course of 1919–20 strikes for higher wages among the boilermakers in London, the printers in the north-west, and the foundrymen and the electricians nationally were all firmly resisted by the employers and ended in defeat. Even at the peak of the post-war boom then, with relatively low unemployment and high trade-union membership, the traditional British pattern of adversarial industrial relations was clearly reasserting itself: business as usual had, after all, no place for a new power in the land.

9

Union Recognition among the Process Workers

The taking over of railways, mines, munition factories, and other controlled establishments during the war, really meant that in the considered judgment of the Government – and a Government not composed of a majority of their own people, but a capitalist Government – the private ownership of these things in time of war was a danger to the State. Why? Because they believed that unrestricted competition and the individual control of the necessities of life in time of war was a menace to the State. If that was their considered judgment in war time, all experience proved that dealing with the State not as bricks and mortar, not as land and railways, but as a mass of human beings, they were equally entitled to say that the same danger existed to the people of the country in time of peace.[1]

This is part of a speech on the task of social reconstruction given by J. H. Thomas MP, during the formulation of the Labour Party's first comprehensive programme in preparation for the general election of 1918. Thomas had been chosen to propose the official resolution on these matters not only because of his extensive parliamentary experience, but also because he was the secretary of the National Union of Railwaymen, one of the largest bodies directly affected by wartime controls, and his remarks therefore indicate some important aspects of the attitudes of the process workers at the time. Clearly the impact of the First World War had weakened the legitimacy of private ownership, as governments faced with a national emergency had demonstrated that they could run major industries both reasonably efficiently and in the public interest. However, this was not to imply that public ownership was the only alternative. Indeed, Thomas consciously defined the problem in terms of unrestricted competition and individual control so that solutions could be found through public regulation and democratic participation. This reflected the wording of the official motion itself, which criticized capitalism but proposed, not socialism, but social reconstruction, defined in terms of 'deliberately planned cooperation in production and distribution', and was itself deliberately vague about who would be involved in this cooperation so that plans could be tailored to the particular conditions within each industry. Indeed, when Thomas later struggled to reduce unemployment under the Labour government of 1929, he focused on carefully selected public works and schemes of industrial re-organization in close cooperation with the businessmen concerned.

Jimmy Thomas had been born in Newport in south Wales in 1874 and, along with a number of his later political colleagues, grew up in the poverty of a single-parent family later compounded by the shame of discovering his illegitimate birth. Following a few local lad's jobs he started on the Great Western Railway as an engine cleaner, gradually working his way up through a decade as a fireman to the lowest rank of driver on a shunting engine. There can be little doubt that his career was hindered by his prominent position in the railwaymen's union, where his energy and outstanding fluency at meetings won him early election as branch chairman and national conference delegate. Moreover, Thomas always refused to bow to pressure: when the company moved him to Swindon to reduce his influence, he responded by getting himself elected on to the union's national executive and eventually in 1906 as its full-time organizing secretary. Thomas was also active in wider politics wherever he lived, as a leading figure in local trades councils, as the first Labour representative on the Swindon municipal authority, and as the main influence behind the emergence of a unified Labour Party in Cardiff. This made him the natural candidate to take over from the previous union nominee as one of the MPs for the railway town of Derby in 1910, in close alliance with a more senior Liberal member. He then moved to London with his family and, with Sir Charles Dilke as his first mentor, began a career in national politics which was to take him to high office as Colonial and Dominions Secretary, and then Lord Privy Seal with responsibility for employment.

In his later memoirs Thomas recalled his attitude on starting out in life:

It was neither the arrogance nor the impetuousness of youth that made me intolerant of the power of capital: it was the sincere belief in the right of every man, no matter what his environment and circumstances, to have a fair chance of making the world better for his having lived in it. It was not equality I wanted, but equality of opportunity. Therefore, I didn't feel it to be incumbent on me to bridle my tongue at any of those political gatherings in South Wales.[2]

His outspokenness as a young man was clearly seen as disruptive to the strict discipline of the railway line but he was never a political extremist; on the contrary, his entry into Parliament under the wing of the Liberal Party strengthened an instinctive sense of fair play and toleration. For example, while keenly patriotic throughout the First World War, he stubbornly resisted the introduction of military conscription and bravely championed Ramsay MacDonald's right to freedom of speech:

I disagree with him on the war, but is there any man who dare ever say that he is actuated by any other motive than the dictates of his conscience? . . . He is at least entitled to respect for having the courage of his convictions, and, if our cause is a good one, we ought not to deny him or anyone else the right of free speech.[3]

As the leading organizer of a massive union in a strategic industry, Thomas was frequently portrayed as something of a revolutionary threat. However, during the first national railway strike in 1911 he played a key role in reducing violence during a preliminary unofficial dispute over wages in Liverpool. Then his main contribution to the subsequent official action was in uniting a number of competing unions behind a focus on recognition by the employers, and it was he who toured the country to secure his members' acceptance of a rather mixed settlement. His distinctive combination of ebullient resistance to the 'petty tyranny' of the railway companies with a strong sense of the need to stay within the limits of the law can be seen in his speeches at the time:

We said to the Prime Minister if you will only bring about a meeting between us and the railway companies, this business will be at an end! But the railway companies not only refused to see us, they even refused the Government's intervention. We would have sacrificed everything if we had done other than accept the challenge of the companies, and said: 'At last we accept the gauntlet that you have thrown down!' . . . Now, men, please obey my request! We want no rioting, no bloodshed. I will do all I can to keep the men in check. Every man who riots, every man who pilfers, immediately goes out of our consideration.[4]

Moreover, as a Member of Parliament Thomas also developed a clear sense of the distinction between industrial and political action: he had no illusion that striking in itself would bring about wider changes and he anticipated the possibility of serious frictions between trade unions and Labour governments in the future. Thus during peaks of unrest on the railways in the last months of the First World War and the immediate post-war period he persuaded local groups of unofficial strikers to return to work by delivering sobering lectures on industrial politics:

Our union is the strongest in the country. We can demand that unless such and such a thing is done, we can paralyse the community. That is our power. I want to examine what is our duty in relation to that power. However strong and powerful we may be, the State is more powerful and more important. Citizenship has a stronger claim than any sectional interest. We as trade unionists have got to keep clearly in mind that we have to make our sectional claims consistent with and part of our duty as citizens of the State. The unfortunate tendency today is to assume that we can hold the State up to ransom at any time. We may succeed and achieve our object, but if we did it at the expense of the State, then as citizens we would have destroyed all our claim to citizenship.[5]

Thus, when the coal miners were considering striking in pursuit of nationalization in 1920, Thomas, as chairman of the TUC, argued forcefully that the appropriate channel for the pursuit of such a goal was Parliament and the election of a Labour government.

Moreover, in all the spheres of his activity Thomas's aims were remarkably down-to-earth. In his later memoirs he recalled with pride not only making the breakthrough as the first Labour member of the Swindon town council, but also being initiated by its accountant into the technicalities of municipal finance and eventually chairing the committee which prepared the local budget. When he called in 1905 for union recognition and conciliation boards on the railways, it was not only as a passionate demand for equal treatment, but also as a proposal with practical benefits for all concerned:

By meeting from time to time, the employees would benefit by the education and business capacity of their employers and so broaden their minds that they could better appreciate the commercial side of the undertaking, and in the same manner the employers would benefit by the brains and practical experience of the workmen, and so assist them to better understand their difficulties and requirements.[6]

Similarly, when he was asked during a speaking tour of the United States in 1917 about the significance of the British government's wartime interventions in industry, he kept bringing the focus back to the question immediately at hand:

It is foolish to boast of the nationalization of England's industries as a victory for Socialism. That is a purely academic question and a very petty one as compared with the real problems with which England is confronted. It is immaterial whether there is a victory for Socialism or not. That is not what England and her labouring people were thinking about. I doubt if as many of the Socialists were, or are, thinking about such a victory as some of their writers claim. We were all thinking about a victory for England and her allies and nothing else, and the nationalization of industries seemed to be one of the wise things to do to further that victory.[7]

Thus in the turbulent years of industrial unrest after the First World War Jimmy Thomas provided an important element of stability. Many other trade unionists were swept along by their unprecedented strength into enthusiasm for direct action in pursuit of political goals, while the government and the newspapers were more than happy to portray strikes in strategic sectors as conspiracies to undermine the fabric of national life on the part of Bolsheviks and anarchists. Thomas meanwhile continued to uphold a set of traditional liberal values: freedom of speech and the rule of law, the submission of national decisions to the whole body of the electors, and a practical assessment of the benefits of state intervention. As one of the outstanding moderates in the trade-union and Labour world he quickly became a prime target for abuse from the far left, his loyalty to Ramsay MacDonald during the cabinet split over benefit cuts in 1931 only putting the final touches to his reputation as an arch-traitor. Thomas's subsequent virtual disappearance from labour history has involved the loss not just of an interesting individual story but also of a set of attitudes which remained more widely representative. During the first Labour government he was regularly attacked by the left for appearing in evening dress at establishment functions but, while he was prepared to alter his external appearance, he never changed his behaviour, usually entertaining those present with an irreverent and earthy sense of humour. For Thomas, pride in his origins and assertiveness on behalf of his members did not require intransigence, and he was prepared not only to enjoy social events but also to look for compromises on matters of national importance. Thus in an interesting counterpoint to craft unionists like John Hill, who were committed to socialism as an idea but did not want immediate public ownership of their own industries, Jimmy Thomas represented a long-standing tendency among seniority unionists to press for increased government intervention on largely pragmatic grounds.

CONCILIATION BOARDS AND SLIDING SCALES

Despite recurrent difficulties, trade unionism had begun to establish a permanent foothold in the cotton and coal industries during the third quarter of the nineteenth century, on the basis of a long period of relative prosperity, the emergence of strong occupational sub-cultures and the support of key measures of state intervention. With public opinion temporarily in their favour, the larger organizations among the process workers had even been able to win formal recognition from their employers, providing them with a minimal safety net during the next two decades of depression and high unemployment. The mere fact of their unprecedented survival then gave these unions a new legitimacy as a focus for organization beyond the individual workplace and locality.

There had been some public discussion of a more regulated approach to industrial relations since the 1850s, resulting in a Conciliation Act in 1867 and an Arbitration Act in 1872. However, this legislation proved largely ineffective because it was only designed to assist in resolving disputes which were already under way, and it contained no compulsory powers. More significant developments had taken place at the level of specific industries, with the Nottingham Board of Arbitration for the Hosiery Trade of 1860 becoming established as a national model through the advocacy of A. J. Mundella, one of the leading figures on the employers' side and later a prominent Liberal MP. The Nottingham board was made up of equal numbers of representatives of the relevant employers' associations and trade unions under Mundella's chairmanship, and also a sub-committee of two employers and two workmen, who could investigate and frequently resolve detailed disputes before they came to the full board. Although there was an element of arbitration in Mundella's casting vote on the full board, this was regarded as a last resort and the aim was primarily to encourage union recognition and consultation, especially over the complexities of piece-rates for this industry's particularly diverse range of products. By the end of the 1860s this model had spread to the Nottingham lace trade, the other Midlands hosiery districts and, following a special effort by Mundella, the particularly strike-prone iron industry in the north-east. These boards generally attempted to insist on the discussion of grievances before any industrial action, and on the passing of a certain number of months between each proposal for a change in wage rates. However, the two sides in the iron industry found it harder to reach agreements on their own and frequently had to call in external arbitrators. They in turn quickly confessed that the intricacies of the industry's payment systems were beyond them and suggested that disputes be resolved by periodic adjustments of wage rates in line with changes in product prices: thus in 1871 what came to be known as a 'sliding scale' of wages had been introduced into the iron industry in the north-east.

Employers began to see advantages in these schemes once they appreciated that the unions were prepared to be reasonable in their demands. For union officials could play an important role in persuading their members to accept agreements and, when this was successful, the reduction in levels of industrial conflict permitted more continuous production. Moreover, by fixing rates of pay for some time to come,

effective agreements could reduce competitive wage-cutting in industries in which labour accounted for over half of costs, and thus permit
more confident business planning. As one manager in the Durham coal
field put it:

A combination of workmen which may take place at an individual colliery
cannot be called a union, because that is a mere family matter. But I think
that immediately it extends beyond the precincts of one colliery, and a combination is made, i.e. between one colliery and another, then it becomes a union
. . . I have not opposed myself point blank to the union; but to a certain extent
so long as they conducted themselves properly, I have admitted a certain right
that they have to have a union. I have not gone dead against it, and perhaps
that is a reason why it may not have affected me so seriously as others.[8]

For their part, the unions had long campaigned for recognition in
the process industries and found that these schemes also gave them
a role in settlements covering unorganized groups, both of which
then encouraged recruitment. Moreover, the unions too had an interest
in reducing levels of industrial conflict, in order to prevent regular
drains on their financial reserves which could threaten them with
organizational collapse.

The long depression which began in the middle of the 1870s led to
such rapidly falling prices and severe rivalry between the hosiery firms
that their model conciliation board collapsed and the sector's unions
were considerably weakened. However, the board in the iron industry
managed to survive and, though not formally recognizing trade unionism, provided a vital support for the skilled puddlers' National Amalgamated Association of Iron Workers, which had previously been close
to collapse. For the salaried secretary of the operatives' side of the
board was in practice also the secretary of the union, and the union
wielded a major influence over the election of the other operatives'
representatives. This was most effective in the north-east, but a similar
scheme was also set up and survived in the Midlands, while in the
Scottish iron industry, where the employers refused to adopt a conciliation board, there was to be no effective trade unionism for twenty
years after the defeat of a major strike in the middle of the 1860s. As
well as providing a shelter for trade unionism, the iron industry's
sliding scale also provided piece-workers with rates which could not

be altered quickly, thus guaranteeing them good rewards for increased output and minimizing workplace conflict over rate reductions. When the semi-skilled smelters and millmen set up their own organizations from the late 1880s they began by struggling for more independence from the sub-contracting puddlers. However, they gradually evolved their own version of conciliation boards and, once they had won the right to piece-rates, they were happy to be included under the sliding-scale arrangements, with the result that iron and steel was able to retain its reputation for unusual levels of industrial peace well into the twentieth century.

Conciliation schemes had also spread to the coal industry on a county by county basis during the 1860s, but they did little to protect trade unionism in the face of rapidly falling prices from the middle of the 1870s. In the west of Scotland and south Yorkshire there were major strikes in resistance to wage cuts, ending in defeats and the virtual collapse of the miners' organizations. In west Yorkshire the union managed to avoid a strike, but large wage cuts imposed through negotiations had an equally undermining impact on membership. In south Wales a major strike in 1875 ended in defeat, a 12.5 per cent wage cut and the introduction of the first sliding scale of wages into the coal industry. This had a mixed impact, for on the one hand employer-coordinated over-production could keep prices and thus wages low, but on the other hand the establishment of a joint committee to administer the sliding scale once again provided recognition and some protection for a considerably weakened union. As a result the desperate Yorkshire miners' unions began to press for the adoption of similar schemes and eventually persuaded their employers in the early 1880s. Meanwhile, Northumberland and Durham were once again able to survive as islands of reasonably strong trade unionism even during a long depression, but only on the basis of minimizing costly strikes and accepting wage reductions, which here too evolved into jointly administered sliding scales.

In the cotton industry the weavers were defeated in a major strike in 1878, followed by a 10 per cent wage cut and then by the emergence of a joint committee to administer a uniform county wage list. This provided a valuable safety net for the survival of trade unionism, albeit only able to organize around a quarter of the workforce before prosperity returned in the 1890s. Despite their tradition of stronger organization, the spinners too lost ground at the onset of the long depression: after the failure of a major strike in the fine-spinning centre of Bolton in 1877 they had to accept three successive rounds of wage cuts over the next two years, resulting in an overall reduction of 20 per cent and a rapid collapse of membership. However, the spinners then proved to be unusually adaptable and far-sighted, not only maintaining their local business ethos by working with the employers for a reduction in Indian protective tariffs and the building of the Manchester Ship Canal, but also undertaking a fundamental restructuring of their own organization. This began in Bolton, where the lessons of defeat were digested quickly: in 1878 a Piecers' Association was set up to collect small contributions towards dispute pay under the supervision of the spinners, in 1879 the minders of self-acting machinery were admitted to the hand-spinners' society, and from 1882 the town's work practices were gradually extended to create a uniform Province of fine-spinning districts. A determined recruitment campaign was also mounted in Oldham, establishing that town as the focus of an increasingly effective Province of coarse-spinning districts: on the basis of their industrial assertiveness and their provision of generous welfare benefits the spinners' organizations were then able to recruit up to 90 per cent of those eligible for membership. Rather than drifting apart, the two reviving centres maintained cooperation through the Spinners' Amalgamation, most notably during a major dispute at Oldham in 1885, when they were able to raise a strike levy from those still in work elsewhere which was large enough to force the employers to compromise.

Towards the end of the long period of mid-century prosperity, permanent organization had begun to emerge among another major group of workers faced with difficult conditions: on the railways. Although not involved in the transformation of raw materials through a succession of stages, the railway workers' responsibilities for handling passengers and freight through a complex transport system gave them a good deal in common with other groups of process workers. Thus high levels of skill were acquired through progression, leaving the more senior workers vulnerable to short-term replacement by junior substitutes. In addition, the railway employers consciously resisted trade unionism by imposing particularly divisive hierarchies of grades and pay, maintaining tight discipline through threats of demotion and dismissal, and providing housing, education and medical care, in return for which they expected strict loyalty. As a result the first moves towards permanent organization had been dependent on outside assistance, particularly from Michael Bass, Liberal MP for Derby and a major railway customer in his role as the head of a brewing company. Thus the significantly titled Amalgamated Society of Railway Servants had been established in 1871 under middle-class patronage, to provide basic welfare benefits and press for parliamentary legislation to reduce the industry's extremely long working hours and rising accident rates. Some success was achieved in gaining special provisions under the Employers' Liability Act of 1880, but there was a good deal of confusion over aims and methods and in the same year some of the more assertive footplate men broke away to form the Associated Society of Locomotive Engineers and Firemen. As experienced railway workers took on the secretaryship, the Railway Servants itself became increasingly dominated by the remaining footplate men and moved more clearly in the direction of collective pressure on the employers. However, this was still limited to the submission of petitions, which were only recognized by the railway companies as long as participation was restricted to their own employees.

THE REASSERTION OF
BARGAINING POWER

The spinners had little difficulty in maintaining their position in the cotton industry into the early twentieth century, for the so-called 'self-acting' mule required more effort and attention, especially for its maintenance, and the new ring-spinning technology from the United States, which could be operated by women, was not widely introduced even for coarser yarns. In general the spinners were able to benefit from increases in technical efficiency through increases in their piece-rate earnings. Moreover, their union was in a remarkably healthy state, having been able to survive the depression years on an industry-wide basis and even begun to extend its influence among the less-skilled piecers. As economic recovery began in the late 1880s the spinners continued their strategy of cooperation with other grades, supporting the launching of an assertive organization by the cardroom mechanics in 1886: this was open to the female workers in the department and soon a majority of its members were women, albeit in a subordinate position to the skilled men. Already claiming 90 per cent unionization in 1888, the spinners' membership only grew slightly from 17,000 to around 24,000 in 1913.

As a result of their compact organization the spinners were able to secure a number of improvements in wages and conditions relatively easily, while the employers remained poorly coordinated. This became particularly evident towards the end of 1892, when a brief return of poor trade led panicky Oldham employers to press for a 5 per cent reduction through a lock-out which went on to last for five months and to involve up to 50,000 workers of all grades. Unable to secure joint action from their counterparts in Bolton and with their own unity increasingly undermined by firms keen to resume production, the Oldham employers eventually settled in March 1893 for a smaller reduction, in return for the spinners' acceptance of regular bargaining procedures. What became known as the 'Brooklands Agreement', after the hotel outside Manchester where the key discussions took place, introduced the principles of the earlier conciliation boards into the cotton industry: no local action before negotiations, along with limits on the frequency of proposals for changes in wage rates.

Under this scheme the employers did indeed gain the expected benefits of a reduction of disruptive disputes and the standardization of wage costs. At the same time, the spinners, increasingly closely allied with the cardroom workers, were able to use peaceful negotiations backed by a large strike fund to improve their position over industry-wide issues such as basic rates of pay and hours of work. Moreover, whenever the employers attempted to introduce a sliding scale into the cotton industry, the spinners were confident enough to insist on their own criteria for the calculation of wages even if it meant that agreement could not finally be reached. Where they found themselves frustrated was over the delays imposed on the consideration of disputes about work practices in particular firms. There were increases in the size and speed of machinery, but these were not usually a source of difficulty as they brought increased earnings to piece-workers. The main problem was the issue of 'bad spinning' in the coarser firms, where employers' cost-cutting use of inferior cotton led to more frequent breakages, more interruptions and reduced earnings, for which the spinners wanted compensation. Revisions in 1906 led to quicker procedures to deal with persistent cases, but these only came into operation several months after an initial complaint, and the following year the union pressed for bad-spinning disputes to be dealt with outside the central procedure. Eventually, as the years of pre-war prosperity led to a surge of assertiveness at the local level, the spinners launched a strike campaign in the Oldham mills where bad spinning was most widespread. This not only meant abandoning the 'Brooklands Agreement' but also the alliance with the cardroom workers, who were unable to take joint industrial action which would bring no direct benefit to their own members. However, the spinners were strong enough on their own to win a new one-clause agreement with the employers in 1913, permitting local strikes over bad spinning if negotiations had not produced agreement within the course of a week.

Meanwhile, the campaign for factory legislation had developed into the United Textile Factory Workers' Association in 1889, involving all grades of mill workers and, with around 120,000 members, constituting one of the largest bodies of organized labour in the country. Despite their smaller numbers the spinners remained the dominant force, partly because of their longer experience, but largely because the majority among the weavers and the cardroom workers, being women, did not have the vote in parliamentary elections. After initial successes in securing acts to control humidity in the weaving sheds and the provision of written particulars of each worker's wage rates, the association began to find the sitting MPs in Lancashire and Yorkshire frustratingly ineffective and seriously considered funding its own parliamentary representatives. However, its members remained fairly evenly divided between the two established parties and the use of old-style pressure was still effective in increasing the Conservative vote in 1895 in protest against the Liberals' acceptance of Indian cotton duties, and in securing a shorter Saturday morning through Liberal amendment of the Conservative Factory Act of 1901. Eventually, the association began to participate within the Labour Party, securing the election of a spinners' leader as one of the MPs for Bolton but retaining its distinctive business ethos, which led to frequent criticism for its willingness to promote legislation jointly with employers.

In mining, the hewers maintained their central position in the extraction process into the early twentieth century, as soft coal and narrow faces made the available machinery largely unsuitable and the most significant technical innovations took place in lighting, ventilation, drainage and haulage to open up deeper seams. In general they too were able to benefit from increases in output through increases in their piece-rate earnings. Moreover, government legislation continued to protect the hewers' organization in the pits, not only by requiring the appointment of checkweighmen, but also from 1887 through safety regulations requiring anyone at the coalface with less than two years' experience to be accompanied by a more senior worker, which made it more difficult for employers to introduce substitute labour during disputes. Given the unprecedented survival of their organizations at the county level throughout a long period of depression, the miners were therefore well placed to embark once again on a period of assertive trade unionism. Moreover, this was underlined by the operation of the seniority system in a period of industrial expansion: increasing demand for the most skilled was met by promotion, which increased the bargaining power of the less skilled and enabled the unions to extend their recruitment beyond the hewers to include other underground and surface workers. Thus estimates of the combined membership of the various regional bodies indicate an impressive six-fold increase from around 150,000 in 1888 to around 900,000 in 1913, which covered 80 per cent of the industry's workforce.

As trade began to improve in the late 1880s the miners became increasingly assertive at the local level, and Yorkshire began to lead a wider alliance of the other domestically oriented coalfields in Lancashire and the Midlands to overthrow the sliding-scale schemes. This resulted firstly in concerted wage strikes gaining increases of up to 40 per cent, then in the reconstruction of a national body to press for state intervention under the experienced leadership of Ben Pickard and Thomas Ashton. Known from 1889 as the Miners' Federation of Great Britain, it focused on a campaign for legislation to achieve Alexander McDonald's old ambition of an eight-hour working day. A brief but severe fall in coal prices then led to employers' counter-pressure for a 25 per cent wage cut in 1893, but this was effectively resisted by the new federation, which now took on an industrial role during an unprecedented four-month lock-out of over 300,000 men. As one prominent employer remarked a few years later:

Experience has shown us that [the strike] cannot be used with effect today as it could have been fifteen or twenty years ago. Organization on both sides has relieved both the individual owner and the individual workman to a considerable extent from the pressure caused by a strike, and what would have been a question of weeks some years ago must now be measured by a much longer period of time.[9]

Moreover, there was considerable disorder in Yorkshire, including the death of two pickets after troops opened fire at a pit near Featherstone, and fuel shortages gradually began to affect other industries. As a result this massive strike led to the first intervention in industrial relations by a Prime Minister, the ageing Gladstone, who insisted that both sides attend a conference chaired by the Foreign Secretary, Lord Rosebery. This produced a compromise settlement, under which the employers were permitted to reduce wages by up to 10 per cent but, in a major concession to strong pressure from the Miners' Federation, the result was to be treated as a minimum and a newly established conciliation board was only to be allowed to consider future adjustments above this level. Organization was significantly weaker in Scotland where an early revival of inter-county action in 1886, with the young James Keir Hardie among its leaders, had led to a disastrous defeat. During a four-month Scottish national strike of 20,000 men in 1894, a parallel Scottish Miners' Federation was set up under the leadership of Robert Smillie of Lanarkshire and Robert Brown of Midlothian, but it was unable to prevent successive rounds of wage reductions until improved conditions later in the decade led to the establishment of a conciliation board in 1899, based on the same principles as that south of the border.

Thus an assertive bargaining position was gradually established throughout the domestically oriented coalfields, which eventually operated from a general national framework through county wage rates down to their application in the specific conditions of individual pits. The Miners' Federation then began to extend its influence into the export-oriented fields of south Wales and the north-east, where, in order to maintain dominance in overseas markets, there had been a greater acceptance of the need for wages to fluctuate along with prices and sliding scales had retained their appeal as a method of setting rates. Since the defeats of the 1870s, trade unionism in south Wales had fragmented to rather deferential pit organizations, and wider links were only maintained at all through the loyalties of Welsh speakers to the charismatic William Abraham, also known by his bardic name of 'Mabon'. Some progress was made over safety arrangements and welfare provision, and in 1889 a holiday on the first Monday of each month was achieved, but the Welsh miners were unable to coordinate effective pressure for higher wages until the improved conditions of the last years of the century. In 1898 they pressed for a 10 per cent increase and did manage to win 5 per cent after a gruelling five-month strike, in a region where trade unionism still covered less than a quarter of the workforce. This initial small success then gave a boost to the formation of a South Wales Miners' Federation, led by Abraham along with William Brace, which rapidly spread its influence and by 1903 had managed to replace the sliding scale with a conciliation board. At the other end of the spectrum, the Northumberland and Durham miners had long benefited from the most effective county-level organizations, had already reduced their standard shifts to seven hours and remained confident that they could maintain their wage rates on an open-ended sliding scale. They did join the national federation briefly in the aftermath of the defeat of their three-month strike against a 10 per cent wage cut in 1892, but left again to avoid getting embroiled in the major dispute of 1893, and only returned after the question of the length of the working day had been settled by Parliament in 1908. From then on, with all the regional bodies involved and their timetables for re-negotiating agreements gradually coordinated, the Miners' Federation of Great Britain could press for industry-wide bargaining and any dispute could become a genuinely national affair with enormous repercussions for the whole economy.

The miners had also continued to be active in political lobbying, building on the concentration of their members in particular constituencies and their ability to influence the outcome of parliamentary elections. There had been a divergence of views between the Miners' Federation and the Northumberland and Durham unions over how to regulate working hours, with the former successfully pressing the TUC to accept its case for eight hours legislation in 1889 and pushing the north-east representatives off the Parliamentary Committee, but failing to displace them as the dominant group among the miners' MPs in the House of Commons. As a result of the continued prominence of miners' political representatives opposed to statutory intervention, progress was delayed until after the progressive electoral landslide of 1906, which saw the emergence of the Labour Party as an alternative source of pressure on the issue. However, the Miners' Eight Hours Act eventually achieved in 1908 was somewhat symbolic, given the improvements already gained on a county basis and the complications of whether or not to include travelling to and from the coalface within the length of the hewers' working day. Moreover, it had unintended consequences in the export-oriented coalfields which threatened to embroil the newly united federation in costly national strikes over local peculiarities.

In the north-east, as long predicted by the miners' leaders in the area, the application of the statutory eight-hour day in 1910 threw established working practices into turmoil. For the norm had been two seven-hour shifts of hewers serviced by one overlapping ten-hour shift of ancillary workers, and a number of employers now proposed to replace the latter with two eight-hour shifts, which would only be economic if accompanied by an additional night shift from the hewers. A major regional strike was only defused by careful pit-by-pit negotiations throughout the early part of the year. Meanwhile, the south Wales coalfield contained many unusually deep and difficult seams and the statutory restriction of the working day to eight hours tended to reduce piece-work earnings. The men stepped up their pressure for compensation for 'abnormal places', leading to a constant rash of local strikes and the tightening up of counter-organization by the region's particularly domineering employers. Finally in the autumn of 1910, disagreement over the rates of pay for a new seam in one of the Cambrian Combine's Rhondda pits escalated into a strike affecting all the company's pits, during which the men's demand was supported financially by the South Wales Miners' Federation and the company's resistance was backed by the regional employers' association. The strikers took what was by this time the unusual step of trying to prevent the safety men from maintaining the pits during their closure, which led to two days of notorious rioting at Tonypandy, heavy-handed local policing and one death. This was followed by the importation of police contingents from outside the area, and finally the deployment of troops, which had been held in the background for as long as possible. However, this was an untypical outburst at the beginning of a very long dispute, which dragged on for ten months and involved around 12,000 men. Eventually the Miners' Federation was drawn into providing additional financial support and strongly pressurized by a group of particularly energetic young local activists to launch wider solidarity action. Despite this attempt to generalize the local grievance, the federation was understandably reluctant to get involved in a national strike over the rates for one seam, instead withdrawing its financial support and forcing the Rhondda men into a settlement.

The unusual bitterness of this Cambrian dispute was the result of a combination of factors connected with the explosive growth of the coal industry in south Wales from the late nineteenth century. This had been accompanied by major waves of migration into the narrow upland valleys of the region, where housing was poor and over-crowded, with the population in the Rhondda being particularly closely packed. It had also been accompanied by the construction of a new sense of identity, in which the resilient life of the nonconformist chapels was complemented by the educational and leisure facilities of the local miners' institutes, and a powerful Welsh revival did not prevent the spread of English as a language unifying natives and immigrants from across the border. Finally, it had been accompanied by a belated catching-up of trade-union organization after a long period of serious weakness, as the South Wales Miners' Federation brought together Welsh and English factions in a network of influential district lodges, and the region began to account for up to 40 per cent of the industry's days lost through strikes. Though the Cambrian strike brought a number of young activists to temporary prominence, their revolutionary attitudes should not be taken as typical of the whole region. At the height of the dispute they did win the Rhondda seats on the executive of the South Wales Miners' Federation, but they failed to repeat this success in the later elections for the region's seats on the executive of the miners' national union. Frustrated by their inability to win support from the other districts in south Wales, their famous 1912 pamphlet *The Miners' Next Step* called for a centralized union with annually elected officials, but when their proposal to do away with the existing district organizations and tenured local agents was put to the test of a regional ballot it was decisively defeated. Thus both the emergence and the ultimate failure of the Rhondda activists' appeal for general class struggle were yet more evidence that the miners' attitudes, in south Wales as elsewhere, were still deeply rooted in very strong loyalties to local institutions and personalities.

The south Wales activists claimed that it was their initiative which eventually won over the national union to a campaign for improved minimum wages, but there was already a good deal of independent interest in this matter in other areas. Moreover, it was chosen as the central issue not so much because it was really fundamental, but rather because it seemed the only sensible basis for unity between the federation's divergent regions. The miners' demands were broadly accepted by the employers in the domestic fields but strongly resisted by those in the export fields and, frustrated by this continued divergence, the federation launched its first national strike early in 1912. The Liberal government under Asquith, having failed to persuade the employers to accept a voluntary settlement, introduced legislation embodying the principle of a minimum wage but leaving the precise figures to be settled by regional joint boards. This fell somewhat short of the miners' demands, but the important concession of principle significantly undermined their unity and they were forced to call off the dispute. Interestingly enough, it was the south Wales men, exhausted by their own long struggle of the previous year, who cast the decisive votes in the ballot in favour of accepting the government's terms. From one point of view the miners had achieved another significant victory, but their staggering ability to mobilize almost a million strikers had been offset by the employers' preparation of large stocks of coal, which became even more valuable once the stoppage began to push up prices. Moreover, the issue of minimum wages had been to some extent an artificial one, the course of the dispute had revealed that the gigantic federation was still prone to regional fragmentation, and once again the miners' eventual success had been dependent on government intervention.

The railway workers were also able to maintain and improve their position into the early twentieth century. Their industry too was expanding rapidly on the basis of existing technology, and with less severe fluctuations, consequently steady workmen could expect fairly rapid promotion on familiar equipment and, unusually for the period, a job for life. The Amalgamated Society of Railway Servants opened a new section in the early 1890s with lower subscriptions for the less-skilled and lower-paid grades, and then in 1913 absorbed two smaller unions of signalmen and station staff to form the National Union of Railwaymen. Its membership grew from around 20,000 in 1888 to almost 270,000 in 1913, while that of its one remaining rival, the Associated Society of Locomotive Engineers and Firemen, grew from around 4,000 to almost 33,000, giving a total coverage of almost 60 per cent of the workforce.

The economic revival from the late 1880s led to a new surge of assertiveness, with the railwaymen beginning to press for union recognition and the extension of best-practice wages and hours into standard national scales. This had some impact among the more skilled grades of drivers, firemen, guards and signalmen, but the union's effectiveness was still limited to lines in the export-oriented mining regions, where the coal companies were highly sensitive to any disruption of their transport links with the sea ports. In south Wales the railwaymen achieved temporary recognition on three small lines in the early 1890s through a conciliation board sponsored by the Mayor of Cardiff, and in 1897 were to produce the union's first outstanding national secretary in Richard Bell. Meanwhile, in the north-east there was one large railway company run by industrialists with long experience of collective bargaining in the local coal and iron industries, who were therefore prepared not only to make concessions over working hours to pressure from their own employees but also to negotiate with union officials. In contrast, a parallel Scottish Society of Railway Servants launched a six-week strike in 1890–91, which won concessions on the length of the working day but was refused recognition. Indeed, the union was so exhausted that in 1892 its remaining members dissolved themselves into the society based south of the border. On the whole, then, trade unionism on the railways continued to be dependent on outside support from Liberal MPs, who succeeded in 1893 in getting the Board of Trade under Mundella to investigate individual complaints about excessive working hours, partly on the grounds of improving passenger safety. However, focusing on the railways as a public service could still cut both ways, as it was precisely this which the companies used to legitimize their strict systems of discipline and their refusal to consider any kind of joint regulation with bodies outside their own sphere of control and responsibility.

By the 1900s industrial relations on the railways were becoming increasingly embittered, as the unions were organizing around a third of the workforce but the employers were still refusing to recognize them and, hemmed in by government limits on their customer charges, were determined to keep labour costs as low as possible and increasingly coordinating their resistance to trade-union demands. In 1907 the railwaymen requested meetings to consider demands for an eight-hour day for the traffic grades, a ten-hour day for the others, and improved wages for all but, with the exception of that in the north-east, the companies refused to meet Richard Bell. Faced with the prospect of the first national railway strike, backed by a massive majority in a union ballot and with ominous implications for the rest of the economy, the Liberal President of the Board of Trade, David Lloyd George, used the threat of compulsory arbitration to force the employers to accept company conciliation boards for each major group of grades. Although the workers' representatives on the boards still had to be elected from within each company's own employees, from the outset the overwhelming majority of them were active trade unionists, so considerable headway had been made towards recognition. However, as the employers continued to adopt a particularly obstructive attitude towards the consideration of their workers' substantive grievances, this apparent resolution only provided a temporary pause in the escalating conflict.

Some small improvements were eventually secured from the conciliation scheme but, especially as the agreements reached were binding for four years, the men soon felt that they were falling behind during the prosperous pre-war years and unofficial wage strikes began to spread. Under the influence of Jimmy Thomas the leaders of the various unions came together on a programme of immediate joint action, ignored promises of an inquiry from the Prime Minister, Herbert Asquith, and launched the first national railway strike in August 1911. Government anxiety about disruption was much greater than during the recently terminated Cambrian coal strike and troops were widely mobilized, resulting in trouble at Llanelli in south Wales, where two strikers were killed trying to stop a strike-breaking train and five more died in an explosion in the freight yard. Once more it fell to Lloyd George, now Chancellor of the Exchequer, to press the employers to compromise, using the old stick of threatened government inter-vention, but now, along with the carrot of increases in customer charges, he managed to secure a settlement within a week. The main concessions were a 6 per cent pay increase and a speeding up of the conciliation boards' procedures. Moreover, while there was still no formal recognition, the employers were forced to meet the union leaders for the first time during a round of national talks and to agree that the workers' representatives on the company boards would no longer be confined to employees. Union officials therefore began to sit alongside their members and to raise a wide range of issues concerning working conditions and individual discipline as well as rates of pay.

Over the two and a half decades from the late 1880s, then, trade unions among the process workers had established improved bar-gaining positions based on their recruitment of the majority of the workers in their industries. Their ability to sustain national strikes, involving tens or hundreds of thousands of members for months on end in strategic sectors of the economy, gave them a position in public life which would have been unthinkable even in the most prosperous years of the middle of the nineteenth century. At the same time, in some contrast to the assembly workers, they were still prone to outbreaks of violence during demonstrations against substitute labour and still dependent on state intervention to shore up their position. The spin-ners, having already gained broadly satisfactory legislative regulation of their working hours and organizing a relatively compact group of workers, were the most independent. They were assertive over stan-dard rates, rejected employer proposals for a sliding scale, and over-threw central bargaining procedures when they found them frustrating in local negotiations. However, even they continued to play a leading role in the parliamentary lobbying of both parties over issues connected with overseas markets and domestic working conditions. Meanwhile the miners, having been much weaker in the preceding depression and suffering from regional variations among their vast membership, were still relatively dependent on the state. Deadlocks in major disputes were only resolved in their favour by Liberal government interventions to secure a floor to collective bargaining and then formal minimum wages. It therefore remained a natural extension of their industrial experience to see central symbolic importance in national legislation such as that for the eight-hour day. Finally the railwaymen, having struggled for longer against stubborn opposition from their employers, had still not achieved formal union recognition. It was almost entirely due to Liberal government pressure that they had managed even to secure a significant foothold on company conciliation boards. More-over, given the direct physical involvement of their consumers as passengers within their industry, it still made sense to phrase their demands for better wages and working conditions less in terms of their intrinsic justice than in terms of improvements to a vital public service.

PROPOSALS FOR PUBLIC CONTROL

The process workers were less directly affected by the recurrent crises of the First World War than the assembly workers in the metal trades. Of course steel, cotton and coal were important primary materials, but they were not immediately required for military purposes, and medium-term increases in demand could be met by reallocations from the high levels of peacetime exports. As a result the main influences on industrial relations in these sectors came through the general con-ditions of the war economy. There were some labour shortages and readjustment due to the recruitment of younger men, but not much replacement by female labour and no intrusion of women into the more skilled jobs, for the seniority systems guaranteed the filling of gaps by promotion of existing male workers from the lower grades. Rapid price inflation naturally fuelled recurrent demands for wage increases which were rarely met in full, though special consideration was given to the least well-paid grades and on the railways the need for enforceable national settlements finally pushed the companies into direct negotiations with union officials. Particularly towards the end of the war there was increasing cooperation between the unions within each sector: an amalgamation movement led to the emergence of the Iron and Steel Trades Confederation in 1917, the spinners, cardroom workers and weavers made their first joint wage claim in 1918, and the piecers were formally admitted to junior membership of the Amalgamated Spinners in 1919. The one exception was on the railways, where the rivalry between the National Union of Railwaymen and the Locomotive Engineers intensified, but this too had the effect of bringing significant gains through competitive leapfrogging. On this basis there was then a general assertion of bargaining power throughout the process industries during the post-war boom, producing a postponed catching up of wage rates and the introduction of shorter working hours, standardized around the eight-hour day. There were also additional bonuses, such as the final abolition of the half-time system of child labour in cotton and the introduction of an annual week's holiday with pay on the railways.

Moreover, these years saw an intensification of the long-standing relationships between the process workers and the state as the pressures of wartime led to increasing government intervention in their industries. Even in textiles, the products of which were least central to the war effort, the government prompted the industry to regulate itself after the German submarine campaign of 1917 began to disrupt supplies of raw materials. A joint Cotton Control Board supervised sales to ensure a fair distribution of materials, regulated the operation of mill machinery to ensure proportional reductions in activity between firms, and administered a lay-off rota and unemployment pay for the workforce. Meanwhile, the railways were such a central part of the country's transport system that they were taken under government control at the outbreak of hostilities, and here too the industry effectively regulated itself through company appointees to a Railway Executive Committee. A Select Committee report of 1918 calling for rationalization of the structure of the industry, in combination with the establishment of a Ministry of Transport the following year, put public ownership on the agenda, but Parliament was not yet prepared to go that far. The 1921 Railway Act only provided for compulsory amalgamation into four private companies, though it did guarantee the continuation of the national negotiating machinery and standard wages which had emerged during the war. Finally, in the coal industry the war saw mounting labour resentment over the high prices and presumed high profits of the employers, especially in south Wales, which provided most of the steam coal for the navy and where the owners remained particularly inflexible in negotiations. Even after the government stepped in to concede most of the demands of a major regional wage strike in 1915, unrest remained endemic so, as a preventative measure, the state took direct control of the south Wales field in December 1916, followed by the rest of the industry two months later. The new Coal Control department of the Board of Trade was concerned primarily with regulating prices, planning distribution and administering an excess profits pool to compensate those firms which suffered from its decisions. However, as well as persuading the miners that their efforts were being made on behalf of the country as a whole, this provided the first viable framework for national pay settlements which were then broadly linked to wartime increases in the cost of living.

The First World War therefore made the intervention of national government in major industries a matter of practical politics, but this was still a novel experience which took some time to digest. Indeed, it seems that most trade unionists in the process industries saw the benefits more in terms of the achievement of national bargaining than the introduction of government administration. Thus, while the Miners' Federation had long been in favour of public ownership in principle and at its 1918 conference unanimously endorsed a south Wales motion to that effect, it was still seen as a somewhat distant objective. In practice the union's immediate focus was on gaining access to the financial details of the existing administration of the industry in order to formulate its post-war wage claim. When this was finally submitted, the demand for a 30 per cent increase in the base rate and a six-hour day was too ambitious to concede, but the miners' industrial strength was too overwhelming to resist. The government therefore compromised with the appointment of a Royal Commission under Sir John Sankey, a judge, with equal representation from the workers and the owners. This was in part a classic delaying tactic, to allow the state to make better preparations to cope with a national stoppage and in the hope that changing conditions might undermine the union's extreme assertiveness. But it was also a product of genuine concern about the organization of the coal industry on the part of the government and the wider public, reflected in Sankey's unrestricted terms of reference and free access to official information. The Miners' Federation therefore agreed to postpone industrial action and take part in the inquiry, which was to provide its leaders with a forum for an unexpectedly serious discussion of the possibility of public ownership.

The Sankey Commission began its open sessions in the King's Robing Room of the House of Lords in March 1919 and the employers were rapidly thrown on to the defensive. For, although the initial stages of the inquiry were supposed to focus on the wage claim, the miners' leaders elected in the last year of the war, Robert Smillie from Scotland, Frank Hodges from south Wales and Herbert Smith from Yorkshire, were all members of the Independent Labour Party and constantly raised wider issues. Moreover, their three other non-union colleagues were all sophisticated intellectual proponents of state intervention: Sidney Webb, a leading Fabian socialist, R. H. Tawney, a prominent economic historian, and Sir Leo Chiozza Money, an economist who had chaired the wartime negotiating body for the shipping industry. For their part, the employers were quite unprepared to deal with anything other than an argument over wage rates. As a result, they responded rather feebly to questions about dangerous working conditions, poor housing and the benefits of government control, and, with generally critical coverage in the press, quickly lost the support of the three independent businessmen on the commission as well as that of the wider public. The commission naturally remained divided over the wage claim, so Sankey put forward a compromise proposal for a 20 per cent increase and a seven-hour day which the miners eventually accepted. Moreover, although they had yet to look formally at the organization of the industry, Sankey and the independent businessmen had already decided that:

Even upon the evidence already given, the present system of ownership and working in the coal industry stands condemned, and some other system must be substituted for it, either nationalization or a method of unification by national purchase and/or by joint control.[10]

However, the miners' leaders' unanticipated success in putting public ownership on the agenda soon proved to be rather hollow. For their withdrawal of the threat to strike over their wage claim defused the dramatic intensity of the situation, especially as there was little evidence of any willingness to strike over nationalization either among their own members or on the part of their closest allies, the railwaymen and the transport workers. Moreover, the replacement of two of the independent businessmen on the commission with less sympathetic individuals reduced the sense of inevitability of continued government intervention. Finally, the owners began to rally their own forces through their district associations and a more effective national presentation of their case. In particular they made it clear that they would not consider any alternatives between continued private ownership or outright state purchase, but that they would give some ground on consultation with the workforce. Thus even though Sankey himself eventually came out in support of public ownership as the only way to restore a degree of trust among the workers in the coal industry, the government was no longer under pressure to go much beyond the limits of its parallel solution for the railways: pressure for amalgamation into larger regional companies and some measure of profit control, along with improved consultation and welfare provision. The miners' leaders and their political allies were deeply disappointed but effectively powerless, for their own members were broadly satisfied with further rounds of improvements in wages and hours, and the publicity campaign 'Mines for the Nation' over the winter of 1919–20 fell quite flat. Their subsequent outright opposition to the government's alternative scheme only led to the eventual abandonment of a set of reforms which in other circumstances would probably have seemed rather radical. Meanwhile the real debate over the future of the industry began to revolve around technical discussions between the government and the owners over price adjustments in preparation for decontrol through the Mining Industry Act of 1920, which came into full force in the spring of the following year. Thus, while private ownership of a major industry had been subjected to unprecedented criticism and public ownership had been briefly considered as a means of pacifying trade-union unrest, there was still no settled political will to find a genuine alternative.

10

New Organizations among the General Workers

Although the Ministry of Munitions had been fully aware of this intention for over six weeks they did not even inform the Ministry of Labour of the pending dismissals, and in some cases when several thousand women were dismissed with only 24 hours' notice, there was no notice to the Labour Exchanges and no railway facilities were thought of or provided for sending these women back to their own homes. Conduct of that kind was calculated to make them feel cynical when they listened to or read the tributes which statesmen were constantly paying to the women war workers of the country. If they were good enough to be paid when they were working they were good enough not to be thrown on the streets without consideration the moment their efforts seemed no longer necessary ... The Labour Party was determined that it would do everything to secure that when the services of war workers were no longer necessary adequate provision should be made for them.[1]

These are extracts from a speech on the emancipation of women given by Mary Macarthur, the secretary of the National Federation of Women Workers, at the Labour conference in 1918 when the party was developing its comprehensive programme for post-war reconstruction as a national alternative to the Coalition government of Lloyd George. Macarthur had been chosen to propose the official resolution on this theme because of the leading role she had played among female trade unionists not only during the war but also before 1914, and her remarks indicate a number of important aspects of the attitudes which had been developing for some time among less-skilled workers of both sexes. Clearly the industrial contribution of women had become more prominent during the war emergency, and the arrangement of their wages and conditions had become a central concern for a number of government ministries. However, this particular passage also highlights the broader principle that the needs of all workers should be considered not only when they were employed but also when they became unemployed: in other words, that the long-term well-being of the nation's labour force was a legitimate matter of public concern. Thus, just as the experience of the war provided new material for the process workers' conceptions of public control of their own industries, so it provided new material for the general workers' conceptions of public intervention in the broader labour market.

Mary Macarthur had been born in Glasgow in 1880, unusually for a leading trade unionist of the period into a prosperous commercial family, for her father had a large drapery business and she had a privileged upbringing and education in the west of Scotland and in Germany. But Mary was a restless girl who needed larger goals to channel her enormous energy: she began by persuading her father to take her on as a book-keeper, which brought her into contact with his female shop workers, and at a memorable public meeting in 1901 she discovered her life's mission in the principles of trade unionism. Her vitality and charisma then fuelled a meteoric rise, with her first year as a member of the Shop Assistants' Union seeing her election as its Scottish President and the next seeing her election as the first female representative on its national executive committee. Although she was a dedicated and efficient administrator, success in a provincial town and one trade union was not enough to satisfy her need for drama, so in 1903 Macarthur moved to London and to prominence as the secretary of a national pressure group, the Women's Trade Union League. She brought to this post not only business experience but also a fiery sense of mission which moved the league on from waiting for affiliations to initiating unionization, culminating in the formation in 1906 of a parallel umbrella union for all-female organizations, the National Federation of Women Workers.

Her early experience with the shop assistants and her contacts with a wide range of new groups gave Macarthur a firm grasp of the vicious circle of low pay: 'women are badly paid and badly treated because they are not organised and they are not organised because they are badly paid and badly treated'.[2] She also quickly learned that it was relatively easy to recruit such low-paid and less-skilled workers into a union during the excitement of strike activity, but much harder to retain them as members:

About the first time I started an open-air meeting I got a number of girls around me on a street corner and I told them about Unionism. I was very enthusiastic, and perhaps I gave it to them in too glowing terms. They believed me, and gave me their names to join the Union. Ten days afterwards the girls looked more inclined to mob me than anything else, and I asked them what was the matter. 'Oh, we've been ten days in the Union and our wages haven't gone up yet!' Of course that taught me it was a mistake. I never speak at a meeting of non-Union girls without telling them the Union is not an automatic machine.[3]

Thus what was required was a combination of enthusiasm and hard-headedness, to rouse the feelings of mass meetings but to make sure that fledgling organizations did not exhaust themselves in pursuit of over-ambitious goals. Moreover, given the relatively weak bargaining power of women and other less-skilled workers even when they were organized, it was also vital to rouse the sympathies of the wider public during disputes. Macarthur therefore developed an impressive ability to secure favourable press coverage, partly by issuing carefully pre-pared case studies of the sufferings of the low-paid, partly through the striking contrast made by her own physical presence, 'a young lady who is not at all like the typical female agitator' but 'blue-eyed, fair-haired and charming'.[4] As one contemporary observed:

With the Federation and the Women's Trade Union League, Mary Macarthur and Miss Tuckwell wrought miracles. With all their camp followers in attend-ance they were no more than a stage army, but they said that they were the women workers of Great Britain, and they made so much noise that they came to be believed.[5]

Having achieved a high public profile, Macarthur was tireless in using it to secure favourable legislation from the more sympathetic Liberal governments after 1906. Her testimony before the Select Com-mittee on Home Work was a major contribution to the passing of the Trade Boards Act of 1909, which made provision for minimum wages for the most deprived groups of women. Her press campaign around the National Insurance Act of 1911 helped to win exemptions from contributions for those on the lowest pay, along with increased provision for girls under twenty-one. She then took part in a further government inquiry into the reasons for the higher level of female claims under the act and, while welcoming its recommendation that maternity benefit should be the property of the woman, issued her own memorandum on the broader causes of women's poor health:

The Act has shown the country what poverty really means. It has shown that people who are underfed, badly housed and over-worked are seldom in a state of physical efficiency; and has expressed in terms of pounds, shillings and pence the truth that where an industry pays starvation wages, it does in literal, sober fact, levy a tax upon the community.[6]

Macarthur's ability to influence the details of legislation as well as grasping the broader issues was intensified by the First World War, during which she played a leading role on almost every committee concerning female workers. As a trade unionist with extensive pre-war experience she was not swept away by the national emergency and, with an eye on maintaining and extending the long-term position of women in employment, she was careful to concede nothing in the way of their wages and conditions to government pressure. Through her role on the Central Munitions Labour Supply Committee she secured a favourable statutory base line and then campaigned tirelessly to see that it was properly implemented.

It was therefore not surprising that Mary Macarthur should have become the first woman selected as a Labour candidate in the 1918 general election, for the west Midlands seat of Stourbridge. However, despite supportive visits from such parliamentary heavyweights as Jimmy Thomas and her own husband, William Anderson, she was unable to prevail against the tide of anti-German feeling which over-whelmed so many of her friends in the leadership of the party. Worse was to come, for William succumbed to the post-war influenza epi-demic in the spring of 1919 and Mary never recovered from the loss, dying herself of cancer just after her fortieth birthday at the end of 1921. She had been outstanding for her inner confidence in approach-ing employers, government officials, and indeed men in general, on a footing of equality. Like her colleagues among male trade unionists she had combined a detailed mastery of practicalities with a clear vision of broader goals and principles. And like those in the other general workers' unions she had focused on the social irresponsibility of low pay, arguing that the long-term costs to the nation's health should be avoided by public intervention to secure an acceptable living wage.

THE CHALLENGE OF ORGANIZATION

Until the last quarter of the nineteenth century there had been few signs of trade unionism among less-skilled workers, frequently referred to as 'labourers' because of the heavy manual tasks they carried out, and regarded as notoriously difficult to organize. For, while they did have some job-specific skills, these were derived more from physical ability and sheer repetition than from long periods of training or technical knowledge: since almost any fit newcomer could make a reasonable start, it was hard to make exclusive claims to particular tasks. Thus, in the absence of core groups with indispensable skills to provide a secure base for the gradual extension of organization, the general workers needed to break through in one step to the widest possible coverage of their industries if they were to establish effective trade unions. For most of the nineteenth century this challenging project had been seriously impeded by the tendency to recruit them from among recent rural immigrants, to employ them on a casual basis in response to immediate requirements and to pay them relatively low wages, thus frustrating the development of stable networks and making it hard to find the money to sustain organizations. However, by the last quarter of the century migration from the country to the city was beginning to slow down, so there were fewer rural workers to draw into such continuously expanding aspects of the urban infrastructure as transport and energy supply: wage rates were naturally beginning to rise and union subscriptions were becoming more affordable. In addition, the numbers employed in the larger firms were increasing, especially in London, so recruiting substitute workers was becoming significantly more troublesome for the major employers: when threatened by effective strike action they were increasingly likely to make concessions. Thus, while the challenge facing the general workers was still an enormously difficult one, it no longer seemed completely impossible and there were bold attempts to tackle it roughly every twenty years, when conditions of economic prosperity coincided with the rise of younger generations with less experience of the costs of failure and more confidence in their own vitality.

The first of these attempts had come in the early 1870s when relatively full employment had presented some groups with a window of opportunity as well as outside assistance from better-organized workers and middle-class sympathizers. The case which received most attention at the time was that of the agricultural labourers, as their harsh subordination in closed rural communities attracted the sympathy of radical liberals already in the habit of seeing the landed aristocracy and the established church as two of their main political targets. The labourers' position had been improving slowly during the middle years of the century, largely because better transport was giving them access to alternative opportunities in urban labour markets as well as permitting more contact between activists in different regions. A long tradition of attempts at organization north of the border had produced a short-lived Scottish Farm Servants' Protection Society in the 1860s. Then a major Methodist revival in the first years of the 1870s provided the confidence for a wave of local union agitations in the arable districts of the south and east of England, where workforces were larger and more detached from their employers than in the pastoral north. The Warwickshire movement, under the charismatic leadership of Joseph Arch, a Primitive Methodist lay preacher, became the focus for the formation of a National Agricultural Labourers' Union in 1872, which could claim a membership of over 70,000 by the end of the following year. However, the onset of the long depression in the middle of the 1870s undermined the labourers' ability to win disputes against determined employers' opposition, which was followed by increasingly undermining divisions within the local organizations. Thus, while Arch himself continued to play an important political role in the agitation for the extension of the franchise in the counties in 1884 and subsequently as MP for north-west Norfolk, union membership collapsed to only a few thousand members of local benefit clubs.

Meanwhile there had been parallel bursts of activity among similar groups in urban areas, above all in the capital. The London gas workers, who had been known to strike as early as the 1830s, formed an Amalgamated Gas Stokers' Union during a strike for shorter hours at the new Beckton gasworks in East Ham in 1872. This was the dispute which produced harsh prison sentences and precipitated the TUC's successful campaign for clemency, leading to the repeal of the Criminal Law Amendment Act in 1875 described in an earlier chapter. Meanwhile, the London dockworkers formed a Labour Protection League to resist a large wage cut in 1871, going on to win increases to a standard 5d. an hour as well as to take part in a federation of transport workers, known as the Amalgamated Labour Union, which included some carmen and railwaymen. In addition, the London builders' labourers, who appear to have been organized briefly during the lock-out of the skilled men in 1859, formed a General Amalgamated Labourers' Union during another dispute in 1872 and claimed several thousand members at their peak. However, despite the welcome they received from the craft unionists on the London Trades Council and their own ambitions to amalgamated status, these bodies failed to survive beyond the middle of the decade with the exception of a few branches of the dockworkers' league, above all among the better-paid stevedores who specialized in shipboard tasks.

However, when the economy began to recover again in the late 1880s there was a sudden revival of organization among the London general workers. At the Beckton gasworks Will Thorne, a socialist stoker, had for some time been trying to re-establish trade unionism among this now relatively well-paid group. When he set up the National Union of Gasworkers and General Labourers in the spring of 1889 with a focus on reducing the length of the exhausting working day, there was an unusually enthusiastic response. Up to 20,000 members joined in the first few months, leading to the concession of eight-hour shifts by the major London companies in June and, though Thorne himself urged a more cautious approach, this initial success inspired the men to increase their demands to include higher rates for overtime. It also helped to inspire the gasworkers' near neighbours in the London docks, many of whom were by then also relatively well paid. Here Ben Tillett, formerly a sailor and shoemaker, had been struggling to build up a small union based in the tea warehouses for the previous two years, and he too was swept along by a new enthusiasm among the men:

Many who had lost heart regained their confidence in combined action ... and the men were already ripe for a contest, when, on August 12th, a dispute at the South West India Dock served as the spark which kindled the blaze. The nature of the dispute – about the division of the 'plus' on a certain cargo – is of little importance, for it was avowedly only the pretext for a revolt against all the grievances which had long rankled in the minds of the dock labourers. The men wanted to come out at once, and their leader only managed to restrain them until he had formulated their demands in writing, and sent them to the dock authorities.[7]

Tillett chose a minimum of half a day's employment and an increase in the standard rate to 6d. an hour as a unifying focus amid the complexities of the highly specialized organization of the port of London, and would have gained some concessions without industrial action had the dockers not insisted on pursuing the full demand. The result was the first big general workers' strike, involving around 20,000 men for over a month and, like all disputes in the capital, attracting more than its share of media attention. More importantly, it also attracted vital support from groups with longer experience of organization. The bodies which had survived among the stevedores quickly joined the action to avoid working alongside substitute labour, and then played a key role in administering the distribution of relief money. In addition a number of socialist engineers, most notably John Burns and Tom Mann, contributed their services as agitators to raise the profile of a series of orderly open-air meetings and marches through the City of London during a particularly warm August. This helped to build up a significant level of public sympathy and financial support, and at a vital moment huge contributions to the relief fund began to pour in from Australian trade unions, eventually totalling around £30,000. A joint committee of employers was formed but, with the rest of the economy booming and the agricultural harvest in full swing, it made little headway in recruiting the huge numbers of substitute workers required, either from the London casual labour market or from the surrounding rural counties. Eventually the Lord Mayor of London and the Roman Catholic Cardinal Manning were able to set up talks at the Mansion House, persuading the employers to concede the 6d. an hour minimum in return for a union guarantee of protection for those who had remained at work. In practice these men left the industry or joined either Tillett's renamed Dock, Wharf, Riverside, and General Labourers' Union on the north side of the river or the revived Labour Protection League on the south side, so, with the smaller bodies of more specialized workers also expanding, trade unionism in the London docks could claim to have made a genuine advance, albeit still far from united.

Outside the capital a new wave of organization already had a momentum of its own. With the encouragement of the miners and other established trade unionists in the north-east of England, Joseph Havelock Wilson had set up the National Amalgamated Union of Sailors and Firemen in 1887. It had spread rapidly to Liverpool and Glasgow, and in the first half of 1889 coordinated a series of brief strikes in most of the major ports, gaining concessions of substantial wage increases and stimulating the Newcastle dock workers to take part in the National Amalgamated Union of Labour. Meanwhile in Glasgow, craft unionists had helped to initiate the National Union of Dock Labourers in February 1889, which rapidly spread down the west coast to Liverpool and the Irish ports and had won concessions in a number of local disputes by the middle of the year. Then, following the well-publicized victories in London that summer, there was a flurry of similar movements in almost every major town throughout the country as general workers' unions became something of a fashion in the last months of 1889. There was even a new wave of activity among the agricultural labourers, especially in the counties within easy reach of London, which were visited by organizers from the gasworkers and the dockers keen to reduce the inflow of rural substitutes.

Some firms were prepared to recognize the new unions but the majority were unwilling to accept the transformation of traditional employment relations which was implied. For the relatively low levels of skill required on entry had previously prevented general workers from establishing monopoly rights over their jobs, but the introduction of trade unionism could provide a new focus for exclusion, and of course the unions would have a direct interest in encouraging this in order to increase the stability of their own memberships. Thus, in addition to the calculation made by the employers of process workers, over whether the advantage of organized bargaining was worth the risk of higher wages, the employers of general workers were faced with an additional calculation, over whether the gain from regular employment of experienced and reliable labour was worth the loss of flexibility and high-pressure working. Most of the large firms involved had strongly established preferences for pliant core workforces with large casual fringes, and they therefore began to coordinate serious counter-attacks against attempts by trade unionists to establish restrictions over the labour employed.

The gasworkers were still able to extend their recruitment into the Midlands and the north, but were easily defeated in their attempt to impose a closed shop in Manchester. Even in their London base they were seriously undermined by the employers' careful preparation of an anti-union drive in early 1890, revolving around substitute labour with effective police protection. Meanwhile, the London dockers were able to spread along the south and east coasts but the employers' mobilization of substitute workers resulted in defeats over union recognition in Southampton and Plymouth, and then over the priority of employment for union members in the capital itself. Similarly, the west-coast dockers were frustrated in their attempts to move towards union priority in Liverpool. For their part, the seamen, while claiming as many as 60,000 members, had been involved in a long-running battle for control of employment through the recruitment of key ships' officers, leading the employers to counter-attack by setting up a high-profile Shipping Federation with its own register of loyal workers prepared to sail with non-union labour. This system was maintained through a national dispute in early 1891 when, once again faced with efficiently organized substitutes under police protection, the union suffered humiliating setbacks in almost every port in the country. This changing balance of power was only further underlined by the disastrous defeat of the London dockers during a dispute over non-union labour in Hull two years' later, which resulted in the disappearance of their organization from the east coast altogether.

The prominence of a number of socialist agitators in the foundation of some of these new unions became a target for exaggerated attacks by employers keen to legitimize their own domineering behaviour.

However, the socialists themselves were generally agreed that they were accepted as leaders despite their political views, not because of them. Thus it was more important that they, and the many liberals who played a similar role, generally came from outside the groups concerned, and brought with them experiences of trade unionism in other occupations. Indeed, this sudden explosion of organization among the general workers at the beginning of another long phase of union growth, like the brief explosion in the early 1870s at the end of the previous one, remained rather too dependent on external assistance. Though the long-term prospects were still improving, the apparent breakthroughs of 1889 were premature: at their early peak the new organizations could claim a total membership of around 350,000, but this explosive growth was halted by the employers' counter-attack and then quickly cut to less than half by the next short economic downturn in 1891.

Those bodies which survived tended to settle over the next two decades at a membership of around 10–30,000 each, putting them on a par with the smaller craft unions but with much less bargaining power. Some had already introduced welfare funds in an attempt to stabilize membership, but their generally low levels of subscription limited what they could offer. The seamen and the National Amalgamated Union of Labour had accident and funeral benefits from their foundation; the west-coast dockers introduced funeral benefit in 1890; their London counterpart followed suit in 1891, and many branches of both set up local sick funds. However, for the rest of the decade turnover remained as high as a third of the membership every year, so those unions which survived could only do so by mounting repeated recruitment drives in new districts and above all by scooping up the members of other bodies which were collapsing. Thus the gasworkers took in local-authority builders' labourers and Birmingham metalworkers and, when the economy revived in the late 1890s, extended even further to include northern telephone operators and Scottish laundry workers. Meanwhile, the London dockers became increasingly dependent on their members in south Wales and took in that region's tinplate workers; and the National Amalgamated Union of Labour established its main foothold among platers' helpers in the northern shipyards. This high priority placed on organizational survival was at least partly motivated by the union officials' desire to keep their own jobs, for, especially on the waterfront, these bodies had tended to be heavily staffed with full-time local officers during their early struggles for recruitment in highly mobile occupations. Thus by a rather random process they began to evolve gradually from unions for 'general labourers' in particular industries into 'general unions' for labourers in almost any industry. However, the sporadic outbreaks of organization resulted in problematic relationships between their officials and their members, for the leaders who struggled to maintain the unions more permanently were faced with long periods of widespread apathy followed by sudden peaks of mass enthusiasm which were hard to contain within the regular procedures of collective bargaining. Moreover, the lack of continuity in branch life produced organizations with under-developed channels of democracy, while the construction of broad federations of very diverse occupations reduced the influence of each group on national policy. Thus even when the general workers' unions seemed to be buoyed up by waves of mass support, their members were usually highly volatile and often rather disaffected.

Twenty years later, between 1911 and 1914, there was another of these bursts of activity, for unemployment was exceptionally low and rapidly rising prices were threatening to undermine real incomes. Once again this wave of enthusiasm was unexpected, catching the employers off guard and resulting in significant initial gains, and, as was now usual, it was accompanied by a fairly high level of intimidation against such substitute labour as was mobilized, especially on the waterfront. There was a marked revival among rural workers whose main organization was now the Eastern Counties' Agricultural Labourers' Union, initially formed under middle-class sponsorship during the Liberal upsurge of 1906 but revolving around George Edwards, whose experience of organization went back to the time of Arch's union in the 1870s. After the bitter defeat of an eight-week strike at St Faith's near Norwich in 1910, the agricultural labourers became increasingly assertive and, with the help of financial support and sympathetic action from the railwaymen, were able to win significant wage increases in Lancashire and north-west Norfolk. Meanwhile, the seamen mounted a vigorous recruiting campaign with the assistance of Tom Mann, recently returned from a stay in Australia, and launched a surprise wave of local strikes beginning in Southampton in June 1911 and spreading even to unorganized ports such as Hull. The employers, keen to take advantage of booming trade conditions and unable to find 120,000 substitute workers all at once, granted wage increases and even recognized the union in some ports. Local solidarity action by the dockers then began to turn into demands for wage increases of their own, particularly in Liverpool where religious sectarianism contributed to several days of turbulence and three deaths, but the west-coast dockers were finally able to win union recognition.

Meanwhile in London, improved coordination through the recently formed National Transport Workers' Federation enabled Ben Tillett to win concessions over wages during the first genuinely port-wide negotiations. However, these were rejected by an excited mass meeting of the men, sweeping the leaders into an official strike of 80,000 dockers in the first two weeks of August. With the assistance of sympathetic arbitration by the Board of Trade, they were able to win formal concessions towards their goals of standard port rates and the reintroduction of union regulation of employment. Inspired by this initial success, the unions continued to press for substantive improvements through local disputes, but the employers had already made more promises than they intended to keep. Rising expectations combined with fear of an employers' counter-attack to create a volatile atmosphere, leading the unions to launch another port-wide strike in the spring of 1912. However, this time the government was unable to persuade the employers to make further concessions and, when the call for national solidarity action met with refusals from the more cautious seamen and west-coast dockers, the strike collapsed. As a result, the employers openly withdrew their concession of union control over recruitment and the return to work was marked by a number of bitter incidents of violence to drive out the temporary replacements. The London dockers and the stevedores both eventually lost up to half of their members and the unions were as far as ever from achieving standard conditions across the port.

Dublin was another major centre of activity in these years, for here the unionization of a wide range of general workers had been proceeding rapidly under the charismatic leadership of the Liverpool-born Irishman James Larkin. Initially sent over to Belfast and Dublin as an organizer of the west-coast dockers, Larkin was influenced by an eclectic mix of British ethical socialism, French syndicalism and Irish nationalism. This led him to set up a breakaway Irish Transport and General Workers' Union in 1908, with a special emphasis on labour representation in local government and the broadening of industrial disputes through sympathetic strikes. As in the rest of the British Isles, disputes over union recognition escalated from 1911, with enough success to allow Larkin's umbrella body to claim 30,000 members and to make progress towards more regular bargaining with the Dublin shipping companies. However, in the summer of 1913 an employers' counter-attack was initiated by William Martin Murphy, a prominent nationalist politician and businessman who owned the largest Irish newspaper and the Dublin tramways. Larkin responded by spreading the dispute from its origins among Murphy's newspaper dispatch workers to include all related groups of transport workers, eventually involving up to 20,000 strikers for eight months. Faced with the usual coercive attitude of the Irish police, the industrial confrontation became increasingly violent, particularly around the picketing of the Dublin tramways at the end of August, which led to two deaths and hundreds of arrests, including that of Larkin himself on charges of sedition. There was widespread concern among British trade unionists about the implications for civil rights of the aggressive attitude of the Irish employers and the coercive behaviour of the Dublin Castle authorities. So, despite criticism from Larkin over their refusal to call for sympathetic industrial action, the leadership of the TUC sponsored a number of delegations to assist with public meetings in Ireland and also set up a hardship fund for the strikers which eventually raised over £90,000. The government attempted to mediate but the employers were adamant in their refusal to deal with the existing union leadership, and the final turning-point came when pro-union candidates failed to make any gains in the Dublin local elections in January 1914: the strike terminated with a gradual return to work over the following month. Larkin's health was undermined by stress and he left the country for a while, but the Irish Transport and General Workers' Union managed to survive, with its combination of aggressive trade unionism and independent labour representation continuing to make a distinctive contribution to the increasingly urgent debate about the implications of Irish Home Rule.

During this pre-war labour unrest the employers, already used to justifying their behaviour in terms of public-spirited resistance to the threat of 'socialism', found another foreign scapegoat in the shape of 'syndicalism'. This was a doctrine drawn from the later phases of the French revolutionary tradition, which rejected political in favour of industrial action, aiming to transform the social order through a widely coordinated general strike. Thus the preparation required was not the building of a revolutionary party but rather the construction of 'One Big Union', ideally made up of coherent industrial units. Tom Mann was particularly enthusiastic in promoting these militant ideas through the Industrial Syndicalist Education League, and they had some impact on G. D. H. Cole's development of a more moderate vision of industrial self-government known as Guild Socialism. In general, however, the influence of syndicalism was diffuse, and those who defined themselves primarily in terms of its doctrines were few in number and widely dispersed between sectors and regions. Moreover, they were prone to division over whether their ideal industrial units were to be achieved through Mann's campaign for an 'amalgamation movement' among those bodies which had already been established, or through the Socialist Labour Party's more sectarian approach of starting afresh with 'dual unionism'. This strategic divergence was accompanied by different conceptions of democracy, with those among the miners in the Rhondda calling for more centralized decision-making within existing bodies, while those among the engineers on the Clyde were calling for new forms of decentralized workshop control. Indeed, it is probably significant that many of these pockets of support were to be found in the 'Celtic Fringe', where the notion of a purely industrial road to a new society seems to have appealed to long-standing regional suspicions of the national political system.

However, with the exception of the building trades and the railways, where there were already strong official tendencies towards union amalgamation, syndicalism found few echoes among those with commitments to existing bodies, whether as leaders who had acquired influence or as members who had invested subscriptions. For their part, the syndicalists were even rather hostile to the less well-established general workers' unions which might have been expected to be their natural allies. For these organizations' creation of umbrellas for diverse groups of less-skilled workers only threatened to create yet another obstacle to the ideal of neat industrial units. If the slogan of 'One Big Union' had some appeal to the followers of James Larkin, it was because the peculiarities of the Irish economy meant that a federation of transport workers and agricultural labourers could realistically expect to become the dominant force in the trade-union world, at least outside Belfast. But in general it would be fantastic to attribute the wave of industrial unrest throughout Britain in the years after 1911 to the influence of syndicalism: where support for those ideas did exist it was a local symptom rather than a significant cause. After all, mass strikes accompanied by relatively high levels of intimidation were the result of the particular problems of unionization among less-skilled workers. And the most threatening stand-offs between capital and labour, in the south Wales coalfield and on the railways as well as on the waterfront, continued to be the result, not of widespread revolutionary aspirations among trade unionists, but rather of an unwillingness to adopt a more constructive approach to collective bargaining among the employers concerned.

Indeed, had it not been for the impact of the First World War, the serious defeats of the large transport strikes in London and Dublin might have been followed by yet another widely coordinated employers' counter-attack. Instead the general workers became a particular target for recruiting and conscription into the armed forces, since their output was even less immediately essential for military purposes than that of the process workers. However, a significant amount of effort was still required to maintain the supply and transportation of food, which became increasingly important as the war dragged on. Thus the smaller labour forces left behind began to benefit from higher wages, increased overtime and generally improved bargaining positions as their large casual fringes were gradually consumed by the endless casualties on the western front. As a result, the decade from 1910 to 1920 was unusual for a continuous growth in strength of the general workers' unions, by a factor of almost ten: resulting in a combined membership of around 3,000,000, and an increase in their share of the total membership of trade unions from around 10 per cent to around 30 per cent.

The agricultural labourers began to benefit from labour shortages early on in the war, winning wage increases and a degree of recognition on a county basis during 1915. Their bargaining power was then significantly improved when a poor harvest in 1916 was followed by the serious disruption of imports as a result of German submarine warfare, and food supply came to the centre of the government's agenda. A Corn Production Act was passed in August 1917, giving farmers guaranteed minimum prices for cereals and setting a national minimum wage which could be adjusted upwards through joint district wage boards. This form of state-sponsored collective bargaining may not have given the labourers in every area as much as they hoped for, but it provided a major incentive to join the union which grew by over twenty times over the next four years, from around 4,000 to over 90,000. However, free access to imported cereals was quickly restored after the war and the repeal of the act in 1921 removed the farmers' guaranteed incomes. Without this statutory framework the agricultural labourers were powerless to prevent successive rounds of wage cuts and lay-offs in response to sharply falling agricultural prices.

The seamen were also able to do relatively well out of a tight labour market from the start, since the need for cooperation was acute when ships were about to sail with vital cargoes: even after increases of over 30 per cent in the first year of the war there was still a constant rash of successful local wage demands. The labour shortage then reached a crisis point in 1917, when Germany launched its campaign of unrestricted submarine warfare, leading to the loss of 30 per cent of the British merchant fleet. The innovation of the convoy system was an effective response to the loss of vessels. The Shipping Federation was persuaded to drop its opposition to national negotiations with the unions and, following a key local dispute in Liverpool in October 1917, permanent procedures were established in the form of a National Maritime Board under the chairmanship of Sir Leo Chiozza Money. The problem of the supply of workers was then tackled by fixing national standard rates of pay at levels roughly double the pre-war rates and by setting up joint district supply boards, thus fulfilling the long-standing union aim for a degree of control over labour recruitment.

Among the dockers, high levels of volunteering for the army reduced the workforce by around 20 per cent, and combined with the concentration of cargoes in London and the western ports to bring more regular work and higher earnings. This in turn encouraged a rapid growth in membership of the dockers' unions, which were able to achieve relatively favourable wage increases along with generous overtime allowances and war bonuses targeted specifically at the less well paid. However, there was still no national employers' organization and indeed, when the Ministry of Labour made a further wage arbitration in favour of the unions in 1918, the Port of London Authority refused to implement it and had to be coerced under the Munitions of War Act. At the same time the war did see some changes in employers' attitudes, as many of them came to accept that the industry could be conducted profitably even with a smaller labour force and a degree of collective bargaining. Attempts were made to reform the practice of casual employment by setting up local port registers to spread the available work among regular dockers. However, since employers were still keen to retain exclusive access to their normal labour, the outcome was not more movement of men to where the work was available but rather an increase in the pressure to report regularly at the usual place. Meanwhile, the unions had become confident enough to put forward their own scheme, advocated particularly strongly by the Bristol organizer of the London dockers, Ernest Bevin. This consisted of union administration of the registers, a guarantee of three-quarters of normal wages whenever a man presented himself without receiving any work, and the funding of the scheme through a levy on all cargoes passing through British ports.

A further pay demand at the end of 1919 led a number of local port employers' groups to suggest an inquiry by an Industrial Court, which the Ministry of Labour set up along similar lines to the Sankey commission on the coal industry: with public hearings in February and March 1920 in front of three trade unionists, three employers and three independent representatives, under the chairmanship of Lord Shaw, a judge. The proceedings opened with an outstanding two-and-a-half-day presentation of the dockers' case by Ernest Bevin, combining distressing details of the hardships accompanying casual labour with a detailed grasp of the finances of the industry, and followed not only by a tough cross-examination of the employers' witnesses over the next month but also by a lucid and reasonable summing-up of the union case. This masterly performance won over the independent representatives to the unions' demand for an improved national minimum wage to foster more cooperative relationships in the industry, along with the establishment of a Whitley Council to oversee the reform of the system of casual employment. For the Shaw inquiry concluded:

The Court is of the opinion that labour frequently or constantly under-employed is injurious to the interests of the workers, the ports and the public, and that it is discreditable to society ... In one sense it is a convenience to authorities and employers, whose requirements are at the mercy of storms and tides and unforeseen casualties, to have a reservoir of unemployment which can be readily tapped as the need emerges for a labour supply. If men were merely the spare parts of an industrial machine, this callous reckoning might be appropriate: but society will not tolerate much longer the continuance of the employment of human beings on these lines ... The time has arrived when the industry out of which the payment of wages will come must also bear a charge in respect of maintenance of unemployed casuals.[8]

The employers' organizations now seemed ready to accept all of this, forming a National Council of Port Labour Employers, conceding the improved wage rates and even participating in talks over the maintenance of labourers through a new Joint Industrial Council. However, as the post-war boom began to fade and unemployment began to rise, they rapidly backed away from the expenses implied by special maintenance arrangements. Their traditional attachment to highly casual labour and non-unionism had been eroded and they did not openly repudiate the outcome of the Shaw inquiry, but they shifted the emphasis away from more cooperative relationships towards the need for maximum efficiency in the use of a smaller labour force. Meanwhile the government had no schemes for the rationalization of production, as it had been responding primarily to union demands for the reform of the labour market. For their part, the unions were increasingly unable to back up their own proposals with threats of industrial action, and indeed the emphasis of national negotiations began to shift towards the size of the next wage reduction. From the point of view of the high hopes inspired by Bevin in early 1920 this was a disappointing outcome, but the survival of national collective bargaining arrangements among such important groups of general workers as the dockers and the seamen was no mean achievement.

WOMEN AND ORGANIZATION

Women in these types of less-skilled occupations were generally regarded as even more difficult to organize. For in addition to the usual problems of casual employment, they were often widely dispersed, either as outworkers in their own homes or domestic servants in the homes of others, and they frequently expected only to work for money until they were married. Even where they were employed in more concentrated and permanent situations, the widespread assumption that their contributions to family incomes were of secondary importance to those of the 'male breadwinners' tended to keep women's wages down to around half those of the equivalent men, and this clearly reduced their resources for self-organization. Moroever, those who were wives and mothers usually had their own priorities for their time away from the workplace, which tended to reduce their participation in formal bodies even further. Female workers therefore had a poor reputation among male trade unionists and became trapped in vicious circles of self-confirming expectations. Among the assembly workers they were usually regarded as lower-paid threats to be excluded from employment, an attitude most prominent among the compositors but also spreading to the spinners in the cotton industry. Elsewhere among the process workers women were restricted to subordinate positions in workplaces and unions, most notably among the weavers and cardroom operatives, who accounted for the vast majority of female union members in the late nineteenth century. Paradoxically, then, the very difficulties of organization among even less-skilled workers could provide unusual opportunities for women: for where the field was still more open, female activists might be able to make more of an independent impact. Nor was the task as unpromising as it might seem, for, despite the difficulty of retaining women in formal bodies, they were far from passively subordinate in the workplace. Indeed, they were just as likely as men to argue back against their superiors and launch informal strikes for wage increases, and when they did so their favoured weapons were ridicule and unruly behaviour:

> Strikers invaded the Cowgate ... 'in a twinkling', a circle, the diameter of which extended from the Queen's Statue to the portals of the shelter was formed, and a couple of score of shrieking, shouting spinners spun round in the gyrations of jingo ring ... ere long Panmure Street was thronged from end to end by an uproarious crowd of lassies. Number gave them the boldness and they made a rush for the shelter, in which for the most part millowners seeking to escape personal allusion and recognition had taken refuge ... A hooting band made for the last door, but the police, who acted with commendable discretion intervened and the portals were closed.[9]

One of the more successful areas for the establishment of permanent unions on the basis of such spontaneous outbreaks was among the less well-organized textile trades, where the cotton model of mixed bodies was extended but with women playing a rather more prominent role. In the Yorkshire woollen industry, for example, female weavers had initiated a successful strike against wage cuts in Dewsbury in 1875, leading to the establishment of the first branch of what was eventually to become the rather grandly named General Union of Textile Workers. As the union spread among woollen weavers, women continued to make up around half of its membership and remained prominent in organization and industrial action at the local level, most notably during an unsuccessful five-month strike against wage cuts at the Manningham mills in Bradford in 1890. However, the prejudice against married women working outside the home led the generally younger female members to see themselves as temporary, and the union's full-time officials were still all men, albeit prominent national supporters of women's suffrage. An even more remarkable example was in the east of Scotland jute industry, where the bulk of the workforce in both weaving and spinning was female, and it was considered normal for married women to continue to go out to work and for single women to form independent households. The jute workers had been in a strong bargaining position in the early 1870s, mounting successful workplace pressure for wage advances and even resisting an employers' attempt at a major reduction through a district-wide dispute involving over 20,000 strikers in 1874. Their first formal organization did not appear until the more difficult years of the subsequent long depression, when further strikes against wage reductions led to the formation of the Dundee Mill and Factory Operatives' Union in 1885. This new, mixed body received no support from existing local unions, was unable to recruit more than a minority of the workforce and failed to influence the course of industrial disputes. However, it had a particular attraction for women because its main public sponsor, the radical Unitarian minister Henry Williamson, was an outspoken proponent of female independence.

The second big wave of organization among the general workers was also paralleled by widespread enthusiasm among women workers. Thus there was an apparent breakthrough in 1888, when the match-girls at Bryant and May's in London initiated a successful strike against dismissals arising out of the exposure of conditions at the works by the radical journalist Annie Besant. Like the dockers a year later, they received a good deal of sympathy from the London middle classes and groups of more-skilled workers, in this case the London Trades Council, which gave them vital assistance in organizing the strike and bringing negotiations to the successful conclusion of union recognition. However, in the course of the 1890s, the limited nature of the advance became apparent. For example, the confectionery girls at Sanders' in Bristol lost a six-month dispute over recognition in 1892, despite significant support from the local trades council, the gas-workers and the dockers. Moreover, when the matchgirls themselves were later faced with determined employer opposition their organization simply collapsed.

Just as in the case of their male counterparts, then, trade unionism among female general workers in the late nineteenth century was still heavily dependent on outside assistance, frequently from middle-class sympathizers. Thus the main instigator of the ambitious Women's Protective and Provident League in 1874 had been Emma Paterson, daughter of a headmaster and an active women's suffrage campaigner, who became convinced of the importance of separate trade unions for women during a visit to the United States. The league offered advice and secretarial assistance in setting up new organizations, with some success among the London sewing trades, such as bookbinders, upholsterers and clothing workers. Paterson's rather over-optimistic feminism had led her to reject the cotton unions' tradition of appealing for special government protection for women and children, as she believed that this would only reinforce assumptions about the inferiority of female workers. While this made the league unpopular with most male trade unionists, Paterson and one of her colleagues had managed to become the first women to attend the TUC in 1875 as delegates from specific female unions. By 1881 ten members of the league were attending in this way and regularly raising issues of concern to their members, in particular the appointment as factory inspectors of women who would be better able to communicate with female workers.

Relations between female activists and established male trade unionists began to improve after Lady Emilia Dilke, the wife of the pro-union radical MP Sir Charles Dilke, took over the leadership of the league in 1886 and promoted a more pragmatic strategy. Within a few years the organization had been renamed the Women's Trade Union League and was modelling itself increasingly on the TUC: a new annual levy scheme was open to any union which recruited women, including the mixed ones in the textile trades, and the league was soon able to claim 70,000 affiliated members. Simultaneously it dropped its opposition to protective legislation and began to lobby increasingly effectively. Thus it helped to shift TUC resolutions towards support for equal pay from the late 1880s, and achieved one of its long-standing goals when the Liberal Home Secretary Herbert Asquith appointed the first female factory inspectors in 1893. On this basis the league was able to mount increasingly ambitious campaigns for the improvement of women's working conditions, most notably through a series of special provisions under the factory acts to reduce the horrific impact of lead poisoning in the potteries. Simultaneously it began to lobby for improvements in women's wages, accelerating after Mary Macarthur took over as secretary in 1903, and initiated a national campaign through the Liberal *Daily News* against the 'sweated' trades, in which women were receiving exceptionally low rates of pay. Following Asquith's election landslide in 1906, and with Sir Charles Dilke and Arthur Henderson playing major parliamentary roles, a Trade Boards Act was passed in 1909 establishing joint bodies of employers and employees to determine minimum wages for ready-made tailoring, box-making, lace-finishing and chainmaking, covering up to 250,000 workers. Though the impact of this first step on incomes was modest, it was still an impressive victory for the female campaigners and an important signal of Liberal intentions, amounting to a form of state-sponsored collective bargaining intended to encourage trade-union membership among particularly deprived groups of workers. Moreover, it was significant enough to stimulate a further successful campaign for the extension of the boards in 1913 to cover five new trades: shirt-making, tin box-making, hollow-ware, sugar confectionery and embroidery.

Meanwhile, in 1906 Macarthur had become convinced that women were still not being effectively recruited or represented by the existing general workers' unions and therefore set up the National Federation of Women Workers to provide a wider network and financial support for female-only bodies. One of its most important campaigns was the initiation of a successful strike among the west Midlands chainmakers at Cradley Heath in 1911 to ensure the enforcement of the Trade Board provisions. The federation then grew rapidly to a membership of 20,000 by 1914, usually by providing organizational and negotiating experience to groups of spontaneous strikers and hoping to secure union recognition after the dispute. It was particularly successful among low-paid factory workers in or near large cities like London, Glasgow and Edinburgh, where there was a greater possibility of additional support from male trade unionists and trades councils.

During the early years of the First World War, the government's policy of dilution of the munitions labour force with female workers was initially highly controversial because the exclusion of women was such a long-standing element of craft regulation. Indeed dilution was only accepted by the craft unions at the 'Treasury Conference' in 1915 on condition that any woman directly replacing a man should receive the established rate for the job, along with a guarantee of the recording and restoration of pre-war practices. However, as it became clear that the bulk of the 800,000 or more women who were drawn into munitions, largely from outwork and domestic service, would be doing repetitive tasks in separate wartime shell shops, posing little in the way of a long-term threat, the craft unions gradually became more open-minded. For example, the electricians went as far as to admit women as auxiliary members in 1916. And while the engineers made no provision for female members, they did enter a formal alliance with the National Federation of Women Workers in the summer of 1915, recognizing it as the legitimate body for women munitions workers in return for agreement that they would be withdrawn at the end of the war. This pushed the government to do likewise, and by 1918 the federation had increased in size by four times, to around 80,000 members.

The implementation of the broad wartime commitment to equal pay left a good deal of room for interpretation, which was handed over to a special committee of the Ministry of Munitions chaired by Arthur Henderson, and including representatives of government departments, the employers, the main craft unions concerned and Mary Macarthur for the federation. This produced Circular L2 of October 1915, which stipulated equal rates for women on piece-work or on fully skilled jobs, along with a safety net of a general minimum wage of £1 a week for female munitions workers. Initially applied only to the government factories, this was extended to all munitions work by the revised Munitions of War Act the following February, largely as a result of pressure from the engineers, keen for a further safeguard for their own members. However, in practice the private employers were still able to evade these requirements by refusing to pay women piece-rates, insisting that in the minority of cases where they replaced skilled men they were not doing exactly the same work and in general treating the minimum rate as a standard rate: on average the earnings of women in munitions tended to remain around half those of men. Meanwhile the government was becoming more concerned about the health of women workers, largely because the huge loss of life in battle was enormously increasing the consciousness of their role as childbearers for the nation. This led to unprecedented improvements in conditions in the munitions works, albeit still under the unilateral control of the employers: above all the provision of protective clothing, canteens, toilets and even a few day nurseries.

During the war there was also a significant increase in the employment of women in transport. One of the first and most important areas to experience this was the buses and trams, where women conductors and drivers were initially resisted by the vehicle workers but then grudgingly accepted in return for strong government safeguards for post-war male employment. Another important area was the railways, where women were increasingly employed as cleaners, sweepers, porters, booking clerks and ticket collectors: here they were accepted more willingly by the railwaymen who admitted women members in 1915, pushed for equal pay for women doing men's jobs, and even accepted that many of them would stay after the war. However, the unions were successful in completely excluding women from the docks, which remained an all-male preserve on the grounds of the alleged dangers and indecency of working conditions. Overall, the war saw female membership of the general workers' unions rise to around 216,000.

However, the major area of permanent increase in female employment opportunities was white-collar work, where the traditional assumption that paid work outside the home was appropriate only for young unmarried women remained strong. The government itself set low standards by taking on an extra 150,000 female clerks as temporary workers, allowing it to pay them lower wages than if they had been permanent staff, to be flexible about their long-term position, and to restrict them to the lowest rungs on the civil service ladder. In the private sector, female white-collar workers usually received better wages, but the flooding of the wartime labour market with inexperienced workers prevented the National Union of Clerks from achieving its aim of equal pay. In addition, explicit marriage bars were operated in the civil service and the teaching profession, and this was followed more covertly by individual employers of shop assistants and typists.

This mass participation of women in the war effort removed the last elements of resistance to the long campaigns for the extension of their civil rights. The Representation of the People Act of 1918 gave the vote to women over thirty, while the Sex Disqualification (Removal) Act of 1919 lifted the legal restrictions on most public offices and on access to the professions. However, as was the case throughout the war, the formal recognition of women's contribution and their substantive treatment diverged markedly. For in general they found they were being pushed back out of their wartime positions in manual employment and bearing the brunt of post-war readjustment. The munitions factories were closing and the returning servicemen had been promised their jobs back. Meanwhile women not only received a lower rate of unemployment benefit, but had it withdrawn if they refused any offer of work, however poorly paid. Thus there was still a good deal of room for assertive collective bargaining and political lobbying on their behalf. By now the number of female trade unionists had risen by three times to around 1,000,000, with the density of organization among women workers increasing from around 5 per cent to around 25 per cent. Moreover, thirty-three new Trade Boards were set up in 1919–20, giving a total coverage of around 3,000,000 workers, mostly women. In 1921 the National Federation of Women Workers merged with the gasworkers, now functioning under the new title of the National Union of General Workers, and the work of the Women's Trade Union League was taken over by the TUC, with two guaranteed seats for women on the general council, a sub-committee for women's interests, and eventually a regular women's conference. This level of recognition from male trade unionists was a remarkable achievement, for it was not long since the organization of women had been regarded as a hopeless cause. However, whether they would fare so well in large mixed bodies remained to be seen. Certainly it was to be a long time before they regained the public prominence they had enjoyed in the heyday of independent women's trade unionism in the first two decades of the twentieth century.

11

Trade Unionists and the Origins of the Labour Party

Was there any Party that ought to be seeking to make its future commensurate with the problems that had to be tackled more than the Labour Party? What were they asking for internationally? They were asking for a People's Peace, broad based upon the will of the people. What were they asking for nationally? They were asking nationally for a reconstruction of society broad based upon the principles of citizenship . . . They could only do so by saying to every man and woman who was a citizen – and even if they had not got the vote but were likely to get it – 'Come along with us, our platform is broad enough and our Movement big enough to take you all'. That was the way to success. That was the way to get hold of the machinery of Government in this country.[1]

These are extracts from a speech on the admission of individual members given by Arthur Henderson MP, the secretary of the Labour Party, at the first of two conferences held in 1918, when it was adopting a new constitution as the basis for fighting the next general election as a fully independent national organization. Henderson had been chosen to propose the official resolution on this matter not just because he was the party's secretary, but also because his strong trade-union background was expected to help in winning over those union leaders who remained sceptical about the admission of individual members, out of fear that this would swing the balance of power towards the party's socialist wing. Moreover, Henderson could be trusted by these powerful union figures because, while the initiative to set up a fully independent party had been his own, it had not been based on a desire to organize around new ideals but rather on a strong feeling that their old Liberal allies had begun to betray their own traditional principles under the pressure of running the war effort after 1914.

When challenged from the left that this approach implied an accommodation with capitalism, Henderson replied that the road to freedom lay through inclusive organization and an appeal to occupations and regions, along with the whole new category of female voters, not previously associated with the party, let alone with any of its affiliated socialist organizations. Thus this passage highlights that, while Henderson was now determined that Labour should govern in its own right rather than acting as a pressure group under the Liberal umbrella, he still saw success coming from the construction of a broad popular alliance around long-established principles of democracy and citizenship.

Arthur Henderson had been born in Glasgow in 1863 and, like Jimmy Thomas, had grown up in the poverty of a single-parent family, once again probably the result of an illegitimate birth. However, Henderson's mother had eventually married when he was eleven and the family had then moved to Newcastle. Here as a teenager he had become deeply involved in evangelical religion through the Salvation Army and the local Methodist chapel, at the same time serving an apprenticeship as a moulder in a local iron foundry. Eventually he had settled as a skilled adult at the celebrated Newcastle locomotive firm of Robert Stephenson and Son, becoming increasingly active in the ironfounders' society, first as secretary of his local branch then as district delegate for the north-east, which had led him to play a prominent role in an eight-month regional strike for a wage increase in 1894. Meanwhile, Henderson had begun to turn his intellectual and organizational talents towards the political arena. He was successful in becoming the first labour representative on the Newcastle municipal authority in 1892, with the support of Joseph Havelock Wilson of the seamen and other prominent local Liberals. Then he was a leading contender for selection as the junior Liberal candidate for the constituency in the parliamentary election of 1895, in which he would have stood alongside Gladstone's former lieutenant John Morley: loyal acceptance of rejection from this role led to his appointment as the Liberal Party's agent for Barnard Castle. In the rather muddled events of the 1903 by-election there, Henderson was successful as a Labour Representation Committee candidate with the support of the national Liberal headquarters, which found him more sound on the principle of free trade than their own official candidate. From then on Henderson was to play an increasingly important role in national politics, first as Labour's chief whip in Parliament, and then from 1912 as the party's formidable secretary during the next two crucial decades of its development.

Arthur Henderson's motivation in standing as an independent labour candidate in local and then in national politics arose not from any major disagreement over the Liberal programme, but rather from a significant disagreement over who should be carrying it out. Following his own election to Parliament in 1903, he declared that:

... the workers of the country had become alive to their interests, and were determined to do their political work in their own way, believing themselves to be competent to do it equally well as those who proposed to do it for them.[2]

Thereafter he remained consistent in his pressure for democratic political reforms, steering a principled line through highly charged contemporary controversies. Thus, as Labour Party secretary, he played a key role in constructing an electoral alliance with the moderate campaigners for women's suffrage in the years before the outbreak of the First World War. Similarly, in the immediate aftermath of the war, he was a leading figure in Labour's brave campaign against the Coalition government's harsh repression in Ireland and for the alternative policy of direct negotiations with Sinn Fein:

By their actions the government's agents had produced in the minds of the Irish people the same effect as a mad dog loose in the public streets would produce ... They had made the forces of the Crown, which existed only to maintain law and order, the instrument of a blind and ruthless vengeance. This was not 'resolute government' but primitive barbarism.[3]

Henderson's wider activities revealed the continuing influence of other long-standing radical traditions: above all popular nonconformity and temperance. He was a prominent figure within Wesleyan Methodist circles both as a regular, and apparently emotional, lay preacher and as an important speaker at national meetings. Thus, while he welcomed the involvement of many other contemporary Christians in movements for social reform, he never neglected their tradition's specifically religious insights:

... there was a tendency for the great mass of the workers to be too willing to come to the conclusion that all reform must be from without rather than from within. If wealth were redistributed it was possible that in some respects we might be worse, unless the redistribution was accomplished by moral and ethical improvement.[4]

One of the most obvious public manifestations of this concern was in his support of the Temperance Fellowship, as a speaker, as an organizer of special meetings at the TUC and Labour Party conferences, and as an MP supporting Liberal initiatives for licensing law reform. In defending these by no means unrepresentative activities against a left-wing critic in the ironfounders' journal in 1907, Henderson replied:

Does he object to my using a portion of my time to propagate principles in which I conscientiously believe? ... It is because I desire to see the workers become the effective instrument of their own economic and social freedom that I desire them not only be independent of the capitalist and the orthodox politician, but also of the brewer and the distiller.[5]

One of the most important results of political independence and moral regeneration would be an increasing awareness of the brother-hood of man in an international as well as in a domestic setting. From early in his political career Henderson therefore placed a major emphasis on the calming of nationalistic passions and the resolution of international disputes through arbitration. For example, as early as 1906 he was dissenting from the Liberal government's foreign policy and its increasing involvement in an arms race with Germany:

... our alleged need for a great Army in addition to a powerful Navy is the result of our present national policy of aggression and of the state of militarism which obtains throughout civilization, coupled with our own method of ruling subject races by force and by refusing them self-government. With the component parts of the Empire and of the world self-governing and self-supporting, and with the rise of the International Labour Movement, the need for great armies disappears. Further, to sanction this scheme would seriously hamper the efforts of those who are seeking to bring about universal disarmament.[6]

Eventually Henderson did reconcile himself to supporting the government when war broke out in 1914, on the grounds that Germany had been the aggressor and that critical support would be the most effective way of defending the conditions of the working population at home. However, when the opportunity presented itself in the final months of the war, he played a leading role in drafting a joint Labour Party and TUC 'Memorandum on War Aims', calling for the establishment of a permanent peace through complete democracy, open diplomacy and general disarmament, supervised by a League of Nations. When such a body was eventually established by the governments of the day, he went on to campaign for its improvement through the inclusion of the defeated nations and the stimulation of wider public understanding and support for its activities, for:

The final safeguard of peace did not lie in machinery of judicial arbitration or conciliation, however skilful it might be devised, security could only be permanently realized in the spirit of friendship and cooperation amongst all the peoples, based upon the fundamental identity of the people's interests.[7]

As a member of subsequent Labour governments and Foreign Secretary from 1929, Henderson was to be a constant critic of the scale of the financial reparations imposed on Germany, an effective champion of the League of Nations' arrangements for collective security and international arbitration, and a tireless campaigner for general disarmament: in recognition of all these efforts he was awarded the Nobel Peace Prize in 1934.

In his maturity Henderson was affectionately referred to as 'Uncle', partly because of his sociable presence at party conferences, partly because he was constantly trying to keep his unruly political brood in line, but mainly because he was widely seen as embodying the best qualities of the Labour family and its traditions: respectable and moderate, but always assertive in the pursuit of equal rights and a decent life for all. Though not generally regarded as much of an intellectual, Arthur Henderson was the main influence on the Labour Party's first two programmatic statements of its aims, *Labour and the New Social Order* (1918) and *Labour and the Nation* (1928). And it is clear, both from these publications themselves and from his other public statements, that his outlook had been fundamentally shaped by the traditions of nineteenth-century radical nonconformity. Indeed, Henderson's tireless efforts to establish a democratic framework for international relations into the increasingly dark days of the early 1930s showed a marked affinity with the idealism of Richard Cobden's campaign for free trade and William Gladstone's resonant slogan of 'Peace, Retrenchment and Reform'.

THE LIBERAL-LABOUR MPS

The concession of the main political demands of the trade unions, for the extension of the franchise in 1867, the secret ballot in 1872 and the reform of labour law in 1871 and 1875, had taken most of the steam out of the preceding extra-parliamentary agitation and left its national leadership exposed as a rather minor pressure group. They were now all loyal Gladstonian Liberals, but still had considerable difficulty in persuading local party organizations to adopt them as parliamentary candidates. Moreover, the emergence of Joseph Chamberlain's National Liberal Federation on the radical wing of the party in 1877 had often made matters worse, for though it had an ambitious land-reform programme and a democratic constitution, its local organizers tended to be drawn from the middle classes and had no particular interest in finding the extra money which would have been required to pay the salaries and election expenses of trade-union candidates. Thus until the middle of the 1880s, the unions had only had two MPs: Alexander McDonald and Thomas Burt of the miners, the death of the former in 1881 being immediately preceded by the election at Stoke of Henry Broadhurst of the stonemasons, following his prominent role in Gladstone's popular campaign against the Turkish massacres in Bulgaria. Moreover, the increasing difficulties faced by individual unions during the long depression from the middle of the 1870s had reduced the resources available for political activity and significantly weakened the influence of their new national bodies: affiliations to the TUC had fallen to half by the end of the decade and the Labour Representation League had eventually been wound up in 1880. Indeed, finances and enthusiasm were so scarce that for a time the political wing of trade unionism became something of a one-man band, with

Broadhurst having to combine his work as an MP with the salaried secretaryship of the TUC Parliamentary Committee, and even paying for his own office furniture.

Meanwhile, the extension of the franchise and the secret ballot, far from producing a permanent progressive majority, had revealed that even among manual workers reactionary attitudes were still very widespread. They were usually connected with the influence of Anglicanism in Church schools and with an attachment to traditional forms of sociability, particularly beer drinking, in contrast to the nonconformist emphasis on self-improvement which was promoted by most reformers. By appealing to these values and stimulating a rising tide of popular nationalism and imperialism, the Conservative Party was able to perform well under the new franchise in many parts of the country. In Lancashire, long-standing Tory support for factory reform in the textile districts had a strong impact, alongside a more dubious appeal to widespread hostility towards Irish Catholic immigrants. In London, imperial expansion made sense to members of the armed forces and other government employees, and here too there was an appeal to aggression against outsiders, this time Jewish immigrants. Finally, in the west Midlands, much of the workforce was employed in small-scale enterprises dependent on the home market and was thus attracted by the idea of moving away from free trade towards protection against manufactured imports, particularly after the depression years of the late 1870s.

That a distinctive agenda of trade-union reforms had been not only maintained but also pressed with some success in these circumstances says a great deal for the sympathies of the Liberal parliamentary leadership, both in opposition and in government. Under Alexander McDonald's influence the trade-union programme focused on issues of health and safety, particularly pressure for employers' liability to provide financial compensation in the event of injuries sustained at work and for an increase in the number of factory inspectors. This led to a Select Committee in 1876, including McDonald as one of its most active members and calling Broadhurst as one of its key witnesses, and soon after the return of Gladstone's second government in 1880 one of its first pieces of legislation was an extensive Employers' Liability Act, followed by the appointment of the first working-men factory inspectors in 1882. In addition there was still room for further political reform, the extension of household suffrage to the counties having been an issue of particular concern to the agricultural labourers and the miners since 1867. The unions therefore made their own distinctive contribution to a wave of mass meetings throughout the country in 1884 in successful protest against the House of Lords' obstruction of the Liberals' Third Reform Act, reaching a peak with a demonstration of over 100,000 people in Hyde Park in the summer.

Once gained, the benefits of the uniform household franchise along with a substantial redistribution of seats permitted the first really significant breakthrough for direct labour representation in parliament, when the 1885 general election led to the return of ten new trade-union MPs. Alongside Thomas Burt there were five additional representatives of the miners' unions, which had been able to take over the constituency organizations of the Liberal Party in the coalfields and to put up well-known local figures as candidates; with Joseph Arch of the agricultural labourers being returned in a similar way for a rural seat. Meanwhile George Howell and three other figures associated with national pressure groups were successful in London constituencies well-known for their radicalism, having been selected as official candidates by local Liberal associations. As a significant group of twelve MPs, the trade unionists soon began to aim for a more effective coordination of their efforts, one of them remarking:

I wish it were possible to have a labour 'party' in the House, and by and by I believe we may have one. We tried in the early part of the last Parliament, and we have appointed Mr Fenwick as the whip; and although we have had no formal meeting in the present Parliament, where our ranks are somewhat thinned, Mr Fenwick acts in that capacity still.[8]

Within a few years Burt could be more positive: 'these members now consult and act together on all matters that specially affect the workmen. On purely Labour questions they are actually, as they ought to be, a party.'[9] Indeed, in recognition of the group's new standing its leader Broadhurst was made a member of Gladstone's third government as a junior minister at the Home Office, as Burt was later to be made parliamentary secretary at the Board of Trade in Gladstone's fourth government. A revival of political optimism led to the establishment of the Labour Electoral Association in 1886, with the aim of increasing the size of the trade-union group in Parliament, but despite the support of Liberal national agents and chief whips, the party's local organizers remained much less responsive and the association was finally wound up in 1895 without having made much further headway.

However, the significant increase in their numbers in 1885 still allowed the trade-union MPs to pursue a broader range of issues more systematically, and following McDonald's pioneering example they raised not only matters of direct concern to their members but also matters of wider national importance. They continued to press for the extension of employers' liability to cover accidents caused by fellow workers, which was embodied in an unsuccessful Liberal bill of 1893. They also gave solid support to Samuel Plimsoll's campaign for improved safety at sea, contributing to the consolidation of a number of earlier gains in the Liberals' Merchant Shipping Act of 1894. And they took up the particular grievances of important groups of government employees, above all in the Post Office and the Royal Arsenals. They were actively concerned with civil liberties issues, protesting over most incidents of heavy-handed policing of industrial disputes and political demonstrations. In addition, following the Liberal split in 1886 and the defection to the Conservatives of most of the Whigs and some of the radicals under Chamberlain's leadership, the trade-union MPs became the most consistent supporters of Gladstone's attempts to introduce Home Rule for Ireland. Indeed, this can be seen as another example of the 'Grand Old Man's' eventual public adoption of a measure which had long been championed by labour radicals inside and outside Parliament. The trade-union group also maintained a continuous onslaught on the constitutional powers of the House of Lords and the high costs of the royal family, and, with their own immediate experiences in mind, repeatedly put forward proposals for the payment of MPs' salaries.

Meanwhile, the persistent campaigning of the Labour Representation League in the 1870s had also opened up new possibilities for the pressing of a distinctive agenda at the local level. For while election to School Boards had been open to all since their creation in 1870, it was only as a result of the league's careful collection of evidence on particular injustices that the property qualification was removed from all other local government bodies, including those administering the Poor Law, in 1878. Under pressure from the trade-union group in Parliament this process of democratization was then extended by subsequent Liberal governments, including the appointment of working men as magistrates on county benches in 1885 and the reform of parish and district councils in 1894. As a result, estimates of the number of labour representatives in local government show a rapid growth from around twelve in 1882, to 200 in 1892 and 600 in 1895, usually as a result of trades-council organization in more or less close cooperation with local Liberals and radicals. One significant result was the spreading requirement for fair wages clauses in local authority contracts alongside improved conditions for direct labour, pioneered by the Progressive Party on the London County Council and soon followed by Manchester, Salford, Liverpool and Sheffield. Of course, as well as such immediate results, this activity gave trade-union activists an invaluable education in the details of practical administration over a wide field, including housing, water supply and the provision of leisure amenities. However, at around the same time the functions of the local trades councils were being displaced by the increasing strength of national trade-union organization and industry-wide collective bargaining. As a result the representatives of the larger unions began to find it less worthwhile to attend and the trades councils tended to become platforms for a new generation of socialist agitators.

The long trade depression of the 1870s and 1880s had made the extremes of wealth and poverty in the capital more marked, while the visible presence there of national government institutions was a provocative target. In this context some of the livelier elements of London popular radicalism moved towards state socialism under the influence of a number of upper-middle-class figures who had been able to read the works of Karl Marx in German or in French. The small Social Democratic Federation led by the Tory radicals H. M. Hyndman and H. H. Champion had the most significant impact on trade unionists, with its campaign against unemployment and its rallying cry of a statutory eight-hour day: it attracted a number of energetic young craftsmen, most notably John Burns and Tom Mann, and one notable labourer in Will Thorne, who was closely connected with Marx's daughter Eleanor. The high point of this development was a series of demonstrations in the centre of the capital in 1886–7, which led to some rowdiness, heavy-handed policing and a great deal of publicity, but which also clarified Hyndman's own view that trade unionism and social reform were only distractions from the preparation for a French-style revolution. Champion and most of the London working men therefore began to move back towards the labour mainstream, but this intense sectarian experience left them with an independent outlook and a close network of like-minded colleagues.

The early 1890s then saw some lively confrontations within the trade-union world, after the involvement of these socialists in the burst of organization among the general workers in 1889–90, described in the previous chapter, was followed by their influx at the next annual conference of the TUC. Gathered together in the face of the established Liberal-Labour leadership and feeling themselves to be part of a younger generation, they began to refer to themselves as 'New Union-ists' and to magnify their distinctiveness. The issue on which they placed symbolic importance was the demand for a statutory eight-hour day, which made a good deal of sense in terms of the general workers' need for government intervention in the labour market. However, while reducing working hours was a long-standing union aim, achiev-ing it by government intervention was more controversial: it was strongly opposed by the assembly workers, who remained committed to self-regulation, and it opened up divisions among the process workers, above all between the Miners' Federation which favoured eight-hours legislation and the miners' unions from the north-east which had already achieved a seven-hour day by industrial action. Thus even at the high-point of their first impact the 'New Unionists' were unable to sway the TUC, and progress towards eight-hours legislation was dependent on the shifting balance of power between the miners' unions. Meanwhile, despite their shared attitude to the eight-hours question, the sudden influx of the 'New Unionists' pro-voked the Miners' Federation to insist on moving away from the rather casual voting by a show of hands of those present, towards a more formal link between each organization's share of the conference votes and the number of members for whom it had paid affiliation fees: what was to become known as the 'block vote'. Since the general workers' unions soon lost half of their members and the remaining loophole of trades-council representation was also closed up, the challenge of the 'New Unionists' was relatively easily contained and the uncompromising socialists were reduced to the status of a permanently disgruntled opposition.

This did not, however, include the most prominent leaders of the general workers, who all found ways of coming to terms with the labour mainstream. Joseph Havelock Wilson of the seamen had long-standing connections with prominent Liberals in the north-east and fitted in smoothly with the Liberal-Labour groups on the TUC Parliamentary Committee and in the House of Commons: he managed to win a seat as an independent in Middlesbrough in 1892, but was subsequently unopposed by the Liberal Party. Will Thorne of the gasworkers was unusual in remaining in the Social Democratic Federation, but he too soon settled down as a constructive member of the TUC Parliamentary Committee, working particularly closely with the group of radical craft unionists around Robert Knight of the boilermakers. Ben Tillett of the London dockers was more erratic than most but, while a founding member of the Independent Labour Party, was also able to cooperate with the Liberals in the Progressive Party on the London County Council. Finally, John Burns of the engineers, who had also played a prominent role in the London dock strike of 1889, became another leading London Progressive, and after winning a seat as an independent in Battersea in 1892 was rapidly integrated into the Liberal-Labour group in Parliament, eventually ending up as one of the outstanding spokesmen of traditional radicalism.

As a result the only true maverick among the leaders of the rising generation was James Keir Hardie, largely as a result of his distinctive early experiences as a coal miner in the west of Scotland. Thus, in contrast to the secularism, collectivism and group discipline of the London socialists, Hardie began as, and in many ways remained, a strong nonconformist, a passionate liberal and a highly wilful individual. Indeed, his stubborn political independence can probably best be understood as an expression of the powerful legacy of the struggle of the seventeenth-century 'Covenanters' in his native region, who had insisted on the self-government of the church against state intervention and lay patronage. Having experienced the failure of his attempts to revive trade unionism among the Scottish miners and to win the support of the TUC conference for personal attacks on Broadhurst, Hardie became increasingly committed to political action. He began by putting himself forward at a by-election in Mid-Lanark in 1888 as an orthodox Liberal-Labour candidate, but when the local Liberal association refused to test his name in a preliminary poll of its members and nominated a London barrister instead, an indignant Hardie refused the national agent's offer of a better seat elsewhere. He persisted in running an independent campaign as a 'Labour and Home Rule' candidate with considerable support from the London socialists, though his programme was still a radical-liberal one and he even declared that 'a vote for Hardie is a vote for Gladstone'.[10] Following the comfortable victory of his official Liberal rival, Hardie resigned from the party and played a leading role in setting up a new Scottish Labour Party, as an alliance of radicals and socialists prepared to run independent election campaigns or to cooperate with other sympathetic candidates. Thus even Hardie's break from the Liberal Party was far from complete and was based more on organizational than on ideological differences: he was merely pushing the traditional Liberal-Labour strategy one step further, from direct representation to independent representation, largely as a result of his own personal disappointment. He still thought it was worthwhile to go back to the TUC with a proposal for a membership levy to put the unions' political activities on a proper financial footing, but though this was passed by the conference it was not pursued enthusiastically by the Parliamentary Committee. The ambiguous nature of Hardie's position was then evident during his successful campaign for West Ham South in the general election of 1892. For while he turned down the Liberals' offer of sponsorship following the unexpected death of their official candidate, he still gave explicit support to their recent 'Newcastle Programme'. As a result, Hardie's first appearance in national politics was as a sort of unofficial Liberal who sat with the Conservative opposition.

Meanwhile broader support was being mobilized for the strategy of independent representation in the north of England. The main catalyst here was the defeat of a five-month strike against wage cuts among the poorly organized woollen workers at the Manningham Mills in

Bradford in 1890–91, during which the Liberal local council tried to prevent strike meetings and approved the calling in of troops and the reading of the riot act. The network of trade unionists, radicals and socialists who had supported the strike set up a Bradford Labour Union and, with the backing of Robert Blatchford's lively and influential *Clarion* newspaper, began to build up links with similar bodies across the northern cities. This was especially effective in west Yorkshire, where a particularly intransigent group of textile employers were dominant figures in the local Liberal associations, and in the early 1890s the independent labour groups took over most of the region's trades councils and began to achieve some successes in municipal elections. A conference to establish a national federal body, called the Independent Labour Party (ILP), was then called in Bradford in January 1893, attended mainly by delegates from Scotland and the north of England, with Hardie taking the chair and exercising a considerable influence over the evolving strategy. While in principle committed to the collective ownership of the means of production, the new party deliberately left the word 'socialist' out of its title because of its lack of popular appeal, strongly voiced by leading trade unionists present. Instead it drew up a familiar programme of Liberal-Labour reforms: improved hours and conditions, work for the unemployed, a shift from indirect to direct taxation, further extensions of the franchise and free non-denominational education. It even modelled its federal constitution on that of the TUC and closed its proceedings in the customary TUC manner with two verses of 'Auld Lang Syne', and it remained deeply imbued with the ethos of provincial nonconformity, including temperance, self-education and evangelical preaching.

By using its socialist commitment largely as a utopian vision, focusing on practical reforms and maintaining a familiar mobilizing style, the ILP was able to establish itself as a focus for the rising generation in mainstream labour organizations outside the capital. It soon had over 10,000 members, was achieving further successes for its candidates in local elections and was beginning to look forward to a breakthrough in the first parliamentary elections after Gladstone's final retirement from the Liberal leadership. However, this proved to be a naïvely optimistic extrapolation of its performance in its strongest centres of support, mainly still in the Yorkshire woollen districts: the

1895 general election saw all twenty-eight of its candidates come bottom of the poll, with Hardie himself losing his seat largely as a result of his constituents' disapproval of his eccentric independence in the House of Commons. In the aftermath of this brutal disillusionment, there was significant support for a shift in a more sectarian direction through fusion with Hyndman's Social Democratic Federation. However, the ILP turned instead towards the more practical business of municipal administration and, as the decade wore on and its founders became more experienced, their attitudes and expectations grew ever closer to those of the Liberal-Labour mainstream. This development was then clinched by the impact of the Boer War in 1899, which led to intense cooperation around the traditional radical issues of anti-militarism and free speech, and brought considerably increased influence within the ILP to another disaffected Scottish Liberal, James Ramsay MacDonald. Indeed, it seems that the strategy of Hardie and MacDonald had by this point become the resurrection of popular Gladstonianism through an anti-imperialist alliance between labour, radical and Irish MPs.

Hardie himself continued his campaign to win over the unions to independent representation, mainly through the Scottish Trades Union Congress, which agreed to set up a joint electoral organization in January 1900, known as the Scottish Workers' Parliamentary Elections Committee and made up of trade unions, trades councils, socialist societies and cooperative societies. At the UK level he found a number of supporters for this model among the railwaymen, who were heavily dependent on state intervention for any progress towards collective bargaining but, in contrast to the miners, were dispersed across the country and less able to exert sufficient local influence to secure the selection of trade unionists as parliamentary candidates. Thus, quite apart from the question of any ILP influence in particular branches, the railwaymen had a strong interest in joint action with other bodies to improve their parliamentary representation, and their west of England organizer, James Holmes, successfully put forward a resolution to this effect at the 1899 TUC conference. By this time there was growing interest in making a third serious attempt to increase trade-union political representation, following in the tradition of the Labour Representation League and the Labour Electoral Association. For the weakness of the Liberal Party following the Home-Rule split had not only reduced the effectiveness of its own administrations but also allowed the political right more room for manoeuvre. Thus the Conservative government elected in 1895 was refusing to meet with union delegations even though their industrial strength was well on the way to recovery from the low point of the 1880s. Meanwhile, the initial shock of the defeat of the engineers in the lock-out of 1897 was leading to increased cooperation between older and younger generations through a TUC sub-committee which drew up a scheme for a General Federation of Trade Unions in 1899. Initially this had the ambitious aim of establishing a national fund large enough to prevent another defeat on this scale, but in the long run it served mainly to provide supplementary services for smaller trade unions and only forty-four organizations with 25 per cent of TUC membership became formally attached.

Even more seriously, the revival of industrial strength was being countered by a new wave of unfavourable decisions in the law courts, mainly affecting the craft unions. While the 1871 legislation had been thought to provide comprehensive immunity from legal action, judges in the 1890s tended towards the opinion that, as representatives of increasingly powerful organizations, union officials should be held responsible under civil law, particularly in cases of injuries to third parties not directly involved in the original disputes. In the case of *Temperton v. Russell* (1893) the Court of Appeal upheld an action for damages against the officials of three Hull building unions which had imposed a boycott on a firm supplying materials to the one with which they were primarily in dispute. Then in the case of *Trollope v. London Building Trades Federation* (1895) the Court of Appeal allowed a firm to recover damages for having been put on a 'black list' of non-union employers. Similarly, the 1875 legislation had been thought to provide for peaceful picketing, but judges in the 1890s seemed to be increasingly of the opinion that the remaining offences of 'watching and besetting' should be interpreted very broadly. In the case of *Lyons v. Wilkins* (1899) the Court of Appeal upheld a decision that the Amalgamated Society of Fancy Leather Workers should only have communicated information during a dispute and that its attempts to persuade others to join the action had been illegal. Indeed, this was such an unsettling departure from previous assumptions that the TUC would have taken the case to the House of Lords had not their solicitor incompetently allowed the opportunity to lapse. Moreover, in the case of *Charnock v. Court* (1899), the Halifax joiners were found guilty of 'watching and besetting' for having sent two men to the port of Fleetwood to persuade workmen arriving from Ireland not to act as strike-breakers. As if all this was not enough, an Employers' Parliamentary Council was set up in 1898 to publicize the advantages contained in these recent legal decisions.

The railwaymen's resolution at the 1899 TUC conference therefore received vital support from the craft unionists who made up the dominant group on the Parliamentary Committee: following the precedent of successful cooperation between the generations in establishing the General Federation of Trade Unions, a similar TUC sub-committee was set up to organize a special conference on political action in London in February 1900. This had the active participation of around half of the affiliated unions, the most notable absentees being the textile workers and the miners, who were largely satisfied with their existing political arrangements. Following the TUC's own procedures, voting was proportional to the numbers represented, so the union delegates, representing over 500,000 members, dominated the conference. However, on the Labour Representation Committee (LRC) set up along the Scottish lines of the previous month, a generous five out of twelve places were reserved for socialist-society delegates representing a nominal membership of 20,000. Significantly enough, Hardie's own role at the conference was to head off an attempt to pass a more dogmatic resolution on socialism and class struggle, both the Social Democratic Federation and the Fabian Society soon lost interest in the new body, and the Cooperative Union declined to participate. Thus in the end the LRC turned out to be an alliance between the ILP and the TUC, with a suitable ambiguity in its strategy: it would sponsor independent candidates, but once elected they would cooperate with other parties prepared to support labour legislation. The selection of its first secretary was also a compromise, for Ramsay MacDonald was the only volunteer for the unpaid post and while he was a member of the ILP he had strong Liberal connections. This basic alliance proved sound enough to survive, though there was to be much jockeying for influence between the two wings of the LRC over the next few years.

Despite the advocacy of their leaders, many trade-union members remained reluctant to pay higher subscriptions for political representation. Even if all the unions represented at the founding conference did decide to join, the relatively modest affiliation fees would do little more than pay for day-to-day administrative expenses: MacDonald, like Broadhurst before him, would have to provide not only his own income but also the facilities for the London office. In the first year he did well to secure affiliations from organizations representing over 300,000 members, but this still left the LRC starved of resources for the sudden general election of 1900, during which it was only able to issue four circulars at a cost of £33. Indeed, out of the fifteen candidates it endorsed, the only two victories came in double-member constituencies. Hardie himself was successful at Merthyr Tydfil on the basis of support from the senior Liberal MP arising from the inadequate parliamentary record of the second official Liberal. Richard Bell of the railwaymen was successful at Derby because, while he stood for the trades council, he received tacit support from the local Liberals, who only had one official candidate. Similarly, two of the three further LRC candidates returned in by-elections in single-member constituencies in the next few years were unopposed by the Liberals, the only victory in a three-cornered contest being at Barnard Castle where Arthur Henderson had the tacit support of the Liberal party's national headquarters against its own unsatisfactory local candidate.

Thus there was no sharp change in either the number or the policies of labour MPs after 1900. In practice the LRC tended to favour trade-union sponsored candidates to socialist-society ones and most of its successes still continued to come from the Liberal-Labour tradition. With the one exception of Hardie, who sat on the cross-benches with the Irish Party, the LRC was an integral part of the Liberal opposition and worked closely with the existing Liberal-Labour group and its long-standing radical allies such as Sir Charles Dilke. In varying combinations these MPs put forward a range of legislation for the alleviation of particular grievances over working conditions and for improved local-government provision of housing, unemployment relief and free school meals. They also struggled to maintain the Gladstonian legacy against the Conservative government's revival of a corn tax to finance overseas militarism and its abolition of democratic local School Boards in the Education Act of 1902. They then became particularly closely allied with the mainstream of the Liberal Party from 1903 in defending free trade against Joseph Chamberlain's new campaign for protection through tariffs giving a preference to imperial imports.

THE PROGRESSIVE ALLIANCE

The increasing concern over the direction of trade-union law became even more sharply focused by a crucial case which arose on the Taff Vale Railway Company in south Wales. A local campaign for improved minimum wages had been followed by the transfer out of the district of one of its main organizers, and this provoked a protest strike in August 1900 among a workforce increasingly dissatisfied at the lack of union recognition. Though the aim was moderate and received a good deal of public support, the firm had been in touch with the Employers' Parliamentary Council and knew that it would be likely to secure an injunction against any picketing action. For its part, the national executive of the railwaymen, against the advice of its secretary and recently elected LRC MP, Richard Bell, decided to give its official support to the local men, and Bell was sent down to Cardiff to coordinate the picketing against the importation of substitute workers. The dispute was soon brought to an end by the mediation of an influential local industrialist, including the reinstatement of all the strikers but not union recognition. However, the firm persisted with its legal action beyond an initial restraining injunction on Bell and was successful in winning a court ruling that the resources of the union itself were liable for damages, opening up the possibility of a much larger award. The union in turn pursued the case to the Court of Appeal, which ruled in its favour that trade unions did not have a legal status as corporate bodies, but in July 1901 the House of Lords unexpectedly reinstated the original judge's decision by ruling that they did. This was reinforced two weeks later by a further Lords' ruling in the case of *Quinn v. Leathem*, upholding an initial judgment over a dispute about the employment of non-union labour, that the funds of the Belfast Journeymen Butchers' Association were liable for damages to a local firm for threatening secondary action against its customers.

Thus the issues which had been resolved in the unions' favour by the Gladstonian settlement were dramatically reopened, to the dismay of such veterans as Broadhurst, who called immediately for the full restoration of legal immunities through the election of a hundred labour MPs. The leadership of the TUC was not so optimistic about persuading public opinion that unions should have no legal responsibility for their actions, so they initially focused instead on pressing the Conservative government for an inquiry into the complex issues involved and drafting specific bills to protect peaceful picketing and welfare funds. However, a parliamentary debate in May 1902 made it clear that this strategy would not lead to any immediate progress, despite significant support from the Liberal shadow cabinet, and the full implications of the Taff Vale case were spelled out at the end of the year when £23,000 in damages and costs was awarded against the railwaymen. The TUC did then move towards a revival of the spirit of the 1860s and 1870s, aiming for the full restoration of previous immunities through a sustained effort to increase the size of the trade-union group in Parliament. This met with an increasingly enthusiastic response from concerned members throughout the country: by the spring of 1903 affiliations to the LRC had more than doubled to over 850,000, drawing in the textile workers, along with a significant increase in affiliation fees to cover MPs' salaries and some election expenses. At the same time the miners had put their own scheme on a more substantial footing, albeit still as an integral part of the National Liberal Federation.

Faced with this rapid revival of one of the country's most effective pressure groups, the two main political parties soon began to make concessions. The Conservative government set up a Royal Commission in 1903 but, since it did not include any trade unionists as members, the TUC withheld its cooperation. The Prime Minister also allowed a free vote on the TUC's bill to protect peaceful picketing, which was subsequently carried with some Conservative support in 1904 and 1905, but so much amended during the committee stage that it was abandoned by its sponsors. More substantially the Liberal opposition, faced with the prospect of increasingly divisive competition over direct labour representation in urban constituencies, agreed in September

1903 to an informal pact for the next general election. The Liberal chief whip, William Gladstone's son Herbert, undertook to persuade local associations to stand aside in up to 30 seats listed by the LRC, arguing that:

I do not see why a candidate of character and capacity, who is ready to support all the leading proposals in which Liberals are interested, would be objected to on the ground that he calls himself a Labour, and not a Liberal, candidate.[11]

For their part the LRC leaders had to maintain a more independent public profile to avoid alienating their local ILP activists, but Ramsay MacDonald undertook to use his influence to prevent competition in other seats and talked of:

a united democratic party appealing to the people on behalf of a simple, comprehensive belief in social reconstruction. The party may not be called Liberal, and it will be as far ahead of Liberalism as Liberalism itself was of its progressive predecessor Whiggism.[12]

At the end of 1905 the Conservative government finally fell apart over Chamberlain's proposals for tariff reform, and the ensuing election campaign saw a decisive rallying of public opinion to the traditional Liberal programme of free trade and non-denominational education. Both sides of the informal electoral pact honoured their promises. On the one hand, Gladstone managed to arrange for thirty-two of the fifty candidates endorsed by the LRC to be given straight fights against Conservatives. On the other hand, MacDonald worked hard to ensure that Gladstone himself would not be opposed by an LRC candidate, and that nothing would be done to divide the votes against the Conservative leader, Balfour. The result was a triumph for careful backroom management, with the total of twenty-nine LRC victories coming to only one fewer than the target set three years earlier. This breakthrough gave it some ground for adopting the rather grander title of the Labour Party, but it was still far from being a national political force. In Scotland and Yorkshire the more conservative local Liberal associations had maintained their stand against any increase in direct labour representation. On the other hand, in London and the coalfields, where numerous trade-union MPs were returned, they were still fairly well integrated into the Liberal Party. Thus one of the main contributions of the Labour Party was to supplement the traditional Liberal-Labour heartlands by winning a dozen seats in Lancashire, where nominally independent candidates could appeal across the party divide to disaffected Conservatives. There was to be a further leap in the size of the parliamentary Labour Party to forty-two MPs in 1909, but this was largely a result of a national decision by the miners to switch their allegiance in the hope of getting more candidates adopted in the coalfields, while their constituency organizations remained largely dependent on local Liberal associations until after the 1910 elections. Thus up to 1914 Labour's position was still that of a junior partner in a 'Progressive Alliance': it still tended to come last in three-cornered contests and it still aimed to wield national influence mainly by putting pressure on its senior partner, the Liberal Party.

In the immediate aftermath of the 1906 election the resolution of the vital issue of trade-union law therefore depended on close cooperation between the Labour Party and the Liberal-Labour group, who could muster up to fifty-four MPs between them, and even more on the support of the Liberal government which had a secure overall majority of eighty-four seats. At first the latter was not forthcoming, as the legal experts on the front bench were opposed to simply returning to the pre-Taff-Vale status quo, an attitude supported by the final report of the Royal Commission on the subject. This recommended the recognition of the right to strike and peaceful picketing, but also that unions should be liable under civil law, as long as their national officials were not held responsible for unsanctioned local behaviour and their benefit funds could be shielded from damages actions. However, while the Liberals initially proposed to use this as the basis for their legislation, the TUC insisted on proceeding with its own bill for the restoration of full legal immunity, and was able to make use of leading Liberal-Labour MPs such as John Burns to persuade the Prime Minister, Sir Henry Campbell-Bannerman, to follow his own traditional radical instincts on the issue. Even then, just as in the 1870s, detailed vigilance over the committee stages was still required to secure a fully satisfactory outcome in the Trade Disputes Act of 1906. David Shackleton of the weavers was now the Labour Party's leading parliamentarian and pressed successfully over the details involved in securing immunity from civil actions for damages, in return for careful concessions over picketing coordinated by the unions' old ally Sir Charles Dilke.

Meanwhile another of the first acts of the Liberal government was aimed at rewarding its trade-union allies before they had even had time to think of mounting any pressure. This was the 1906 Workmen's Compensation Act, initiated by Herbert Gladstone as Home Secretary and embodying all of the TUC's own proposals for reform, including the improvement of scales of compensation for industrial injury and the extension of coverage to all workers unless specifically excluded. In addition, as has been seen in the previous discussions of particular industries, the following years saw the development of a new style of progressive government involvement in industrial relations, unambiguously favourable to the union side. Once again, it was Gladstone at the Home Office who set the ball rolling by introducing the government's bill for the eight-hour day in the coal mines in 1908, though this was then pursued even more energetically by the younger radicals at the Board of Trade. David Lloyd George became the preferred trouble-shooter for the railways, gradually pushing the employers towards union recognition from 1908, and his successor Winston Churchill introduced the government's bill for the enforcement of minimum wages through Trade Boards in 1909. Trade unionists were not only consulted over the details of this wave of legislation but also given the opportunity to participate in its administration, as factory inspectors, industrial conciliators and eventually insurance officials: by 1912 there were up to 400 trade unionists working for the government in these sorts of posts.

Among these the most prominent was John Burns, with a post in the cabinet as President of the Local Government Board intended to encompass a wide responsibility for initiating new measures of social reform. Rapid progress was achieved over a private members' bill to permit local authorities to provide free school meals, introduced by the recently returned Labour MP for Lancaster, W.T. Wilson of the joiners. However, over measures which had more expensive implications there was something of a tussle between Burns on the one hand, who tried to postpone decisions until after the report of a comprehensive Royal Commission on the Poor Law, and the Labour Party and the TUC on the other, who organized national campaigns and parliamentary pressure to secure speedier action on old-age pensions and unemployment relief. The first result was Herbert Asquith's initiation of a preliminary pensions scheme in his preparations for the 1908 budget, significant not only for its modest impact on the budgets of a majority of the country's working households, but also as the first public recognition of the dignity of old age. This was quickly followed by an increase in the exchequer grant to support local authority unemployment relief schemes. Then, after Asquith had become Prime Minister, his role as Chancellor was taken over by Lloyd George who, along with Churchill taking his place in turn at the Board of Trade, became closely associated with an even more ambitious programme of social reform. Partly inspired by the contemporary model provided by Bismarck's Germany, this development was funded by taxes on unearned incomes and wealth, and carefully side-stepped Burns's continued reluctance to sanction major increases in national government intervention.

While broadly accepted by organized labour as a useful beginning, these 'New Liberal' or 'social democratic' schemes also included a number of centralizing and bureaucratic implications which soon aroused suspicions similar to those of John Burns in the minds of many other trade unionists. In the first place, they had personal experience of the complex range of working conditions and family situations which would have to be addressed by any new measures, along with a stronger motivation to achieve real improvements for the least well-off. At the same time, many of them still had an underlying dislike of state hand-outs, along with a marked preference for the independence and self-organization which came with full employment at fair rates of pay. As a result the Labour Party in Parliament subjected the Liberal legislation to a barrage of detailed amendments which pushed it in directions at once more practical and more generous. Moreover, when in 1909 Churchill proposed Labour Exchanges to ease the flows of information and of available workers, and thus help to reduce periods of transitional unemployment, the trade unions were outspoken about their concerns over the potential for the supply of substitute labour during industrial disputes, the delay in the appointment of their own representatives to local advisory committees and the attitudes of those who were being appointed as full-time administrators. Even when in 1911 Lloyd George began to provide public finance to support contributory insurance schemes for the health of all adult male workers and the unemployment of those in severely cyclical industries, he had to compromise by making the existing trade unions and friendly societies the 'approved societies' for the operation of the new national arrangements and by promising a full review of the first two years' operation of the schemes.

While the Labour Party therefore played an increasingly distinctive role within the 'Progressive Alliance', the corresponding eclipse of the Liberal-Labour group did not take place without resistance. This took its most dramatic form in a legal case initiated by W. V. Osborne, the secretary of the Walthamstow branch of the railwaymen, within the ranks of which there had long been friction between the Liberal-Labour attitudes of their MP, Richard Bell, and the socialist views of the majority on the union's national executive. Osborne was a supporter of Bell and, feeling that the Labour Party was selecting too many socialist candidates, wished to prevent it from receiving his political levy. Nor was he an isolated individual: in an internal ballot of the railwaymen his position was supported by a significant minority of 20 per cent, and his subsequent legal battle was funded by donations from branches of a number of other unions. However, during a two-year process of hearings, the courts began to discuss the matter rather differently and in December 1909 the House of Lords, keen to re-assert the view that unions should be treated as corporate bodies, ruled that political activity as such lay outside the existing statutory definition of a trade union. Naturally there was a major campaign by the TUC and the Labour Party for a legislative reversal of this judgment, and Asquith's Liberal government, re-elected without an overall majority in 1910 and therefore concerned to secure trade-union support for its campaign to reform the House of Lords, was in principle prepared to reciprocate. However, it was faced with some disquiet within its own party over the risks of political compulsion of individual union members, so it moved by stages, beginning in 1911 with the introduction of the state payment of MPs' salaries to ease the financial pressures on the Labour Party in particular. Then in 1913, as the next general election began to approach, it passed an act to reaffirm the legitimacy of trade-union political activity, but with a number of safeguards: a union could only have the necessary separate political fund if it was approved by a majority in an internal ballot, and individual members who disagreed were to be allowed to opt out of paying the political levy. A continuing sense of uncertainty about the role of the Labour Party, even among the process workers who had their own long traditions of political representation, was indicated by the many narrow margins in favour of setting up political funds in the subsequent ballots: 56 per cent among the weavers and 57 per cent among the miners, only rising to 75 per cent among the railwaymen. Thus even after over a decade of independent labour representation, many trade-union leaders were still faced with an uphill struggle to persuade their members that this was a better use of their money than their traditional arrangements with the Liberal Party.

AN INDEPENDENT LABOUR PARTY

Having weathered this financial crisis, the Labour Party was then faced with the possibility of a serious split over international affairs. For, on the outbreak of the First World War in August 1914, the ILP MPs, led by Ramsay MacDonald, decided to withhold their support from the national effort. Meanwhile the trade-union MPs, led by Arthur Henderson, went along with the steadily rising tide of patriotic feeling, the TUC having pledged to use its influence to reduce strikes and support the recruiting effort for what was assumed to be a short military campaign. However, as the war dragged on this initial division turned out to be rather less clear-cut than might have been expected. On the one hand, MacDonald joined up with a number of prominent Liberals to form the Union of Democratic Control, campaigning for open diplomacy and a negotiated peace, towards which Henderson always showed considerable sympathy. On the other hand, Henderson was instrumental in setting up the War Emergency Workers' National Committee, acting as a watchdog over everyday living standards and working conditions, which became a forum for cooperation between moderate pacifists and sane patriots within Labour and the unions. Henderson's expertise was then put at the service of the government by his inclusion in Asquith's 1915 coalition cabinet, a position which was to involve severe conflicts between his role in the government and his loyalties to trade-union colleagues.

However, Henderson's awkward situation apart, the labour campaigns of the period were conducted with a remarkable degree of unity. Thus, the unrest over leaving certificates on the Clyde in the autumn of 1915 produced a coordinated and successful campaign to amend the Munitions Act, involving key moderates in the ILP such as John Hill of the boilermakers and W. C. Anderson, the recently elected MP for Sheffield Attercliffe. Similarly, the introduction of military conscription early in 1916 met with initial opposition right across the parliamentary Labour Party, from critics of the war such as Ramsay MacDonald to champions of voluntary recruitment such as Jimmy Thomas, though in the end it was accepted by the trade-union majority as the price of remaining in the government. Thus the unions and the Labour Party were not only able to maintain a reasonably united front but also to develop a shared definition of popular patriotism. This focused on the decency of ordinary working people and the demand for equality of sacrifice, permitting effective defences of established practices against unnecessary state interference, alongside powerful criticisms of the selfishness of war 'profiteering' by private businesses.

In some contrast, the unity and ethos of the Liberal Party was undermined by its responsibility for leading national administrations during an exhausting European war. Although it was successful in presenting its international policy as a moral crusade against Prussian despotism, a series of military crises drew it into coalition with the Conservatives and increasingly illiberal measures at home: intervention in economic markets, restrictions of press and parliamentary scrutiny, repression in Ireland, and above all military conscription. These were tolerated by many Liberals as temporary necessities, counter-balanced to some extent by consultation with union leaders and the inclusion of Labour MPs in decision-making. But other Liberals became disillusioned, some began to collaborate with Labour pacifist critics of the government, and a number of key figures among the younger progressives joined the ILP. A further set of military defeats finally provoked the restlessly ambitious Lloyd George to push out Asquith in December 1916 and to lead a Conservative-dominated coalition committed to an even more interventionist war effort. Lloyd George's attitudes soon seemed to have more in common with those of his Conservative ministers, while Asquith and the Liberal majority were too compromised and too tired to establish a meaningful opposition. Thus the Labour Party was increasingly seen as the guardian of the conscience of the 'Progressive Alliance', while still able to maintain its vigilance over the conduct of the war by accepting a place for Henderson in Lloyd George's inner War Cabinet as well as appointments to head the major new ministries of Labour and Pensions.

Labour's increasing occupation of the centre of political interest was further highlighted by events in Russia in 1917. The initial February revolution was greeted with general enthusiasm, for it removed the embarrassment of having the autocratic Tsar as an ally, opening up the possibility either of a more effective pursuit of the war on the eastern front or of serious steps towards a negotiated peace. Arthur Henderson was sent to keep the Russians in the war, but was deeply alarmed by the threat of Bolshevik subversion and came back urging the vigorous pursuit of a negotiated peace as the only way to shore up the Mensheviks' precarious provisional government. One promising avenue was a proposed International Socialist Congress in Stockholm, where delegates from the Labour Party might open discussions with German socialists, but this smacked too much of fraternization with the enemy for Conservative ministers and Lloyd George therefore withdrew his support from Henderson's activities. Moreover, this growing divergence of views was handled very roughly. In the famous 'doormat incident' Henderson was summoned to a meeting of the cabinet and kept waiting outside the room while his colleagues discussed his behaviour, and in the government's public statements his position was increasingly misrepresented and discredited. Eventually he decided to resign and, while agreeing that his place in the cabinet should be taken by George Barnes of the engineers, he also initiated the process which led to Labour's decisive break from its traditional alliance with the Liberals.

In this delicate situation Henderson's first challenge was to persuade the Labour Party and the TUC to see these events from his point of view. His careful speeches at a series of turbulent conferences led to wholehearted support for his controversial foreign-policy initiative and then to the drafting of an important joint 'Memorandum on War Aims', calling for peace without annexations and the establishment of a League of Nations. A small minority of more patriotic British trade-union leaders were still in favour of a fight to the finish, especially Havelock Wilson of the seamen, whose members had been suffering particularly badly from German submarine warfare, but the majority followed the lead of the TUC Parliamentary Committee, and the Labour Party therefore withdrew from its participation in the government as soon as Parliament was dissolved. Thus Labour's pro- and anti-war factions were fully reconciled in open opposition to the Conservative-dominated coalition, and aimed to fight the next election as a party with a high national and even international profile, contesting over 360 seats across the whole country. The fundamental change in attitude involved was clearly articulated by one of the party's rising young parliamentary stars, William Anderson:

Labour said that the Government must act, must lead and show them the way, but there was something even more important than that, and that was that Labour must organise on the industrial and political fields with full unity, with a full sense of its power, that Labour must conquer the Government, that Labour must be the Government, and that Labour must make laws, not for a small section, but for the happiness and the freedom of the whole people.[13]

Some progress had been made with local organization in the seats already held before the war, largely on the basis of financial backing from the miners and the railwaymen, and the potential to add to these was improved by the re-drawing of constituency boundaries in the 1918 Reform Act, increasing the number of seats in the coalfields and in London. The simultaneous extension of the franchise had a less clear-cut impact on the relative position of the parties, for those who gained the vote were mainly the wives and sons of previously enfranchised male voters, and their political loyalties still tended to be influenced by the lead of their household head. In any case, there had been hardly any extension of Labour's local organization outside its existing heartlands: as late as 1917 many affiliated unions were still finding difficulties in getting their branches to pay the political levy, there were only fifty members of the party's agents' society and the Women's Labour League had only eighty branches.

Out of necessity, then, the Labour Party fought its first fully independent election campaign less on the effectiveness of its organization than on the appeal of its policies: not only could it now present itself as having considerable experience of national administration, it also put a major effort into constructing and publicizing a comprehensive programme for government. In its new constitution of 1918 Labour declared its full-blown party status by admitting individual members for the first time, while aiming to maintain its existing role as a federation of pressure groups, among which the Parliamentary Committee of the TUC would remain the most prominent. Thus alongside the socialist commitment to 'the common ownership of the means of production', later to be known as 'Clause Four', there was a parallel radical-liberal commitment to 'the Political, Social, and Economic Emancipation of the People'.[14] When it came to more specific matters it was clear that the latter tradition was still the dominant one, for at its conference in 1918 Labour not only increased the representation of the unions on the National Executive Committee but also adopted the whole of the traditional radical agenda: complete adult suffrage, the abolition of the House of Lords, home rule all round within a federal constitution, stronger local government as the main agency of economic and social reform, and equal access to a high-quality education system. As far as the more recent lessons of the war years were concerned, 1918 also saw the effective re-integration of the three main attitudes and factions which had emerged. First, the principled critics of military involvement such as Ramsay MacDonald had their views recognized in the party's commitment to frontiers based on self-determination and an end to secret diplomacy. Secondly, the pragmatic guardians of working-class conditions such as Arthur Henderson had their views recognized in the commitment to pay off the war debt by a temporary capital levy and the recognition of equality of sacrifice. And thirdly, the trade unionists who had kept their distance from the government, such as John Hill, Jimmy Thomas and Mary Macarthur, had their attitudes embodied in the commitment to public control of the mines and railways, and the maintenance of gains made through wartime collective bargaining.

Indeed, much of the assertiveness of Labour in 1918 came from this latter group, with its confidence based on considerable increases in trade-union strength achieved in tight wartime labour markets, along with the emergence of a shared conception of a new role for the state. As with the party's programme as a whole, this was not the result of the simple application of an intellectual principle, but rather of dialogue and accommodation between views based on particular experiences. Thus the craft unions in the assembly sectors such as engineering and shipbuilding pressed for the withdrawal of government restrictions on industrial bargaining along with some form of continuation of the social safety nets of rent control and food rationing. Meanwhile, the seniority unions in the process sectors such as coal mining and the railways pressed for guarantees of the continuation of national bargaining through some form of public control of their own industries, widely referred to as 'nationalization' but not always implying state ownership. Finally, the federal unions among the general workers and women workers pressed for novel forms of labour market regulation, sometimes involving legislation at a national level, sometimes involving joint control of particular industries. By 1918 these distinct outlooks had come to be seen as sharing a common ground as practical schemes to promote full employment and effective collective bargaining, tailored to the specific conditions of each industry. This was an evolution out of traditional liberalism towards an open-ended future and, though ILP activists could see it as a step towards their socialist utopia, the party leadership deliberately adopted the more neutral title of 'the New Social Order'.

Having maintained a broad appeal to progressive opinion as a matter both of political principle and of electoral pragmatism, it was a major advantage to Labour that the Liberal Party remained seriously divided, with Asquith and his followers waiting for a move towards reunification, while Lloyd George was enjoying his pre-eminent international role too much to give up the premiership of the victorious coalition. No national leadership or programme was provided to resolve the ensuing disarray and, with the Liberal Party thus either absorbed by the Conservative Party or paralysed, the Labour Party's claim to have inherited the mantle of popular radicalism began to receive the endorsement of an influential section of the Liberal press.

In fact Labour did not immediately improve much on its pre-war results, still only winning fifty-seven seats, mainly in traditionally Conservative industrial constituencies and formerly Liberal mining constituencies. However, this disappointing result was accompanied by significant increases in Labour's share of the vote and its ability to beat Liberals in direct contests, and indeed it had already overtaken the Asquithian Liberals, who now had only thirty-six seats. Moreover, Labour could expect to improve its results in the very near future, as this first general election after the war had been fought on an inaccurate register, with particularly poor arrangements for the young men still in the army, and at a peak of anti-German and anti-Bolshevik feeling cynically manipulated by Lloyd George's campaign. In the local elections of 1919 the Labour Party was already making a considerably stronger showing, taking control of twelve of the twenty-eight London boroughs as well as three counties in the north-east and in Wales; and it was able to win fourteen out of fifteen by-elections fought over these four years. By the time of the 1922 general election, the number of local parties and the number of full-time agents had both doubled, and on this basis Labour was able to make breakthroughs in some previously strong Liberal seats in London and the north-east. Moreover, with the Irish Party removed from Westminster by the establishment of the twenty-six-county Free State, Labour was also able to pull in most of the Irish vote in Liverpool, Glasgow and other northern industrial cities. Thus the Labour Party won 30 per cent of the vote and 142 seats and became the official opposition, for even if the divided factions of the Liberal Party were counted together they only had 116 seats between them.

The validity of Labour's new independent strategy had already been amply confirmed by the post-war development of the Coalition government. For following its overwhelming victory in the 1918 general election, from which it emerged with a massive overall majority of more than 300 seats, the Coalition began to backtrack across the range of reforms which had been anticipated in the last years of the war, especially in the areas of housing, public control of the utilities, and agriculture. Instead, the restoration of unrestricted private enterprise became the government's main priority, the Federation of British Industry having been established in 1916, the British Employers' Federation in 1919, and such hard-nosed businessmen as Eric Geddes having come to the fore within the Conservative Party. Thus the progressive reconstruction programme of the Coalition Liberals was sidetracked and the Conservatives gradually became confident enough of their grasp of the national mood to dispense with Lloyd George altogether in 1922 and to reshape the focus of their electoral appeal from being anti-Liberal to being anti-Labour.

PART FOUR

The 1920s to the 1970s

12

Shop-floor Bargaining among the Assembly Workers

Scanlon confirmed, on being challenged by Mrs Castle he was in effect man-
oeuvring in order to defeat the entire legislation, that his motive in supporting
the TUC had nothing to do with seeking to deal with the problem of strikes
and that it was legislation he was against not strikes. He cheerfully admitted
this and so did Jones, because he said the question of legislation raised a
fundamental principle about unions and about the whole system of collective
bargaining. Once this principle was admitted there was no limit to the extent
to which it could be pushed. There was clearly some fear that an incoming
Tory government would seek to go very much further but the two union
leaders were totally confident on their ability to make Tory-type legislation
unworkable and drew pictures of British industry stopped by a series of
shorter or longer strikes in a large number of industries.[1]

This is an extract from a record of the views expressed by Hugh
Scanlon, the president of the engineers, during an informal meeting
over dinner in June 1969 with Harold Wilson, the Prime Minister, and
Barbara Castle, the Employment Secretary, at a crucial stage in the
discussion of their Labour government's proposals for legislation to
curb a rising wave of unofficial strikes, especially in key export sectors
of the engineering industry. Though Scanlon was particularly forceful
in his opposition to any move away from the existing system of
voluntary collective bargaining, he was backed up by his colleague
Jack Jones, the secretary of the transport workers, and as a result of
their stubborn insistence on this principle they became known as the
'Terrible Twins'. It was a sign of the increasing power of the craft
unionists that their most important representative was no longer challenging the government from a distance but rather face-to-face over

the Prime Minister's own dining table, and it was certainly a new experience for Labour ministers to face such determined opposition from the national leaders of the largest trade unions, whom they had been used to regarding as their closest allies. However, although these new features of the situation at the end of an unusually long period of full employment made it possible to portray Scanlon as some sort of revolutionary, the principle he was pursuing would have been equally close to the hearts of his apparently quite moderate Victorian counterparts of 100 years earlier. Indeed, as has been seen in earlier chapters, following the hearings of extensive Royal Commissions, the principle of non-intervention in industrial relations had twice been enshrined in Liberal legislation in 1871 and 1906, and the Royal Commission set up by Harold Wilson himself in 1965 had only recently reported in favour of the re-statement of this policy in a revised form adapted to new circumstances. Paradoxically, then, in their defence of this voluntarist tradition the 'Terrible Twins' could plausibly have presented themselves as the true conservatives in the field, and the eventual transformation of an apparent extremist into the establishment figure of Lord Scanlon of Davyhulme may be less mysterious than it might at first seem.

Hugh Scanlon had been born in Australia in 1913 and, his father having died soon afterwards, his mother had returned to her parents' home in Davyhulme, Manchester, and worked in the local Cooperative soap factory.[2] This had clearly placed major financial constraints on Scanlon's education, leading him to take on part-time work while still at school and to leave at the age of fourteen for full-time work at the huge Metro-Vickers engineering plant in Trafford Park. However, he must have been a bright lad, as he had managed to secure a highly technical apprenticeship as an instrument maker. Having already been subject to the influence of his grandfather, active in the local Labour Party and keen for him to read the novels of Jack London and Upton Sinclair, Scanlon had soon been drawn into National Council of Labour Colleges' evening classes to catch up on his education, particularly in economics and industrial psychology. He had simultaneously been initiated into membership of the engineers' union, gradually moving through the ranks of its lay officials as a shop-floor representative and district-committee member to become full-time chairman of the works committee in 1945 and then full-time organizer for the north-west region two years later. Having given up his earlier membership of the Communist Party in the middle of the 1950s, Scanlon had finally been elected on to the engineers' national executive in 1963, a position he was able to use creatively to build a united left-wing movement among the membership, eventually securing him the presidency of this massive and vital industrial organization in 1967.

Soon after this emergence to national prominence, he gave a revealing interview to a group of young Marxist intellectuals who hoped to find him advocating a new form of industrial militancy to force an immediate transition to socialism. As a trade-union activist with many years of practical experience, Scanlon's response was more cautious and more concrete. He saw the new mood of rebelliousness as a product of youthful impatience, stressed the ambiguous position of shop-floor representatives caught between pressures from their members and pressures from management, and emphasized the constitutional limitations on his own power. His own leftism therefore took a more traditional form, turning questions about the upsurge of militancy and the imminence of socialism into answers about the procedures of labour institutions and the details of collective bargaining. The core issue of his presidential campaign had been resistance to the increasingly restrictive incomes policy of Harold Wilson's Labour government. However, while accepting that in such a context ordinary economic demands were likely to have political implications, Scanlon was still hesitant about taking industrial action for directly political ends and still hoped for an understanding response from Labour ministers:

With all the very close ties that the government has with the organized trade-union movement, I would hope that if the government saw the trade-union movement's determination to give effect to its own policy, and if it saw the futility of its own economic policy, it would in fact change the policy which might be the cause of a clash.[3]

Thus the trade-union campaign would be conducted not through political strikes, but rather through the existing channels of the TUC, with closer cooperation between the leftist leaders of the larger unions securing, first the passing of resolutions at annual congresses, and then adherence to them by the General Council in its discussions with the government throughout the rest of the year. Moreover, the demands being pursued would be the familiar ones of traditional collective bargaining:

... the Engineering Wages application itself which we have just presented to the engineering employers ... asks for a substantial wage increase without any strings attached – in other words, without any productivity deals, with all that implies for the Prices and Incomes policy – for a shorter working week, increased holidays and holiday pay, increased overtime premiums and a better guaranteed week. Together with the establishment of illness and pension benefits.[4]

Similarly, though a number of his speeches at this time resulted in Scanlon becoming closely associated with the notion of 'workers' control', his own understanding of this widespread catchphrase remained close to the realities of everyday trade unionism. Thus, in the foreseeable future, he took it to mean the formalizing of traditional craft regulation of training, manning, and hiring and firing, extended to include ratification of the appointment of supervisors at shop level and scrutiny of the decisions of managers at enterprise level. Indeed, at the heart of his conception of workers' control was his own experience as a local union activist during the Second World War and the long post-war boom:

Never has the labour movement in this country been stronger, more confident and more experienced largely as a result, not only of technological change, and the integration of white collar 'specialists' within the Labour Movement, but because of relatively full employment. Trade Union membership has doubled since the 1930s and the increased confidence of workers has reflected itself in the development of strong shop floor organizations, which have been able not only to bargain very effectively for increased earnings at a local level, but also question the 'prerogative of management'.[5]

Even in his more utopian sketches of a fully democratic, socialist future he still foresaw the survival of powerful roles for technical staff and managers alongside the adversarial pressure of independent trade unions. Much of the language was new and the overall tone was more assertive, but the fundamental goals expressed by Scanlon in these speeches would have been familiar even to the more moderate among his predecessors. For the core of his vision was a challenge to the parasitic power of international financiers and the creation of a cooperative atmosphere within British industry to release the full potential of the workforce, which would be further enhanced through shorter hours and life-long access to education and training:

Fundamentally, the aim within public ownership is the wearing down of sides in industry, with no 'superiors' or 'inferiors' but only differences and functions based on knowledge and ability . . . Ideas, aspirations and intentions need to have full access and be encouraged upward, whilst explanations, snags and problems should move downward for discussion and the creation of an informed working populace.[6]

It was therefore entirely consistent that Scanlon should have served on a number of joint industrial bodies, including the Engineering Industry Training Board, represented the unions on a number of regulatory bodies, including the Metrication Board and the British Gas Corporation, and taken part in a government inquiry into the teaching of mathematics in schools. For from his point of view all of these would have been seen as steps in the direction of 'workers' control', even if they also contributed to the eventual award of a life peerage after his retirement in 1978. Hugh Scanlon's vigorous leadership of the reform movement within the engineers in the 1960s had given rise to exaggerated expectations on the far left, while his determined opposition to state intervention in industrial relations had then provoked a shocked reaction from the Labour leadership. However, in almost every respect his attitudes and actions fell squarely within the centuries-old tradition of British craft unionism.

THE EMERGENCE OF
SHOP-FLOOR BARGAINING

The collapse of the reconstruction boom after the First World War had led to a sharp rise in unemployment and the re-assertion of the pattern of fifty years earlier: a long period of prosperity and apparently irreversible growth in union strength had been followed by a long period of economic instability and defeats for even the strongest of the craft organizations. Thus in 1921 the engineers were faced not only with the removal of their wartime bonuses but also with the beginning of a long process of cuts in standard rates eventually amounting to over 30 per cent. Then in 1922 they were defeated by the employers in another national lock-out over the re-assertion of managerial pre-rogatives, this time aimed specifically at the skilled men's attempt to use overtime bans to cushion themselves against rapidly rising unemployment. This had a much more serious impact than the famous 1897 lock-out, for in 1922 the engineers were not only forced to accept the employers' domination of national bargaining procedures but were also bankrupted and had their membership cut in half. Meanwhile the boilermakers and the compositors, who had initially been more stubborn in their resistance to wage cuts, soon found themselves forced into line, having both experienced major defeats of their own in national disputes during the course of 1923. With high unemployment persisting in the heavy engineering and shipbuilding districts well into the 1930s, the unions were faced with a continual erosion of their capacity to provide welfare benefits and defend their members' pos-itions in the workplace. As a result, even in the old centres of craft regulation management was able to press successfully not only for the introduction of piece-rates but also for the employment of youth and female labour.

Moreover, these years were seeing another major structural and regional shift in the assembly sectors, away from the heavy industrial regions of the north and towards lighter centres in the Midlands and the south, manufacturing electrical goods, aircraft and above all motor vehicles. Having been a slow starter, Britain emerged as Europe's leading car producer during the 1930s and then the world's leading exporter during the years of economic dislocation immediately after the Second World War. As a result, the car assembly plants became the backbones for whole new industrial districts of component suppliers, eventually accounting for over 750,000 workers at the height of the long post-1945 boom. This was closely connected with equally impor-tant developments in the economic infrastructure and in social behaviour: a suburban house-building boom and the establishment of a national electricity grid, accompanied by new patterns in the use of leisure time and in consumer spending. Thus the skilled assembly workers were faced with another major challenge of organization which it took them some time to tackle effectively.

However, despite the major shift in regions and products there were also significant continuities within the new sectors. Even in the case of the car industry British firms were generally competing for well-off customers on the basis of distinctive models, so, though their plants might have looked like those of their mass-production counterparts in the United States, their smaller production runs made it more difficult for them to integrate the supply of standardized parts and establish machine-paced assembly lines. As a result they followed the heavier assembly sectors in continuing to rely on outside component suppliers and relatively specialized and independent labour, motivated through systems of payment by results rather than close supervision. The significant new feature of the car firms was that they could pass on costs to their consumers, and they were therefore able to allow their workforces relatively high earnings to secure intensive effort. However, maintaining the desired pace of work was also dependent on retaining control over rates of pay, so, like their predecessors in heavy engineering and shipbuilding fifty years earlier, this new generation of independent-minded entrepreneurs began by resisting all attempts to introduce unions into their factories, using fluctuations in production as opportunities to weed out activists. This was if anything easier for the high-volume producers in the industry to enforce, for though they had larger workforces they had built them up by attracting large numbers of young, long-distance migrants to new plants in rural areas without strong traditions of trade unionism, such as Morris at Cowley east of Oxford and Ford at Dagenham east of London.

Under the unprecedented conditions of virtually full employment during the Second World War and the long post-war boom, the balance of bargaining power was bound to shift back towards key skilled and semi-skilled workers and trade unionism was bound to re-assert itself. However, by then a major new factor had been introduced into the situation, for, profoundly influenced by the spirit of national co-operation under state direction which had emerged between 1939 and 1945, and desperately in need of foreign currency to pay off remaining war debts, governments of both parties had new ambitions to promote peaceful industrial relations in the assembly sectors as part of a drive to boost the export of manufactured goods. On the one hand, Labour governments began to call on the political loyalties of trade-union leaders to control wage demands as an integral part of national incomes policy, beginning with a stiff voluntary pay freeze between 1948 and 1950. On the other hand, Conservative governments began to overcome their political distance from the unions by leaning on employers to be more flexible during wage bargaining, bringing a major national dispute in engineering and shipbuilding to an end in 1957 by insisting on a generous settlement. However, Labour's approach tended to widen the gap within the unions between national officials and their local members, while the Conservatives' approach tended to undermine the attempts by employers' organizations to maintain coherent industry-wide strategies. As one of the regional leaders of the engineering employers argued in the aftermath of the imposed compromise of 1957:

We cannot expect our members repeatedly to go through all this formality of voting, and then accept with complacency results diametrically opposed to the purpose of their votes . . . We must agree amongst ourselves whether or not government intervention is inevitable, and if so whether we must yield to it . . . If this great Federation of ours is to maintain its position in the national economy of our country, we must do something different. If we carry on in the same old way, we shall become less and less effective if, indeed, we do not disintegrate altogether.[7]

Unintentionally, then, these attempts by post-1945 governments to create a new form of national industrial order contributed to an increasingly fragmented pattern of bargaining among the assembly workers. For, in the absence of the hard lessons learned through unrestrained conflict and the costs of major disputes, the employers and the unions failed to develop integrated and disciplined forms of organization to cover the new sectors in the Midlands and the south. Thus within the Engineering Employers' Federation the northern firms continued to press for realistic national rates which would provide a basis for refusing further local demands, but the car firms preferred to set only minimum rates at the national level and then make generous supplements on a plant-by-plant basis. There was even some talk of the motor employers setting up a breakaway organization, and the only reason they did not do so was because some of the larger car firms preferred to retain their independence by not joining any organization at all. Since the skilled and semi-skilled workers in the motor industry and its component suppliers were able to win substantial wage increases through pressure in specific plants, and their industrial actions were not restricted by wider forms of employer organization, trade unionism in the new sectors began to assume an unusually decentralized form. Moreover, this was reinforced by a change in the way strikes were financed. For, since strikers' dependants had become eligible for state 'supplementary benefit' with deductions made for any union strike pay over £4.85 a week, the unions had a strong incentive to keep their strike benefits low. Money which might have gone into central funds was therefore retained in the hands of the members and strikes came to be financed mainly from individual savings, supplemented not only by state benefits but also by the increasing likelihood of spouses' earnings. This combined with the uneven application of wider procedural structures to reduce national union control over local bargaining, which came to focus on the increasingly important figures of the shop stewards.

Shop stewards had been a significant part of craft-union organization for many years, initially as the vigilant eye of the district committee in the workplace, making sure that new arrivals were union members and reporting any significant changes in wages and conditions. During the First World War, the very tight labour market and the urgency of resolving minor disputes in the metalworking plants had given their shop-floor representatives increasingly independent bargaining functions, and the role of democratically elected stewards had been recognized in post-war adjustments of procedure, especially in the engineering industry. Somewhat unexpectedly, the long inter-war depression had then turned this in favour of the employers, as the new procedures they were then able to impose meant that disputes could not be pursued officially at the district and national levels unless they had first been raised at the shop level, while individual workers understandably became increasingly reluctant to take on the role of shop steward when threatened with long unemployment queues. The balance of power was shifted back again by the full employment of the Second World War and the long post-war boom, but although taking on the steward's role was becoming less risky, it still usually involved loss of earnings while attending to grievances during working hours. Thus the emergence of effective shop-floor bargaining in the assembly sectors depended not only on a new set of background conditions, but also on the unusual commitment of large numbers of individual activists.

Shop-floor bargaining was an ambiguous solution to industrial relations: when it worked it led to the speedy resolution of disputes, but when it broke down it produced highly fragmented conflicts. Eventually the disadvantages came to be exaggerated and the positive aspects overlooked, so it should be stressed that shop stewards were only able to resolve disputes because they could exercise some discipline over their members, and also that they took over many of the traditional functions of gang leaders in the assembly sectors, including making sure that work flowed smoothly and allocating overtime and piece-rates to individual members. However, when industrial action did break out it tended to disrupt the work of neighbouring gangs, and when it was successful it resulted in gains for particular individuals rather than coherent occupational categories. As one car worker at a leading Coventry firm in the early 1950s recalled:

The Standard, when I started there was all little empires, every shop was a little empire, all getting different bonuses, all earning different money, and all 'You ain't coming onto our gang' or 'We ain't getting enough bonus. We got to get some off our gang on to their gang' and all that business, at the Standard. Although it was union it was all different empires. It weren't like I always thought the union was, you know, all brothers together. They were all brothers in their own little circles.[8]

It is therefore not surprising that even at the plant level joint shop stewards' committees were only effective in developing coherent policies when led by powerful full-time conveners, while organization at the company or industry levels remained an elusive ideal. Of course, this was also a result of the general lack of interest in the details of industrial relations on the part of senior managers, who remained either indifferent or hostile towards shop-floor organization. As a result, despite the increasing ineffectiveness of national bargaining structures, few of the major engineering firms bothered to develop their own formal procedures for handling disputes at the plant, let alone the company, level.

The pattern of industrial relations which emerged in the assembly sectors after 1945 was therefore almost a mirror image of that which had been established in the previous long period of trade-union growth: it lacked the organizational advantages of national uniformity and coordination, but it appealed to the craftsmen's longer-standing preferences for self-government and independence. Some of their leaders even began to use it as the basis for an ambitious new vision of the potential of trade unionism to transform employment relations by referring to the practices of shop-floor bargaining as manifestations of 'workers' control'. This overlapped with the discussion of more formal schemes of industrial democracy, above all employee representation on the boards of companies. However, these tended to appeal to those with less direct influence at the point of production, such as the general and white-collar workers, while the skilled workers in manufacturing preferred to rely on the extension of adversarial collective bargaining. At the very least, this allowed them to use their role as an independent opposition in the workplace to exercise some joint control over routine productive activity, and as this role expanded it was matched by management attempts to channel it into new schemes of consultation and information sharing. At a more ambitious level, the adversarial approach allowed skilled workers to mobilize their knowledge and experience to produce alternative business plans in the face of redundancies by proposing viable new products or even, most notably at Upper Clyde Shipbuilders, by demonstrating the capacity to keep firms going after the removal of normal management. Both the routine and the more unusual cases combined to inspire a spreading view that, at least in a period of sustained economic prosperity and full employment, trade unionism might be able to move on from the satisfaction of immediate material needs to the stimulation of new democratic processes, increasing the opportunities for creativity, self-expression and participation in everyday working lives.

TRENDS IN NATIONAL BARGAINING

At the same time this rising tide of shop-floor activity was still dependent on the rebuilding and maintenance of the unions' position within a wider institutional framework. The engineers had renewed their formal commitment to the recruitment of semi-skilled workers following a further round of mergers into the Amalgamated Engineering Union in 1920. However, as a result of their defeat in the 1922 lock-out and the following long period of high unemployment, their district organization had been seriously undermined and the bulk of members of the new semi-skilled section turned out on closer examination to be fully skilled men doing less-skilled work and opting to pay lower union subscriptions. It was only once the rearmament recovery was well under way after 1935 that the union was able to rebuild its local branches and begin the serious recruitment of less-skilled grades: its membership then doubled to reach just over 390,000 in 1939 and doubled again during the Second World War to a peak of 825,000 in 1943. Even before the war broke out the engineers had been able to make significant progress over national wage rates, shorter working hours, paid holidays and even the right to negotiate for apprentices, following a wave of local strikes by the youths themselves which began on Clydeside in the spring of 1937. Then during the Second World War they were able to make further major gains on the basis of the urgent need for armaments and the generally favourable framework of government policy resulting from Winston Churchill's inspired appointment in May 1940 of Ernest Bevin, the experienced leader of the transport workers, to the key post at the head of a considerably enhanced Ministry of Labour and National Service.

First of all Bevin ensured that he had all the compulsory methods he could possibly need to organize the nation's manpower under a comprehensive Emergency Powers Act, then he did everything he could not to use them, instead pressing the employers and the unions to reach voluntary agreements under threat of compulsory arbitration. As both sides in the assembly industries had absorbed the lessons of the previous war, this worked out much more smoothly than it had done in 1914–18: the employers knew that they would benefit from cost-plus munitions contracts and the unions expected that dilution would be temporary. There were some special cases, such as the need to guarantee the time rates of skilled men in the toolrooms and the need to persuade woodworkers to adopt piece-rates in the aircraft factories, but on the whole the wartime adjustment of the skilled men's wages and hours proceeded relatively quietly. Meanwhile Bevin was ensuring that the employers would be more responsible about labour mobility by drafting an Essential Work Order in 1941, which permitted his officials to allocate skilled workers where they were needed and to ensure that they were employed under trade-union conditions, including guaranteed wages and protection against arbitrary dismissal. Once again this was used as little as possible, instead acting as a powerful incentive towards industrial consultation and cooperation, and promoting a significant extension of national bargaining arrangements.

Women were mobilized to a much greater extent in 1939–45 than they had been in 1914–18: not only were there twice as many of them in industry (over 2 million) and five times as many of them in the armed forces (over half a million), this time many of them were conscripts rather than volunteers. As a result the government took more immediate responsibility both for their efficiency at work and for their domestic roles, particularly through improved public funding of day nurseries and maternity support. Learning from the difficulties of the First World War, female substitutes in previously male jobs in munitions were quickly given a guarantee of existing standard rates, and once again this significantly limited the impact of dilution schemes. For direct substitution no longer produced any immediate financial advantage for the employers, but it did threaten to undermine their established principle of lower pay for women throughout metal-working. As a result, such dilution as did occur was accompanied by the re-labelling of jobs as women's work or the re-organization of the tasks involved, so that only a very small minority of women were on equal pay or work classified as fully skilled. Women were considerably more prone to join unions during the Second World War, their numbers among those affiliated to the TUC rising from just over 500,000 to just over 1.3 million, though this was still a minority of those eligible and it took place without any corresponding increase in their representation in the ranks of union officials. In the absence of an independent body such as the National Federation of Women Workers, the need for regulation of the employment of female workers in munitions to protect the position of the skilled men led the engineers themselves to open a special section for women at the beginning of 1943. By the end of the year this leading craft union had recruited almost 140,000 female members and had begun to adopt an increasingly strong line on their right to equal pay as a central element of its campaign to regulate the wages and conditions of all semi-skilled workers in the war industries. While most female war-workers were once again pushed out of their emergency tasks at the end of the hostilities, the structural and regional shift in the assembly sectors between the wars had also begun to affect the pattern of women's employment. There was a continuous decline in domestic service and outworking, accompanied by a long-term increase in white-collar and lighter factory work, particularly in electrical engineering, in which women came to make up around a third of the labour force. This was usually still in sexually segregated tasks, but it was in overall environments which were significantly more favourable to trade unionism, if only somebody was prepared to persuade female workers of the benefits of formal organization.

It was only to be expected that favourable wartime conditions would have most impact in munitions works, which, despite the construction of 'shadow' aircraft factories alongside some of the southern car plants, were for the most part still located in the heavier engineering and shipbuilding districts: thus even in 1945 unionization in the car firms was still nowhere higher than 50 per cent and usually nearer 30 per cent. This was due partly to the companies' anti-union policies, but partly also to the initial ineffectiveness of the unions themselves. As an assembly sector it was to be expected that the motor industry would be plagued by multi-unionism, and indeed the engineers found themselves in direct competition with a number of other craft bodies, particularly the National Union of Vehicle Builders and the Sheet Metal Workers' Union. But what was unusual for such an important industry was that the two largest organizations involved still had the main focus of their attention elsewhere and were slow to adapt to conditions in the new sectors. The engineers were still mainly concerned to defend their status as highly skilled timeworkers in the heavier sectors in the north: so, while they were able to play an important role in organizing toolmakers and bodymakers in the motor industry, they tended initially to neglect the semi-skilled piece-workers being employed in increasing numbers in the Midlands and the south. This left an opening for the rapid recruitment of these machinists into a dynamic new body known as the Workers' Union in the years before and during the First World War; then, following an equally rapid collapse during the inter-war depression, the remnants found refuge in 1929 within the ranks of the transport workers. However, this federal union was still mainly concerned with its traditional membership in the docks and initially continued to be rather passive in its approach to the engineering industry.

In general the craft unions only began recruitment drives among semi-skilled men and women in the new assembly sectors when they felt encroached upon by other bodies, especially in the Coventry area, where the transport workers' district organizer, Jack Jones, was unusually interested in extending his federal union's membership among metalworkers. In some cases the various bodies were then able to cooperate on joint shop stewards' committees within the plants, particularly during the enforcement of overall closed shops, and this was supported by the national guidelines of the Confederation of Shipbuilding and Engineering Unions. In other cases the different aims of craftsmen and semi-skilled workers led to serious disagreements over the priorities for joint shop stewards' committees, particularly when it was the semi-skilled who were under more pressure, and this plant sectionalism was reinforced by long-standing rivalries between the national unions involved. However, an overall arrangement did begin to emerge, under which the craft unions tended to retain exclusive control of certain jobs and high wages for all their members, while the transport workers were able to gain more than proportional increases for those in their ranks, significantly reducing wage differentials and sometimes even securing the same rates for all production workers.

Meanwhile the re-assertion of the craft unions' bargaining strength during the long post-war boom was most strikingly visible over the issue of working hours, with the length of the standard week being pushed down from forty-eight to forty-four hours in 1945–7 and then even further to forty hours by the mid-1960s. Since the time actually spent at work remained more or less the same, average earnings were being boosted by the working of considerably more overtime, on time-and-a-half in the evenings and double-time at weekends. This achievement through national bargaining therefore contributed to the increasing role of the shop stewards at the local level, first, because the allocation of overtime to individuals became one of their major functions, and second, because it increased the effectiveness of over-time bans which could be undertaken at minimal cost to those involved and without national union support. The period also saw a further spread of piece-rates to cover over 40 per cent of workers in manufac-turing by the early 1960s, with a further marked impact on the role of shop stewards, for fixing the rates for new jobs and haggling over bonuses and allowances for interrupted work became the bread and butter of shop-floor bargaining. The importance of this process was then reflected in the accelerating drift of average engineering earnings above the industry's standard rates, a gap which widened from around 10 per cent in 1938 to around 90 per cent in 1967.

Moreover, a marked tendency towards the amalgamation of craft unions into much larger bodies during the post-war boom also tended to encourage the increasing importance of shop-floor bargaining. This mirrored a major wave of mergers between companies which was producing far more multi-product firms and much larger plants, and it was made easier by the 1964 Trade Union (Amalgamations) Act, which reduced the voting requirements to a simple majority in favour in the union or unions concerned. The emergence of larger craft unions probably contributed to the fragmentation of bargaining by increasing their members' self-confidence while simultaneously reducing their satisfaction with the representation of their particular interests at a national level. Among the smaller and more cohesive bodies, each with around 100,000 members in 1976, were the boilermakers, who had already merged with their main rivals the shipwrights and the black-smiths between 1961 and 1963 in response to a major restructuring of the production process in shipbuilding, and the compositors, whose London and provincial sections had amalgamated into the National Graphical Association in 1964. A much larger body emerged in the building industry as a result of the amalgamation of the carpenters, bricklayers and painters into the Union of Construction, Allied Trades and Technicians in 1971, with around 300,000 members. Meanwhile, the electricians, recruiting in a newer occupation, had been growing even more rapidly: doubling their membership in the 1930s and tripling it again in the 1940s, they amalgamated with the plumbers in 1968 and had a combined membership of almost 500,000 members by 1976. While this made them the second largest body in the engineering industry, they were still completely overshadowed by the engineers themselves, who absorbed the foundrymen in 1971 and whose membership doubled again from its wartime peak to reach almost 1,500,000 in 1976, making them the largest occupational body in the country, ahead of even the miners and the railwaymen. This helps to account for both the fragmentation of bargaining in the industry and its absorption of much of the public attention of the period.

Significant exceptions to the trend towards shop-floor bargaining were to be found in the building and printing trades, as they were relatively protected from foreign competition and developed more effective national bargaining arrangements. In building the prevalence of smaller firms and more casual employment made the employers keen to take wages out of competition and the unions keen to secure the protection of genuine standard rates. In the immediate aftermath of the First World War a strong union federation had achieved a favourable system of national bargaining over graded district time rates linked to the cost of living in each area, which aimed to equalize real wages across the industry in return for a significant reduction in local disputes. This had survived the ensuing long depression more or less intact, despite temporary breakaways by the bricklayers and the plasterers, and the inevitable imposition of wage cuts by the employers had been somewhat curbed by their even greater preference for keeping the national bargaining arrangements in place. Workplace bargaining did emerge after the Second World War on some of the larger construction sites, where piece-rates and special bonuses were introduced, but shop-steward organization did not put down deep roots in the building industry, as networks of activists were inevitably broken up when work at each site was completed. In printing too, the years immediately after the First World War had seen a union federation achieving a favourable system of time rates graded by district, though further complicated by the distinctive situations in newspapers and in London.

The relatively low levels of unemployment during the inter-war depression had given the industry's workers something of a cushion against wage cuts, and in the tighter labour market of the Second World War the employers had conceded significant increases to maintain the national bargaining arrangements in the face of widespread threats of industrial action. This then provided the basis for the persistence of the printing craftsmen's traditional position throughout the post-war boom: they were able to use national arrangements to maintain differentials, limit women's employment and secure favourable workplace consultation over such issues as apprentice ratios and payment by results.

CRAFT UNIONS AND THE CRISIS OF INDUSTRIAL RELATIONS

However, it was not these cases which attracted the most attention, as from the late 1950s it was the car industry which became increasingly prominent as the scene of industrial disputes: having previously been relatively strike-free it now saw a seven-fold increase in days lost, mainly due to short unofficial strikes of less than a week. Simultaneously, the issues under dispute shifted from a focus on union recognition and basic wage rates towards such classic aspects of the assertion of craft control as security of employment, wage differentials and overtime. This assertion was most marked in the component suppliers and in the smaller assembly plants around Coventry, but the struggle to establish effective shop-floor organization was beginning to penetrate into the larger, previously less unionized, plants, and into the ranks of the semi-skilled as well as the skilled workers.

With the benefit of hindsight the economic implications of this strike wave can be seen to have been considerably exaggerated, for lost production was quickly made up through more overtime working and, even if the wage/effort bargain was shifting in favour of the workforce, the labour share of total costs remained relatively small. The underlying realities were that, once Germany and Japan had recovered from the destruction of the Second World War, the British motor industry could not hope to maintain its unchallenged dominance of export markets and that management was slow to respond to the loss of its temporary economies of scale. Even after a wave of company mergers, too many models were still being assembled in too many plants with too little analysis of costs, leading to falling profits and accelerating under-investment. Scapegoating shop-floor militancy was simply an easier option for managers than putting their own positions at risk during a fundamental restructuring of the industry.

Meanwhile, in the immediate aftermath of a particularly intense phase of the 'Cold War' between the West and the Soviet Union, there were frequent claims that the sharp increase in industrial disputes in such a strategic sector was the responsibility of small groups of politically motivated, and by implication anti-patriotic, agitators. Certainly the demands of the shop steward's role were such that the inclination to take it on, particularly in the more permanent form of senior steward or convener, would usually have come from some political commitment. However, in the majority of cases this was active membership of a local Labour Party, which could hardly be portrayed as subversive, and even for the minority of cases further to the left the desire and the ability to create industrial disruption was much more limited than was widely assumed. In order to clarify this point it will be necessary to give a brief survey of the history of the revolutionary left in Britain since the aftermath of the First World War.

The Communist Party of Great Britain had been formed from the fusion of a number of extreme-left groups in 1921, to promote proletarian revolution in the west in support of the fledgling Soviet Union. Its industrial wing had drawn heavily on syndicalist currents, including the veteran Tom Mann himself as well as shop stewards from among the engineers and local activists from among the south Wales miners. Two of its most prominent figures in the inter-war years had been Wal Hannington of the engineers, who had played a leading role in campaigns among the increasing numbers of unemployed assembly workers, and Harry Pollitt of the boilermakers, who had quickly become the party's most significant industrial organizer and been elected regularly as one of his union's delegates to the TUC. Otherwise, the Communist Party had been restricted to a position on the fringes: it had been able to retain only a few thousand individual members, it had been unable to persuade the TUC to adopt the syndicalist model of industrial unionism, and it had failed in all its attempts to build up a 'National Minority Movement' as an alternative centre of revolutionary leadership within the unions.

However, as a result of its relative unimportance within the Communist International, the British Communist Party had gained some much-needed room for manoeuvre towards a more realistic strategy, while still appearing to follow the Moscow line. Particularly after Pollitt had taken over as general secretary in 1929, its industrial activists had been allowed to concentrate on the pursuit of conventional trade-union goals, albeit with the longer-term aim of establishing themselves in leadership positions in preparation for the long-anticipated 'revolutionary crisis'. During the course of the 1930s this carefully disguised turn towards moderation had been successfully entrenched as the new orthodoxy in Britain, as one activist in a Communist stronghold in aero-engineering later recalled:

We had a great deal of influence in the factory from the point of view of friends in management. People in management were impressed by organized labour and realized that men who had worked at Napier's for 20–25 years had taken our stand on the side of the working class. That integrity got through. We learned how to use our power. It was straightforward as long as you knew what you wanted. The transition to this position was smooth as long as the demand you were making was not extravagant.[9]

This emerging 'British Road' had then been strongly underwritten by a shift in the policy of the Communist International towards building a 'United Front' against the rise of fascism and, above all, by the Soviet Union's entry into the war on the Allied side after Hitler's invasion of Russia in the summer of 1941. As a result party membership had come to be regarded as something of a badge of honour on the shop floor, for the new Moscow line had demanded the rapid resolution of disputes and the maximization of Allied munitions output. This unusual convergence of international socialism and common patriotism had allowed British Communists to channel their energies and ambitions into playing leading roles on plant-level Joint Production Committees sponsored by the government, and the party had reached an all-time peak of over 50,000 members. Among the assembly workers its influence had been particularly marked among the highly skilled men in the rapidly expanding sectors of aero-engineering and electrical contracting, leading to a wave of Communist successes in elections to office within the craft unions at district and even national level.

After 1945, the 'United Front' against fascism had gradually been replaced by the 'Cold War' division between East and West, and Communism had consequently come to be associated with a sinister international conspiracy, despite the British party's open adoption of parliamentary socialism in 1951. Its membership had fallen to settle at around half its wartime level, but its industrial organization had been able to maintain some momentum into the post-war years, particularly where its activists had been able to secure official union positions. In the case of the engineers, the London district committee had been dominated by Communists for some time, a 'fellow traveller', Jack Tanner, had become the union's national president as early as 1939, and two party members, one of them Hannington, had been elected as full-time national organizers by 1945. However, during and after the war Tanner himself had begun to move towards a more mainstream position, and widespread disillusionment over Krushchev's official acknowledgement of the Stalinist terror, immediately followed by the Soviet invasion of Hungary in 1956, led to the success of a moderate movement within the union in electing the Roman Catholic Bill Carron as his successor. In the case of the electricians, the Communists were once again strong in the London area and three of them had been successfully elected as national president, secretary and assistant secretary by 1948. They had then determinedly resisted a moderate opposition through the cynical manipulation of branch meetings and widespread ballot-rigging, but in 1961 they too were finally overthrown by an alliance of Catholics and disillusioned former Communists, following five years of highly damaging revelations about the conduct of the union's internal affairs. These battles over national union posts after 1956 were given extensive media coverage, which strengthened the widespread image of Communists as subversive political agitators at the very time their link with the Soviet Union was becoming a liability on the left and they were failing to attract younger activists. Thus even in such strongholds as the British Leyland car plant at Longbridge in Birmingham, where they remained well represented among the shop-stewards and managed to retain control of the main convener's post into the 1970s, they were never more than a large minority and were unable to sustain effective leadership of unofficial strikes without the support of the other stewards. And most importantly, where they did continue to wield any influence it was because they had long given up pursuing a revolutionary line and become much more used to urging the acceptance of negotiated compromises than pursuing militant action for its own sake. That their influence was based mainly on their reputations as effective bargaining representatives rather than any broader ideological appeal was strongly underlined by the restriction of the party's recruitment to less than 1 per cent of the membership of the unions concerned.

The search for politically motivated industrial disruption would therefore have to be conducted elsewhere, perhaps among the various Trotskyist groups which had emerged since the Second World War. However, they were only functioning on a similar scale to the revolutionary Communists of the 1920s, and without the advantage of a link to an actually existing socialist state to restrain an endemic tendency towards personality clashes and sectarian splits. They came out of their initial isolation with an appeal among those radicalized by the 'student revolt' of 1968, subsequently establishing ginger groups on the left of some white-collar unions, but never achieving more than an extremely patchy and fragile presence in industrial organizations. Even the exceptional influence of the Workers' Revolutionary Party at British Leyland's car plant at Cowley in Oxford in the early 1970s was due to the manipulation of key individuals among the conveners, rather than any genuine appeal to the wider body of trade unionists in the factory. As the leadership of the rival Socialist Workers' Party itself concluded after a decade of intense industrial agitation:

Despite the increase in membership we have not gained a proportionate increase in striking power. We are very weak in the workplaces. The November Rank and File Conference was not a significant advance on its predecessors held when we were smaller. We are not stronger and may well be weaker at shop steward and lower echelon trade union machine level . . . What can we actually deliver? The answer turned out to be in terms of industrial action, as opposed to lower level solidarity work, effectively zero.[10]

Thus the Trotskyists were only learning the lesson of the inter-war 'Minority Movement' all over again: that in Britain it was futile trying to establish a politically motivated alternative to mainstream trade unionism.

Although the economic impact of the unofficial strikes in the key assembly sectors was marginal and the allegations of their roots in political subversion were implausible, governments of both parties were soon following the media in exaggerating their disruptive and sinister aspects. It was the Conservative Minister of Labour, Edward Heath, who set the precedent in 1960 by initiating a series of meetings between the main motor employers and unions, at which they were called on to commit themselves to responsible industrial relations. But this was followed by Labour in government setting up a motor industry Joint Labour Council in 1965 which carried out a major inquiry under Jack Scamp, a personnel manager sympathetic to the unions, highlighting the increasingly disorganized nature of shop-floor bargaining. This process had the advantage of bringing together federated and non-federated employers at a national level for the first time, but it provided no methods for dealing with the unions' loss of authority over their own local memberships. Indeed, the initial cooperation of the moderate leadership of the engineers with the employers in enforcing official disputes procedures and weeding out pockets of Communist activists was not met with any significant concessions over wages. As a result it only encouraged members to transfer to more assertive rival organizations, and contributed to the increasing popularity of the 'Broad Left' within the union, leading eventually to the election of the former Communist Hugh Scanlon as the engineers' national president in 1967. Meanwhile, the employers continued all of the managerial practices which encouraged shop-floor assertiveness, especially their stubborn resistance to the unions in official national negotiations followed by rapid climb-downs in the face of unofficial local action.

As a result, the only way forward the motor employers would consider was more restraint on unofficial action and, given the ineffectiveness of their own national organization, they looked increasingly to the government to provide statutory enforcement of formal bargaining procedures. They managed to persuade both the Engineering Employers' Federation and the National Confederation of Employers'

Organisations to make this the substance of their submissions to the Labour government's Royal Commission on Trade Unions and Employers' Associations under Lord Donovan, an Appeal Court judge, which began its lengthy sessions in 1965. However, when this inquiry eventually produced the Donovan Report in 1968 it favoured the continuation of the voluntarist tradition in British industrial relations: recognizing the increasing role of shop-floor bargaining in a period of full employment, highlighting poor management practice as a major source of increasing disputes, and recommending a more sustained pursuit of plant-level negotiations to fill the gap between formal and informal agreements. This was in large part because of the influence of a number of distinguished figures in the university and legal worlds who expounded a vigorously explicit pluralism which had its roots in the social-democratic opposition to the rise of dictatorship in inter-war Germany. First, there was a group of industrial-relations academics influenced by Allan Flanders of Nuffield College, Oxford, who had joined a tiny but highly influential German ethical-socialist sect in the late 1920s, returned to Britain in 1933 when his German colleagues had gone underground, and then been sent back to Germany in 1946 by the British government to assist the revival of the social-democratic movement. His unusually explicit ideas on voluntary social co-operation were to be a powerful influence on his close colleagues Bill McCarthy and Hugh Clegg, who played leading roles during the Donovan Commission. The former acted as its research director and ensured the avoidance of simplistic condemnations of shop stewards as political agitators, the latter wrote the central chapters of the final report rejecting the employers' arguments and championing the formal recognition of shop-floor bargaining. Second, there was a group of academic labour lawyers influenced by Otto Kahn-Freund of the London School of Economics and Oxford University, who had been a member of a brilliant circle of Jewish social-democratic intellectuals in Weimar Germany and, shortly before his flight into exile in 1933, had made a brave decision in the Berlin Labour Tribunal in favour of trade unionists dismissed from the state radio station by the Hitler regime. Kahn-Freund himself served on the Donovan Commission and proved to be the decisive influence on its rejection of statutory intervention, while his close colleague Bill Wedderburn was to be a particularly outspoken critic of the later Conservative act of 1971 and subsequently the major legal adviser to the TUC during the drafting of Labour's eventual legislation to repeal it in 1974.

However, despite the prestige of these intellectual figures and the effort which had been put into gaining familiarity with trade-union attitudes, it was the contrasting employers' approach that began to appeal to Barbara Castle, the Employment Secretary responsible for drafting Labour's white paper *In Place of Strife* in January 1969, at a time when the government was hard-pressed by economic difficulties. This report included, and the subsequent parliamentary bill focused exclusively on, provisions for statutory conciliation pauses and strike ballots to establish more centralized controls over local bargaining. Though this came from a Labour government it was bound to encounter strong opposition from the unions, particularly the craft bodies which had traditionally been at the forefront of resistance to state intervention in industrial relations. Sure enough, with Hugh Scanlon of the engineers taking the most intransigent position, the TUC insisted that penal legislation would be unacceptable to the majority of its members and that the most it could offer was a 'solemn and binding' commitment to support the leaders of its constituent unions in restraining unofficial strikes. The novelty of this undertaking helped the Labour government in its public presentation of a humiliating 'U-turn', but could not disguise its original intentions or prevent a significant erosion of confidence among its core supporters, paradoxically resulting in the election in 1970 of a Conservative government even more committed to the legislative restraint of trade-union power.

The subsequent Industrial Relations Act of 1971 not only contained provisions for statutory conciliation pauses and strike ballots but also introduced the notion of 'unfair industrial practices', permitted the prosecution of unions for breaches of written agreements, and undermined existing arrangements for closed shops. However, by this time close relations between the Labour front bench and the TUC had been restored and a united opposition was soon in place, involving careful restraint in the use of strike action to maintain a public reputation for constitutionalism, a national petition with over half a million signatures, and a march to Hyde Park attended by over 140,000 demonstrators. Though this failed to prevent the passing of the

Conservative legislation, it succeeded in laying the basis for a gathering momentum of union refusals to register under the act, in anticipation of its repeal by a Labour government in the near future. Within this context Scanlon was able to lead his own union in a particularly intransigent campaign of one-day protest strikes and outright boycotting of the provisions of the legislation. Severe penalties were then imposed on the engineers in two cases of contempt of court, with fines of £55,000 over the 'unfair' maintenance of a closed shop and £75,000 over local action on union recognition. Jack Jones and the transport workers followed suit, leading to an even more controversial case of contempt of court, with a fine of £55,000 and the highly symbolic imprisonment of five of their docker members over local actions against new container terminals. Despite these penalties the days lost due to strikes continued to rise sharply to over 24 million in 1972, the highest figure since the General Strike of 1926. Meanwhile, the ineffectiveness of the central provisions of the act had already been exposed during a national dispute on the railways, when two conciliation pauses failed to produce an agreement, the statutory ballot produced a majority of six to one in favour of strike action among the railwaymen, and substantial concessions therefore had to be made. By this stage the main employers' organizations were understandably becoming disillusioned with the legislation, so it was only a matter of time before Labour was re-elected with a clear mandate to repeal it.

During the early 1970s the engineering employers were therefore forced to accept that the tradition of voluntarism in the private sector would continue and that they would have to rely on their own initiative to deal with their industrial-relations problems, particularly their highly fragmented arrays of piece-rates, by this time only loosely connected to occupational categories or even to actual output. Just as in the years immediately after the First World War they began by making progressive noises, but eventually revealed that they were unwilling to abandon their adversarial approach to industrial relations. Thus, on the one hand, there were some moves towards an accommodation with the long-term growth in union strength, seen for example in employers' increasing willingness to recognize closed shops and even to act as agents for the collection of union subscriptions through 'check-off' pay arrangements. But simultaneously, instead of building up appropriate bargaining procedures within their firms, they were trying to arrange once-and-for-all buy-outs of shop-floor organization. Thus British Leyland, a recent amalgamation of all the British-owned car firms, negotiated 'measured day work' rates which guaranteed earnings as long as output exceeded a certain minimum level. However, the emphasis of shop-floor activity then simply switched from increasing piece-rates, which was no longer possible, to decreasing work effort, which no longer incurred the same immediate financial penalty. Similarly, Ford negotiated the abolition of bonuses in return for increases in standard hourly rates and, following a nine-week strike which eventually became official, even began to incorporate shop-stewards into its national bargaining procedures. However, the firm's traditionally strict attitude to discipline on the shop floor remained intact and was experienced as increasingly irksome in this new context: vicious cycles of unofficial action and severe retribution were to characterize its industrial relations for the rest of the decade.

In short, the employers' eventual moves in the direction of the reform of industrial relations in the assembly sectors failed to resolve deeply rooted problems. For, while they did amount to an explicit acknowledgement of the futility of national bargaining, they were launched without the experienced personnel required to replace payment by results with direct supervision, and without any commitment to genuine consultation on the shop-floor. There was, indeed, a significant decline in the number of small, sectional strikes, but only to be replaced by bigger and longer strikes at the plant or company level. Thus the craft unions, even at this peak of strength when they were developing an ambitious new vision of their democratic potential in modern industrial society, had been cast in a largely negative light: reduced to vetoing ill-considered government interventions and undermining poorly planned employer initiatives.

13

Industrial Decline among the
Process Workers

There is no question of a voluntary agreement on wages whilst we are confronted by a Government such as the one we have which has been responsible
for the biggest rise in the cost of living in any one single period of government
in this last hundred years. It is impossible to get members of the NUM, and
workers in general, to accept lower wage increases when they can see their
cost of living, and their standard of living being eroded week in and week out
. . . when the chips are down, the miners will struggle for the right wage for
the job, the wage which I have said previously must be the highest industrial
wage in Britain, because the job warrants that wage.[1]

This was part of a speech to the annual conference of the National
Union of Miners by its president Joe Gormley in July 1973, in the
run-up to a major industry-wide strike which was to play a significant
role in the downfall of the government of the day. Gormley was widely
regarded as being both perceptive and outspoken, so his remarks are
worth careful attention for what they reveal about the attitudes both
of his own members at that moment and more generally about those
of the process workers throughout the period. The first thing which is
clear is the gritty realism of concern over wages, prices and standards
of living. These men were proud of their efforts at work, keenly aware
of the value of their contributions to the incomes of their families and
sensitive about their relative positions in the national earnings league.
The second thing which emerges clearly is the focus on central government as the key influence on these matters. The state may have been
taking more responsibility for the economy in general as the twentieth
century went on, but its role was particularly acute for the process
workers, who were increasingly facing it as their main counterpart in

wage bargaining. Major disputes in these sectors were therefore likely to have significant political repercussions even though the mass of workers involved were not primarily motivated by political considerations. Indeed Gormley himself, though he led two major challenges to the government in 1972 and 1974, was anything but a threat from the far left, being rather a notable presence on the moderate wing both of his own union and of the Labour Party.

Joe Gormley had been born in the Lancashire village of Ashton-in-Makerfield in 1917 into a family of coal miners of Irish descent, and his early memories were made up of all the classic elements of 'rough' northern culture: domestic violence, pigeons, ferrets, illegal gambling and a regular diet of soup and potatoes. Indeed his family was so large and poor that, although he had the ability, he had not been able to attend grammar school and instead had to start down the local pits at the age of fourteen, gradually working his way up the seniority system from haulage lad to face-worker. This was a world of tight-knit family and workplace loyalties. Both his mother and mother-in-law having been founder members of the local women's section of the Labour Party, it had seemed only natural to become involved himself, first as a delegate to the monthly meetings of the National Union of Labour Clubs, then as chairman of the local Labour Party, a district councillor and eventually leader of the Labour group. Indeed his interest in the possibility of a parliamentary career had been the motivation for taking night classes for his mining deputy's certificate and for considering going on to further courses in management. These experiences gave Gormley a strong sense that political decisions should be made by democratically elected representatives, that it was not the role of trade unions to interfere in the choice of government and, indeed, that if they did so it was only likely to provoke a dictatorial reaction from the far right:

So I say that, when the people of Britain have decided . . . to vote Tory rather than Labour, no group of unions . . . has the right to say, 'Well, the people have voted Tory, but we think they're wrong, and therefore we will immediately set out to destroy the Tory Government'. Because that leads to the total breakdown of democracy.[2]

Throughout his early years Gormley's attitude towards trade unionism was indeed a form of particularly blunt economic pragmatism: he simply wanted to earn enough to keep his own family comfortable. As he advanced in the pits he had frequently bargained over rates of pay for himself and his work teams, and this bred an assertive and independent manner:

I would occasionally meet the union branch secretary and have a chat with him, but I never bothered to attend branch meetings, simply because I always did my own negotiating. Right from the start I'd fought for better conditions, but as an individual.[3]

This had led him to initiate brief unofficial stoppages, from which it was only a few short steps to serving on his local branch committee, as branch delegate to the Lancashire area meeting and eventually as a rank-and-file representative on the miners' national executive, even though he had never seen trade-union activity as being particularly high on his own agenda. In fact in all of these roles he retained his reputation for dogged independence, having become most widely known for resisting the implications of an area-wide concessionary coal package which implied reductions in the benefits he had already won for himself:

Well, I was one of the leaders in that fight, but it was one I lost, even though we had legal opinion to back us . . . It was only fair, of course, but it did mean that in place of those twenty-four hundredweight of coal at ten shillings, delivered every six weeks, we got just six tons a year at £2 a ton. All those wonderful socialist ideals become a bit harder to accept when you're on the losing side of the deal![4]

Of course Gormley himself saw socialism less as a matter of ideals than as a matter of business. He always accepted the distinction between the roles of management and unions even within nationalized industries, and his later arguments for a national energy policy were based on a pragmatic appreciation of the need for expert evaluation of the relative efficiency of different fuels and for large injections of public money for new projects. Moreover, he also accepted that the unions existed within a larger framework of privately owned capital and urged them to use their own resources for the maximum benefit of their members, for example investing their pension funds with an eye on the immediate financial return as much as on the broader social benefits.

As he continued to rise in the union during the 1960s, first as Lancashire area secretary then finally as national president, Gormley's experience in struggling against pit closures led him to develop a distinctive approach: he came to accept that the coal industry was in irreversible decline, but he fought hard for the best possible short-term deal for those still employed in it. This was to result in two dramatic confrontations with the Conservatives in government in 1972 and 1974, but Gormley himself had a traditional trade unionist's dislike of the expenses and risks involved in such actions. Of the run-up to the first of them he later recalled:

I can't say it was all that happy a Christmas, nor New Year come to that. We didn't *want* to strike. We were all perfectly well aware that any gains as a result of a strike would be offset by loss of wages while it was going on. What's more, we were novices at the strike business – in the quarter century since the NUM was formed, we'd never *had* a national strike. But, as far as we were concerned, we had an absolutely just case, a case in which we had the support of many other unions. And, if striking was the only way to get that case answered, then so be it.[5]

Indeed, if a dispute was to be fought out, it should be done as forcefully as possible in order to keep it as short as possible, and it was this attitude which led to the evolution of the tactic of 'secondary picketing', to prevent the movement of coal and oil stocks to power stations and thus ensure that the withdrawal of labour from the pits would have the maximum impact.

Although his members' position as prominent public employees also added significant political implications to the conduct and the outcome of these national disputes, and though some of his colleagues in the leadership of the miners' union welcomed this, Gormley was always clear that strikes were about economic, not political, matters. Thus he recalled that in the run up to the confrontation of 1974 he declared in a meeting with the Conservative Prime Minister Edward Heath:

'I'm not here to talk about changing the Government. *We* are here as the NEC of the NUM, discussing the possibility of ending an industrial dispute, and trying to get the right wages for the men on the job. That's our position. When you go to the country, you go to the country. You'll decide that. And I shall decide to oppose you at that time, and I shall work like all holy hell to get you defeated at that time. But this strike is not about that. This strike is about wages, and that only.'[6]

Indeed, in unsuccessful attempts to head off this second confrontation he suggested in private conversations, first with Heath and then with his employment minister, that the miners' relative standing might be maintained through special payments for unsociable working hours or for waiting and bathing time. Moreover, it had been Gormley who had earlier worked tirelessly to bring the 1972 strike to a conclusion, for, when it had become clear that there would be no further improvement in the wage increases being offered, he had largely fulfilled his members' expectations by negotiating successfully over a long shopping list of other fringe benefits.

Joe Gormley, then, would have been the least likely person to lead the miners into a politically motivated strike, and most of them would have been reluctant to follow such a lead in any case. For the miners, and for the seniority unions in general, trade unionism was about industrial issues and, as employees in large-scale processing enterprises with little influence over working methods and conditions, that meant above all the size of the weekly wage packet. Moreover, since they knew, either from direct experience or collective memory, that industrial action in their sectors would be large in scale and very expensive, they were far from strike-happy. Finally, when it did come to politics their sense of 'socialism' was primarily a matter of local loyalties, reasonable standards of living and safety nets for those unable to work, not much more than an extension of ordinary trade unionism. Thus, while Gormley led the miners assertively in the national strike of 1972 and was a willing figurehead in that of 1974, his outlook was not that different from such apparently more conciliatory predecessors as Jimmy Thomas. These men were above all pragmatic masters of the technical detail and group psychology of collective bargaining, and they took far more satisfaction from achieving favourable settlements than from engaging in dramatic industrial action: as Gormley commented himself in a sort of personal epitaph, 'negotiating has been my life'.[7]

CONFRONTATION OVER COAL

While the diversification of modern metalworking offered new opportunities to those assembly workers who were prepared to move between cities and sectors in search of employment, Britain's loss of its overseas markets for such staple goods as coal, cotton and steel confronted the process workers with a long-term decline in their prospects from the early 1920s. As they also frequently lived in smaller, single-industry towns, this had a traumatic effect on ways of life which in some areas had only recently become reasonably settled. Many of them experienced industrial conflicts in the years immediately after the First World War as opportunities for idyllic escape from the routine grind, but these temporary shut-downs can now be seen as prophetic anticipations of permanent closures and the ultimate disappearance of their communities. Thus while there were around 1,200,000 coal miners in 1920, this was already down to 700,000 in 1945, and it fell by half again to 300,000 in 1970: as a result the membership of the miners was cut in three over the period as a whole, from around 900,000 in 1920 to only 300,000 in 1970. Similarly, while there were around 750,000 railway workers in 1920 and this was maintained reasonably well at 600,000 in 1945, the numbers employed then began a rapid decline to only 250,000 in 1970: the membership of the railwaymen over the period as a whole was therefore cut by more than half from around 450,000 in 1920 to 200,000 in 1970. Again, in cotton there were around 600,000 workers in 1920, this had already fallen to a third of that number at 200,000 in 1945 and it fell by half again to only 100,000 in 1970: as a result the spinners, who had begun the period with around 50,000 members, had virtually disappeared by 1970 with only 1,000 remaining. The one exception was in the case of iron and steel for, although suffering just as severely from the inter-war depression, this sector's structural collapse was postponed until after 1980: over the period as a whole employment tended to fluctuate between 250,000 and 300,000 and, aided by the prosperity of the long boom after the Second World War, the main steelworkers' union grew from around 50,000 members in 1920 to around 100,000 in 1970.

The common experience of most of the staple export sectors led to growing bonds of sympathy between their workforces and, when this resulted in coordinated industrial action, it posed a significant threat to the running of the whole economy and looked rather like the 'class struggle' long anticipated by the political left. Thus paradoxically a powerful image of the 'traditional working class', predominantly male, manual and prone to mass strikes, became entrenched in public consciousness just when the groups which made it up were beginning a long process of decline. Moreover, because of the particularly turbulent nature of events in coal just after the First World War, it was the miners who became the central figures in this twentieth-century industrial and political drama. For collective bargaining took a more peaceful course in the other process industries, largely because their decline was less sudden and their employers could afford to be more reasonable in their demands for post-war wage reductions.

The railways began to encounter their first significant competition as inner-city tramways were supplemented by more flexible motor-bus services able to penetrate suburban and rural areas. However, at first the impact was largely restricted to local passenger routes: the steam engine still retained its dominance on long-distance passenger and freight routes, while further innovation intensified its appeal to machine enthusiasts. A favourable settlement achieved by the railwaymen under the adroit leadership of Jimmy Thomas in 1920 was shored up by the Railway Act of 1921, which gave statutory backing to continued national negotiations and standard rates of pay. As a result, the long inter-war depression did little to damage the union and produced only relatively minor wage reductions. An employers' demand for a general pay cut in 1925 was eventually restricted to new entrants, renewed demands in 1927 and 1930 resulted in compromise cuts of around 2.5 per cent for all employees from directors downwards, and a further demand in 1932 was dropped in the face of a national strike threat. Higher wages were then gradually restored through concessions to a series of union counter-claims beginning in 1934. In effect, having been forced by the government into recognizing trade unionism, the railway companies found little difficulty in establishing a new form of cooperation around a joint commitment to providing a safe and reliable service.

Cotton began to encounter serious overseas rivalry in the inter-war years as nations in the Far East asserted their independence, with India erecting protective barriers against British textiles and Japan setting up a competitive export industry. However, since the loss of foreign markets was initially restricted to the coarser branches of the trade, there was little sense of crisis and reasonably amicable negotiations between employers and unions produced reductions in post-war wage rates broadly paralleling the fall in the cost of living. The worsening of the depression in 1929 did lead to more friction as the employers' demands for reductions bit deeper, but by this time the spinners' financial reserves were being weakened by the heavy burden of unemployment benefits. As a result they were only reluctantly drawn into a national dispute by the less well-paid weavers, they went for a marginally unfavourable arbitration after only three weeks, and they accepted a further negotiated reduction in 1932. Meanwhile, the spinners' traditional businesslike approach led them to prefer immediate schemes for the contraction of the industry rather than the long-term goal of nationalization. They supported the Lancashire Cotton Corporation's use of bank finance to scrap excess machinery, they drew up their own proposals for a Cotton Control Board to enforce output quotas, and they joined the employers in sponsoring a 1939 Cotton Industry Bill to coordinate further reductions in capacity.

In the case of steel, prices began to fall drastically from the early 1920s as a result of renewed competition from larger, more integrated and better-equipped firms in the advanced economies of Germany and the United States. The Iron and Steel Trades Confederation, an all-grades union formed by amalgamation in 1917, found that its least well-paid members were suffering particularly severely from the automatic reductions in wage rates which followed as a result of the industry's traditional sliding-scale arrangements. In a series of complex negotiations which went on until 1929, this sector's reputation for cooperation was confirmed both by the absence of any strike threats and by the resolution of the problem through the higher grades' unusual acceptance of reductions of 10–30 per cent in return for much-needed increases for their lower-paid colleagues. The sliding scale then continued to operate peacefully, with the iron and steel trades experiencing particular benefits from the re-armament boom beginning in the early 1930s.

In the coal industry, however, disputes over inter-war wage reductions took a much more dramatic course, involving not only national miners' strikes but also an unprecedented degree of solidarity on the part of other major unions. Indeed a similar pattern was to be repeated in 1920–21 and 1925–6: at first the support of the other unions seemed to produce favourable state intervention, but then a shift in government attitudes towards determined resistance led to the withdrawal of that support, leaving the miners isolated and vulnerable to crushing defeats.

Under the leadership of Robert Smillie of the miners a 'Triple Alliance' had already been set up in June 1914 to promote solidarity between his own union, the railwaymen and the dockers in the event of any one of them being involved in a dispute. The aim was not so much to increase the effectiveness of strikes but rather to make disruption in any one of these key sectors less likely by using the threat of combined action to press for government intervention. Moreover, as each union retained its right to act independently and had no formal obligation to come to the aid of the others, the alliance was little more than a significant but rather loose statement of intent. Then in the aftermath of the war there was another move towards an even more ambitious form of coordination, this time through the influence of the transport workers (formerly the dockers) on the re-organization of the TUC. Initiated by Harry Gosling, fleshed out in more detail by G. D. H. Cole and officially adopted in 1920, this scheme replaced the old Parliamentary Committee with an enlarged General Council made up of thirty-two members, both more representative of and more knowledgeable about the whole range of occupations. The change of title also signalled a shift in focus from parliamentary to industrial matters, which made sense following Labour's emergence as an independent political party. In principle the TUC now had a greater capacity to coordinate joint industrial action but, like the 'Triple Alliance', its original aim was to reduce the likelihood of stoppages in key sectors by demonstrating the potential for wider solidarity, and there was no formal infringement on the autonomy of the member unions.

In the autumn of 1920 the 'Triple Alliance' became something more than a vague aspiration when the miners, still confidently making the most of the immediate post-war boom in export coal prices and rejecting Smillie's own preference for arbitration, decided to launch a strike in pursuit of further wage increases. Faced with the possibility of major disruption in coal and transport, and still exercising its wartime controls over prices and wages in the mines, Lloyd George's coalition government conceded the whole claim on a short-term basis. However, this apparent victory was in reality a significant turning-point towards the decline of the miners' position, for after two months wage levels were to be re-negotiated with the owners and were to be linked to export prices, thus displacing the union's wartime achieve-ments of government intervention and a link to the cost of living. Then, to the miners' dismay, when the reconstruction boom began to break in the winter of 1920–21, coal export prices fell by half and undermined their high wages on grounds to which they had themselves just agreed. Moreover, the government was now worried that its administration of the industry might soon involve large subsidies, so the decontrol of both the mines and the railways was brought forward by six months from the autumn to the spring of 1921. This sudden change of circumstances clearly implied a new confrontation with the owners, not only over wage levels themselves but also over the issue of distinct agreements for the domestic and export coalfields.

Indeed, at the very moment of decontrol on 31 March 1921 the employers presented demands for wage cuts of up to 50 per cent in the export districts and the next day a national strike was in full swing. The miners were prepared to accept some reductions but they mis-judged the attitude of the government, which was no longer mobilizing all of the nation's resources for war but rather running fast from the prospect of large peacetime subsidies. Once again the miners called on the 'Triple Alliance' for support, but their case was weaker than in the previous year, for the deepening depression was bringing about wage cuts throughout the whole economy, and their refusal to enter negoti-ations without a prior guarantee of a national settlement seemed excessively stubborn to other union leaders. When the support initially promised by the railwaymen and the transport workers was withdrawn by Jimmy Thomas in the course of confused discussions with the government on 15 April this became known as 'Black Friday'. While the presentation of this as a straightforward betrayal was too simplistic, it was not surprising considering how much the miners and their families suffered when their isolated struggle dragged on for another three months. By the end of June they were forced to give in and accept district settlements and substantial reductions, albeit phased in more gradually on the basis of a limited government subsidy and still protected by the pre-war minimum wage arrangements.

In 1923 and 1924 the British coal industry experienced a deceptive recovery as a result of the temporary disruption of German output by the French occupation of the Ruhr, and this was accompanied by small increases in wages. However, these soon proved more than usually temporary when the inevitable resumption of falling exports was aggravated by the over-valuation of the pound during the Conservative government's return to the gold standard at pre-war parity in 1925. The owners therefore began to press for further wage cuts of around 10 per cent along with an increase in the length of the working day back to eight hours. The miners, despite their already rapidly falling membership, were determined to resist and began to revive arguments about the need for a living wage and the country's duty to support its key workers. Persuaded of the justice of their case, the TUC General Council called on the railwaymen and the transport workers to place an embargo on the movement of coal stocks, which resulted in speedy intervention by the Prime Minister, Stanley Baldwin, on 'Red Friday', 31 July 1925. However, while Baldwin announced an interim subsidy to maintain the status quo and set up a further Royal Commission to make a comprehensive inquiry into the industry, this was only by way of preparing the ground for a more decisive confrontation. For the new inquiry, headed by the Liberal statesman Sir Herbert Samuel, included no trade-union representatives and, while it urged systematic amalgamation of small companies and opposed increases in working hours, served mainly to educate the public in the government's firm opposition to continued subsidies and its belief in the need for further wage cuts. Meanwhile, behind the scenes the Conservative administration was building up the resources of its regional emergency Supply and Transport Committees and welcoming the initiatives of the volunteer lorry drivers in the Organisation for the Maintenance of Supplies.

Thus when the mine owners announced further wage reductions of up to 25 per cent in the export districts the following spring and the miners decided on resistance under the slogan 'Not a penny off the pay, not a minute on the day', the government was prepared to sit out the General Council's coordination of solidarity action across most of the country's essential services in what became known as the 'General Strike' of 4 May 1926. Indeed the escalation of the dispute to this level, instead of focusing on another embargo on the transport of coal, weakened the TUC's position by turning an industrial issue into a constitutional confrontation and alienating much of the public. After just over a week the General Council, desperate to extract itself from an impossible situation, agreed that the Samuel Report could be taken as the basis for renewed negotiations over the coal industry, despite their knowledge that the miners were bound to disagree. Unfortunately, in its rush to call off the solidarity action on 12 May, the TUC did not insist on clear guidelines for the return to work and subsequent cases of victimization, especially among transport workers, made it seem like a humiliating surrender. Even more unfortunately, the miners' own struggle carried on for another six months, less because of the much-publicized outbursts of such far-left figures as A. J. Cook, the volatile national secretary from south Wales, than because of the extraordinary determination of the mining communities themselves, better represented by the more moderate Herbert Smith, the stubborn national president from Yorkshire. As one observer had commented at the end of the 1921 dispute:

Whatever is thoughtful and foresighted and faithful in the miners' movement cries out. 'We want education and art and culture and a finer way of living. We don't know very exactly what it's all like, and we suppose it's too late for us as individuals, and we all drink too much beer, and bet too much, and all that, but we want what we don't understand, and perhaps shouldn't recognize, for our children's children. And, meanwhile, if you lay a finger on that usual quarter of an hour Saturday that's always been customary at our pit, we stop the whole coalfield till we starve. For that we do understand.'[8]

However, such a desperate war of resistance was one which the miners were bound to lose in the end. Despite considerable welfare support for their families from sympathetic local authorities, there was spreading poverty and the threat of the serious under-nourishment of whole industrial districts during the approaching winter. A slow return to work began in September and in the middle of November the miners' national leaders advised their members to make their own district settlements, generally involving slightly smaller wage reductions in return for significant increases in the length of the working day.

In the end, then, the miners' stubborn defence of the wages and hours they had achieved at the end of a long period of prosperity only resulted in their loss of national negotiations, the exhaustion of their federation and a turn back towards the fragmented pattern of organiz-ation which had characterized the previous long depression of the 1870s to 1880s. In October 1926 the secretary of the Nottingham-shire miners, George Spencer, had already arranged for the majority of his members to withdraw from the national strike and accept a compromise settlement with the employers in this more prosperous domestic-oriented district. This then led to the establishment of a permanent employer-sponsored organization, with an impressive record on welfare issues and around 18,000 members, which spread into Derbyshire and, in the face of high unemployment and widespread victimization, found imitators in other coalfields including even south Wales. Meanwhile in Scotland a split was initiated by younger local activists on the far left, in the form of a rival executive in Lanarkshire and a breakaway union in Fife, which then amalgamated into the Communist-backed United Mineworkers of Scotland in 1929 with around 10,000 members.

When economic recovery began to bring its benefits to the miners, a good deal of energy therefore had to be devoted to resolving the frictions between these rival organizations in the regions. A recovery in the position of the south Wales miners began in 1934 under the leadership of James Griffiths from the traditionally more prosperous anthracite district, who brought in democratic reforms of the union's executive, launched a major recruitment campaign, and encouraged local actions against employer-sponsored unions, most notably a several-week-long 'stay-down' strike at Nine Mile Point colliery in October 1935. Having re-established the predominance of the South Wales Miners' Federation within the region and of pragmatic policies within the union, the Welsh miners then began to win modest increases in the wages which had been enforced in the 1920s, as a result partly of Ministry of Labour intervention and partly of the public reaction to an appalling disaster at Gresford in north Wales, where over 260 men had died in an explosion in September 1934. Meanwhile in Nottinghamshire, grievances at Harworth over wage deductions for dirt in the coal combined with growing hostility to the employer-sponsored union among emigrants from Durham to produce a six-month-long local strike. Spencer himself offered to support reunification on condition that he was guaranteed an official post in the new body, but the employers stubbornly refused to recognize the Miners' Federation. The only option left was the threat of a national strike in May 1937, which produced the desired government intervention to push the employers into accepting the reunification of the Nottinghamshire organizations under Spencer's presidency, though not surprisingly leaving unresolved tensions within the union at both the county and the national levels.

Once again, then, what might look from the outside like the natural solidarity of the miners had to be consciously created, and it was based not only on the painstaking reconstruction of local organizations but also on the continuous cultivation of local identities. Although most of the cultural leaders still tended to come from Methodist backgrounds, the centre of their activities was shifting from the chapels themselves to the local working-men's clubs, which had begun to spread when the impulses of the more liberal employers had been made a general requirement under the welfare provisions of the 1920 Mining Industry Act. As well as laying on talks by visiting speakers these clubs provided a regular stream of newspapers and books alongside an ongoing experience of self-government, contributing towards a shift in the imagery and language of the banners of the miners' lodges. These now focused increasingly on secular forms of welfare provision, cooperative stores, aged miners' homes and the local welfare halls themselves, while in a long period of severe conflict over wage levels it is not surprising that references to 'brotherly love' should have been increasingly replaced by calls for unity among 'the workers of the world'. More systematic educational classes for the long-term unemployed also encouraged a rich vein of autobiographical and fictional writing, particularly in south Wales, where the publication of some outstanding work made a national and even international impact: especially B. L. Coombes's authentic memoir *These Poor Hands* (Left

Book Club, 1939) and the middle-class Richard Llewellyn's more sentimental novel *How Green Was My Valley* (1939), which was turned into a successful Hollywood film.

THE IMPACT OF NATIONALIZATION

By the end of the 1930s the chronic depression in the export markets for coal was compounded by the beginning of a decline in domestic demand. For up to 30 per cent less coal was needed in more energy-efficient processes, both where it was directly used in industrial production and where it was transformed into the intermediate resource of electricity, and alternative primary fuels were becoming more common, not only gas but above all oil. Moreover this period also saw the widespread introduction of more productive methods of extraction: by 1939 around 60 per cent of British coal was being cut and conveyed mechanically, with ominous long-term implications for the need for labour. Almost a third of the industry's workforce had been unemployed for many years and now looked redundant to its long-term needs, a problem which was particularly acute in the export districts of the west of Scotland, the north-east of England and south Wales. Schemes of company rationalization to reduce the industry's capacity had been discussed at length since the early 1920s, but it had become clear that left to themselves the owners were unlikely ever to undertake the private sacrifices required to achieve such a wider public benefit. In 1930 a Labour government therefore initiated intervention to protect British coal prices through the statutory requirement of district output quotas. Then in 1936 the Conservative-dominated National Government supplemented this with joint selling organizations, along with a further commitment to public ownership of the coal in the ground as the lever to bring about a major restructuring of its commercial extraction. However, the scale of the problem and the need to carry along the party's backbenchers and the business interests concerned delayed legislation until 1938, and the outbreak of war came before it was clear just how much compulsion over private property the Conservatives were prepared to sanction.

Since governments had become used to thinking about the problems of the coal industry in terms of over-capacity, an optimistic view was taken of its ability to respond to the demands of the Second World War and fewer controls were set up than in 1915. Not only the management of production but also prices and local allocations were left in the hands of the owners, with the state only exercising loose overall supervision of distribution. Too many young face-workers were then allowed to enlist and coal output began to fall to dangerously low levels: even the application of the Essential Work Order to the industry and appeals for men to return from the armed forces had little effect. Moreover, the bitter legacy of the inter-war defeats and mass unemployment made those left in the mines reluctant to maximize their effort, while the chronic lagging behind of their wages increased the likelihood of damaging local strikes. As a result, in the spring of 1942 the government took a decisive step towards direct intervention in the industry by establishing a Ministry of Fuel and Power, with a new scheme for the redistribution of profits between companies, regional controllers to oversee production methods and labour management, and the re-establishment of national wage bargaining, subject to arbitration by an independent tribunal under Lord Porter. However, despite these new measures, output continued to fall as the ministry's attempts to ensure the concentration of work on the most productive pits and the introduction of machinery from the USA were obstructed, both by the unwillingness of owners to write off existing assets, and by the unwillingness of workers to leave familiar areas or abandon customary practices as long as the mines remained in private hands. Moreover, although there were other significant improvements in pay, the Porter Award of increases in minimum wages in January 1944 led to a wave of local unrest over the maintenance of differentials which could only be settled by further government intervention, including an increase in coal prices.

The miners' lack of enthusiasm for war production and their willingness to pursue wage increases at the expense of higher prices may have been eroding some of their public support, but the government was finding the system of dual control increasingly unsatisfactory. By early 1945 there was a wide consensus among politicians, civil servants and many company managers that only a more whole-hearted scheme of public intervention could address the industry's chronic problems of fragmented ownership, under-investment and poor labour relations. Even authoritative business commentators began to reject the mine owners' counter-proposals, in the words of the *Economist*:

There would be no effective movement towards closer integration – for at this time of day it is simply impossible to believe that voluntary methods plus an appeal to the Coal Commission will achieve anything. There would be no drastic re-equipment – because the capital does not exist within the industry and cannot be raised on market terms. There would be no improvement in the labour position – because the men would regard the scheme as reactionary . . . the plain truth is that the industry is past self-help . . . neither the owners nor the miners can put the industry on its feet, neither separately nor together. The State, the Government, the public, will have to abandon the role of neutral umpire and evolve their own plan.[9]

Labour's landslide election victory in the summer of 1945 then merely guaranteed the rapid implementation of a policy which was no longer controversial. Despite the new government's historic links with the miners' union, the mine owners gave in to political reality and received independently assessed and reasonably generous financial compensation when their physical assets were transferred to the National Coal Board on 1 January 1947. Moreover, this new body was deliberately established as a public corporation serving the interests of the nation as a whole. Its labour relations were indeed to be worked out in close consultation with the unions, but its overall management was to be based on technical expertise, independent both of party politics and of sectional groups within the industry.

Given the central role it had played in the miners' demands for half a century, the final advent of public ownership was a surprisingly low-key affair: local celebrations were muted and the adversarial nature of industrial relations remained largely intact. During the war the strength of the miners had substantially recovered through the successful imposition of the closed shop, the re-establishment of national wage settlements and the virtual doubling of their members' earnings. Their leaders were determined to use nationalization to press for further improvements in wages and conditions, and even before the industry's assets had been transferred into public hands they were demanding a five-day week with no loss of pay. Meanwhile at the local level, many of the managers from the private companies remained in place and unofficial disputes over the fixing of rates for particular jobs were still endemic. However, once the National Coal Board was fully established there was a substantial improvement in labour relations. For an increasing sensitivity to the industry's problems led the miners to channel their regional and national grievances through official procedures and to moderate their demands to levels which could usually be conceded, while still maintaining the relatively high wages they had achieved during the Second World War. Although it was only to be expected that local unofficial strikes would increase in a period of virtually full employment, it was still possible to create a better atmosphere in the pits through extensive investment in the moderniz-ation of equipment and substantial advances over such traditional welfare issues as safety and compensation for injury, pit-head baths and pensions. Even when rationalization required closures to focus resources on the more productive inland seams, there was extensive consultation, government subsidy of generous redundancy payments and a real effort to secure alternative employment, either in other pits or in new industries stimulated by broader regional policies for the old exporting districts. It was a remarkable achievement that, in such a massive public enterprise with such an appalling legacy of industrial relations, there should have been no national strike for twenty-five years, accompanied by a downward trend in the loss of output due to disputes of all kinds.

There was a similar story on the railways, which had for many years had their charges and wages regulated by the state in the interests of consumers and workers, and had then suffered seriously from war damage, over-use and acute under-investment between 1939 and 1945. As a result their nationalization on 1 January 1948 was not particularly controversial, especially as it was part of the wholesale public ownership of land transport, with the aim of providing a coordinated modern infrastructure under another public corporation, the British Transport Commission. The railway workers, having been barely dented by the inter-war depression and then seen their earnings double during the Second World War, had higher expectations than the coal miners and consequently expressed more discontent over the limits of nationalization. They were less sympathetic to Labour calls for wage restraint, more resistant to the introduction of new work practices and more prone to threaten national strikes and operate local 'go-slows' in order to defend their position in the earnings league. However, they were also weakened by their continued division into the rival organizations of the railwaymen and the locomotive engineers, which made the coordination of national strike action virtually impossible. Then from the early 1950s railway freight traffic began a sudden and sustained decline as a result of the restructuring of the long post-war boom. For the rapid rise of motors involved not only a major relocation of manufacturing but also the emergence of a powerful new rival form of transport; the equally rapid decline of coal produced both a loss of traffic and an increase in railway fuel costs. These trends were strongly underwritten by a switch in Conservative government policy in the early 1960s towards a marked preference for road-building, and the publication in 1963 of the high-profile report by Dr Richard Beeching on *The Reshaping of British Railways* advocating the extensive closure of branch lines. Potential union opposition was simply bought off with major wage concessions, which had been a feature of Conservative policy since the middle of the 1950s, and, while subsequent Labour governments were able to introduce productivity considerations into bargaining, they also offered generous redundancy payments. Although arguably rather costly in financial terms, the overall result was still a remarkable achievement for such a strategic sector in such rapid decline: not only were there no industry-wide strikes, but the first quarter of a century of public ownership also saw significant increases in all physical measures of efficiency.

Cotton experienced a brief period of reprieve between 1939 and 1951, due to the disruption of its overseas competitors followed by the increased domestic demand of post-war reconstruction. However, its subsequent collapse was then even more rapid, as Third World producers not only recovered but even began to penetrate the British market for cheap textiles. While there was no sustained debate over public ownership of the industry, the state was heavily involved in its planned contraction along the lines of the inter-war interventions in coal and the railways. Thus the 1945 Labour government proposed the amalgamation of firms, with a quota system to ensure long runs of production and an improved wage structure to attract young workers.

However, its eventual legislation in 1948 had little impact, for, while it offered subsidies for re-equipment when accompanied by amalgamation, the employers were too preoccupied with reaping the short-term profits of the post-war boom. Under the pressure of growing import penetration, the subsequent Conservative government then proposed generous subsidies for the scrapping of equipment on condition that the employers set up their own redundancy scheme. Under the new economic circumstances, this legislation of 1959 proved to be much more decisive and indeed effectively signalled the end of the industry as many firms used the compensation to pull out altogether. Meanwhile, the war years had seen a recovery in the spinners' wages followed by further negotiated increases on an almost annual basis right up to 1957. They had been consulted as equal partners in the development of Labour's plans for the industry and, though marginal to the Conservatives' considerations, had continued in close agreement with the employers in pressing for restrictions on imports. Eventually the spinners felt they had no option but to accept the redundancy payments offered and peacefully accept the demise of their once great industry: consequently the union went into a rapid decline after 1960 and was formally disbanded in 1976.

The state had been involved in steel since the imposition of high tariffs against imports by the Conservative-dominated national government in 1932. As this protection had been conditional on the domestic firms re-organizing themselves, they had rather reluctantly set up the British Iron and Steel Federation, but only to fix prices for each major section. The industry's traditionally cooperative labour relations reduced the pressure for public ownership from the left, while its capacity to make profits as a supplier to the new assembly sectors increased the resistance to it from the right. Steel then produced the only serious controversy over the 1945 Labour government's industrial programme, with nationalization being delayed until 1951, immediately reversed by the incoming Conservative government the following year, and then reinstated by Labour almost as a point of principle in 1968. Thus for most of the long post-war boom the industry was unusual among the process sectors for being both relatively prosperous and still in private hands. As a result the average plant remained relatively small, there was only patchy investment and re-organization, and Labour's ambitious plans for modernization in the 1970s came too late to save the industry from terminal decline in the face of foreign competition, now especially from Japan. Equally, there was no progress towards a unified system of collective bargaining, leaving considerable room for final adjustments of production workers' rates at the plant and even departmental levels, as well as for friction between unions over the differentials of ancillary craftsmen and the recruitment of white-collar staff. However, expanding output and relaxed management attitudes towards manning continued to guarantee the employment and earnings of the core process workers and unusually peaceful industrial relations for such a strategic branch of manufacturing.

SENIORITY UNIONS AND THE CRISIS OF INDUSTRIAL RELATIONS

The nationalization of the process sectors, then, was a relatively uncontroversial response to the problems of inter-war under-investment compounded by wartime exhaustion, and it was generally accompanied by significantly improved industrial relations. However, with the benefit of hindsight some more unsettling features can be detected in the coal industry even in the heyday of public ownership. In the first place it was still a declining industry. The Second World War and the post-war reconstruction boom had led to a period of unusually buoyant domestic demand when the mines were under pressure to maximize output, but even in this period there were closures of uneconomic pits. Then, from the middle of the 1950s, long-term decline began to re-assert itself as coal was increasingly replaced by oil and then by natural gas, and the programme of closures inevitably accelerated. In the second place, despite their falling numbers, the miners' industrial power was growing. In part this was a result of the technical innovations which had been introduced into the industry since the 1930s, with mechanical cutting and conveying leading to the replacement of individual work sites with 'longwall' faces. These methods reduced the autonomy of the senior hewers, integrated them into larger skilled work teams, and focused each shift on either cutting, conveying or setting up a new face. Thus the whole underground workforce became increasingly aware of its interdependence, especially after the National Power Loading Agreement of 1966 absorbed the remaining piece-workers into day-wage arrangements with provisions for more equality between grades and districts. At the same time, the miners' union had consolidated its thirty-seven existing local organizations into a more coherent National Union of Mineworkers in January 1945. Though it still had twenty-one separate districts each with independent funds, the public ownership of the industry itself provided a centralized focus for bargaining and facilitated the union's long-term aim of harmonizing existing local settlements into a common national wages structure. Even some groups of specialized surface workers saw advantages in merging with the miners, for example the winding-enginemen in 1951 and the supervisory staff in 1970, while agreements were reached with the craft unions involved in the industry for the miners to represent their members in all collective bargaining matters.

When dramatic industrial unrest eventually broke out in coal mining in the 1970s it was widely blamed on political extremists, so, as with the assembly workers, a brief review of the longer history of the Communist Party's role in the industry will be necessary to demonstrate how inappropriate such allegations were. In the 1920s the employers' imposition of major wage reductions in the export-oriented coalfields had indeed created fertile soil for Communist agitation: it had been here that the attempt to build a revolutionary 'Minority Movement' had met with most success and, though contributing less to the actual course of events than its activists would have liked, it had undoubtedly heightened the melodramatic atmosphere of the period. However, following the shift in international policy towards the 'United Front' against fascism, Communists among the miners had been allowed to associate more closely with the official mainstream and had become militant but realistic builders of reunified organization. During the 1930s the charismatic Arthur Horner, a former Baptist preacher, had played a leading role in rebuilding the South Wales Miners' Federation and gone on to succeed James Griffiths as its president. The Scottish emigrant Mick Kane had been prominent during the Harworth dispute against company unionism in Notting-hamshire, and the separate United Mineworkers of Scotland had been dissolved against the wishes of the majority of its own members by the national leadership of the Communist Party. In some contrast to the burst of interest in the newer branches of engineering, there had been no noticeable increase in Communist Party recruitment in the coal industry. The high profile of some of its activists among the miners' regional and national officials was based solely on their reputations as effective trade unionists and was no indication of the political views of the mass of the union's members. As in the case of engineering, the Soviet Union's entry into the Second World War on the Allied side in 1941 had then turned these prominent Communists into enthusiastic proponents of increased output, considerably enhancing their post-war credibility as leaders keen to make a success out of the nationalization of the mines in cooperation with a Labour government. This was particularly marked in the case of the two national secretaries from south Wales, Arthur Horner himself, followed by Will Paynter, who between them ran the miners' union from 1946 to 1968: they were acutely aware of the contraction of the industry and were prepared to trade off smaller pay increases against the protection of jobs. There was some shift in emphasis under their Scottish successor Lawrence Daly, also a Communist until the disillusionments of 1956, but though he campaigned on a platform of assertiveness over wages, once in office he became significantly more concerned to maintain the integrity of the national organization. Moreover, even though another Scottish Communist, Michael McGahey, was elected as national vice-president in 1973, the union continued to balance its left-wing secretaries with a moderate majority on the national executive as well as a succession of presidents representing more moderate regions: Will Lawther from Durham, Ernest Jones from Yorkshire, Sidney Ford from the union's own staff and, during the turbulent 1970s, Joe Gormley from Lancashire.

In short, the dramatic industrial unrest in coal mining in the 1970s was the result of widespread economic grievances which could no longer be contained by either the moderate or the left-wing union leaders. For by the late 1960s wage increases in other industries along with general price inflation were contributing to a serious erosion of the miners' relative and real earnings. Not only was the union's leadership still mainly moderate, but most of its members were still reluctant to engage in all-out national action, so the first signs of unrest were at the local level. However, the uniform wage structure now restricted the scope for local bargaining and it soon became clear that significant increases for skilled underground workers in the better-paid districts could only come on the back of large increases for the lower paid across the whole country. In 1971 the miners therefore demanded general increases of around 40 per cent, but the Coal Board reckoned the industry's performance would only allow 6 per cent, even less than the rate of inflation. Following a leadership recommendation and majority approval in high turn-outs at pit-head ballots, the miners' first national strike in almost fifty years began in January 1972 and, in the traditional manner, once it was under way it was solidly supported by the whole workforce even though the union could not afford any strike pay. Despite attempts by a Conservative government to persuade the miners to accept improved offers, the strike dragged on for six weeks. Indeed, increasingly effective mass picketing and support from other unions prevented the movement of coal stocks and led to power cuts and closures in other industries, particularly steel and cotton. Moreover, the miners continued to receive widespread support from the general public, often in the very useful form of accommodation for pickets away from home.

This escalating crisis was brought to an end only by the appointment of a Court of Inquiry under Lord Wilberforce of the Court of Appeal. A remarkably speedy two-day hearing included evidence from experts called in by the miners: Hugh Clegg, Professor of Industrial Relations at Warwick University, argued for less restraint on public-sector bargaining in general, and Michael Meacher, MP for Oldham West, highlighted the problems of low pay in a wider context. Like Sankey just over fifty years previously, Wilberforce then not only endorsed the miners' case for a wage increase to be supported by state subsidies, but also gave a much-appreciated public acknowledgement of the exceptional conditions of their industry:

The large group of men underground but not at the face do work which is heavy, dirty, hot and frequently cramped. In this day and age when physical conditions in other jobs have improved greatly the relative discomforts of working below ground become greater. Other occupations have their dangers and their inconveniences, but we know of none in which there is such a combination of danger, health hazard, discomfort in working conditions, social inconvenience and community isolation. The men working on the face and associated with the face, who are in the key jobs winning coal, not only suffer the problems of other people below ground but they may need to work in dust masks and suffer considerable noise and are at maximum danger risk.[10]

This was clearly a major victory for the miners, especially as in addition to the basic pay claim a whole series of their other demands were also conceded, covering not only further detailed wage adjustments but also subsidized transport to work and more paid holidays.

However, when this settlement ran out in February 1973 the government was attempting to contain high levels of inflation through a statutory wage freeze, so the miners' position soon began to lag once again behind that of workers with less centralized and less visible bargaining arrangements. To restore the position they felt they had only recently been assured by the state, the miners formulated a new demand of around 30 per cent, to which the Coal Board responded with an offer of only 7 per cent, which it reckoned was the maximum legally permitted. The personal intervention of the Conservative Prime Minister, Edward Heath, only served to confuse the process of negotiation without producing any significant concessions, even though war in the Middle East and rapidly rising oil prices were increasing the strategic importance of coal. When the miners launched a systematic overtime ban in November to bring about a reduction in stocks, the government began to treat the dispute as a constitutional challenge which had to be resisted. Heath immediately declared a state of emergency, put industry throughout the country on a three-day week to preserve fuel in preparation for a long confrontation, and ignored a TUC offer to treat any wage increase in coal as a special case. Then, when the miners, again armed with a large ballot majority, announced the escalation of their action into another national strike in February 1974, the Conservatives responded with the highly unusual step of calling a general election over the issue of 'Who Governs Britain?' At this point the miners' president, Joe Gormley, wanted to postpone the strike until the outcome of the election was clear and, though the union insisted on continuing anyway, this industrial action was deliberately kept more low-key than that of two years before. The public responded with a small swing towards Labour which, as anticipated, brought the dispute to an end by permitting a large wage increase to restore the Wilberforce conditions, along with yet more improvements in paid holidays and retirement benefits. For the rest of the decade the miners' position was impregnable and they were able to gain regular wage increases of anything up to 30 per cent a year.

The most obvious immediate cause of the disruptions in coal mining in the 1970s was to be found in the Conservatives' unnecessarily confrontational approach. Thus their persistent, and surprisingly effective, tendency to blame left-wing extremists for the crisis in the country's industrial relations can be seen at least partly as an attempt to distract attention from the extent to which the responsibility really lay at their own door. The workers in coal were only trying to keep up with the wage gains made by those in cars and other assembly sectors, even if the nature of their industrial action was quite different. It was indeed the opposite, for the miners were employed in a declining sector in which districts which might have been able to afford increases for key workers were restrained by the rigidity of national bargaining, and the result was massive industry-wide strikes. Moreover, the miners had a much stronger sense of the past so their victories of the 1970s, achieved alone and in the face of government opposition, replaced the bitter memories of the 1920s with a euphoric sense of omnipotence, which in the end could really only lead to a tragic downfall.

14

Federal Organization among the General Workers

I tried to explain that the words 'free collective bargaining' did not of themselves get rid of inflation, put right thirty years of neglect of our manufacturing industries, or create a million jobs. What was wanted was not slogans but *real* wage increases, employment security, and greater influence in the running of their industries. In the light of subsequent events, including the 'winter of discontent', there is little satisfaction for me in the knowledge that I warned that a mad scramble for larger wage increases would only make our troubles ten times worse in the years to come. 'The benefits of North Sea oil and an improved balance of payments are on the horizon. If this Government fails you will hand these to the party of privilege. You will put back the mighty in their seats and kick the people of low degree in the teeth. That is the danger . . .'[1]

This was the recollection of his speech to the biennial conference of the transport workers in 1977 of their general secretary Jack Jones, as he stood up to the lay delegates' determination to break through a Labour government policy of a firm ceiling on wage increases. Jones himself had been one of the major architects of a TUC-Labour Party agreement known as the 'Social Contract', under which voluntary wage restraint had been traded for a package of economic and social reforms. However, he had also been warning the government for some time that it ought to be preparing for a return to free collective bargaining, and he was not surprised when his appeal failed to sway the local activists at the transport workers' conference. Thus Jones's difficult position at this crucial time illustrated the dilemma of trade unionism as it had developed among the general workers over the course of the twentieth century. As the leader of what was by then the largest union in the country, he was caught between his strong sense of the need to support a precarious Labour government and his clear awareness of the growing economic discontent among his members. The very diversity of their occupations and conditions of employment made the union's high profile in forming Labour policy an attractive focus around which to unite, but in a period of rapidly rising inflation this proved ultimately insufficient to distract them from the pursuit of their more immediate economic demands. It is also significant that even this late in the twentieth century, when faced with the need to appeal to his members at a moment of crisis, Jones should have laced his speech with the traditional language of nonconformity and popular radicalism. For, whether consciously or not, he echoed Mary's song of thanksgiving for her pregnancy at the beginning of St Luke's gospel, 'he hath put down the mighty from their seats, and exalted them of low degree', as well as the key phrase in Benjamin Disraeli's famous polemical novel *Sybil*, 'the Privileged and the People formed Two Nations'.[2]

Jack Jones has been born in Liverpool in 1913, the son of a docker and grandson of a boilermaker, so he had vivid childhood memories of a range of waterfront industries and a typically rough neighbour-hood of crude housing, heavy drinking, domestic violence and poor schooling. He had begun an engineering apprenticeship but, since the engineers did not have an active youth section, joined his father's organization, the Transport and General Workers' Union. His outlook was already being shaped by a long period of defeats and trade-union weakness: the depressing aftermath of the 'General Strike' in 1926, the major split in the Labour Party in 1931, the 'hunger marches' and personal unemployment following the closure of his own workplace. Through his father's influence he had eventually been able to get work again in the docks, where he experienced at first hand the particularly authoritarian attitudes of the transport workers' full-time officials. He soon became an active member of his branch and a local delegate on the union's national docks committee, an outspoken champion of improved safety and compensation for injury, and the founding editor of an unofficial news-sheet:

I began to question whether the members themselves were being encouraged to play a big enough part in the work of the union. Surely, I argued, the union shouldn't be seen as just another insurance company. There should be more meetings of members in addition to the so-called 'statutory' branch meetings held every three months. My efforts were opposed by officialdom ... To speak your mind in the union then was like walking on glass![3]

As an idealistic and energetic young man, he had also become heavily involved in the local Labour Party and in workers' education classes. Partly through these and partly through the international contacts made at work in the docks, he became increasingly concerned about the rise of fascism on the continent and was eventually accepted as a volunteer for the International Brigade in the war against Franco in Spain, where he was badly wounded during the Ebro offensive of 1938. By the time war against Hitler's Germany broke out the following year, Jones was back home as the transport workers' full-time district organizer for Coventry, where he experienced at first hand the heavy bombing of the city on 14 November 1940. Because he already saw the conflict as an extension of his Spanish experiences, he threw all his energy into building up the morale and organization of semi-skilled workers in the local engineering industry, with the dual aim of improving their conditions of work and contributing to the war effort. This was achieved by taking a leaf out of the craft unions' book and building organization from the ground up:

The early 1940s in the Coventry area saw a remarkable transformation in attitudes on the shop floor. At the start managements had done everything possible to prevent people from recruiting for the unions ... Step by step we inched forward until it became commonplace for shop stewards to be elected at shop-floor meetings, to hold committee meetings during working hours, and to report back, after meetings with management or the works committee, to members on the shop floor.[4]

By the time he began to rise within his union, Jack Jones therefore had two contrasting but equally intense industrial experiences: the problems of the casual system on the docks during the inter-war depression and the emergence of shop-floor bargaining in engineering during the Second World War. As the union's assistant secretary from 1963, and then general secretary from 1969, he was keenly aware of the need to keep in touch with the different situations of key groups of his members, travelling around the country, visiting workplaces, attending meetings of local lay officials and socializing in the evenings. Whereas the older generation of the union's officials tended to regard local unrest as the result of subversive political agitation, Jones was more sensitive to the range of real grievances involved. In 1967 for example, during a major dispute on the Liverpool docks:

Our officers were not talking to the unofficial strike committee, and although they had made various efforts to secure a resumption of work the men were out, solid. I caused some consternation by announcing that I would hold talks with the unofficial committee . . . I met them in a smoky meeting-room and invited them to put their cards on the table and tell me what they saw as the main problems. I took voluminous notes and promised to talk with the employers. The men on the committee, I was sure, realised that I was taking their case seriously and would do my damnedest to make progress.[5]

Despite this energetic approach to ordinary bargaining, Jones had also long held the view that the simple pursuit of high wage settlements was too narrow, and that more thought should be paid in trade-union circles to productivity bargaining and industrial democracy, as well as to life after work: shorter hours, paid holidays, proper redundancy arrangements and more generous pensions. His impatience to get things moving and his own need to be at the centre of events placed him on the left of the TUC and brought him into contact with equally powerful personalities on the left of the Labour party, with whom he did not always see eye to eye. For Labour politicians of all shades in this period saw public ownership in terms of centralized planning and wage restraint, whereas Jones saw it as an opportunity to experiment with new forms of industrial democracy. During discussions with Barbara Castle after her appointment as Minister of Transport in 1965, for example:

. . . Barbara thought my ideas 'way out', 'syndicalist' even 'anarchist'. I found her reaction incomprehensible, for I was simply urging that when she came to set up regional transport authorities, working people in the employment of the authority, such as busmen, should be appointed to serve on the board. She conceded that it would be useful to have people on the authorities with practical experience, but did not agree that they should *represent* the workers.

Neither did she agree that employees should serve on the authority in which they worked . . . In my many dealings with Barbara Castle I found her anxious to do things *for* the workers but not *with* them. Her outlook was not all that unusual in politicians of the Left.[6]

Naturally enough their disagreements came to a head over Castle's attempt, as Employment Secretary, to introduce statutory restrictions on industrial action. Having taken part in heading off both this and the similar challenge from Edward Heath's subsequent Conservative government, Jones began to establish better links with the politicians of Labour's centre and right and went on to play a leading role in rebuilding relations between the unions and the party in the run-up to the election of 1974. His constructive attitude towards governing partnerships with Harold Wilson and James Callaghan during their periods in office then allowed him to play a high-profile role in a major public inquiry into employee representation on the boards of large companies.

To Jack Jones the red thread running throughout his life was clearly the struggle for democracy, first of all in his own union, then in the affairs of the workplace more generally. His sense of the importance of this activity was strongly reinforced by the enormous size of the transport workers, both as an industrial organization and in terms of their block votes at the TUC and the Labour Party conference. Confident that he represented his members' views, Jones was not averse to throwing his weight around and this gave him a significant role in national politics which could be both obstructive, as in the case of trade-union legislation, and constructive, as in the case of the 'Social Contract'. However, as was seen in the opening account of the union's 1977 conference, democracy could cut both ways, especially in a large federal organization embracing many diverse groups of workers. Behind their progressive adoption of democratic procedures and their impressive political influence, the history of the transport workers in the twentieth century was therefore rather more complex than might at first appear.

TENSIONS AMONG THE
TRANSPORT WORKERS

As in the case of the craftsmen, the years of optimism just after 1918 had seen a range of talks about amalgamation among the labourers' unions. By the end of 1920 Ernest Bevin had used his unique powers of persuasion to rally all the members of the Transport Workers' Federation, with the one exception of the seamen, into a single national organization of port and road transport workers. A few years later in 1924 the gasworkers also merged with a number of other general unions to form the National Union of General and Municipal Workers. Meanwhile, the agricultural labourers struggled to remain independent until the drastic decline in rural employment finally forced them to accept absorption into the transport workers in 1982. Indeed, as time went on, the growth of Bevin's transport workers began to outpace that of the municipal workers more and more significantly: 300,000 to 255,000 in 1924, but 1,200,000 to 800,000 by 1945, and 1,500,000 to 800,000 by 1970, making them by far the largest body of organized workers in the country. This was partly because the transport workers tended to be stronger in the Midlands and the south, and as their bases in traditional forms of transport were eroded they were able to penetrate such new growth sectors as the car industry. The municipal workers on the other hand tended to be stronger in Scotland and the north, and as they were faced with increasing competition from new public-sector unions there were few other opportunities for recruitment in these declining regions. Moreover, the faster growth of the transport workers soon became self-confirming, as they found it easier to persuade smaller unions of the advantages of merger into an apparently highly dynamic body.

However, in this type of organization large membership was not a direct indicator of the popularity of the national leadership or even of the effectiveness of local bargaining power. From their earliest years the general workers' unions had tended to be rather top-heavy, with full-time officials struggling to establish continuity among the casually employed, who for their part had only a sporadic interest in permanent organization while being prone to periodic outbursts of highly

335

ambitious demands. The formation of the two gigantic federations in the 1920s did help to stabilize long-term membership but did not remove the internal tensions, for their leaders were reluctant to use the full fighting force of their organizations to support specific sectional demands. Indeed in order to safeguard against this, their constitutions had been deliberately designed to place a clear distance between national policy and local interests. The transport workers functioned as a federation of trade groups, while the municipal workers functioned as a federation of regions, but in both cases the national executive retained control of finances and the power to authorize strikes within particular sections. Moreover, their general secretaries, rather than being subject to regular re-appointment, were elected for life, which gave them a good deal of leeway to pursue policies which might be unpopular with large sections of their members. And their other full-time officers, rather than being directly elected by the membership, were appointed by higher national or regional bodies, which gave them a good deal of room to impose compromise settlements at all levels of negotiation from the country as a whole down to the individual plant.

If this degree of top-down leadership was unusual among British trade unions, its origins were understandable: the insecurity and fear of those casual workers who had formed the original basis of the membership, underwritten by the difficulties the large federations had faced in the first years of their existence during the long inter-war depression. As Bevin himself commented during the founding conference of the transport workers:

I have never funked a fight, and I never will, but I do not want to be in a position to sacrifice the men or to victimize them before I am sure of their strength ... I have had Hell's own work to hold them together in an arbitration, to say nothing about a strike, on more than one occasion, and I know the difficulties that have to be overcome in building up these movements ... Friends, do not let us live in a fool's paradise. We have brought into the Union men and women, and we are proud of it, but they are not yet out of servility; confidence has not been established, and it has got to be established.[7]

The legacy of these difficult origins was thus to leave the federal unions poorly equipped for the long economic boom after 1945 when the confidence of many groups did finally begin to grow. The transport workers in particular, having adopted a trade-group structure, were to be plagued by constant running battles between their better-organized sections and their national leadership, which were only addressed by the rather belated increase in responsiveness to local activists during Jack Jones's period in office in the 1970s.

The dockers remained at the core of the transport workers' membership but their industry began a process of long-term decline in the years just after the First World War: the number of dockworkers fell from around 120,000 in 1920 to only 80,000 in 1945 and then even further to 60,000 in 1970. As in the other traditional export-oriented sectors, this was due first to the loss of Britain's dominant position in overseas markets for staple goods and second to the impact of innovations in technology. For the latter ensured that the further loss of business to a rival sector, in this case air transport, was compounded by the impact within the older sector itself of labour-saving devices, in this case cranes, fork-lift trucks and containers. However, in some contrast to the process workers, who were organized into more or less industrial unions, the dockworkers, subsumed within the massive federal body of the transport workers, found their local grievances increasingly hard to pursue within the recognized channels of collective bargaining. Whereas cotton, steel, the railways and, following nationalization, even coal experienced relatively peaceful industrial relations after 1945, under the impact of renewed full employment the docks became one of the most strike-prone sectors, with around half of the workforce involved in unofficial industrial action every year.

The seemingly endless series of proposals to reform the system of casual labour on the docks had continued to come to nothing in the years after the First World War, as both sides in the industry expected the other to cover the costs of rising unemployment. At the same time, both sides were agreed in continuing to resist state intervention, with the port employers fearing it would be biased in favour of the unions, while the transport workers were wary of being drawn into enforcing government schemes on their members. This indeed pointed to an increasingly significant stumbling block for, while Ernest Bevin remained committed to decasualization as the best way to secure more stable union membership and job monopolies, many of his members in the docks began to re-evaluate their situation during the 1920s and 1930s. First, they remained attached to their specialized manual abilities, for, though the demand for these was uneven, this in itself gave them their traditional freedom to alternate periods of work and leisure, and even to move in and out of the industry. Second, they were finding that small improvements in their position were tending to consolidate this way of life. For the establishment of continuous trade-union organization was helping to increase their pay for short periods of intense effort, while the relaxation of unemployment insurance regulations during the inter-war depression was allowing some of them to claim state benefits even when they were working up to three days a week. Finally, and perhaps most importantly, they began to realize that, in an industry undergoing long-term decline, reforming the system of casual employment was likely to imply a significant reduction in the size of the workforce through compulsory redundancy, and as increasing numbers of them were ageing this was widely felt as a source of serious concern. Thus many ordinary dockers were becoming more suspicious of decasualization. Even at its best it was likely to increase the time they would have to spend within the workplace without increasing their earnings, and at its worst it might put them out of a job altogether. As early as 1932 there was a breakaway on the Clyde to form a separate Scottish Transport and General Workers' Union in opposition to the centralization of power within the national body and its support for port registers as a way of bringing about decasualization, and there were signs of growing discontent over similar issues among the transport workers' local branches on the Mersey and the Thames.

The Second World War, like the First, put strains on the country's ports through the loss of labour to the armed forces and the redirection of sea-borne traffic, with the pressure on the western ports being even greater than before as a result of the combined impact of the German bombing of London and the running of the north Atlantic convoy system. This gave Bevin, now heading the Ministry of Labour, the opportunity to introduce his long-cherished programme of registration and maintenance, beginning with Glasgow and Liverpool in 1941, and extended throughout the rest of the country the following year under the control of a new National Dock Labour Corporation. The demands of the war effort ensured that this scheme would not only cover a broader range of workplaces than previously envisaged but also include a greater degree of discipline. Thus guaranteed wages were dependent on regular attendance, the acceptance and completion of suitable jobs, the working of overtime and, of course, the suspension of the right to strike. The larger port employers came to accept that something along these lines would be continued after 1945, given Britain's key position on the Atlantic seaboard during the post-war reconstruction of Europe, and focused their energies on influencing the level of the guaranteed wage and the independence of local port bodies. There was therefore no serious opposition to the Labour government's establishment of a permanent National Dock Labour Scheme in July 1947, which included equal representation for the transport workers on its national and local boards of management and disciplinary committees.

The union officials saw this as a victory for their long campaign for security of employment, a closed shop and minimum wages, along with an unprecedented degree of worker participation in management. However, their members, while appreciating that these were indeed real improvements, were also soon involved in daily battles against the equally real restraints involved. Since the post-war scheme did nothing to reduce the marked unevenness of well-paid work on the docks, high levels of absenteeism and refusal of allocated tasks remained endemic, with the result that up to 20 per cent of the workforce were soon appearing before the disciplinary committees every year. A rapid build-up of resentment over the one-sided impact of the ensuing penalties was inevitable, and a growing alienation of members from their own organization was only to be expected given the transport workers' joint responsibility for the administration of the disciplinary procedures. Moreover, the union's further aim of revising wage rates into a uniform national structure, along with the continuation of compulsory arbitration until 1951, threatened to weaken the dockworkers' highly localized bargaining power, which was at its most effective in short-term actions by small groups unloading urgent cargoes from specific ships. In the years after 1945 there was therefore a major wave of unofficial industrial action in the docks, much of it in protest over such disciplinary issues as the imposition of overtime, which might initially have applied to only a few men but frequently escalated into port-wide disputes, particularly in London. Indeed, as the immediate post-war pressures began to ease off, this local resistance was eventually successful in persuading the employers to give up using the disciplinary provisions of the scheme, on the grounds that they were counter-productive. However, by then divisions within transport workers had become entrenched because the union was also seen as increasingly ineffective in securing satisfactory wage increases for its members on the docks, which led to major unofficial strikes in 1945 and 1951, accompanied by the growth of a particularly powerful protest movement in Liverpool. As a result there was a degree of coordination of a national unofficial movement around the common demands of successive 'Dockers' Charters', and even the formation of breakaways in the northern ports to join the transport workers' old rival, the stevedores.

The press, politicians and the transport workers' own leaders jumped much too quickly to the conclusion that this high level of disruption had to be the result of political agitation, largely because the first wave in the late 1940s coincided with the height of the 'Cold War' against the Soviet Union. In this context the leading figures in the union tended to treat it very seriously because of the strategic position of the ports for the Labour government's export drive, and also very personally because Ernest Bevin was by then at the head of the Foreign Office: Communist Party members were banned from holding office among the transport workers in 1949. These assumptions about subversion had become so deeply entrenched in the public mind that they re-emerged twenty years later when another Labour government was facing a major wave of unofficial strikes over a further programme of decasualization, even though by then changed political circumstances allowed the transport workers' leaders to deny that their members' local actions were politically motivated and to lift the restrictions on office-holding. There were indeed some Communist Party members among the leaders of the unofficial protests over disciplinary and manning issues in London, with Jack Dash becoming particularly prominent in the 1950s and 1960s. But even here their influence was largely limited to the Royal Docks, while in the northern ports their comrades were regarded with suspicion and even hostility because the Communist Party tended to stick fairly close to the union mainstream and opposed large unofficial wage strikes. This gave rise to an unusual opportunity for a few Trotskyist activists, particularly in encouraging the stevedores' competition over recruitment and recognition, but their success was rooted in the widespread membership hostility to the transport workers' policies rather than in any particular political appeal.

The genuine organizational tensions on the union side were eventually resolved during a process of industrial modernization which began to accelerate in the 1960s, and promised to replace dockworkers' wide range of specialized manual abilities with standardized machine-handling of pre-packed containers in a smaller number of larger firms. As this would also involve further reductions in the size of the workforce and a shift towards harbours outside the Dock Labour Scheme, such as Felixstowe and Dover, widespread resistance was only to be expected. One of the first acts of the Labour government of 1964, keen to boost the economy through export-led growth, was therefore to appoint a committee of inquiry into port transport under the High Court judge Lord Devlin. Although his recommendations the following year had little to add to the long-familiar case for reducing the number of firms and increasing the size of the permanently employed labour force, these now seemed more appropriate to the processes already under way in the industry and they became the focus for the final ending of the casual system through port-by-port negotiations. At first this only exacerbated the problem of unofficial action, as London and Liverpool dockers resisted changes in established manning practices, but substantial government subsidies were quickly made available to fund generous redundancy payments. Moreover, the transport workers gave their assistant secretary Jack Jones a special brief to tackle their chronic problems of organization in the docks. He then used this opportunity to recognize the role of the unofficial movement, to establish a system of locally elected shop-stewards, to succeed in recruiting members in the non-scheme ports, and even to reach more amicable arrangements with the stevedores, who were eventually fully absorbed in 1982. This improved coordination on the union side permitted the disciplined conduct of two major official strikes in 1970 and 1972 to secure an increase in the national time rate and to retain control over the handling of containers around the ports, which resulted in substantial increases not only in wages but also in labour productivity. Indeed, the legitimacy of the transport workers had been so restored that they were able to persuade the Labour government to support a special Dock Work Regulation Bill in 1976, aiming to preserve container work for registered dockers.

Part of the reason the docks as well as the railways began to decline from the 1920s was because new motorized vehicles were taking their place for road passenger transport and road haulage. Something of the expansion in the workforce involved in this can be gauged by the increase in the membership of the relevant trade groups within the transport workers' union. That for passenger transport already had over 150,000 members in the 1930s and was still stable at this level in the 1970s, while that for haulage rose from around 40,000 in 1922 to 140,000 by 1945, and then to 190,000 by 1970. However, although these numbers were impressive their bargaining impact was weak, as the employees involved spent most of their time working in isolation and were also relatively easy to replace.

In road passenger transport the impact of collective organization was further reduced by the wide variety of alternatives available to the public in cases of industrial action: trams, buses, trolleybuses and eventually privately owned cars. However, in the capital the main employers', and later London Transport's, willingness to recognize trade unionism and accept a virtual closed shop among the busworkers provided a degree of protection for a lively left-wing leadership from the time of the First World War onwards. Indeed, the unusual strength of this group was recognized during the formation of the transport workers by the establishment of a London Central Bus Committee bypassing the union's national passenger transport trade group. Periodically, the solidarity and independence of the 25,000 workers in the capital's garages could overcome the intrinsic weakness of their position and force the union's national leadership to press for improved settlements and even, somewhat reluctantly, sanction successful district strikes over shorter hours in 1937 and higher wages in 1958. This relationship was constantly plagued by moves towards breakaway organization, but once again the Communists involved played a largely stabilizing role from the early 1930s, consistently arguing for a loyal opposition within the transport workers' union: their reward was the election of their leading figure, Bert Papworth, to the union's national executive as early as 1933 and to the TUC General Council in 1944. The imposition of the Cold-War ban on Communists holding office within the union in 1949 was therefore particularly counter-productive in this case and proved to be unenforceable, though the problem was eventually resolved by the declining appeal of Communism after the shocks of 1956. Moreover, in the longer run the capital's busworkers as a whole were experiencing a marked erosion of their special position. For, as individual car ownership began to reduce the demand for public transport, declining employment was accelerated by the spread of one-man bus operation, and traditional networks of solidarity were threatened by the increasing employment of women and immigrant workers. Up to the middle of the 1960s the London busworkers were still able to organize effective political lobbying and overtime bans to win improved wages and hours, but thereafter were notably absent from the rising wave of industrial unrest.

Meanwhile, the road haulage industry was plagued by small firms, the prevalence of casual labour, and the tendency for the men to spend increasing amounts of time on their own and far away from their home bases. Despite the merger of a number of smaller bodies into the road transport commercial trade group of the transport workers, organization remained ineffective throughout most of the period. In 1938 it was the larger employers, keen to exclude the worst cases of exploitation from the fringes of the industry, who persuaded the National Government to supplement the existing company licensing scheme with a statutory minimum wage overseen by a special joint board, and this proved reasonably resilient even under the pressures of the Second World War. The tendency of the transport workers' leadership to see such legislative intervention as a necessary basis for trade unionism was then reinforced by the brief nationalization of the industry under a new Road Haulage Executive as part of Labour's general transport strategy between 1947 and 1953. However, no real progress was made either by the employers or by the state towards establishing collective bargaining over substantive issues, the union itself remained rather passive over recruitment, and the real dynamic of organization was shaped from below. First by groups with some traditional independence, such as the drivers at London's Smithfield meat market, who mounted effective unofficial strikes in 1947, 1950 and 1958, then, as the demand for labour increased even more rapidly in the 1960s, by the drivers in new branches such as oil contracting, and in particularly buoyant districts such as Birmingham. It was this spread of unofficial action which pushed the employers into forming effective district organizations of their own and seeking out counterparts for disciplined bargaining in the local branch officials of the transport workers. By the 1970s they in turn were therefore able not only to support their members' demands for better pay but also to press increasingly successfully for comprehensive district and company settlements including sickness and pension schemes.

The transport workers were also faced with tensions due to the increasing employment from the late 1940s of black immigrants from the West Indies and the Asian subcontinent, particularly in road passenger transport but also in important areas of semi-skilled manufacturing. The general line of the unions, while rather ambiguous about how many more immigrants should be allowed into the country, was always strongly in favour of equal rights for everyone already working in Britain. However, some local groups of white workers still displayed significant degrees of hostility, usually as a result of basic economic concerns about the lowering of wages or the loss of jobs. From the first decades of the twentieth century the seamen had campaigned with some success against the employment of cheaper Asian labour in the British merchant marine, and from the 1950s similar attitudes were becoming evident among London transport workers. In other cases, these motivations could be intensified by the clearly visible differences in colour and culture, particularly in the west Midlands, where busworkers were able to insist on more or less formal controls over the number of black workers employed.

The leadership of the transport workers attempted to set a good example at the national level, with their general secretary, Frank Cousins, taking up the first chairmanship of the Community Relations Commission set up under the Race Relations Act of 1968. However, since ethnic minorities remained seriously under-represented among the union's own branch and full-time officials, it is not surprising to find a number of cases indicating persistent reluctance to recruit black workers and support their industrial disputes. Most notoriously, at Imperial Typewriters in Leicester in 1974 there was an unsuccessful ten-week strike by Asian workers. Many of them were women from east African backgrounds, and during the dispute the original issue of reductions in bonus payments rapidly became compounded by complaints over the lack of effective trade-union representation. For not only did the transport workers refuse to give official recognition and strike pay, their local negotiator remained wilfully deaf to his own black members' views:

The workers have not followed the proper disputes procedure. They have no legitimate grievances and it's difficult to know what they want. I think there are racial tensions, but they are not between the whites and coloureds. The tensions are between those Asians from the sub-continent and those from Africa. This is not an isolated incident, these things will continue for many years to come. But in a civilized society, the majority view will prevail. Some people must learn how things are done.[8]

If this sort of remark caused less alarm in the union than might have been expected, it was because the case of ethnic minorities was only one among many. The transport workers had put a good deal of energy into resolving the tensions between local activists and full-time officials in the car industry and the docks, but those among the London busmen had only died down because of changes in the labour market, and there was still something of a dual organization among the road haulage workers. Indeed that could be said of the union as a whole even after Jack Jones's moves towards reform: the role of shop-stewards was given considerably more recognition and full-time officers were increasingly appointed from among them, but the centralized consti-tution remained unchanged. Thus the welding together of the different levels of the organization, and the different occupations and regions within it, still depended above all on the qualities of leadership pro-vided by the general secretary, and personalities such as Bevin and Jones were rare. This was not a stable basis for the country's largest trade union.

WHITE-COLLAR AND
PUBLIC-SECTOR WORKERS

Although their levels of recruitment tended to be significantly lower, white-collar workers had a history of organization almost as long as that of the general manual workers. Indeed their first bodies had emerged as early as the end of the long phase of union growth between the 1850s and the 1870s, at the same time as the major burst of organization among the London casual labourers. Initially the most significant in terms of size had been the National Union of Elementary Teachers, representing a profession already faced with pressure to raise standards while salaries were falling, and further stimulated into action by the intense public debate surrounding the 1870 Education Act. The subsequent expansion of elementary schooling had then led to a long-term increase in the literate and numerate population, permitting a major expansion of white-collar employment in the late nineteenth century. Though non-manual work was initially seen as more desirable and higher in status, larger offices and increasingly impersonal supervision were soon undermining the ambition of the young men attracted into it, leading to the emergence of trade unionism in the biggest organizations, most notably the Post Office. With the recovery from the intervening long depression, the 1890s had then seen a significant burst of organization among white-collar occupations paralleling that among the gasworkers and the dockers: among the many new non-manual unions founded were the National Union of Clerks (1890) and the National Amalgamated Union of Shop Assistants (1891). These bodies had continued to expand even in the early 1900s when union growth as a whole was levelling off, and then shared in the more rapid growth of the years after 1910, but in 1920 they still had only around 750,000 members out of a total white-collar workforce of around 4,000,000.

Organization was strongest in the standardized, hierarchical offices of the public sector, where there was also either only one employer, as in central government departments, or a group of employers susceptible to pressure for common wages and conditions, as in local government offices. The Civil Service Clerical Association, formed in 1920 through the amalgamation of a number of earlier bodies, saw itself as a full-blown trade union and, though hindered between 1927 and 1945 by prohibitive legislation, had every intention of being affiliated to the TUC and pursuing its members' interests in an assertive manner. On the other hand, the National Association of Local Government Officers had been established as an amalgamation of provincial friendly societies in 1905 and, though increasingly involved in collective bargaining after 1918, remained divided over affiliation to the TUC and felt inhibited from taking industrial action by its sense of responsibility to the public. Organization was also relatively strong in transport and finance, where waves of recruitment followed major company mergers and the subsequent creation of much larger offices in which there was less contact with management. The Railway Clerks' Association (1897) saw itself as a full-blown trade union, affiliated to the TUC almost from the outset, and was increasingly able after the First World War to use strike threats to secure major concessions from the employers, including recognition and a favourable national wage scale. On the other hand, the Bank Officers' Guild (1918) steered a more cautious line, playing down the possibility of industrial action because it was faced with serious competition from company-sponsored staff associations, but still deciding to affiliate to the TUC in 1940. Meanwhile, organization in the generally smaller offices throughout industry and commerce remained very weak, amounting only to isolated pockets of association dependent on contact with sympathetic employers: some of the London newspaper printing firms, paternalistic Quakers in the cocoa trades, and committed activists in the offices of trade unions, friendly societies and cooperatives. However, the National Union of Clerks, as its title declared, always considered itself as a full-blown trade union affiliated to the TUC, and was prepared to pursue its members' interests both through industrial action against the employers and through vigorous competition for members with other unions.

Non-manual employment and self-organization proved relatively resilient during the inter-war depression. As the additional stimulus of supportive government wartime labour policy was maintained in the public sector and the newly nationalized industries after 1945, more white-collar organizations were able to secure employer recognition and most of them continued to move in the direction of mainstream trade unionism. However, in the first two decades after the Second World War their membership still only just kept pace with the rate of growth in employment: rising from 2,000,000 to 2,500,000 members and barely maintaining a 30 per cent recruitment rate. The late 1960s then saw a major burst of organization among white-collar workers, as for the first time their bodies were able to recruit more quickly than the growth of their occupations, and they consequently began to make up an ever-increasing proportion of the country's trade unionists. Even among office workers in industry and commerce recruitment increased from around 15 per cent at the end of the 1960s to 45 per cent by the end of the 1970s, and the growth among the already better-organized public-sector workers was even more impressive, soon reaching over 80 per cent coverage.

It was also clear that those white-collar bodies which were growing most rapidly were those which were adopting the federal ambitions of the large general manual workers' unions and pursuing expansionist membership drives and amalgamations. Thus the significantly renamed National and Local Government Officers' Association not only continued to recruit throughout the whole of the public sector except for the civil service, but also followed its core occupations into all of the nationalized public utilities except the railways: with over 700,000 members by 1979, it had become the fourth largest union in the country. Similarly a number of existing technical associations joined together to form the Association of Scientific, Technical and Managerial Staffs in 1968, went on to seek out further mergers with bodies among insurance and medical staffs, and pursued a policy of vigorous recruitment in the engineering industry, reaching a membership of over 400,000 by 1979. Simultaneously there was even more explosive growth among the National Union of Public Employees, originally focused on local government domestic staff but expanding into the health service and also taking in some nurses and white-collar workers, and resulting in a membership of over 600,000 by 1979.

Perhaps, then, it is not surprising that in their internal arrangements these new white-collar bodies tended to mirror some of the shortcomings of the older manual federations. Their full-time officers were usually appointed rather than elected, and they usually saw their role as diffusing the benefits of national agreements from the top down. Meanwhile, their shop-stewards still tended to be weakly organized, and they were poorly integrated into the branch and district procedures. Inevitably particular occupations sometimes felt it was harder than it should have been to secure a sympathetic hearing at the higher levels of the unions. These organizations had originally been built on the vision and energy of outstanding individuals, most notably two Welshmen: Bryn Roberts at the National Union of Public Employees from the 1930s to the 1950s, and Clive Jenkins at the Association of Scientific, Technical and Managerial Staffs in the 1960s and 1970s. But as the new federations reached previously unimagined levels of recruitment they clearly needed more sophisticated arrangements to bridge the gap between their national leaders and the growing ambitions of many of their local members.

Moreover, although the emergence of larger white-collar unions did lead to some reduction in the number of organizations, it still left considerable room for competition and overlapping. Since both the transport workers and the municipal workers were also increasingly active in this field through their own white-collar sections, in local government in particular there could be up to seven major unions involved, leading to significant demarcation disputes and complex annual pay rounds. Two of the recommendations of the 1968 Donovan Report might have helped to simplify the situation. The official registration of company agreements might have encouraged cooperation between all the unions involved, and the establishment of a fund for loans and grants to aid amalgamation or membership transfers might have produced some structural re-organization. However, while both of these recommendations were adopted by the Labour government, the Conservative election victory in 1970 led to them being shelved.

Finally, since they represented direct employees of the state, the large public-sector unions were bound to pursue the strategy of trying to influence government policy in pursuit of their members' interests and for this reason they all affiliated to the TUC. However, the older manual unions were reluctant to give up any of their influence in that national forum. Supported by the custom that once elected to the General Council one remained there until the normal retirement age, until as late as 1982 they resisted the pressure from the white-collar unions that every organization with over 100,000 members should automatically be given a seat. Consequently, the interests of the growing numbers of members of these new bodies remained for a dangerously long time under-represented within the policy-making procedures of the TUC and the Labour Party.

Overall then, while the white-collar and public-sector unions were emerging as a major dynamic force in British trade unionism during the 1970s, their organization was still inadequate in a number of areas: internally in relation to their own members, externally in terms of competition between themselves, and more broadly as a result of their unsatisfactory position within the TUC. Moreover, although it was one of the major employers concerned, the only government contribution to the situation was a constant focus on maintaining incomes policies, most vigorously enforced in the public sector and bound to cause maximum dissatisfaction among those who had traditionally been poorly paid but were beginning to experience new levels of confidence.

This issue also increasingly involved a gender dimension, for, whereas in the nineteenth century women's paid work had generally taken the form of demanding manual jobs at widely dispersed sites particularly in domestic service, in the course of the twentieth century, fuelled in part by the rise of the welfare state, it shifted towards lighter white-collar jobs in larger, public workplaces. There were, for example, increasing opportunities for women as secretaries, typists, telephonists, nurses and teachers. Significant improvements in conditions and an increase in part-time work made permanent employment a more attractive option, while the lifting of marriage bars after the Second World War made it a feasible one. As a result, the number of women going out to work rose from around 3,000,000 in 1920 to 5,000,000 in 1945 and 9,000,000 by 1970, and the proportion of them who were married rose from around 10 per cent to around 50 per cent. Now that they were healthier, more concentrated and more likely to regard themselves as long-term employees, recruiting women into trade unions became easier and, as in the case of white-collar and public-sector unionism more generally, the main burst of activity began in the late 1960s. In 1945 there were around 1,600,000 female trade unionists, growing only gradually to 2,200,000 by 1965 but then rising more steeply to 3,900,000 by 1979. Thus, whereas in the first two decades after the war women's share of the country's trade unionists had remained constant at around 25 per cent, by 1979 it had risen to almost 40 per cent.

The organizations involved had all experienced campaigns for the recognition of women's right to equal pay, which were strongest where white-collar unions themselves were strongest, in the public sector. Having been undermined by the high levels of unemployment in the 1920s and 1930s, their revival during the Second World War still met with little success. For although a Royal Commission on Equal Pay was set up in 1944 and reported in 1946, it resisted strong pressure from the TUC, focused on pre-war examples, and emphasized the physical weakness of women and the traditional notion of the family wage. It therefore concluded that there was no justification for equal pay in the private sector or in manual work in the public sector, though conceding that it might be appropriate in teaching and the higher levels of the civil service. Moreover, the following year the Labour government announced that, while it did approve of equal pay in principle, its implementation anywhere in the public sector at that time would be inflationary. Eventually freed from this wage freeze by the election of a Conservative government in 1951, the civil servants, the local government officers and the teachers mounted coordinated campaigns which won firstly equal pay for teachers, spreading out at the local level from London in 1952, and then an important concession of the principle for the civil service in 1955, eventually extended to administrative grades throughout local government and the public sector.

Determined to follow in the wake of this breakthrough, the private-sector unions led by the shop workers brought about a shift in TUC policy in 1963, away from the pursuit of equal pay through collective bargaining towards a demand for legislative intervention by the next Labour government. However, little was achieved in practice until the summer of 1968, when a strike for recognition of their skilled status by female sewing-machinists at Ford's Dagenham works led to the sympathetic intervention of the Labour Employment Secretary, Barbara Castle, and inspired other women in the private sector to become more assertive. Under further pressure from the National Joint

Action Campaign Committee for Women's Equal Rights, which began to organize large demonstrations and encourage the recruitment of more women into individual unions, Castle then committed herself to the immediate introduction of legislation. However, the 1970 Equal Pay Act, by allowing a long run-in period of five years, gave employers plenty of time to re-organize the allocation and titles of jobs to make it difficult to claim that their female employees were carrying out equal work. As a result, while the most poorly paid women did experience a substantial catching up, the overall advance was limited: the average female weekly wage began to rise from its previous level of around 50 per cent of the male one but levelled off at around 60 per cent in the late 1970s.

Clearly, then, there were other major issues which remained to be tackled, above all equality of opportunity. The increase in women's determination to enter employment on a fairer basis and to secure improvements in their general rights as citizens was such that even Conservative governments had been forced to consider legislation. Some male trade unionists found this new attitude threatening, particularly in the Post Office, but in general the response of the national leaderships was to develop increasingly comprehensive and sophisticated equal opportunities policies and to broaden recruitment criteria so as to include more female members. Labour's Sex Discrimination Act of 1975 then required most jobs to be open to both men and women, and set up an Equal Opportunities Commission to deal with cases of complaint. However, it was still up to individuals to initiate their own cases and to provide proof of discrimination: only around 10 per cent of such attempts were successful, and even then the compensation awarded was minimal. Moreover, there was only a slow recognition of the conditions which would be required to allow women to take advantage of any improved opportunities. Thus, while union campaigns for paid maternity leave led to its inclusion in Labour's Employment Protection Act of 1975, the provision of affordable child-care facilities and equal access to training was still a long way off.

Trade-union pressure and Labour government responses had therefore led to a historic improvement in women's formal rights at work during the 1970s. However, the remaining major loopholes left it up to local groups and individuals to take action to secure more equal treatment in practice. Moreover, if the legislative recognition of their important economic contribution helped to boost women's assertiveness, it did nothing to ensure their integration into trade-union organization. As Mel Read of the Scientific, Technical and Managerial Staffs recalled:

Things did change in the 1970s and I think many trade unions, including my own, were acutely aware that they had fairly radical policies with regard to women but relatively few active women certainly at regional and national level . . . In 1974–5 the union set up its first ever Women's National Committee. There was a considerable battle about this but eventually it was established and I was its first chair. I held this office probably for eight or nine years and this saw a time when women's structures were established, sometimes at branch, more usually at divisional or regional level . . . All of this coincided with the growth of the women's movement generally and a much more vigorous agenda for and by women.[9]

Given that the union concerned was in the middle of a seven-fold increase in its female membership, something of the sort was indeed required. But by the end of the period the overall picture was still not a positive one: there were eleven significant trade unions each with a majority of female members, but overall only 15 per cent of their national executive members and only 7 per cent of their full-time officials were women. Even in the case of the shop workers, with their long experience in this field of recruitment and a female membership share of almost 60 per cent, only four out of 149 full-time officials were women. And in the case of the public employees, whose explosive growth saw their transformation into a union with a 65 per cent female membership, only two out of 120 full-time officials were women. No doubt this was as much a result of female unionists' own decisions to give priority to their family responsibilities as it was of male unionists' prejudices against them, but it was an organizational shortcoming in urgent need of attention.

THE FEDERAL UNIONS AND THE
CRISIS OF INDUSTRIAL RELATIONS

Paralleling the major burst of organization among white-collar and public-sector workers in the late 1960s, there was a general increase in assertive industrial action among their ranks. The technical and managerial staffs, for example, pursued a vigorous strategy from the outset, aiming for exemplary wage settlements in the larger private corporations as well as giving more emphasis to health and safety issues. Even the more moderate body which had evolved out of the National Union of Clerks, now known as the Association of Professional, Executive, Clerical, and Computer Staffs, was drawn into a high-profile dispute at a film-processing firm in the north London borough of Brent. Many of the workers concerned at Grunwick were Asian women from middle-class east African backgrounds, now casually employed, low-paid, and forced to work long hours to keep up with the good weather in the summer of 1976. A protest against unfair dismissal in one particular group escalated into a two-year-long strike for union recognition supported by the clerical staffs and the local trades council, and sustained by increasingly dramatic confrontations with an employer determined on a last-ditch resistance to collective bargaining:

... outside the factory gates of Willesden the High Road suddenly exploded into a blaze of colour. Down the road, banners flying, swept hundreds of demonstrators, led by Indian workers. In the vanguard, saris swirling, were the Indian women. Not submissive housebound women but Grunwick strikers – fists raised in anger. Not the inarticulate immigrant women we are often told about. Hardly. For at every building they passed, they shouted their one resounding slogan: 'Union! Union! We want union!'[10]

Even in the spring of the following year the employer, George Ward, was still refusing to accept a recommendation of the official conciliation service in favour of union recognition, despite its being upheld in the High Court. By June 1977 support from other unions and women's groups was leading to an escalation of mass picketing at Grunwick, while unusually heavy-handed policing was raising serious allegations of sexism and racism. To defuse the situation the Labour government set up a Court of Inquiry under Lord Justice Scarman, who produced a careful and balanced report once again in favour of union recognition as well as the reinstatement of the strikers. However, Ward, now supported by the leading far-right Conservative MP Sir Keith Joseph, simply ignored the Scarman Report and went on to get the High Court overruled by both the Appeal Court and the House of Lords.

The increasing assertiveness of previously under-confident groups had even more dramatic repercussions in the public sector. It led the local government officers to sanction industrial action for the first time in 1969, and to go on to demonstrate how easily they could create administrative chaos during local strikes in Leeds and the inner-London boroughs, and to win a 12.5 per cent national pay increase in 1970 by threatening to disrupt the running of that year's general election. While the post office workers were almost crippled by their defeat in a seven-week-long national strike over pay in 1971, they were still able to win major concessions through unofficial overtime bans in the London area later in the decade. Similarly, the civil servants' rebellion against pay restraint through sporadic strikes across the country in 1973 resulted in substantial pay increases. This pattern was also matched among the more manual public-sector unions led by the public employees. They first flexed their muscles successfully in 1970 through selective action by their dustmen members, who could cause considerable unpleasantness by leaving piles of uncollected refuse, and were consequently able to secure most of their wage demands in the face of government attempts at pay restraint.

This rising wave of membership ambition fulfilled mainly through local disruptions of public services then came to a head in a wave of action over wages early in 1979, soon to become notorious under the title of the 'Winter of Discontent'. The main dynamic came from those members of the public employees working in highly sensitive areas but still receiving low pay because so many of them were female or black, or both: nurses, hospital ancillary workers, ambulance personnel and gravediggers. Following the pattern of previous successes, the union's national leadership left the local branches to decide on which groups to involve and what action to take, and there was little or no attempt at coordination with the other unions involved in the workplaces affected. Indeed, there were serious frictions with the municipal workers and the Confederation of Health Service Employees, who both felt that the public employees were encouraging unrealistic expectations in the hope of poaching their members. As a result, the wave of industrial action launched on 22 January 1979 manifested all the familiar weaknesses of federal unionism: it was an upsurge of discontent from below, which swept along a reluctant and unprepared leadership, and it could only hope to succeed by appealing to a wider national sense of the unacceptability of poor wages and conditions. However, the workers concerned were portrayed by remarkably hostile and sensational media coverage as causing shocking harm to the very audiences whose support they so desperately needed. Short of a painful and futile confrontation with a Labour government, the public employees were therefore forced to accept an immediate 9 per cent increase and the submission of their broader case to a new Standing Pay Commission on Comparability which, even though chaired by a well-known friend of the unions, Professor Hugh Clegg, rejected most of their claims later in the year. Above all the commission rejected the union submission that the low pay of women in the public sector should be addressed by setting a minimum wage at two-thirds of the national male average, and instead made its main comparisons with the only slightly less poorly paid women in the private sector. In the end the public employees therefore had to settle for a fairly modest wage increase at the cost of a major undermining of their position in the eyes of the nation.

The media portrayal of some sort of acute crisis in late January 1979 was intensified by the coincidence of this fragmented industrial action in the public sector with the height of a more effective stoppage in the equally sensitive road haulage industry, which had threatening implications for essential supplies. As this too had traditionally been a dispersed, casual sector with weak trade unionism, both the employers and the government were slow to appreciate how much the organization and determination of its workforce had increased over the previous decade. In the autumn of 1978 they seriously underestimated the difficulties that would be involved in enforcing a stiff Labour 5 per cent pay norm, and a 20 per cent rise had to be awarded to the oil-tanker drivers to stave off industrial action and the disruption of fuel supplies in the middle of winter. The transport workers' national leadership, significantly weakened by the recent retirement of Jack Jones, tended to be rather indecisive, but its local organizers were confident of their ability to press their case and, through a series of unofficial delegate meetings, launched a national strike of the rest of the road haulage drivers on 2 January 1979. This received enthusiastic support throughout the well-organized districts, and included highly effective and largely peaceful picketing to close the country's ports as well as large food distribution centres which were attempting to make their own emergency arrangements. After this momentum had been sustained for a week, the union's national leadership was forced to give official endorsement to the local initiatives, though it never managed to regain control over the course of events. After another week, the government was forced to drop the application of its wage freeze to road haulage. And after a third week, even the employers' resistance crumbled on a district-by-district basis. The surprising effectiveness of the drivers' local organization thus ensured that they ended up with similar wage increases to those already achieved by the oil-tanker drivers. However, in the meantime, some individual firms had won court rulings to outlaw the picketing of distribution centres on the grounds that they were remote enough from the main dispute to be classified as 'secondary'. Moreover, increasingly hostile media coverage had followed the unsubstantiated claims of the far-right leader of the Conservative opposition, Margaret Thatcher, that these actions also involved widespread intimidation. Thus though most of the exaggerated press and television reports of early 1979 focused on the disruption of the public services, it was the lorry drivers' strike which provided the decisive focus for a rallying of those anti-union forces which had been becoming increasingly outspoken over the previous few years.

In retrospect, the controversial events of the late 1970s had many of the hallmarks, not of unions that were too strong, but rather of unions that were not strong enough to channel a rising tide of membership grievances. These sharp conflicts can thus be seen as the predictable long-term pay-back for employers who had determinedly resisted effective trade unionism among their workforces. The deeply misleading media coverage persuaded much of the public into taking the opposite point of view, causing not only panic among the middle classes but also divisions among the working classes, which were then exploited for political gain by Margaret Thatcher's forceful attack on the Labour government's ineffectiveness. This then laid the basis for the construction of a new alliance of those who were determined that the weakest members of society should be made to know and kept in their places.

15

Trade Unionists and Labour in Power

'Objectives for 1980: Reduction of inflation below 5 per cent and unemployment below 3 per cent; a manageable balance of payments; Devolution within the United Kingdom, and the country to play a leading role in European, Commonwealth and world affairs; to resume our social aims in housing, education, health and welfare to build a cohesive society; and to win the general election for Labour.' We had a few successes, there were some near misses and the rest were failures. The critics may be scornful but I would claim that although we were a Government without a majority, it was better for us to have some long-range objectives than to live from day to day.[1]

These were the recollections of James Callaghan of some of his thoughts soon after taking over as Prime Minister in the Labour government of 1976, and as such they reveal a good deal about the long-term attitudes and objectives of the party over the twentieth century as a whole. Naturally as professional politicians Labour leaders were keen to gain and retain power; however, given the origins of their party in extra-parliamentary social movements, they usually also retained a strong sense of using that power in order to achieve things on behalf of their supporters. This distinguished them not only from some of their parliamentary rivals but also from some of their extra-parliamentary critics, for the emphasis on practical achievement led them to tone down some of their earlier ambitions and to pursue instead a more limited list of aims within the existing political and social framework. As the century went on, an ever-higher priority was given to managing an economy which looked increasingly weak in comparison with its major competitors, for the Labour Party never really escaped from inherited assumptions about Britain's claim to a leading role in world affairs. At the same time there was still a commitment to a particular tradition of domestic reform, with an emphasis on improving the material well-being of ordinary people in order to create a society which would be not so much more equal as more inclusive. This adoption of a more pragmatic outlook was accompanied by a growing appreciation of the peculiarities of parliamentary procedures and, particularly in Callaghan's case, by a modest and good-natured assessment of the degree of success achieved. However, this immersion in the day-to-day details of the political system did not preclude a sense of underlying principles, even on the part of the most moderate Labour leaders. Thus in Callaghan's recollections his specific shopping list was preceded by more general reflections on his life-long commitments to increasing the equality of opportunity, 'that men and women may be enabled to lead the fullest possible lives', and to governing through discussion and understanding, 'to reconcile differences between groups, to persuade them that they are all part of the common weal which determines the quality of our society as a whole'.[2]

James Callaghan had been born in Portsmouth in 1912, his father having been a naval petty officer and then a coastguard, and the family fairly comfortably off until his early death as a consequence of military service in the First World War. Callaghan's by then twice-widowed mother found some consolation in the local Baptist chapel and Callaghan was given a very strict religious upbringing, as well as being pushed into educational achievement as the only route towards secure employment in the increasingly uncertain inter-war years: he had eventually passed the civil service examinations and begun work as an Inland Revenue clerk in Maidstone. Here he remained active in Baptist circles while simultaneously absorbing a good deal of socialist political literature, particularly the pluralist theory of Harold Laski, which gave him a lasting commitment to the idea of autonomous voluntary associations. It was this which inspired him to join the Labour Party and the small white-collar Association of Officers of Taxes, later merged into the Inland Revenue Staff Federation. As an early pioneer of white-collar unionism Callaghan had played a leading role in an unofficial movement for improved pay and promotion for the younger clerks, eventually resulting in his election at the age of only twenty-four to the post of the union's full-time national assistant secretary in 1936. In this role he quickly came to resent the Conservatives' restrictive legislation of 1927 prohibiting civil service bodies from affiliating to the TUC, and equally quickly picked up much of the art of bargaining, recalling that on one occasion:

We had a good case and it fell to me, as principal spokesman, to put it. I was eloquent and forceful, pressed it to the extreme, rebuffed the rather weak opposing arguments with ease and with scorn, and altogether gave what I thought was a brilliant display of fireworks. But pride goes before a fall and, at the end of the afternoon, despite the easy wicket I had been batting on, our team came away without having gained a single halfpenny. I was furious and could not understand what had gone wrong. But D. N. Kneath, one of the older and more silent members of the negotiating team from south Wales, knew. And the next day he told me. 'Remember, my boy, more flies are caught with honey than with vinegar.' And that has remained one of my negotiating maxims ever since.[3]

Following a rather uneventful period of war service in the navy, Callaghan, representing South Cardiff, had then joined the new influx of Labour MPs swept into Parliament by the party's landslide victory in 1945. This inevitably prevented him from resuming his full-time position with the Inland Revenue Staffs, but his responsibilities with them had already produced an unusual level of confidence and independence for a young back-bencher. Meanwhile, the location of his constituency was to bring him into close and sympathetic contact with the south Wales miners and dockers. Moreover, he was still able to use his trade-union skills directly when he served for a decade in political opposition as the principal pay negotiator for the Police Federation, with considerable success in winning concessions from their local authority employers.

All of these experiences naturally left their mark, and throughout the long and distinguished political career which followed Callaghan remained an archetypal product of the traditions of popular nonconformity and trade unionism. His tendency to stick to the party mainstream and keep his distance from factions may have helped to promote his own ambitions, but it was largely the product of his powerful sense of the importance of organizational loyalty. His toughness and skill in bargaining were fully revealed during his period as Foreign Secretary in the middle of the 1970s, particularly during his re-negotiation of the terms of Britain's membership of the European Economic Community. His high priority on education as a means of acquiring skills, opening up opportunities and developing citizenship was then given prominence when as Prime Minister he launched a 'Great Debate' on the nation's schools. Meanwhile, his commitment to local democracy had already been demonstrated when, as Home Secretary in the late 1960s, he had launched a programme of Community Development Projects:

... to encourage those who lived in the most poverty-stricken areas of inner cities to recognize that they themselves possessed the capacity to manage the affairs of their neighbourhoods, to reduce their reliance on outside help and, in the process, to achieve greater control over their own lives and more satisfaction from them. We laid down the basic condition that the schemes must involve the people directly concerned, by finding out their views of their needs, and not by imposing ours ... that officialdom did not know the answers and that we could find them out only with the active cooperation of the local people.[4]

Above all, his early background gave Callaghan a consistent sympathy with the point of view of trade unionists. For example, as Chancellor of the Exchequer in the middle of the 1960s he benefited from the restraining impact of statutory incomes policy on wages and prices, but deeply regretted that such coercion was necessary:

My own trade union experience had taught me that anomalies would be thrown up, and none of us could judge how far wage increases were only postponed, not forgone. I held strongly to the view that the country would get the best results when the unions themselves recognized the wisdom of voluntarily and freely linking their pay claims to increased productivity.[5]

The consistency of this attitude was more dramatically revealed a few years later, during the Labour government's attempt to introduce legal restrictions on industrial action, when, as Home Secretary, Callaghan emerged as the leading dissident within the cabinet. He was emphatic that collective agreements should be strictly observed, that arbitration should always be preferred to industrial action and that the unions should find ways to restrain unofficial strikes. But he was also outspoken in his objections to the Employment Secretary's proposals, on the grounds that legal intervention was unlikely to be effective and that rushing it through without giving the unions time to reform their own affairs would only serve to undermine the normally close relationship between the industrial and political wings of the Labour Party. Addressing the Nottinghamshire miners at the height of the crisis he remarked: 'I was told recently by someone skilled in public relations that it is unpopular to speak up for trade unionism in this country today. If that is true so much the worse for the future.'[6] His willingness to press this issue to the point of his own resignation initiated a major swing of opinion within the parliamentary party, and the Employment Secretary and Prime Minister were forced to back down.

Thus it was later no surprise that Callaghan's own period as Prime Minister from 1976 to 1979 should have seen one of the closest partnerships between a peacetime government and the TUC, which gave strong support and understanding to his constant struggle to manage the country's chronically weak economic position. Unfortunately, this formal support from the unions' national umbrella body could not withstand mounting pressure from the local membership of its constituent organizations, and Callaghan was eventually confronted with the distressing experience of an uncontrolled wave of pay strikes in the highly sensitive public sector. As an outspoken advocate of the autonomy of voluntary associations, this normally decisive politician could only stand by and watch as they learned from their own mistakes:

Both the Labour Government and the trade unions had become widely unpopular. It was but the latest demonstration of a truth we have all uttered to the effect that the fortunes of the unions and the Labour Party cannot be separated. As one trade union leader told his colleagues during the worst of our troubles, 'The TUC can either have a Labour Government with some unpalatable policies, or a Conservative Government with disastrous ones.' The serious and widespread industrial dislocation caused by the strikes of January 1979, short-lived though they were, sent the Government's fortunes cascading downhill, our loss of authority in one field leading to misfortune in others just as an avalanche, gathering speed, sweeps all before it.[7]

Behind the affable and relaxed public face which gained him the nickname 'Sunny Jim', James Callaghan was, then, very much the embodiment of the mainstream values of British trade unionism. Loyal, intelligent and tough, committed to producing genuine improvements for his supporters but realistic about the compromises that would be involved, it was deeply ironic that his own background had been in exactly the type of white-collar and public-service unionism that was to cause so much disruption in the 1970s and that he himself had first come to wider notice as just the sort of angry young man who was to bring down his own government in 1979. But this was the underlying paradox of the Labour Party as a whole: its aims rooted in the idealism and commitment of extra-parliamentary movements for social justice, its methods constrained by the pragmatism and constitutionalism of working within the existing political system.

LABOUR'S FIRST GOVERNMENTS

The years immediately after the First World War had seen a continued high demand for labour, accompanied by an unprecedented peak of trade-union strength and very intense levels of strike activity. The great bulk of disputes had still revolved around specific occupational demands, initially for higher wages and shorter hours and then, as the post-war boom began to break, to defend gains against counter-pressures from the employers. However, as these strikes tended to happen at the same time and to involve workers in transport and energy supply, it repeatedly appeared as if the whole country was going to grind to a halt. Moreover, trade unionists' confidence, along with their wartime habit of expecting favourable government responses, led them to consider using this industrial power to pursue broader ends. The confrontations in the coal industry discussed in an earlier chapter were one of the most persistent and dramatic instances of these developments. For the miners' own strikes in pursuit of occupational demands were serious enough, and when they received the broader support of other major unions the consequences could seem potentially catastrophic. There were also flurries of union interest in 'direct action' whenever there were any signs of escalating British military intervention in Russia, motivated more by the strength of anti-war feeling than by sympathy for the Bolsheviks. These came to a head in August

1920 when the coalition government seemed to be about to mount a major expedition on the side of Poland, leading to a joint statement by the Labour Party and the TUC calling for the setting up of local 'Councils of Action' to mobilize opposition. However, the diplomatic tension eased quite quickly and the real determination behind this joint initiative was never put to the test. On the whole, trade unionists were too divided among themselves for such threatening noises to come to much: they did not agree either on the issues involved or on the advisability of using industrial action for political ends, and they continued to resist any centralization of authority in the hands of the TUC General Council.

By the end of 1920 it was clear that the post-war boom was over, trade-union membership and bargaining power were being seriously undermined by rapidly rising unemployment, and each organization was faced with a lonely defensive battle. With the partial exception of a brief trade recovery in 1924, this was to continue for longer and lead to more serious defeats than anyone had anticipated. By 1926 the unions had been experiencing an overall decline in their position for five years, and the attempt to mount a 'General Strike' in support of the miners was a sobering experience. This was partly because it became clear that industrial action could only be used as a demonstration of opinion and, if the government did not make immediate concessions, trade-union leaders would not be prepared to sustain a lengthy political confrontation. And it was partly because the aftermath saw not only the victimization of individuals but also the Conservatives' restrictive Trade Disputes and Trade Unions Act of 1927. This outlawed attempts to coerce the government by organizing strikes of workers outside the industry immediately concerned, limited the freedom of action of civil service and local authority unions, and altered the arrangements for the trade-union political levy from contracting-out to contracting-in. In practice, however, the anti-strike clauses of the act were never used and there was a concerted effort by major public figures to emphasize a return to normality in industrial relations. Thus talks were initiated in 1928 by Sir Alfred Mond, chairman of Imperial Chemical Industries, and received an enthusiastic response from Ben Turner, chairman of the TUC General Council: these well-publicized meetings resulted in a statement by some of the larger employers in favour of collective bargaining, followed by a revival in the public standing of the TUC.

The unions were obviously going to survive as industrial bodies, albeit seriously weakened by a long period of high unemployment, but their wider ambitions had received a severe blow, for not only had the events of 1926 set clear limits to the use of strikes, the legislation of 1927 had reduced their political funds by around 30 per cent, as many who had previously not bothered to contract-out now did not bother to contract-in. The lessons of the 1920s were therefore clear: in peace-time the unions could not expect to exercise political influence through industrial action and they were still in need of powerful parliamentary support to protect them against restrictive initiatives. By 1927 such a central figure as Ernest Bevin of the transport workers was not only beginning to revise his previously low opinion of politicians but was also emerging as a supreme advocate of political realism within the Labour Party:

If Trade Unionism had been successful in getting men and women to unite on the industrial field, give them a chance to try to convert them to political consciousness. He thought he knew their people, and he wanted Labour in power, but the first Labour Government could not accomplish Socialism, and they might as well face it. The first Labour Government could not achieve all the dreams of the biggest dreamers. It might provoke a nightmare if they did. All the same he wanted them in office. He thought they would make mistakes if they were in office. He did not want to paint the picture to their people too much and then find them disillusioned after the first term of office. He would rather see a short programme of immediate objectives that Labour could really hope to accomplish, and then they could go back and say, 'At least we have done what we said we would; we have delivered the goods.'[8]

Interestingly enough these lessons were becoming so clear that they were eventually digested even by the revolutionary minority, now focused on the Communist Party of Great Britain, established as an affiliate of the Moscow-based Third International at the peak of the post-war boom in 1920. This new party was formed by the unification of a number of pre-war Marxist sects such as the British Socialist Party, but soon came to be dominated by a network of younger activists whose attitudes had been shaped by their wartime experiences of trade-union power. However, the timing of its foundation was unfortunate, for the onset of the inter-war depression began to undermine the basis of the industrial movement and the Communist Party was unable to expand its membership beyond a few thousand activists, smaller even than the pre-war sects it had replaced. Like other tight-knit groups the Communists were able to exercise an influence disproportionate to their numbers, particularly through the miners' 'Minority Movement', which added its weight to the confrontations in the coal industry. As a result the calling-off of the 'General Strike' and the painful defeat of the miners in their long lock-out was a decisive turning-point for the far left in Britain. For these events dissipated the dream of a revolution exploding out of ordinary industrial conflict, permanently confined the Communist Party to isolated pockets of local support and, after the brief dead-end of a shift further to the left, turned it back towards mainstream trade unionism and an explicitly parliamentary road to socialism.

The increasingly obvious weaknesses of industrial movements therefore brought the Labour Party more and more to the centre of trade unionists' political attention, especially as it was able to form two governments surprisingly early in its existence as a fully independent organization. The first was for a brief period of seven months as a distinctly minority administration in 1924, when the Conservatives were once again undermined by their championing of economic tariffs and the Liberals were still shattered by the First World War. The second was for a longer period from 1929–31, now as the largest party though still without an overall majority, when the Conservatives were discredited by their failure to address the problem of rising unemployment. However, despite this sudden surge to the centre of public life, Labour was only slowly constructing its position as a genuinely national party. In 1924 it still had only 113 full-time local agents, few of its constituency branches had significant individual memberships and, though it increased its seats in Parliament to 191, this was achieved without any improvement in its share of the overall vote. By 1929 its national status was more secure, for by this time a decade of hard organizational work had produced 169 full-time agents, more active branch life, particularly among women and in London, and an increasing ability to field candidates and win seats in local government elections. This culminated in the return of 287 Labour MPs with 37 per cent of the overall vote, on the basis of major gains in constituencies in London, the Midlands and the north-west.

Moreover, James Ramsay MacDonald had consolidated his position as an outstanding strategist and charismatic leader of the parliamentary party. He was sometimes worn out by his self-imposed workload and frequently distant from his colleagues, but he was establishing Labour as an indispensable part of the national political scene by steering a careful course around the temptations of coalition with the Liberals, excessive attachment to socialist rhetoric and too much concession to trade-union pressure. An understandable lack of government experience led to reliance on former Liberals who had come across to Labour during the wartime crises, or in some cases even more recently, and this was particularly obvious in MacDonald's first cabinet in 1924. But there was also a principled adoption of traditional Gladstonian policies, above all the commitments to free trade and international cooperation, balanced budgets and low levels of taxation. This was usually enough to ensure the Liberals' cooperation in the House of Commons, shored up in 1930–31 by a loose agreement that they would support MacDonald's second administration in return for a measure of electoral reform. Meanwhile the distinctive Labour contribution to the progressive tradition in domestic policy was maintained even in a difficult period of economic depression: through the Housing Acts of 1924 and 1930, which provided subsidies for local authority building and protection for tenants against unfair eviction; through increased funding for local schools; through the Coal Mines Act of 1930, which reduced the miners' working day to seven and a half hours; and through schemes of industrial re-organization and public works to reduce unemployment, alongside more generous benefits for those unavoidably out of work. Similarly, a distinctive emphasis in foreign policy was pioneered through unilateral reductions in military spending, multilateral agreements on wider disarmament, the strengthening of the League of Nations, the reduction of the burden of post-war reparations on Germany and the re-establishment of economic relations with Russia.

While establishing this wide policy base as a responsible party of government, MacDonald was careful not to be seen to be caving in to sectional pressures from his closest supporters. Admittedly a major dock strike during the first few days in office in 1924 was settled quickly by a court of inquiry, and a few weeks later a London tram-workers' strike ended in a compromise settlement, with the companies granting a pay advance in return for legislation to coordinate the capital's passenger transport system. However, MacDonald simultaneously made it clear that Labour's role as a national administration might require it to make use of emergency powers during disputes which threatened major disruptions of public services. Moreover, the second Labour government was responsible for a number of arbitrations involving wage reductions, albeit less than those initially demanded by the employers, most notably in cotton in 1929 and in wool in 1930. Indeed MacDonald kept the unions at arm's length while in office, acutely sensitive that any regular consultation with outside bodies could be portrayed as a breach of his responsibilities to Parliament. He encouraged the withdrawal of members of his cabinets from their seats on the TUC General Council, a reduction in the frequency of meetings of the Joint Committee of the Labour Party and the TUC, and the separation of the previously shared research, publicity and international departments. This was matched by the unions' own move away from intimate involvement with the party, as the increasing pressure of industrial responsibilities meant that their national officers were less likely to sit in Parliament, while the experiences of 1924 quickly revealed the possibility of conflicts of interest with a Labour government. As the number of Labour MPs grew, the union-sponsored share fell steadily from fifty out of sixty-one in 1918 (80 per cent), to 102 out of 191 in 1924 (53 per cent), and to 115 out of 287 in 1929 (40 per cent). Politicians from trade-union backgrounds were still given seven out of twenty places in the cabinet of 1924, and six in 1929, their leading statesmen including Arthur Henderson of the ironfounders as Home Secretary and later Foreign Secretary, Jimmy Thomas of the railwaymen as Colonial Secretary and then Lord Privy Seal in charge of tackling unemployment, and J. R. Clynes of the municipal workers as Leader of the House of Commons and later Home Secretary. However, functioning at this level of responsibility, they were largely absorbed by the developing ethos of the parliamentary party.

Some signs of tension then began to appear between the Labour leadership and the unions as the world economic depression deepened following the Wall Street crash of 1929. For it became painfully clear that Labour's attempts to tackle unemployment were not working and that the burden of benefit payments was approaching crisis levels. As a result the government came under increasing pressure from the other parties and the media to find ways to cut public expenditure in order to avoid further tax increases. A Royal Commission on Unemployment Insurance was set up in December 1930 without prior consultation with the TUC, which then only reluctantly submitted evidence and objected strongly to the final report recommending reductions in benefits and limitations on entitlements. In the end, the Labour government itself was not ready for such a tough policy and compromised on smaller savings through closing up a number of loopholes and anomalies. However, at the Liberals' insistence a further Economy Committee had already been set up under Sir George May, the secretary of the Prudential Insurance Company, and its report in August 1931 predicted even higher levels of government debt and recommended major reductions in public spending including, once again, reductions in unemployment benefit. This unfortunately coincided with a spreading European banking crisis and panic withdrawals of investment funds from London. The Labour government therefore agreed that public spending would have to be reduced substantially to restore the confidence of overseas lenders and maintain the value of the pound. However, almost half of the cabinet was opposed to any cuts in the level of benefits, shored up by the re-assertion of the firm position of the TUC. Understanding that the attempt to steer a compromise course between these positions was doomed, MacDonald offered his resignation, but was persuaded by the King and the leaders of the other parties to stay on himself at the head of an emergency administration to push through the controversial cuts and stabilize the economy. However, the bulk of the Labour Party now refused to follow his leadership, much to the dismay of MacDonald and his small group of loyal supporters, who were left at the head of a Conservative-Liberal coalition.

Despite this National government's gradual abandonment of liberal economic principles, including the gold standard and free trade, the

Labour Party was unable to mount a coherent opposition. For, persuaded of the seriousness of the crisis, the public was now prepared to swallow not only benefit cuts but also a weakened pound and even economic tariffs. Moreover, many of Labour's influential figures, including Arthur Henderson who had reluctantly accepted election as leader, still hoped for MacDonald's eventual return. The Labour campaign in the general election of October 1931 was therefore rather confused and was further undermined by exaggerated government claims that the unions had brought unconstitutional and selfish 'dictation' to bear during the national crisis. In the face of this onslaught, Labour sustained its share of the vote fairly well at 29 per cent, but the major reduction in the number of three-cornered contests badly affected the outcome in terms of seats: the National government's candidates won 554, squeezing Labour down to only forty-six, with most of its experienced parliamentarians failing to secure re-election. Thus far from demonstrating the excessive influence of the unions, the crisis of 1931 had demonstrated the opposite: more than half of the Labour cabinet including the Prime Minister had been prepared to cross the TUC and, when the latter put its case to the country, Labour was reduced to a tiny rump. After the first promising steps into government in the 1920s the Labour Party was more or less back where it had started, as a small trade-union pressure group based heavily in the coal-mining constituencies, without a charismatic leader or any experienced statesmen.

THE ERA OF CENTRAL CONTROL

This crisis was a sharp reminder that effective parliamentary support for trade unionism could only be achieved through the success of a progressive party with a wider popular appeal, but it was no longer clear what shape such a party should take. For the departure to the right of the MacDonald group in the leadership in 1931 was soon followed by the departure to the left of most of the rest of the ILP in 1932, convinced that mass unemployment was a symptom of the final 'crisis of capitalism': within a few years it had declined to the status of just another marginal sect. The electoral defeat of most of Labour's experienced MPs produced a nominal swing to the left in the parliamentary party, with George Lansbury as leader assisted by Clement Attlee and Stafford Cripps, who also played a leading role in rallying the remnants of the left around the Socialist League. However, this was rather an extremist and patronizing body with few organizational roots in the country or links with significant social movements, so there was no obvious way of reconstructing the alliance of the TUC and the ILP which had given Labour so much of its national identity and local dynamism. As a result, although it could hardly fail to improve on the electoral disaster of 1931, the party seemed condemned to permanent opposition.

Given the urgency of the situation, real progress was made in doubling the individual membership to around half a million, developing the life of the branches, and giving constituency delegates increased representation on the National Executive Committee. However, even under the impact of contracting-in to the political levy after 1927, the number of trade unionists affiliated remained at around 2 million: so it was still they who were providing the backbone for most local committees and election campaigns, it was still their financial resources which were keeping national organization afloat and it was still their votes which dominated the party's annual conference. Behind the scenes Ernest Bevin of the transport workers had become increasingly influential, especially after the opening of Transport House in May 1928 as the offices not only of his own union but also of both the TUC and the Labour Party, as well as through his virtual control of the trade-union newspaper the *Daily Herald*. Although his intuitive temperament made him very different from the more systematic Walter Citrine, the secretary of the TUC, the two men were in agreement on most major issues and the General Council was therefore able to make a coherent claim for a substantial voice in the processes of party policy-making. This led to the revival of the TUC-Labour National Joint Council, given the more high-profile title of the National Council of Labour in 1934, with a trade unionist in the chair guaranteeing an in-built union majority. Moreover, this was matched by the increased predominance of trade unionists both in the parliamentary party and on Labour's National Executive. With this more than adequate counterweight to the intellectual left, the party moved decisively towards immediate practical reforms and realism in foreign policy, as well as maintaining a negative position on repeated Communist Party appeals for a united front against fascism and admission as an affiliated socialist organization. Indeed the National Joint Council made its position very clear in *Democracy versus Dictatorship* (1933), which condemned both fascism and communism equally, and the TUC General Council went on to encourage its affiliated bodies to impose bans on office-holding by members of both movements.

However, the nature of Labour's own appeal to the public needed considerable re-thinking, as the bedrock of nineteenth-century liberal assumptions had been swept away in the storm of 1931. Reports from the Soviet Union were convincing even those who were opposed to that regime's undemocratic methods that mass unemployment was not inevitable, and this revived memories of Britain itself during the 1914–18 war, when physical controls over manpower and materials had proved effective in defending national security. Even for those who were less enamoured with centralized planning, including most trade unionists, the 'New Deal' in the United States was demonstrating the effectiveness of large-scale public works in providing employment. Meanwhile, although the promised social reconstruction had never materialized in Britain after 1918, subsequent governments of both parties had seen a gradual drift towards increasing state intervention in domestic affairs. The social services had continued to expand, particularly through the central government provision of unemployment benefits but also through local government improvements in health care; there had been some subsidies for housing and road building; and the National government not only carried through Labour's plans for London passenger transport but also introduced its own legislation for the regulation of road haulage. Many of these schemes included a willingness to consult the unions concerned, to which both the individual organizations and the TUC General Council responded with enthusiasm. For example, within two weeks of the National government taking office in 1931, the annual congress of the TUC was welcoming its policies for planned industrial development and regulated overseas trade. And by 1935 the presidential address to the TUC, drafted with the help of Walter Citrine's staff, was arguing that:

Trade union recovery is most marked . . . in the change that is taking place in the attitude of people towards the social and economic policy our movement has advocated. Economic planning and social control of the mechanism of industry and trade are no longer regarded as the impracticable dream of Trade Unionists and Socialists – they are principles which capitalist Governments and employers' organizations recognize and accept. Not in theory only, but in practice, the unbridled individualism which determined the policy of Governments in the past had been discarded.[9]

Within this context of a broad trend towards the acceptance of increasing state intervention in economic life, public ownership began to assume a higher profile in Labour's domestic policy. The 1934 programme, *For Socialism and Peace*, included the nationalization of land and public utilities, now more broadly defined to include banking and iron and steel, alongside the more familiar transport, coal, power and water supply. However, Labour's conception of how this would operate drew on the London Passenger Transport Board initiated by Herbert Morrison in the 1929 government. It was based on fair compensation for the private owners and their replacement with small boards of expert administrators responsible to the minister concerned and, while these would include some trade-union nominees, the unions would otherwise play their normal adversarial role rather than taking any direct part in management. Moreover, this was only part of a broader package for dealing with unemployment in a mixed economy which, by the end of the 1930s, depended more on public control than public ownership. Indeed, its main devices built on the approach of the National government: a proposal for a National Investment Board and a willingness to use such Keynesian tools of demand management as budget deficits and interest-rate adjustments. Thus a major change in style was more significant than any of the changes in substance: Labour's programmes had become strategic and specific rather than idealistic and vague, and they were backed up by an increasingly focused understanding of how to use the existing machinery of central government. That pragmatism rather than socialism was still the dominant influence was also evident in foreign policy, which moved gradually back from a brief flirtation with pacifism towards a more traditional emphasis on the provision of collective security against aggressor states through the League of Nations and eventually, under the impact of the Spanish Civil War, towards passive approval for rearmament in 1937. Consequently, in the following years Labour was firmly opposed to the Conservative tendency to appease Hitler's Germany and quite ready to accept an early declaration of war. As Bevin put it in 1936:

The whole position that has arisen as between the democratic and peace-loving states and the Fascist menace of war demands that there should be the most careful re-examination and a statement issued to the Movement after the closest consultation with the Party in the light of these developments . . . If in certain respects it means uprooting some of our cherished ideals and facing the issue fairly in the light of the development of Fascism, we must do it for the Movement and for the sake of posterity.[10]

Despite the survival of Labour after 1931 on the basis of trade-union organization and the redefinition of its programme on the basis of trade-union realism, there were still no signs that it could reconstruct its appeal as a successful national party. The importance of the Second World War therefore lay not in any redefinition of Labour's identity, but rather in the recovery of its credibility as a party of government as a result of its leadership's high-profile position in the wartime cabinet from 1940 onwards. Because of the widespread unpopularity of Hitler's dictatorship, there was little resistance to Labour's participation in a coalition as long as it was not led by Neville Chamberlain, whose reputation had been stained by appeasement; and the parliamentary party was able to play a significant role in bringing him down in May 1940 by moving a vote of censure over the inadequate resistance to the German invasion of Scandinavia. As a result, the new government formed under Winston Churchill gave a disproportionately large role to Labour ministers, partly to make it look like a genuine coalition and partly to ensure the maximum cooperation of trade unionists in the war effort. The leader and deputy leader of the party, Clement Attlee and Arthur Greenwood, joined the five-man inner war cabinet: the former with responsibility for Food and Home Policy and eventually taking on the role of Deputy Prime Minister, the latter with responsibility for Production and Economic Policy. Just as importantly, Ernest Bevin, who was not even an MP at the time, was appointed as Minister of Labour and National Service, while a number of other leading Labour figures took on significant ministries, for example Herbert Morrison at the Home Office and Hugh Dalton at the Ministry of Economic Warfare and then at the Board of Trade. As it was largely responsible for the domestic administration of the country from early in 1940, there could no longer be any doubt that Labour was a national party. Meanwhile, the wartime experiences, not only of the effectiveness of large-scale state intervention in the economy but also of the great difficulties and costs of securing the defeat of Germany, made the policies of the pre-war national governments look increasingly misguided. Moreover, in even longer memories the experience of the 1920s undermined the credibility of a post-war coalition, with the likelihood of a repeat of Conservative backtracking on the mood of national cooperation in the face of an emergency.

The Labour Party was therefore ready to contest an early and relatively low-key election in July 1945, and the appeal of its plans for post-war reconstruction based on the needs of the majority of the population produced its first overall majority in Parliament: 48 per cent of the votes cast, resulting in 393 seats against the other parties' combined total of 247. This was accompanied by the party's marked recovery of its ability to break out of its northern heartlands, taking clear majorities of the seats in the Midlands and London, and even penetrating into the traditional core of rural Liberalism in north Wales and the south-west of England. The 'Progressive Alliance' still survived at the level of policy-making, with highly significant contributions from leading Liberal intellectuals on key issues, such as the 1942 report of William Beveridge on social security and the evolving ideas of J. M. Keynes on economic management. However, the 1945 election saw the end of the Liberal Party as an effective national organization: it was reduced to a small rump of only twelve MPs, and any future alliance would clearly be a Labour-Liberal one.

In the course of the 1940s the Labour leadership also became considerably more powerful within its own party, due to the seriousness of the national emergency combined with the highly effective working relationship which developed between Attlee, Bevin and Dalton. After 1945 they consistently supported each other in their respective roles as Prime Minister, Foreign Secretary and Chancellor of the Exchequer, making all rivalry for the top positions futile and all opposition factions marginal. Meanwhile, participation at the centre of the war effort followed by the smooth transition to a post-war Labour administration entrenched the trend towards statism already evident within the party in the 1930s. For its leaders formed an increasingly favourable view of the apparatus of central government, admiring the war-time model of a small cabinet with clear-cut functional responsibilities, increased government control of the parliamentary timetable and further reductions in the power of the House of Lords. The party's strategy therefore moved sharply on to the offensive, seeing war-time controls as the basis for top-down economic and social reconstruction. From as early as 1942 it was confidently demanding full employment, social security, a national health service and education reform. From 1944 it was demanding continued public management of the economic infrastructure in order to ensure sufficient investment and adequate coordination. This domestic programme was then implemented at a remarkable pace after 1945, with the added urgency of war damage and post-war shortages giving further legitimacy to state controls over such areas as urban rebuilding, the food supply and steeply progressive taxation. In foreign policy Labour maintained its commitment to realism, demanding that Germany as a whole be held responsible for the war and made to pay reparations, and anticipating the continuation of military service into peacetime in order to support the occupation of German territory. This was further stiffened after 1945 by Bevin's close cooperation, and eventually formal alliance, with the United States in resistance to the Soviet Union's tightening grip on Eastern Europe and in the building-up of nuclear armaments during the intensifying Cold War.

In principle, war-time legislation made industrial action illegal after 1940, but Bevin at the Ministry of Labour had been very reluctant to initiate prosecutions, preferring instead to maintain an atmosphere of maximum cooperation by emphasizing negotiations. Thus, while there were around 10,000 disputes resulting in around 12 million days lost between 1939 and 1945, there were only 109 prosecutions involving just over 6,000 individuals, and the normal sentence was a small fine. Indeed there was only one case of imprisonment, when the Minister of Mines prosecuted three local union officials in 1941, and the dispute was soon settled on the strikers' terms and their leaders released. The maintenance of voluntarism in industrial relations was, then, the major exception to the extension of state controls and this remarkably harmonious relationship between the government and the unions was maintained largely intact after 1945. One of the first measures of the new Labour government was the long-awaited repeal of the 1927 Trade Disputes Act, removing the prohibitions on general strikes and the restrictions on civil service and local authority unions. While the war-time emergency legislation did remain in place, it was only used twice to fine small groups of strike leaders among the gasworkers and the dockers, just before its eventual repeal in 1951. Thus the Labour government continued to rely on responsible collective bargaining rather than state control for the achievement of its aims in the fields of wages and productivity. For their part trade-union leaders and most of their members accepted the need for continued restraint and cooperation during the period of reconstruction, accompanied as it was by the urgency of repaying post-war loans to the USA and correcting the balance of payments by boosting export earnings. They even accepted the Labour government's unilateral call for a voluntary wage freeze between 1948 and 1950, for this was counter-balanced by the maintenance of strict controls over prices. The growing tensions of the Cold War in the later 1940s led to increasing paranoia about Communist subversion and a repressive attitude towards unofficial strikes on the part of some Labour ministers and trade-union leaders. However, as has been shown in earlier chapters, this was a serious misunderstanding of the industrial situation and in reality the level of strikes between 1946 and 1951 remained remarkably similar to that of the war years: there were around 10,000 disputes resulting in around 11 million days lost.

The close relationship between Attlee and Bevin within the cabinet reduced the role of the National Council of Labour in setting Labour's policy framework, but the unions still remained the dominant force within the party's organization. By returning from contracting-in to contracting-out, the repeal of the 1927 Trade Disputes Act in itself more or less automatically increased Labour's affiliated trade-union membership by around 25 per cent. In addition, the continuous increase in the unions' own membership from around 6 million in

1939 to around 8 million in 1945, continuing to grow to almost 10 million by the early 1950s, ensured that the numbers affiliated to the party would follow a similar course from just over 2 to 2.5 million during the course of the war, doubling to over 5 million by the early 1950s. Thus, despite a significant increase in individual membership from around 400,000 in 1939 to over 500,000 in 1945, continuing to rise to a peak of over a million in the early 1950s, the unions retained their massive preponderance of 80 per cent of the votes at the party conference. The most influential figures in this period were Arthur Deakin of the transport workers, Tom Williamson of the municipal workers and Will Lawther of the miners, all solid moderates and anti-Communists, so a safe passage for leadership policies was guaranteed within both the TUC and the Labour Party against any criticism from factions on the left.

The union-sponsored share of Labour MPs continued its long-term decline to only 124 out of 393 in 1945 (32 per cent), but the Attlee cabinets retained the traditional handful of ministers from trade-union backgrounds. Ernest Bevin as Foreign Secretary was the outstanding figure among them, performing a crucial mediating role as, on the one hand, the highly respected voice of the unions within the cabinet on a wide range of both foreign and domestic issues, and, on the other, the deeply trusted representative of the transport workers and the TUC, able to guarantee the loyalty of the unions at times of tough economic decisions. The close wartime cooperation between government and unions continued in a more general way with the TUC's representation on official committees increasing from twelve in 1939 to sixty in 1949, dealing with such issues as productivity, technical education, regional policy, rationing and prices. This was a mutually beneficial relationship, for the unions now had a high public standing as a result of their exemplary participation in the war effort, so the Labour government was able to benefit from its close association with them. For their part the unions were compensated for their self-imposed industrial restraint with careful consultation over the package of wider policies on social welfare, public ownership and above all full employment, which they had been actively pursuing since the 1930s.

THE RE-ASSERTION OF
TRADE-UNION AUTONOMY

With its programme of reconstruction largely fulfilled and its leading figures worn out by a decade of extraordinary stress, by the beginning of the 1950s it was no longer clear what Labour's further aspirations were. The party continued to attract widespread loyalty; however, a redistribution of seats and some marginal swings produced a majority of only five in a general election early in 1950. Cabinet divisions over rearmament and a revival of Conservative organization then combined to produce defeat in a second election towards the end of the following year and, despite initial assumptions that this would only be a temporary interruption, the Conservatives went on to win again with increased majorities in both 1955 and 1959. This was partly a result of Labour's own loss of direction, which worsened as continuing divisions over rearmament began to combine with personal rivalries to polarize opinion between a moderate majority around Hugh Gaitskell and a well-organized left-wing minority around Aneurin Bevan. However, it was also partly a result of the Conservatives' acceptance of the popularity of the main pillars of the post-war settlement: the mixed economy, full employment and welfare safety nets. Consequently, their aims in office were limited to reducing economic controls and taxation in order to stimulate private enterprise and personal consumption within that overall framework.

Over the next thirteen years this combination of Conservative governments and full employment led to a marked re-assertion of trade-union autonomy. For not only were the unions no longer constrained by traditional party loyalties, the Conservatives were determined to replace quasi-political bargaining over comprehensive social wages with purely industrial bargaining over narrower money wages. As a result they pared back state food subsidies and rent controls, while encouraging pay settlements which were broadly favourable to the unions. The TUC pursued a moderate line, keen to maintain its responsible image and its involvement in national policy-making, but its member bodies had little choice but to abandon a self-restraint which had already been stretched to its limits. As one union leader had already remarked in the last years of the Labour regime:

Our movement is basically a sectional movement for the benefit of small sectional interests, but now we are expected to give them up for the benefit of the nation. But can we do that without being disloyal to our members and giving up the tasks for which we are appointed? We were not meant to be public servants to guard the interests of the nation; we were appointed to protect our members and to guard and further their interests within the framework of the law. Does anyone ask the employer to have the national interest in mind instead of the interest of his firm? It is all right having the national interest in mind but we are not the right people to have it.[11]

Thus, whereas between 1939 and 1951 there had been around 20,000 strikes, this rose to around 30,000 between 1952 and 1964, with the average number of days lost each year doubling from 1.7 to 3.5 million. Moreover, the impact of this on the public was further intensified by additional threats of strike action as well as the high profile given to such problematic issues as multi-unionism in engineering and local indiscipline in the docks. As a result it was at this time that the media began to give more serious attention to what were to become familiar proposals for fundamental reforms of the country's industrial relations practice: above all the introduction of compulsory strike ballots and compulsory arbitration, and the effective outlawing of unofficial action. On the whole, the Conservative leadership continued to favour voluntarism and a rather lax line on wage settlements to boost the electorate's sense of prosperity, even though this was also producing a rising tide of imported consumer goods and growing deficits in the balance of payments. These economic pressures did eventually lead to more restraint in public-sector pay settlements and the conception in the early 1960s of an embryonic incomes policy, including the review of significant wage claims by a National Incomes Commission and the inclusion of the larger unions in discussions of future prospects at meetings of a National Economic Development Council.

In this way the unintended consequences of its own policies began to push the Conservative Party on to its opponent's ground, for it was still the Labour Party which had the better reputation for controlling wages by involving the unions in the formulation of national strategies.

As a result, the fifteen years from the middle of the 1960s were to see another era of Labour in power, though this time with a specific brief of damage limitation rather than a broad mandate for social reconstruction. This was reflected in the party's general inability to secure strong parliamentary majorities and its tendency to become increasingly dependent on the support of Liberal MPs. Thus Labour's initial victory in 1964, like its previous one in 1950, produced a majority of only five seats. Greater enthusiasm produced a ninety-seven-seat margin in 1966, but subsequent disillusionment led to a low turn-out in 1970 and a rather unexpected Conservative majority of thirty. Labour was then twice confirmed as the public's overall preference in the elections of 1974, first as a minority government, then ending the period back where it had begun with an overall majority of only three seats. This weak parliamentary position was a result of a long-term decline in Labour's share of the vote, the return to power in 1964 seeing no increase on the 44 per cent which had lost it the previous election, and the brief recovery to 48 per cent in 1966 falling to only 37 per cent and 39 per cent in the elections of 1974. A pattern was also beginning to emerge of decisive swings taking place in the west Midlands, and to some extent in Lancashire, where widespread unease over increasing numbers of coloured immigrants was giving rise to more or less open racism and the renewal of popular Conservativism. However, small majorities were still possible for Labour on low shares of the overall vote, because both of the main parties were losing ground to the Liberals and to the Welsh and Scottish Nationalists.

As a result of Labour's relatively poor electoral performance in this period its leadership was more vulnerable to pressure from dissatisfied minorities within the parliamentary party than it had been during its previous period of power in the 1940s. Since it could only sustain its administration by containing back-bench revolts, the personal paranoia of Harold Wilson, its leader for most of the period, was not completely misplaced. Consequently, there was not only considerable re-shuffling of ministerial positions to distract and divide potential rivals at the top, but also unusual lip-service paid to the ideas of the left within the party more generally, especially during the period in opposition in the early 1970s. However, the real priority in government was correcting the chronic tendency towards deficits in the balance of payments inherited from the preceding period of Conservative economic opportunism. Tariffs on imports and devaluation of sterling were used as emergency measures, but the key to long-term success was seen as the setting of a firm ceiling on wage costs through the restraint of trade-union demands. Labour's overall style of government therefore tended to become even more technocratic and corporatist: its focus was firmly on centralized management of such economic matters as the balance of payments, exchange rates and incomes policies, and one of its main methods was negotiation behind the scenes to ensure the support of trade-union leaders for government projects. Although Wilson tried to enthuse the party and the public with a vision of the modernization of industry through the application of scientific knowledge and the tackling of regional inequalities, in practice the main issues of the day took a great deal of explaining and were not very exciting or easy to identify with. Pent-up passions were still released in fierce disputes between the left and right of the party over foreign-policy issues, with the established division over nuclear armaments being extended to include the United States' intervention in Vietnam, levels of spending on overseas aid and membership of the European Economic Community. However, even though the Labour Party tended to be rather defensive and fragmented throughout this period, its continued responsiveness to rising public expectations and pressure from single-issue campaigns enabled it to build on its long record of social reform. This was manifest not only in traditional Labour areas such as the expansion of spending on education, housebuilding and benefits for children and the elderly, but also in traditional Liberal ones such as the relaxation of legal restraints on abortion, divorce and homosexuality. Moreover, a serious beginning was also made in tackling the questions raised about the legitimacy of the British state by the resurgence of nationalist sentiment throughout the Celtic Fringe, with the first intervention in Northern Ireland in the late 1960s and the first attempt to introduce devolution for Wales and Scotland in the late 1970s.

However, given its economic priorities Labour soon became increasingly anxious about the behaviour of the unions. It set out with the goal of reviving the type of voluntary incomes policy achieved through consultation with trade-union leaders which had served the country so well during the crises of the 1940s. But it soon found that in the changed circumstances of the 1960s and 1970s this was continually challenged by the increasing assertiveness of trade-union members, encouraged as they were by a sense of growing bargaining power during an exceptional period of peacetime full employment. Indeed, this produced a number of serious political crises, threatening to undermine the government's export drive in the 1960s and its restraint on the public sector in the 1970s. Thus, a two-month official strike by the seamen in the spring of 1966 secured higher wages for that particular group, but also provoked intense speculation against the pound on the international money markets, which was only overcome through a year-long statutory freeze on other British pay settlements. Just as this situation was easing, unofficial strikes among the dockers caused further disruptions of trade in the autumn of 1967, accompanied by more speculation against the pound, which was only overcome by a significant currency devaluation in November 1967 and a systematic attempt to link pay increases to a new emphasis on productivity agreements. The unfortunate conjunction of industrial unrest and international financial pressure then worked the other way round in the 1970s, when yet another sterling crisis was only overcome with loans from the International Monetary Fund conditional on deflationary cuts in public spending which, to avoid a repeat of the 1931 split over reductions in unemployment benefit, focused instead on job cuts and pay restraint. However, this only served to deflect the source of the eventual crisis, and a wave of local strikes for higher wages among the public employees early in 1979 became the basis of the disastrous imagery of the 'Winter of Discontent', fatally undermining Labour's reputation as the party which could deal with the unions. Indeed, although these years in office saw no particularly marked increase in the overall number of strikes, they did see a further doubling in the average number of days lost each year from 3.5 to 8.5 million. As a result, throughout the period harassed Labour ministers were all too prone to denouncing such damaging industrial disputes as the result of the covert influence of politically motivated minorities, actively reviving the myth of Communist subversion in the 1960s and displaying open hostility towards public-sector strikes in the 1970s.

Labour governments throughout this period were therefore caught between two contradictory pressures, on the one hand from the speculative activities of financiers overseas, and on the other from the rising expectations of working people at home. That it was the former which predominated in the governments' overall considerations demonstrated only too clearly a major limitation on the power of British trade unionists, even in this period of rapidly increasing membership. However, away from the substantive issue of the level at which wages should be set, there was considerably more room for manoeuvre around the procedural issues of how that should be achieved, and Labour governments were generally able to work closely with leading figures within the TUC to improve the legal framework of industrial relations.

This was, of course, the result not only of the long-standing relationship between these two bodies but also of the continued influence of the unions within the party's own internal procedures. Indeed, if anything, this influence was increasing during the long post-war boom. Thus, while there was a long-term fall in Labour's individual membership through the constituency parties from a peak of over 1 million in the early 1950s to only half that by the late 1970s, the membership affiliated through the unions remained buoyant at between 5 and 6 million. Along with the massive majority of the annual conference votes which this gave them, the unions also retained twelve places out of twenty-seven on the party's national executive, while the proportion of union-sponsored MPs even began to rise again from 120 out of 317 (38 per cent) in 1964 to 127 out of 301 (42 per cent) in 1974. It was often remarked that, despite this predominance within the party, the unions intervened relatively infrequently over policy-making in the years after 1951. Moreover, when they did do so, they increasingly found themselves on opposite sides of the debates, as the compact group of moderate leaders characteristic of the 1940s began to break down from the time Arthur Deakin was replaced by the more left-wing Frank Cousins at the head of the transport workers in 1956. However, this in no way meant that, over such matters of trade-union law as had led to the original founding of both the Trades Union Congress and the Labour Representation Committee, the unions would not still be able to find common ground and not still be keen to exercise their influence.

While there were fewer trade unionists in the Wilson and Callaghan cabinets than had been the case in previous Labour governments, they still held significant positions. Thus on Labour's return to power in 1964, Frank Cousins himself was given the new responsibility of heading a Ministry of Technology at the heart of the high-profile agenda of industrial modernization. A number of former union officials were also prominent in related areas: James Callaghan from the Inland Revenue staffs was at the Exchequer, George Brown from the transport workers was in charge of overall planning at Economic Affairs, and Ray Gunter from the transport salaried staffs was at the Ministry of Labour. Admittedly, when wage freezes began in 1966 Cousins resigned his cabinet post to resume his independent union role as a high-profile opponent of compulsory pay policy, when coherent economic planning collapsed later that year Brown followed him, and as tensions over the government's handling of industrial relations mounted Gunter eventually also resigned in 1968. However, on the return to office in 1974 there was once again a small group of trade unionists in significant cabinet posts, including Roy Mason from the miners at the Ministry of Defence. Moreover, throughout the whole period Callaghan continued to hold a series of posts at the highest level, moving on to the Home Office and then the Foreign Office, before becoming the first trade unionist to move into 10 Downing Street itself in 1976.

As a result of this close involvement of the unions at all levels of the party, one of Labour's first steps on returning to power in 1964 was to pass a Trade Disputes Act in 1965, closing up a loophole over union liability to damages actions in cases of individual exclusions from closed shops, which had been opened up when the case of *Rookes v. Barnard* had been upheld in the House of Lords the previous year. Equally, the new government was careful to secure union participation in its Royal Commission on Trade Unions, including the full member-ship of George Woodcock, the TUC general secretary at the time. Even when the recommendations of this inquiry were ignored, Barbara Castle as Employment Secretary initially seemed to be getting a hearing from Woodcock for her alternative proposals. The eventual lack of wider support for *In Place of Strife*, particularly among such powerful craft unions as the engineers, in combination with the impact of successive pay freezes, did lead to a serious breakdown of cooperation between Labour and the TUC, with the latter in effect blocking the government's publicly stated policy. As a result the party's share of the vote among manual workers fell from a peak of 69 per cent in the election victory of 1966 to only 58 per cent in the defeat of 1970. However, this sobering development helped to restore the customary close relationship, especially through the joint campaign of opposition to the incoming Conservative government's passage of restrictive trade-union legislation. Under the influence of Jack Jones of the transport workers this evolved into the establishment of a powerful Labour-TUC Liaison Committee which, like the National Council of Labour before it, gave important union leaders a direct role in overseeing the development of party policy.

By the time Labour was restored to office as a result of the Conservatives' inability to cope with the demands of the miners under Joe Gormley in 1974, its approach to government had replaced earlier attempts to enforce compulsory incomes policies with a high-profile partnership with the TUC. Thus the 'Social Contract' was a sustained attempt to revive a full-blown social wage, with self-imposed restraint in pay bargaining being exchanged for a package of price controls and welfare reforms, alongside a major wave of labour legislation championed particularly by the general and white-collar unions. Not only was the Conservative Industrial Relations Act repealed, an Employment Protection Act of 1975 was largely drafted by the TUC: it extended employee rights to appeal against unfair dismissal and trade-union rights to recognition by employers, made provision for six weeks' maternity pay, set standards for employers' disclosure of information relevant to collective bargaining and established a new Advisory, Conciliation and Arbitration Service. A Health and Safety at Work Act of 1974 was toughened up by TUC amendments, a Sex Discrimination Act of 1975 gave much-needed back-up to the earlier Equal Pay Act, and was followed by a Race Relations Act in 1976. The highest point of this tide was marked in 1977 by the report of a committee of inquiry into industrial democracy chaired by Lord Bullock, a distinguished historian and biographer of Ernest Bevin, with Bevin's successor at the transport workers, Jack Jones, among its most influential members. This recommended substantial representation on the boards of large companies in the form of worker-directors elected through trade-union channels: widely regarded as quite normal in many other European countries, forms of participation of this type were still seen as almost revolutionary in Britain and stiff employers' opposition combined with craft-union reservations to produce inaction. Finally, even after the credibility of the 'Social Contract' had been fatally eroded in the public mind by the widespread discontent within the ranks of the public-sector unions in early 1979, the Labour government was still able to work closely with the TUC in drawing up a voluntary code for future trade-union self-restraint, covering the desirability of strike ballots, limits to picketing and the closed shop, and the need to maintain essential services during industrial action.

On the whole, then, the economic situation in the 1960s and 1970s was increasingly difficult but the prospects for constructive working relationships between Labour governments and the unions were still good. Indeed, paradoxically, the close relationships between Labour ministers and key individuals within the TUC seem to have become part of the problem, as they repeatedly led politicians into serious misjudgements of the wider mood among trade unionists. Moreover, this blind spot on the part of Labour's leaders was heavily reinforced by their strong attachment to the memory of the wartime mood of self-restraint. However, the traditional links between Labour and the TUC also ensured that it was only during the Conservative interregnum that a government persisted in head-on confrontation which, given the peak of trade-union strength, was bound to lead to humiliating defeat. In contrast, TUC pressure on the Labour Party eventually forced its leaders to abandon their attempt at restrictive legislation in the late 1960s, while the real consequences of the challenges to the strict pay norms of the late 1970s were not nearly so disastrous as portrayed by a hostile media. With both wage increases and the rate of inflation continuing to fall in the course of 1979, Labour was able to demonstrate that it was indeed still capable of stabilizing the economy by working with the unions, even in a period when their membership was over half of the labour force and industrial relations had become increasingly antagonistic. However, there was a growing feeling among almost all shades of political opinion that it was somehow demeaning to have to take so much account of the views of ordinary working people and that there was an option worth exploring once again: a more carefully prepared and determinedly pursued version of direct confrontation.

Epilogue

16

The End or a New Beginning?

If democracy requires the existence of popular rights, the British constitution provides for none. Parliament may make provision for freedom of expression, for regular elections, for freedom of the individual from arbitrary or unnecessary interference. Parliament may legislate to increase equality in any or all of its manifestations. However, Parliament need do none of these things and it has the ultimate authority within the Constitution to abolish popular rights, and to rewrite the constitutional documents that have hitherto enshrined them.[1]

This was the critical assessment of the British political scientist Judith Mather, undertaking a systematic comparison of provisions for democracy in Britain and in the European Union in the year 2000. Clearly a great deal had changed since eighteenth- and early-nineteenth-century French observers such as Montesquieu and Tocqueville had enthused over the advantages of the British limited monarchy in comparison, not only with continental absolute monarchies, but also with continental republics. For the freedoms which they had initially found so unusual, but had come to value so highly, had been allowed to emerge because of the plurality of centres of power within British society and politics. Unfortunately, however, Tocqueville seems to have been justified in fearing that the extension of democracy, in the sense of the right to vote, might well be accompanied by a centralization of power and reductions in all kinds of freedom.

The observations of these early French liberals have turned out to be particularly perceptive in their pinpointing of the issue of checks and balances within the constitution itself. For in their time there had indeed been restraints on the sovereignty of the British Parliament, because that body was not just the Commons, but also the Lords and even to some extent the Monarch. Thus the hereditary peers in the upper chamber had the power of veto over the elected representatives in the lower chamber until, following the stalemate around Lloyd George's proposals to increase the tax burden on land, the House of Lords was reformed in 1911. This removed its power over financial bills altogether and limited its power over others to providing advice, a degree of revision and, in cases of opposition, delay for a short period. Similarly, although the King or Queen had originally exercised some real powers, by the twentieth century these had become largely symbolic: opening and closing parliamentary sessions, inviting the leader of the largest party in the Commons to form a government, and giving formal assent to bills before they became law. What remained of the Royal Prerogative was then exercised by the relevant members of the cabinet, giving them a degree of independence from Parliament, above all in matters of external relations with other states, such as making treaties, declaring war and peace, and commanding the armed forces. Moreover, there had been no innovation to create new checks and balances, above all because the British political system was a matter of informal practice rather than formal prescription: there was therefore no possibility of establishing a superior court to scrutinize proposed parliamentary legislation in relation to a written constitution. Between periodic elections, then, the largest party in the House of Commons had become effectively unrestrained and the survival of the liberties of the country's citizens had come to depend on that party continuing to follow customary guidelines in exercising its power.

In this way, as John Stuart Mill, one of Tocqueville's leading British followers, had pointed out in his powerful analysis *On Liberty* in 1859, an apparent increase in democracy might only produce a 'tyranny of the majority'. To make things even worse, as Mill had also predicted, that 'majority' might turn out on closer examination to be an active minority, and as such was more likely to come from among the educated and resourceful middle classes than from among the greater numbers of ordinary working people. Thus under Britain's 'first-past-the-post' electoral system it was quite possible for a majority of seats in the Commons to be won without an overall majority of votes in the country. Indeed, in recent times the Conservative Party between 1979 and 1997 and the Labour Party thereafter have both been able to secure around 60 per cent of the parliamentary seats with only around 40 per cent of the national vote. Moreover, as the franchise has been extended there has been a significant erosion of the traditional idea that the economic and social background of the representatives should roughly reflect that of those who had elected them. In recent times 90 per cent of MPs have been from professional or business backgrounds, only 10 per cent have been from manual or non-manual employment; similarly, 90 per cent have been over forty and 90 per cent have been men. Once again, then, the survival of a genuinely democratic element in British government has not been guaranteed by institutional arrangements, but rather has become increasingly dependent on the willingness of the dominant male, middle-aged and middle-class party to take account of the wider state of public opinion. As Mather concluded on these issues:

... the House of Commons is an inadequate vehicle for democratic input. MPs do not empower their constituents. There are three main reasons for this: the doctrine of parliamentary sovereignty, the theory of representation that is practised (which is the only one possible given the way in which the electoral system is organized), and the authority of party. The people function only as a mechanism for installing a ruling government. Their faith in their representatives (government support) and in the system that supplies them (regime support) provides the necessary ingredient of consent to enable the system to function.[2]

There is one other very significant way in which the concerns of the early continental admirers of liberty have proved to be justified in the British case: through the erosion of the independence of local government. Representatives on local authorities have indeed been elected ever since the Whig reforms of the 1830s and subsequent reforms have extended the range of their activity and size of their electorates. However, since all this has been the result of parliamentary legislation it has actually undermined the autonomy local councils had previously possessed under royal charters: what was given by Parliament could also be taken away by Parliament. As the central state had an increasing sense of its responsibility for all aspects of economic and social life, it was probably only a matter of time before it became more interventionist, but the actions of the cost-cutting

Conservative governments of the 1980s and 1990s took a shockingly abrupt form. For the London-wide tier of local government was simply abolished, around forty acts were passed to restrict local revenue and expenditure, many local services were contracted out to unaccountable organizations, and in the key areas of housing and education local authorities were increasingly subject to strict instructions from the centre. As Mather concluded: 'in the UK case, the extent to which Parliament has concerned itself with other sources or potential sources of elected political authority illustrates not only the supremacy of Parliament, but also its determination that such supremacy should not be successfully challenged'.[3]

Thus the confrontations which began to take place at regular intervals in the late twentieth century between the trade unions and the state can be seen as the result, not only of short-term increases in union strength, but also of a longer-term trend towards the centralization of political authority. More and more the majority party in Parliament expected to have untrammelled control over the behaviour of all of its subjects. In a way that would have greatly surprised earlier generations of foreign observers, British constitutional critics and trade unionists themselves therefore began to look towards continental institutions to provide some safeguards for their traditional liberties. Thus political scientists such as Judith Mather began to take an interest in the way initiatives coming from the European Union might have the potential to bypass Parliament and strengthen regional and local government, potentially closer to the lives and interests of their citizens. Meanwhile trade-union leaders such as John Monks of the TUC began to take an interest in the way existing European Union guidelines might be used to extend British employees' rights to representation and consultation within the workplace.

GOVERNMENT AGAINST THE UNIONS

Elected in 1979 in the aftermath of the media outcry over the 'Winter of Discontent', one of the main mandates of the Conservative leader Margaret Thatcher was to curb the growth of trade-union power. Beginning with a fairly moderate response to the immediate legacy of indiscipline in the public sector, her tighter control over the media following the Falklands War and her improved parliamentary majority in 1983 allowed the expression of a deeper personal hostility towards trade unionism as such. Though the Conservative majority was reduced in 1987, Thatcher remained firmly in power and her hysterical condemnation of the unions as the 'enemy within' became ever more deeply entrenched as a central orthodoxy of public life. Even after her removal in November 1990 by an unprecedented coup within the Conservative Party as a result of her stubborn attachment to a highly unpopular 'Poll Tax', the new Prime Minister, John Major, continued the momentum of the anti-union drive. In more coherent moments, neo-liberal economic rhetoric was used to present union restrictions on the labour market as the root cause of the country's economic problems, as well as to paint a picture of an ideal 'free society' in which no interference with individual choice could be tolerated. As far as trade unions were concerned, this clearly meant outlawing as many as possible of their customary methods of regulating the behaviour of employers and employees through a radical reversal of the century-long trend of parliamentary legislation which had favoured collective bargaining. However, acutely conscious of her predecessor Edward Heath's humiliating defeat over his interventionist Industrial Relations Act in 1971, Margaret Thatcher and her key advisers proceeded with this change of course through a series of careful steps which were always presented as working with the grain of the voluntarist tradition.

Somewhat to his own surprise, the first appointment as Employment Secretary was the traditional 'one-nation' Tory James Prior, who had already been shadowing this post in opposition and who was generally in favour of continuity and consultation. His task in the Conservatives' first Employment Act in 1980 was merely to bring in widely acceptable changes: reducing the possibility of mass picketing by limiting such action to strikers' own place of work, requiring 80 per cent support in ballots for the setting up of any new closed-shop arrangements, and making public funds available to support trade-union secret ballots for the election of full-time officers and for the approval of strike action. But this attempt to adjust the balance between employers and employees, and between coercion and choice, was far from the end of the story, for a series of aggressively reactionary successors, particularly Norman Tebbit, Norman Fowler and Michael Howard, soon set out to undermine the whole position of trade unions within the established system of collective bargaining. Thus they withdrew the legitimation of the union contribution to public life by abolishing such tripartite bodies as the National Economic Development Council and the Manpower Services Commission. And they pursued an increasingly ideological reduction of the rights of free association through three further Employment Acts in 1982, 1988 and 1990, a Trade Union act in 1984, and a Trade Union Reform and Employment Rights Act in 1993. Moreover, their attention was focused not only on increasing the restrictions around closed shops and secret ballots, but even more crucially on reopening the old issue of the financial liabilities of trade unionists, significantly raising the stakes for any disobedience of the government's other requirements.

Thus in 1982 the union immunity from common-law claims which dated back to 1906 was fatally undermined by the provision for the award of damages of up to £250,000 for any officially sanctioned unlawful actions carried out in the course of industrial disputes. This also implied that unions would be subject to court injunctions against any such actions, as well as to fines for contempt in cases of failure to comply with these injunctions which could be far larger than the penalty if found guilty of the original offence. Moreover, their remaining immunities were significantly curtailed by the redefinition of legitimate industrial disputes: requiring that they be between workers and their own employers, and that they be wholly or mainly concerned with wages and working conditions, rather than merely connected with them. This therefore excluded inter-union disputes over recognition, many forms of solidarity action against other employers, and any public-sector strikes judged to have significant political agendas. Eventually, unions were also required strictly to repudiate unofficial action if they were to retain their immunity to liability for its consequences. Meanwhile, pre-1980 closed shops were only allowed to continue if they secured 85 per cent support in ballots, and it became unlawful for companies to be refused contracts simply because they did not operate union-labour-only policies. Eventually it was made illegal for unions to strike in pursuit of closed shops or for firms to refuse employment over the question of union membership, and finally the closed shop was simply outlawed altogether.

Most of this legislation covering industrial disputes did have a voluntarist form, in so far as it aimed to undermine trade-union power not through direct government interference or special tribunals but rather by giving employers considerably more scope to take their own legal actions in the normal civil courts. However, in its legislation covering trade-union democracy, the Thatcher regime was prepared to be more openly interventionist. Thus in 1984 the long-standing assumption that the unions should be left to decide how to conduct their own internal affairs was fundamentally breached by the requirement that secret ballots be held for the regular re-election of national officials, immediately before the launching of any industrial action and in order to approve the continued use of trade-union funds for political purposes. Not only were the procedural requirements for these ballots repeatedly tightened up by the government to make decision-making more awkward, but in addition members were given immunity from discipline by their own organizations if they refused to take part in industrial action, even when this had already received majority support in the required ballots. By this point it had become all too evident that the cynical use of individualist rhetoric had taken over from any coherent vision of democratically run voluntary associations.

This impressive battery of legislation would inevitably have had some restraining effect on the behaviour of the country's trade unionists, though how much is not clear. For equally, if not more, important was Margaret Thatcher's simultaneous abandonment of the cross-party commitment to full employment which had been in place since 1945. Once again a rationale was provided in terms of monetarist economic rhetoric about the need for high interest rates and restricted public spending to control the rate of inflation, but prominent ministers were also quite open about the attraction of sharp deflationary measures and rising unemployment as a way of weakening trade unionism. Thus a government-induced business recession increased the number of the unemployed to over 2 million by the end of 1980, and Thatcher's stubborn attachment to this particular brand of monetarism ensured that the figure continued to rise to over 3 million by 1986, possibly over 4 million if changes in government statistics are taken into account. Naturally enough, the proportion of the workforce in trade unions fell from more than 50 per cent to less than 40 per cent over the course of the decade. Consequently, though the practice of organized bargaining declined more slowly than the government would have liked, the proportion covered by collective agreements also fell from around 70 per cent to less than 50 per cent. Similarly, the number of strikes was cut by half and the number of working days lost due to industrial disputes was cut to around a quarter of its earlier level.

The impact of this strategy was focused on those manufacturing sectors which had remained the key centres of trade-union organization among the assembly and process workers: engineering and shipbuilding, and the steel industry. But simultaneously, the Thatcher regime removed the legislative framework which had gradually been built up to protect less well-organized general workers. This increasingly regressive strategy was veiled by a superficially progressive rhetoric on the 'enterprise economy' and 'job creation', but it soon became clear that this meant little more than the reduction of wages and the spread of casual employment. Significantly enough, this was accompanied by an open repudiation of the whole trend of Tory paternalism which had sought to protect the weakest members of society, traceable back to the early-nineteenth-century factory acts. Thus the government abolished the Fair Wages Resolution guaranteeing industry-standard wages to those employed on public authority contracts in the private sector, which had been a Conservative measure in 1891. Similarly, it removed those under the age of twenty-one from the protection of the Wages Councils and then simply abolished those councils, which had been established in 1909 by no less iconic a figure than Winston Churchill. Remarkably enough, it even reversed the impact of the Truck Acts of the 1830s, by reintroducing the possibility of extensive non-cash remuneration for labour, and it removed the prohibition on women working underground in the mining industry.

This openly reactionary drive was also accompanied by an increasingly passionate repudiation of the pressures arising from Britain's membership of the European Community, which was attempting to maintain at least a minimal framework for a socially regulated economy. Thus the Thatcher regime began by dragging its feet in implementing a number of significant Community Directives, to the extent of having several proceedings successfully taken against it in the European Court of Justice over the unequal treatment of women in paid work. The British government then went on to use its presidency of the Council of Ministers in 1986 to secure reformed decision-making procedures exempting most of its own employment policy from new Community legislation. Finally, in 1989, it simply refused to sign the European Social Charter, the drafting of which had in part been provoked by what was increasingly perceived as the danger of its own policies: seen by neighbouring states as both unjustly oppressive in social terms and unfairly competitive in economic ones. As two legal experts commented in 1992:

By the early 1990s, there did indeed seem to be a real opposition between the extreme economic liberalism which had come to inform the employment law of the UK, and ideals of social citizenship in industrial society of which the European Community had become the most important champion – or, at least, the most obvious rallying-point. From a standpoint in 1950, 1960, 1970, or even 1980, this would have seemed a scarcely predictable state of affairs, an unlikely way in which the government would be defining its policy objectives for employment law.[4]

Naturally enough, all this was accompanied by tight limits on pay increases where the government could exercise direct control, in the public sector. Relatively easily imposed on the weaker federal unions in education and health, initial attempts at applying restraint to the stronger seniority unions in steel, railways and coal mining had rather mixed results, as these bodies were still in a confident mood. This contributed to the government's determination to reverse the measures of 1945–51 and dispose of the nationalized industries altogether. For privatization would not only allow it to dispense with its responsibility for public-sector pay policy, the selling of assets would also allow it to increase its short-term revenues. Moreover, a further advantage would be the opportunity once again to undermine an established system of collective bargaining by making national agreements increasingly irrelevant. Thus the public utilities of water, gas, electricity and tele-communications were simply sold off to a large number of regional limited companies theoretically in competition for customers. Mean-while, local government was required to put out its contracts for services to external competitive tendering, and local authority control of schools was weakened by allowing opting-out as independent trusts and enforcing delegated budgets on those which chose to remain within the public sector. Similarly, regional pay bargaining and eventually 'internal markets' and separate trusts were introduced into the National Health Service, while the central government Civil Service was divided into almost 100 distinct agencies, and what was left of the Post Office was split up into sixteen main bargaining units.

Given its previous history, it is perhaps not surprising that the epic battle of resistance which came to dominate the decade took place in the coal industry. Following the major strikes of the early 1970s, employment relations had stabilized considerably around the National Coal Board's Plan for Coal of 1974, committing it to a long-term expansion of mining in order to provide an alternative fuel for electricity generation in the new context of unpredictable increases in the price of imported oil. This assumed large government subsidies for deep mining, assessed closures of older pits in terms of physical exhaustion rather than commercial viability, and proposed a number of major new investment projects, including a complex of new mines at Selby in Yorkshire. It was also accompanied by an incentive scheme implying greater differentials between face-workers in different regions, eventually accepted by the area organizations of the miners' union even though it had initially been rejected in principle in national ballots. This loosening up of previously over-rigid wage bargaining promised to provide the opportunity for skilled workers in the more dynamic regions to secure major improvements in their wages without the need to rely on national strikes.

However, even this sort of progress within the old framework of economic assumptions was unlikely to survive long in the Thatcher era. Indeed, one of the new regime's first moves was a special Coal Industry Act in 1980 to reduce subsidies and make the industry pay its own way, naturally leading almost immediately to proposals for major pit closures. A wave of protest strikes in the areas most likely to be affected, above all in south Wales, then forced the government to back down, maintaining a generous level of subsidy and feeding the illusion that the miners' industrial organization might indeed still be impregnable. However, this was a fatal under-estimation of Margaret

Thatcher's personal tenacity as well as her political determination to even up the score over the defeat of Conservative governments by the miners' industrial action in the 1970s. As far as the coal industry itself was concerned, she immediately set about building up stocks at the power stations and promoting tougher figures within the relevant government departments. This culminated with the appointment to the head of the Coal Board of Ian McGregor, an outsider from the United States, and already responsible for cutting the workforce of the British steel industry in half. More generally, the consolidation of the regime in the aftermath of the 1982 Falklands War permitted Thatcher to begin a more aggressive assault on 'the enemy within'. The first step came in December 1983 when the Prime Minister in her role as Minister for the Civil Service gave an instruction that the staff at the Government Communications Headquarters intelligence centre in Cheltenham were no longer permitted to belong to national trade unions. Perhaps it was not surprising that, though the white-collar bodies involved initially secured a High Court judgment in their favour, this was overruled on grounds of national security in both the Appeal Court and the House of Lords. However, what was revealing about the government's new approach was that the TUC's attempts to construct a compromise around a no-strike deal were simply rejected out of hand by the Prime Minister, on the grounds that there was an inherent conflict between membership of a union and loyalty to the state.

With the government determined to reverse the legacy of 1945 and the miners' union in a confident mood after its victory in 1981, some sort of costly dispute was probably inevitable unless its members could be persuaded to digest the real lessons of their forerunners' experiences during the 1920s. This, however, was ruled out by the meteoric rise within the union of Arthur Scargill from the Yorkshire area, which guaranteed that the conflict would be particularly controversial, drawn-out and eventually disastrous for ordinary working miners. Although a former Communist and able to call on the deep loyalties of leftist networks, Scargill had imbibed little or nothing of the industrial realism and political constitutionalism of the post-war British Communist Party. His intransigent personality and bitterly satirical sense of humour initially appealed as a counterpoint to Margaret Thatcher, but in electing him as their national president with a landslide majority in 1981 the miners probably got rather more than they bargained for. Thus, on their side, electoral support for Scargill's vigorous defence of the legacy of the 1970s and the promised expansion of the industry was not maintained in any of the three national ballots held during his first two years in office which would have committed them to industrial action. Meanwhile, on his side, Scargill's determination to have a final showdown with the Conservative government over its latest plans for pit closures finally led him to launch a major strike in March 1984 without the ballot on national action required by the union's constitution. Instead he and his far-left supporters on the executive aimed to build up support district by district, allowing the more assertive areas (especially Yorkshire) to initiate strikes and send out mass pickets to rally the more moderate areas (especially the Midlands), and relying on the miners' deeply felt loyalties once action was under way. This did work to some extent in the short run, even in those older regions now regarded as peripheral coalfields and deeply demoralized by the extent of the closures which had already taken place. In south Wales, for example, the members were divided at the outset and the district leadership remained deeply suspicious of Scargill's tactics throughout the strike, but, as long as it was on, it was supported by 94 per cent of the local men, accompanied by tremendous solidarity action on the part of their wives.

However, in the longer run this proved to be a disastrously backward-looking strategy which failed to take account of the government's determination to maintain public order, of the working miners' willingness to take advantage of the new trends in union law and of other unions' reluctance to prejudice the position of their members in a period of deep economic uncertainty. Already in the aftermath of the successful mass picketing during the 1972 strike, local police chiefs had been considering coordinated activity through a National Reporting Centre, but had held back from action because of the cost implications as well as their traditionally neutral role in industrial disputes. Now Thatcher gave this initiative the government's full financial and political support, to the unprecedented extent of setting up a mobile force of 20,000 police drawn from forty-three different forces. This eventually cost over £200 million and carried out over 11,000 arrests, while on the miners' side the union's federal structure still left picketing in the hands of its area organizations. As a result, the immense police operation of 1984 succeeded in maintaining long-term access to the collieries, and by doing so turned mass picketing from the ultimate weapon of trade unionism into a mere public-order nuisance comparable to football hooliganism. Simultaneously, the union was finding its position increasingly vulnerable to court actions taken against its constituent areas by those members who did wish to carry on working. When it failed to comply with the rulings obtained against mass picketing, it had all its national assets sequestered in October 1984 and was put into receivership a month later. Meanwhile, the electricians were unwilling to risk their members' long-term positions through solidarity action in the power stations, which in any case had plenty of coal to see them through their slacker summer period; the steelworkers were worried about the prospects for their industry and cooperated with management to secure coal supplies; and the transport workers were unable to prevent many of their local members from driving coal delivery lorries.

Since Scargill's strategy had left the miners' union vulnerable to heavy-handed policing and to civil actions through the courts, and had failed to secure effective support from other organizations, it was only a matter of time before the strike collapsed. The national leadership belatedly accepted defeat in March 1985 after an epic fifty-one weeks which had secured no concessions, resulted in the loss of almost £10,000 income to each striker, and led to bitter divisions within the union. In particular, the Nottinghamshire miners, who had mostly stayed at work, now as in the 1920s, broke away to form their own Union of Democratic Mineworkers, which soon spread into south Derbyshire and secured a significant pay rise. Moreover, despite the enormous show of solidarity within many other mining communities, the scale of the defeat only hastened the very process the strike had been called to prevent. For with its overall position even more deeply entrenched, the Thatcher regime proceeded to privatize the electricity supply industry and gave it a free hand to use not only other types of fuel but also cheaper imported coal. A wave of pit closures over the next five years reduced the workforce in British coal mining by 50 per cent and the membership of the miners' union from 200,000 to only 40,000. Despite a brief rallying of the union and of public sympathy for its members' plight in the early 1990s, the inexorable decline of British coal could not be halted: ten years after the strike there were only seventeen deep mines left in the country, manned by only 11,000 miners.

Similar factors ensured the equally complete defeat of what had previously been seen as one of the country's strongest groups of craft unionists, the printers in the newspaper industry. In a dispute with the maverick publisher Eddie Shah in the winter of 1983–4 they had already found themselves fatally entangled in the new legislation. An injunction against pickets acting away from their own place of work had led to increasingly heavy fines for contempt of court when they refused to give in, and eventually to the complete sequestration of their financial assets. Then, in the aftermath of the miners' strike, the News International company of Rupert Murdoch was prepared to dismiss all 5,000 of its existing employees, to move to a new production site away from Fleet Street, and to rely on aggressive action from the Metropolitan Police to run its restructured operation in a virtual state of siege. Once again the printers were ultimately undermined by heavy fines and the sequestration of their assets, eventually conceding defeat in February 1987.

With these epic struggles ending firmly in its favour, the Thatcher regime seemed to have achieved all it had set out to do in the sphere of policy on trade unionism. For through its general approach it had managed to shift the balance of legislation firmly against the unions and thoroughly deregulate the labour market in the context of rapidly rising unemployment. And through its specific handling of the miners' strike it had shown that long-standing corporatist understandings would not be allowed to stand in the way of re-organizing the public sector, and that major unions were vulnerable even when fighting over such general social issues as jobs and the survival of whole communities.

PATTERNS OF INDUSTRIAL RELATIONS

By any standards this was a sustained and shocking assault on the historic rights of long-standing voluntary associations, and it was perhaps not surprising that in her twilight years Mrs Thatcher became embroiled in the public defence of visits to Britain by the Chilean former dictator General Pinochet. However, as always in the history of national policy-making, a major question remains about the impact of all this at the level of everyday, local behaviour. Thus one of the surprising findings of research carried out during the 1980s was that employers in general were making relatively little use of the new legislation which had been passed supposedly at their request and in their interest. There was not much widespread removal of formal recognition from trade unions: only fifty-six cases up to the end of 1988, mainly in newspaper printing and the docks. And there was little use of the new laws in the course of industrial disputes: only 114 injunctions against unions between 1983 and 1987, in which period there were still around 1,000 strikes a year.

New approaches were being introduced by overseas companies. For example, 'human resource management' was favoured by North Americans such as IBM, offering high salaries and promotion linked to individual effort, in return for the acceptance of company culture and non-unionism. And 'single-union agreements' were favoured by Japanese such as Nissan, recognizing the trade union of their choice in return for a no-strike agreement and the acceptance of all-or-nothing 'pendulum arbitration'. However, though heralded by some as the wave of the future, neither of these approaches became particularly widespread in Britain. Performance-related pay and some other elements of the human-resource approach did become more widespread, but it was rarely adopted as a complete package. The most notable omissions were naturally in the traditional blind-spots of British management: investment in the provision of systematic training and the direct control of production. Similarly, single-union agreements were actively championed by such craft bodies as the electricians and the engineers as a way of surviving in a hostile environment. But there were still only around 200 by 1993, covering only around 200,000 workers, and they tended to take the form of traditional union recognition: only 1 per cent of workplaces which had unions had adopted pendulum arbitration.

More significant was the simple refusal to recognize trade unions in new workplaces as the economy and the workforce entered yet another phase of sectoral and regional restructuring. For the early 1980s saw a sharp acceleration in an existing trend away from traditional engineering in the north and the Midlands, towards high technology and private services, such as finance, distribution and catering, heavily concentrated in London and the south-east. As in the past, this was accompanied by aggressive new entrepreneurs pushing for tight control over the use of technical innovations and working methods, and pressing their employees to accept long hours and intensive levels of effort. Moreover, with large numbers of married women still in the workforce, this phase of restructuring was also accompanied by a marked increase in part-time work, sub-contracting and short-term employment.

However, this kind of approach tended to produce an increase in workers' discontent which could not always be bought off even with higher financial rewards. For intense effort all too often led to a deterioration in health and safety, while the segmentation of the workforce frequently led to a build-up of dissatisfaction over differential treatment. The strong drive towards unilateral domination of the new workplaces therefore tended once again to produce just what it had aimed to prevent: a collective response from employees. As a result there was evidence of an interest in joining trade unions among a significant number of those in new firms in the south-east, not only among semi-skilled assembly workers, but also among highly skilled technical workers and poorly skilled service workers. What was missing was an effective union presence, due in part to the unions' own lack of sufficient local staff and information, but mainly to employers' persistence in non-recognition.

Meanwhile, there was a marked trend in the longer-established sectors to move away from multi-employer national bargaining towards single-employer, organization-wide or even workplace bargaining. Though this was exactly what had been widely condemned as the central weakness of the country's system of industrial relations a decade earlier, it was now vigorously promoted in a context in which workers' assertiveness had been on the wane since the re-emergence of significant levels of unemployment in the middle of the 1970s. National negotiating procedures were wound up in retailing and banking in the late 1980s and replaced by unilateral, organization-wide decision-making. A similar trend was evident in the public sector following the increasing fragmentation of pay determination imposed by government policies. Meanwhile, in manufacturing the trend was towards unilateral decisions at the level of the workplace, finally symbolized by the abandonment of national procedures in engineering in 1990. These significant shifts in formal structures were an integral part of tougher management attitudes, involving non-negotiable offers in a context of large-scale redundancies and the easy dismissal of trouble-makers. An increasing ability to bypass trade-union channels was sometimes accompanied by the communication of new plans to employees through direct personal mailings, followed by their ratification through special workplace ballots. Sometimes referred to as 'macho-management', this trend began in the car and steel industries, spread into the public sector in the aftermath of the miners' defeat, and also found some high-profile champions in newspaper publishing.

However, it is also significant that in most cases tough attitudes in the older sectors did not involve attempts to eliminate unions altogether. This was because few of those involved at the more practical level shared the Prime Minister's conviction that trade unionism as such was a major threat to economic competitiveness. On the contrary, most of them found that established relations with unions still made a useful contribution to communication with their employees and were preferable to untested, and often expensive, innovations in personnel management. Moreover, even the most 'macho' were still looking for new forms of agreement with their employees, even if these were increasingly imposed within a general climate of insecurity and fear. Thus as the author of one survey carried out in the middle of the 1980s remarked:

The evidence does not then support the view that the emerging trend of industrial relations is based on an aggressive management attack on established trade unions: a more subtle process seems to have been taking place in which firms have certainly been trying to change working practices but in which cooperation and involvement have been seen as important.[5]

As a result, even at the end of almost twenty years of Thatcherism, the authors of the 1998 Workplace Employee Relations Survey (partly financed by the Department of Trade and Industry itself) were prepared to observe:

Still, unions have a foothold in just over half of workplaces, and in five out of six of these workplaces there is union recognition. These workplaces are, on the whole, larger than average such that 62 per cent of employees work in workplaces with union recognition. Thus, an engagement with a union presence is still part of the work experience for two out of three employees, even if only half that number are actually union members. This leaves plenty of scope for new recruitment, if unions are able to persuade these employees to become members.[6]

Their evidence also led them to conclude that British employees' perceptions of fair treatment were still generally associated with one main model: the presence of a recognized trade union combined with union representation on a formal consultative committee. What held membership down, then, was not workers' hostility towards the unions, or indeed any fear of joining them, but rather the feeling that at that point in time they were not making much impact on everyday working situations.

NEW UNIONS, NEW LABOUR

Perhaps understandably, the unions were slow to drop the attitudes they had acquired during the 1960s and 1970s, and slow to appreciate the novelty and resilience of the Thatcher regime. The TUC refused to cooperate with the trade-union legislation of 1980 and 1982, imagining that such a boycott might still mean something, and still assuming that rising unemployment would be unpopular enough to make the return of a Labour government inevitable. However, the Labour Party began to swing to the left and to find itself increasingly driven back into its electoral heartlands in the north and the 'Celtic Fringe'. For, when Callaghan retired as leader in the autumn of 1980, the veteran Bevanite Michael Foot beat the veteran Bevinite Denis Healey in voting by the parliamentary party. The party conference then went on to introduce a new system of choosing the leader through a broader electoral college, in which the parliamentary party would have only 30 per cent of the vote while the generally more left-wing constituency parties would also have 30 per cent, and the unions the remaining

40 per cent. At this point a number of the more moderate Labour MPs split away to form the Social Democratic Party and, since they took a significant body of left-of-centre opinion with them, the electoral opposition to Thatcherism was fatally divided. It took the severe shocks of Labour's worst post-war election defeat in 1983, followed almost immediately by the equally dramatic defeat of the miners' strike, to wake up the party and the unions to the full extent of their new situation: a major change of attitude which came to be known as the 'New Realism'.

Since the TUC's attempts at dialogue with the Conservative government were not reciprocated, it was left up to individual unions to find their own ways of protecting their members' interests. At first the new initiatives tended to be controversial and divisive, and the TUC had something of an uphill battle to maintain a united front. For example, leading craft unions such as the engineers and the electricians led the way in accepting government financial support for internal ballots, and were also unusually enthusiastic in entering single-union agreements, leading inevitably to charges of poaching on the territory of other bodies. However, in the longer term, one of the most obvious responses to the resilience of Thatcherism was closer cooperation through a wave of defensive union mergers, eventually leading to the construction of a handful of massive conglomerates which began to cross the traditional boundaries between the main types of organization and to drop any specific occupational references in their titles. In one of the earliest of these moves, the long-established craft boilermakers joined forces with the more recent federal municipal workers in 1982 to create the GMB, a title which had echoes of its constituent bodies but was meant to be understood mainly as a set of initials. In less unusual moves the scientific and technical staff amalgamated with the technical and supervisory staff in 1988 to form the Manufacturing, Science and Finance Union, or MSF, while in 1992 the craft engineers sought refuge with their close neighbours the electricians: but ten years later these two bodies then began a further process of merger to form a new conglomerate union to be called Amicus. Meanwhile, the public employees had already joined forces with their close neighbours the local government officers and the health service employees in 1993, to form the huge conglomerate Unison. In 2001, Unison had 1.3 million members, the two wings of Amicus had 1.1 million members between them, the transport workers had 0.9 and the GMB 0.7. The strong possibility of a further merger between the latter two bodies suggests that the future may see one major body each for public sector workers, for skilled assembly workers and for general workers, with the effective disappearance of long-standing distinctions between manual and non-manual organizations. The major absence, which could hardly have been imagined a century ago, is that of a major body for process workers. But the long-term decline of cotton, coal, steel and the railways has meant that what was once regarded by many as the core of the labour movement has turned out to be only a temporary phenomenon, at least in the case of Britain.

By pooling their financial resources, membership and bargaining power, the massive new conglomerates have not only ensured the long-term survival of British trade unionism, but also begun to address one of its long-standing problems. For, while the TUC has never been in a position to coordinate collective bargaining by its numerous constituent bodies, the new conglomerates could in principle do just this. Moreover, the wave of formal mergers not only reduced the number of separate unions to almost half its previous level, it was also accompanied by a significant increase in 'single-table' bargaining in which all the recognized unions were prepared to negotiate jointly. In workplaces where collective bargaining was still the norm in pay-determination, single-table bargaining increased from around 40 per cent to almost 80 per cent of cases during the 1990s. Since this was particularly marked in the public sector, it seems that one of the major problems in the background of the disorganized disputes of the 1979 'Winter of Discontent' may now have been substantially resolved.

In itself the introduction of the legal requirement to hold secret postal ballots has probably not improved internal union democracy, as turn-outs have generally been lower than in the previous workplace meetings and ballots, while the role of national factions and slates of candidates has increased. However, the general climate of government and media hostility has pushed the unions into establishing better lines of communication with their members. In addition to more attractive union magazines and periodic membership mailings, the larger bodies have all begun to provide wide ranges of individual services. As in the case of many other voluntary associations in this period, there was a new interest in securing preferential financial deals for their members for such services as mortgages, loans and insurance through the establishment of the joint Unity Trust Bank in 1984. But the unions were also concerned to provide other services more closely linked to their own traditional spheres of expertise, above all legal advice over industrial illness and injuries, through which they secured annual compensations totalling hundreds of millions of pounds a year during the 1990s.

Meanwhile the unions were also making significant progress towards addressing the under-representation of women and ethnic minorities within their own internal affairs. More women's officers have been appointed and more special women's conferences and education courses have been established. Some of the unions with predominantly female memberships have initiated positive discrimination through reserved seats on their representative committees. Thus by 2001, in Unison women made up around 70 per cent of the members, 65 per cent of the executive and 50 per cent of the national full-time officers; among the teachers the equivalent figures were 75 per cent, 50 per cent and unusually in that year 0 per cent; among the shop workers they were 60 per cent, 60 per cent and 65 per cent; and among the public and commercial service workers they were 60 per cent, 45 per cent and 35 per cent. Female trade unionists continued to be assertive, with a high profile in campaigns to defend employment in the health service and education, along with an increase in the number of women's places on the TUC General Council from two to twelve. Similarly, there has been increasing openness to the recruitment of black members, the appointment by some unions of racial-equality officers up to national level and significantly improved opportunities for participation within the TUC. Already by the mid-1980s this had produced equal densities of union membership. However, although the Jamaican-born Bill Morris emerged at the head of the transport workers in 1991, this was still all too untypical: in 2001 less than half of the major unions had any black full-time officers, and among the transport workers themselves there were still only seven in the 320 national and regional positions.

The TUC gradually came to accept its much reduced significance

413

in public life with the demise of tripartite bodies and the closing of ministerial doors, and returned to its original role as an umbrella pressure group focusing limited resources on key campaigns. For example, it took overall control of the campaign against further pit closures in coal mining in the early 1990s and continued its campaigns against sexual and racial discrimination. However, its most notable contribution was as a broker between British trade unions and the European Union. Under the leadership of John Monks it promoted an increasingly integrated Europe as a potentially progressive influence: as a stronger economic competitor in world markets, as an initiator of protective social legislation to counter-balance the Thatcher regime, and as a source of financial subsidies for development in deprived regions. Indeed, given the Conservative government's growing hostility towards Europe, the TUC even came be seen as a useful ally by some of those continental figures leading the moves towards closer integration. Thus what had long been a source of uncertainty and division in British trade-union attitudes was firmly resolved in a direction appropriate to the changing international circumstances.

Despite the Conservative attempt to undermine the link between the unions and the Labour Party through its 1984 legislative challenge to the continuation of political funds, the relationship remained very close and in some respects became even closer at the height of Thatcherism. In the first place, a carefully thought-out campaign secured massive successes in the ballots required over the political funds. By 1986 all thirty-eight unions which already had them in place had held membership ballots, resulting in an overall 83 per cent vote in favour of retaining them. Meanwhile, over the next five years another twenty trade unions, mainly white-collar ones, decided to set them up for the first time, though not all of these newcomers went as far as to affiliate to the Labour Party straight away. As union contributions represented over 80 per cent of Labour Party income at the time, this success was vital in securing the survival of an effective parliamentary opposition to Thatcher's far-right Conservatism. In the second place, the fall in individual party membership meant that the union share of the conference block vote reached 90 per cent by the 1980s. Moreover, decisions about how to allocate these votes were in the hands of fewer, larger organizations: for example, the transport workers on their own could easily out-vote all the constituency parties together. Finally, the hostile political environment stimulated a revival of the traditional practice of union sponsorship of MPs, paying most of their election expenses and supporting the employment of a constituency agent, in the hope of increasing the effectiveness of their parliamentary lobbying. This involved around 40 per cent of Labour MPs in the 1970s, but rose to almost 60 per cent by the early 1990s, and was backed up by the increasing appointment of full-time union political officers.

Learning from the marked weakening of Labour's electoral performance during the early-1980s atmosphere of factionalism and splits, the unions quickly united in agreeing that they would not support any further initiatives to change the party's constitution or any further challenges to the leadership. They then made a major contribution to the stabilization of the party through their reliable support for a succession of increasingly moderate Labour leadership teams, from the left-right alliance of Neil Kinnock and Roy Hattersley, through the right-left alliance of John Smith and Margaret Beckett, to the closer partnership of Tony Blair and Gordon Brown. As a result, beginning with a debate over the causes of the 1983 election defeat, and moving on through a comprehensive Policy Review following a further defeat in 1987, the party gradually overhauled its public commitments in a strategic move back towards the centre-left. By the early 1990s the far-left shibboleths of withdrawal from the Common Market, unilateral disarmament and further rounds of nationalization had been replaced by something more like Labour's original radical-liberalism. The emphasis was now on international cooperation and the limitation of the state's economic responsibility to the provision of a stable monetary framework: implying the reduction of unemployment in the context of a market economy, the maintenance of public services in the context of a relatively low-tax regime, and the introduction of constitutional reform to decentralize power. The bulk of this transformation was accepted by party activists under the reassuring leadership of the former left-winger Kinnock, with the more openly centrist Blair only adding the final touches when he dropped the formal commitment to public ownership in 1995 and successfully projected the image of 'New Labour' during the landslide election victory of 1997.

As in the 1930s, then, a temporary crisis in Labour's relationship with the electorate was tided over by the unions providing the bedrock of the party's organization and supporting its shift in a more pragmatic and more popular direction. However, in contrast to that earlier period, the deep unpopularity of the unions both with the wider public and with many left-of-centre activists, arising from perceptions of their excessive power in the 1970s and their role in the fall of the previous Labour government, led to a reduction in their direct influence within the party's policy-making processes. Thus both the National Executive Committee and the Liaison Committee with the TUC were marginalized, while senior figures in the Shadow Cabinet and, above all, a much-enlarged Leader's Office emerged as the main sources of policy innovation. Moreover, faced with relentlessly hostile right-wing media coverage, the party also set up a Campaigns and Communications Directorate responsible for monitoring public opinion and presenting a professionally coordinated image, which led immediately to a new emphasis within existing policies and in the longer run to a new input into policy-making itself. As a result, earlier commitments to repeal all of the Conservative trade-union legislation were dropped, and the Labour leadership announced that it was prepared to accept the framework of state-imposed ballots, the liability of the unions to common-law damages for industrial action and the prohibition of closed shops. This was then pursued into the reform of the publicly embarrassing predominance of the unions within the party's own constitution as they were progressively reduced to more equal partners. Their share of the vote at conference came down by stages to 70 per cent in 1992, and then 50 per cent in 1995, and was to be cast by individual delegates rather than as union blocks. Similarly, in 1993 their share of the college for leadership elections was reduced to one third, to be determined in prior internal ballots of declared Labour supporters, and the principle of 'one member one vote' was introduced into the local selection of parliamentary candidates. Finally, in 1996 the procedures for union sponsorship of MPs were replaced by looser links with constituency parties. Meanwhile, especially under Blair, there was a successful drive to reduce the party's financial dependence on the unions by increasing individual membership and donations, including many large ones from sympathetic businessmen.

For their part the unions accepted all this in good faith as necessary stages along the road to the restoration of Labour's status as a genuinely national party capable once again of securing a governing majority. In return they were guaranteed the enactment of a minimum trade-union programme on the long-awaited return to power. By the mid-1990s this consisted of pledges to sign up to the European Social Chapter and to legislate for a minimum wage and statutory enforcement of union recognition. Following the 1997 Labour landslide many trade unionists felt that, while Blair's government did indeed meet these pledges, it also pressed for a lower definition of the minimum wage and a more demanding threshold of employee support for recognition than had been hoped for. Moreover, although dialogue between ministers and union leaders was re-established after many years of exclusion, it was widely felt that the Blair leadership was more comfortable in the company of senior figures from the world of business. Similarly, while there was much union enthusiasm for Labour's second-term increases in spending on education and health, there was also much dismay over its continued reliance on Private Finance Initiatives at the core of its strategy for rebuilding public services. The relationship between Labour and the unions therefore became increasingly tense: but, despite many forecasts of its final dissolution, it did still remain in place. For, as the party became more confident of its grip on government, it became less nervous about public perceptions of its dependence on the unions. Meanwhile, a myriad of specific reforms across a wide front of government activity really did make a difference to the living standards of ordinary working people, and the New Labour team's remarkable success in achieving something close to full employment through careful management of the economy reaffirmed its convergence with the traditional priorities of British trade unionism. However, early in 2003 Tony Blair's passionate advocacy of the invasion of Iraq in the face of remarkably widespread extra-parliamentary opposition seemed to confirm New Labour's drift to the right. Individual unions and the TUC were notably anti-war and, particularly if concerns over the foreign policy of the USA continued to destabilize the economy, they were increasingly likely to find themselves being pushed once again into playing a high-profile role in redefining Labour's overall strategy or in an even broader process of political realignment.

In the opening years of the twenty-first century British trade unions are still at rather a low point. Their membership has stabilized after falling constantly for twenty years, but it shows no signs of rising again and they are still marginal to the nation's public life. Thus, in looking to the future, the first important question to consider is that contained in the title of this chapter: will the unions recover anything like their previous position, or at the end of this book have we also reached the end of their historical significance? If past precedents are still a reliable guide, they suggest that, on the contrary, we are about to see a major revival of British trade unionism. After all, one of the organizing principles of this historical account has been a pattern of cycles around fifty years in length. We have seen the unions hitting low points in the 1870s to 1880s and again in the 1920s to 1930s, suggesting that the same was likely to happen again in the 1970s to 1980s. This did indeed occur and, though that downswing has lasted for longer than the previous ones, it has not taken membership levels anything like as low as before, suggesting that the unions may now be well placed for a more rapid recovery. How will this come about?

Despite understandable concerns about the impact of recent legislation and the hostility of new employers, the key is in the national labour market. As unemployment falls, there will be less competition for jobs and employees will soon come to feel more secure. This is likely to lead to an increasing unwillingness to accept poor conditions, low pay and part-time work, manifesting itself through individual mobility and small-group disruption in the workplace. Thus managers will, sooner or later, be reminded of the advantages of collective bargaining and the value of trade-union involvement in contributing to a more orderly working environment. Once their role has been reactivated from above, this is likely to be followed by a revival in interest and membership from below which, given the widespread survival of positive attitudes towards trade unionism, may well be surprisingly rapid. While this will probably be more marked in the older sectors, where collective organization was stronger in the past, the unions have also shown an increasing interest in recruiting in the newer sectors, as well as an increasing awareness of the particular problems of those who work in them. In similar situations in the past new types of workers have repeatedly defied widespread assumptions that they could not be organized to emerge as some of the largest components of British trade unionism. Thus the sort of developments which took place among transport workers from the 1890s, and among white-collar workers from the 1960s, may well be repeated among private-service workers over the next few decades. Meanwhile, large groups of professional workers, such as nurses, doctors and teachers, have already moved closer to the trade-union mainstream than would have been thought possible before the unexpected pressures which began to affect the public sector in the 1980s.

The concern then arises, even in the minds of many trade-union activists, that this will only mean a return to the widely perceived chaos of the 1970s, which in turn prompts the question whether there is any possibility of more orderly collective bargaining and more coordination of sectional demands during a new upturn in union strength? As we have seen in earlier periods, there are a number of ways in which this might be brought about. For example, there might be changes in the nature of employment relations, with increases in consultation and company welfare provision helping to reduce adversarial attitudes. However, past precedents suggest that, though more generous approaches are likely to spread among employers as the labour market gets tighter, they are also likely to remain a small minority in the British case.

Alternatively, coordination might be imposed from above through a government incomes policy, with firm limits on overall increases in the national wage bill and clear targets for specific occupations. However, past precedents suggest that such attempts are likely to founder on the inability of the TUC to impose restraint on its member organizations, as well as on many employers' willingness to make pay concessions to gain short-term advantages over their rivals. Thus the most likely option in a traditionally voluntarist industrial relations system is that the unions themselves might organize a better-coordinated annual pay round, spending more time on the negotiation of realistic initial settlements which would then be accepted by both sides as guidelines for the remainder. One major recent change already noted may help in this regard: the emergence of a handful of 'mega unions', automatically reducing the amount of coordination required between separate organizations. But if such bodies as Unison and Amicus do indeed begin to act as 'mini-TUCs', will they be able to impose restraint on specific groups among their own members? Success will depend on making sure that each of the internal sections is fully integrated into the union's national policy-making process, not only by being given full accounts of the basis of decisions but also by being provided with effective channels of representation and flexible responses to their particular situations. Unfortunately past precedents suggest that large federations formed with defensive attitudes in periods of high unemployment may not be well equipped to respond to their members' rising expectations in periods of greater prosperity. Whether or not this can be improved upon is likely to be one of the main influences on the future of British trade unionism.

Another question much discussed is whether the British industrial relations system will indeed retain its traditional voluntarist form? For, faced with extremely tough times in the 1980s and 1990s, trade unionists began to press for a wide range of legislative protection for all employees, some of which have been granted by New Labour in office. However, as we have seen, this has long been a characteristic of the non-craft bodies which had less effective bargaining power within the workplace. For example, pressure for legislation on reasonable minimum wages and conditions was central to the very existence of unions among process workers in cotton and coal, while the current pressure to prevent discrimination and unfair dismissal is only one manifestation of older campaigns for legislation to regulate the labour market among general workers such as those in the docks. More novel is the interest in emulating the European model of positive rights for employees to secure workplace representation and consultation, and for trade unions to secure freedom of association, bargaining recognition and even some basic forms of industrial action. But while it is true that this would break away from the British legal preference for making provision through immunities from the impact of the common law, most of these positive rights would only provide an enabling foundation, and only the definition of legitimate forms of industrial action would really diverge from the voluntarist tradition. Since such an innovation is unlikely in the absence of sustained trade-union pressure, much will depend on the influence of the long-standing champions of voluntarism among the assembly workers and, since their craft bodies have now been merged with other types of organization, we face once again the intriguing issue of the relationships between distinctive groups within the new conglomerate unions.

Whichever currents of opinion turn out to be predominant among British trade unionists in the future, their ability to exercise influence on wider public issues would seem to have been significantly undermined by the removal of their traditionally privileged position within Labour's policy-making processes. How will they respond? Past precedents suggest that they will probably reconstruct themselves as a more effective pressure group, for, after all, they had been remarkably skilful in securing major legislative concessions long before the foundation of the Labour Party. Current signs are that union delegations to that party's annual conferences will construct a more coherent front on a narrower range of issues of direct concern to their members. For the time being, these are likely to focus on the management of the public sector, which remains both a major concentration of trade-union membership and a major concern to those dependent on its services. In the longer run, as they grow in strength and confidence, they are likely to seek relief from their current liability to common law damages, which was after all the issue which launched the Labour Party in the first place. In order to achieve this they may consider running more active trade unionists as MPs to create a powerful block within the legislature itself: indeed, the old Liberal-Labour target of a group of fifty senior trade unionists in the House of Commons would be an interesting tradition to revive. As in the past, they could be ready to take their own whip on issues of direct concern to their own organizations and could aim to exercise a substantial influence on broader policy issues by producing statesmen of the calibre to guarantee them places at cabinet level. Of course all this will depend on their extra-parliamentary standing and influence, so another key to the future of British trade unionism will be its ability to adapt to new circumstances and new media and to win wider public support for its demands.

In the opening years of the twenty-first century the British tradition of liberal pluralism is still at a low point. Having finally achieved office, New Labour moved quickly with an ambitious programme of constitutional reform, but, despite its formal proclamations, it has taken only limited steps towards the real decentralization of power. Thus the House of Lords has had its hereditary element removed, but has been given no new powers to check the House of Commons. Similarly, regional bodies have been introduced for Scotland and Wales, and revived for London, but the Labour leadership has interfered in the selection of key candidates and shows no signs of enthusiasm for the revival of the independence of local government. If there is indeed a popular desire to restore elements of pluralism and decentralization, professional politicians' natural reluctance to give away their power will have to be overcome by organization and pressure from below. This is where British trade unions have the opportunity to play a key role, not only in promoting their own members' interests, but also in contributing once again to the general public good. The main challenges facing them during a period of major recovery in their strength will be to maintain a largely voluntarist system of industrial relations, to achieve a degree of coordination of their economic demands, and to regain a significant influence within national, regional and local politics. All the signs are that these challenges will prove just as demanding as those we have seen being faced and overcome by their earlier pioneers.

Acknowledgements

The books listed over the next few pages are meant not only as an introduction to some further reading on British trade unionism, but also as an acknowledgement of my main intellectual debts in writing about it. In the case of some of these authors I have been able not only to read their work but also to benefit from their advice. For the following colleagues and friends have read some, or even all, of my chapters and offered much-valued comments and support: John Benson, Eugenio Biagini, Ken Brown, Margaret Dyson, Roger Fagge, Alan Fowler, Garry Runciman, Barry Supple, Duncan Tanner, Miles Taylor, Pat Thane, Steve Tolliday, Noel Whiteside, Simon Winder and Jonathan Zeitlin. I would like to pick out three of these for special thanks. I was lucky enough to collaborate closely with Jonathan Zeitlin and Eugenio Biagini at key moments in the development of my thinking: seeing the field through their eyes has made a vital contribution. I have also been very lucky to have been sharing my private life with Margaret Dyson: her enthusiasm and sympathy for the subject and my struggles with it has made all the difference. Finally, I would like to mention the late Henry Pelling, who started the whole thing off by putting me in touch with his publishers, took a keen interest in the early chapters and was a living example that, even in these hard times, it is still possible to be a scholar and a gentleman: this book is dedicated to his memory.

Further Reading

Surveys

For guides to the debates among historians in this field see K. D. Brown, *The English Labour Movement, 1700–1951* (Dublin, 1982), and K. Laybourn, *A History of British Trade Unionism, c. 1770–1990* (Stroud, 1992). For surveys of trade-union history against its wider social background see E. H. Hunt, *British Labour History, 1815–1914* (London, 1981), J. Rule, *The Labouring Classes in Early Industrial England, 1750–1850* (Harlow, 1986), and J. Benson, *The Working Class in Britain, 1850–1939* (Harlow, 1989). For a parallel account of trade unions, friendly societies and cooperative societies see E. Hopkins, *Working-Class Self-Help in Nineteenth-Century England. Responses to Industrialisation* (London, 1995). For surveys of industrial relations in the twentieth century see H. A. Clegg, *The Changing System of Industrial Relations in Great Britain* (Oxford, 1979), C. J. Wrigley (ed.), *A History of British Industrial Relations* (3 vols., Brighton and Cheltenham, 1982–96), and H. F. Gospel, *Markets, Firms and the Management of Labour in Modern Britain* (Cambridge, 1992). For the state of the unions in the 1970s see R. Taylor, *The Fifth Estate. Britain's Unions in the Seventies* (London, 1978), and for subsequent developments see R. Taylor, *The Trade Union Question in British Politics. Government and Unions since 1945* (Oxford, 1993), and J. McIlroy, *Trade Unions in Britain Today* (2nd edn, Manchester, 1995).

For a survey of the history of trade unionism among women see S. Boston, *Women Workers and the Trade Unions* (2nd edn, London, 1987). For the wider social background see H. Bradley, *Men's Work, Women's Work. A Sociological History of the Sexual Division of Labour in Employment* (Cambridge, 1989), E. Roberts, *Women's Work, 1840–1940* (2nd edn, Cambridge, 1995), and K. Honeyman, *Women, Gender and Industrialisation in England, 1700–1870* (Basingstoke, 2000).

For surveys of the history of trade unionism in Wales see the relevant sections of K. O. Morgan, *Rebirth of a Nation. Wales, 1880–1980* (Oxford, 1981), and J. Davies, *A History of Wales* (London, 1993). For Scotland see W. H. Marwick, *A Short History of Labour in Scotland* (Edinburgh, 1967), and for the wider social background see the relevant sections of T. C. Smout, *A History of the Scottish People, 1560–1830* (London, 1969), and T. C. Smout, *A Century of the Scottish People, 1830–1950* (London, 1986). For Ireland see E. O'Connor, *A Labour History of Ireland, 1824–1960* (Dublin, 1992), and for the wider social and political background see the relevant sections of R. F. Foster, *Modern Ireland, 1600–1972* (London, 1988).

For the trade-union involvement in politics see P. Adelman, *Victorian Radicalism. The Middle-class Experience, 1830–1914* (Harlow, 1984), D. G. Wright, *Popular Radicalism. The Working-Class Experience, 1780–1880* (Harlow, 1988), B. Pimlott and C. Cook (eds.), *Trade Unions in British Politics. The First 250 Years* (2nd edn, London, 1991), H. Pelling, *A History of British Trade Unionism* (5th edn, London, 1992), D. Tanner, P. Thane and N. Tiratsoo (eds.), *Labour's First Century* (Cambridge, 2000), and A. Thorpe, *A History of the British Labour Party* (2nd edn, Basingstoke, 2001).

For short extracts from sources illustrating all the main events in trade-union history see J. T. Ward and W. Hamish Fraser (eds.), *Workers and Employers. Documents on Trade Unions and Industrial Relations in Britain since the Eighteenth Century* (London, 1980). For a guide to the development of individual unions including lists of official histories see W. Maksymiw, J. Eaton and C. Gill (eds.), *The British Trade Union Directory* (Harlow, 1990). For accounts of individual lives see J. M. Bellamy and J. Saville (eds.), *Dictionary of Labour Biography* (London and Basingstoke, 1972–).

1 From Medieval Guilds to Modern Trade Unions

For a history of ideas about the role of occupational interest groups see A. Black, *Guilds and Civil Society in European Political Thought from the Twelfth Century to the Present* (London, 1984). For important continuities in the long pre-history of British trade unionism see R. A. Leeson, *Travelling Brothers. The Six Centuries' Road from Craft Fellowship to Trade Unionism* (London, 1979). For industrial disputes in the eighteenth century and the role of the local magistrates see C. R. Dobson, *Masters and Journeymen. A Prehistory of Industrial Relations, 1717–1800* (London, 1980), and for parallel developments in Scotland see W. H. Fraser, *Conflict and Class. Scottish Workers, 1700–1838* (Edinburgh, 1988). For the more technical aspects of the legal history of the period see J. V. Orth, *Combination and*

Conspiracy. A Legal History of Trade Unionism, 1721–1906 (Oxford, 1991). For a survey of the wider social background to early trade unionism see J. Rule, *The Experience of Labour in Eighteenth-Century Industry* (London, 1981). For the subordinate position of women see A. Clark, *The Struggle for the Breeches. Gender and the Making of the British Working Class* (London, 1995).

2 Local Organization among the Assembly Workers

For a colourful account of local club activity drawing in detail on the records of one early craft society see W. Kiddier, *The Old Trade Unions. From the Unprinted Records of the Brushmakers* (London, 1930). For the activities of the London trades see I. J. Prothero, *Artisans and Politics in Early Nineteenth-Century London. John Gast and His Times* (London, 1979), and for the wider economic and social background see L. D. Schwarz, *London in the Age of Industrialisation. Entrepreneurs, Labour Force and Living Conditions, 1700–1850* (Cambridge, 1992). For a detailed account of the development of the tramping system see R. A. Leeson, *Travelling Brothers. The Six Centuries' Road from Craft Fellowship to Trade Unionism* (London, 1979).

3 Problems of Organization among the Process Workers

For the cotton spinners see A. Fowler and T. Wyke (eds.), *The Barefoot Aristocrats. A History of the Amalgamated Association of Operative Cotton Spinners* (Littleborough, 1987). For the handloom weavers see D. Bythell, *The Handloom Weavers. A Study in the English Cotton Industry during the Industrial Revolution* (London, 1969), and N. Murray, *The Scottish Hand Loom Weavers, 1790–1850. A Social History* (Edinburgh, 1978). For the coal miners see M. W. Flinn and D. Stoker, *The History of the British Coal Industry. Volume 2. 1700–1830. The Industrial Revolution* (Oxford, 1984), A. B. Campbell, *The Lanarkshire Miners. A Social History of their Trade Unions, 1775–1874* (Edinburgh, 1979), and for a survey of their broader social experience see J. Benson, *British Coalminers in the Nineteenth Century. A Social History* (Dublin, 1980). For physical coercion see E. J. Hobsbawm, 'The machine breakers', in *Labouring Men. Studies in the History of Labour* (London, 1964), pp. 5–22, E. J. Hobsbawm and G. Rude, *Captain Swing* (Harmondsworth, 1969), M. I. Thomis, *The Luddites. Machine-Breaking in Regency England* (Newton Abbot, 1971), and J. E. Archer, *Social Unrest and Popular Protest in England, 1780–1840* (Cambridge, 2000).

4 Trade Unionists and Extra-parliamentary Radicalism

For the London trade clubs and radicalism, including a detailed account of the Queen Caroline Affair, see I. J. Prothero, *Artisans and Politics in Early Nineteenth-Century London. John Gast and His Times* (London, 1979). For the handloom weavers and radicalism see D. Bythell, *The Handloom Weavers. A Study in the English Cotton Industry during the Industrial Revolution* (London, 1969), N. Murray, *The Scottish Hand Loom Weavers, 1790–1850. A Social History* (Edinburgh, 1978), and for a detailed account of the Peterloo Massacre see D. Read, *Peterloo. The 'Massacre' and its Background* (Manchester, 1958). For the legal aspects of the combination laws see J. V. Orth, *Combination and Conspiracy. A Legal History of Trade Unionism, 1721–1906* (Oxford, 1991), and for the cooperation between Francis Place, John Doherty and John Gast around their repeal see D. Miles, *Francis Place, 1771–1854. The Life of a Respectable Radical* (Brighton, 1988), R. G. Kirby and A. E. Musson, *The Voice of the People. John Doherty, 1798–1854, Trade Unionist, Radical and Factory Reformer* (Manchester, 1975), and Prothero, *Artisans and Politics*, listed above.

5 Financial Centralization among the Assembly Workers

For the experiences of emigrant skilled workers as recorded in their own letters see C. Erickson, *Invisible Immigrants. The Adaptation of English and Scottish Immigrants in Nineteenth-Century America* (London, 1972), and for numerical measurements of population movement in the period see D. Baines, *Migration in a Mature Economy. Emigration and Internal Migration in England and Wales, 1861–1900* (Cambridge, 1985). For the evolution of tramping networks into coordinated trade unions see E. J. Hobsbawm, 'The tramping artisan', in *Labouring Men. Studies in the History of Labour* (London, 1964), pp. 34–63, and R. A. Leeson, *Travelling Brothers. The Six Centuries' Road from Craft Fellowship to Trade Unionism* (London, 1979). For case studies of rivalries between craft unions see R. Harrison and J. Zeitlin (eds.), *Divisions of Labour. Skilled Workers and Technological Change in Nineteenth-Century Britain* (Brighton, 1985). For the trades councils and the public profile of trade unionism see W. Hamish Fraser, *Trade Unions and Society. The Struggle for Acceptance, 1850–1880* (London, 1974).

6 State Intervention among the Process Workers

For the social background to cotton workers' trade unionism in the north-west see J. K. Walton, *Lancashire. A Social History, 1558–1939* (Manchester, 1987), and for a survey of the development of organization among the spinners see A. Fowler and T. Wyke (eds.), *The Barefoot Aristocrats. A History of the Amalgamated Association of Operative Cotton Spinners* (Littleborough, 1987). For the defeats in Lancashire in 1829–31 see R. G. Kirby and A. E. Musson, *The Voice of the People. John Doherty, 1798–1854. Trade Unionist, Radical and Factory Reformer* (Manchester, 1975), for the defeat in Glasgow in 1837 see W. H. Fraser, *Conflict and Class. Scottish Workers, 1700–1838* (Edinburgh, 1988), and for the important dispute in Preston in 1853 see H. I. Dutton and J. E. King, *'Ten Per Cent and No Surrender'. The Preston Strike, 1853–1854* (Cambridge, 1981). For the long campaign for state intervention see J. T. Ward, *The Factory Movement, 1830–1855* (London, 1962). For the social divisions among coal miners in the west of Scotland see A. B. Campbell, *The Lanarkshire Miners. A Social History of their Trade Unions, 1775–1874* (Edinburgh, 1979), and for the social basis of organization in the north-east of England see H. Beynon and T. Austrin, *Masters and Servants. Class and Patronage in the Making of a Labour Organisation. The Durham Miners and the English Political Tradition* (London, 1994). For south Wales in the 1830s see D. J. V. Jones, *Before Rebecca. Popular Protests in Wales, 1793–1835* (London, 1973), and for the attempt at national organization in the 1840s see R. Challinor and B. Ripley, *The Miners' Association. A Trade Union in the Age of the Chartists* (London, 1968). For a survey of industrial relations see R. Church, A. Hall and J. Kanefsky, *The History of the British Coal Industry. Volume 3. 1830–1913. Victorian Pre-eminence* (Oxford, 1986). For McDonald's campaigns of pressure for state intervention see G. M. Wilson, *Alexander McDonald, Leader of the Miners* (Aberdeen, 1982).

7 Trade Unionists and Popular Liberalism

For a survey of the involvement of trade unionists in radicalism and Chartism see M. Chase, *Early Trade Unionism. Fraternity, Skill and the Politics of Labour* (Aldershot, 2000). For the London assembly workers see I. Prothero, *Artisans and Politics in Early Nineteenth-Century London. John Gast and his Times* (London, 1979), and D. Goodway, *London Chartism, 1838–1848* (Cambridge, 1982). For two of the major Chartist episodes among the provincial process workers see D. J. V. Jones, *The Last Rising. The Newport Insurrection of 1839* (Oxford, 1985), and M. Jenkins, *The General Strike of 1842* (London, 1980). For middle-class radicalism see N. McCord, *The Anti-Corn Law League, 1838–1846* (London, 1958). For surveys of labour campaigns from the 1850s to the 1870s see F. E. Gillespie, *Labour and Politics in England, 1850–67* (London, 1927, reprinted New York, 1966), and W. Hamish Fraser, *Trade Unions and Society. The Struggle for Acceptance, 1850–1880* (London, 1974). For the integration of labour within the Gladstonian Liberal party see E. F. Biagini and A. J. Reid (eds.), *Currents of Radicalism. Popular Radicalism, Organised Labour and Party Politics in Britain, 1850–1914* (Cambridge, 1991), and E. F. Biagini, *Liberty, Retrenchment and Reform. Popular Liberalism in the Age of Gladstone, 1860–1880* (Cambridge, 1992). For the more technical aspects of the legal history of the period see J. V. Orth, *Combination and Conspiracy. A Legal History of Trade Unionism, 1721–1906* (Oxford, 1991), and K. D. Brown, 'Nonconformity and trade unionism: the Sheffield outrages of 1866', and J. Spain, 'Trade unionists, Gladstonian Liberals and the labour law reforms of 1875', both in Biagini and Reid, *Currents of Radicalism*, listed above.

8 National Bargaining among the Assembly Workers

For the extension of craft regulation see the relevant sections of H. A. Clegg, A. Fox and A. F. Thompson, *A History of British Trade Unions since 1889. Volume 1. 1889–1910* (Oxford, 1964), H. A. Clegg, *A History of British Trade Unions since 1889. Volume 2. 1911–1933* (Oxford, 1985), and R. Harrison and J. Zeitlin (eds.), *Divisions of Labour. Skilled Workers and Technological Change in Nineteenth Century England* (Brighton, 1985). For the wider social vision involved see A. J. Reid, 'Old Unionism reconsidered: the radicalism of Robert Knight, 1870–1900', in E. F. Biagini and A. J. Reid (eds.), *Currents of Radicalism. Popular Radicalism, Organised Labour and Party Politics in Britain, 1850–1914* (Cambridge, 1991), pp. 214–43. For employers' attitudes see A. J. Reid, 'Employers' strategies and craft production: the British shipbuilding industry, 1870–1950', and J. Zeitlin, 'The internal politics of employer organization: the Engineering Employers' Federation, 1896–1939', both in S. Tolliday and J. Zeitlin (eds.), *The Power to Manage? Employers and Industrial Relations in Comparative-Historical Perspective* (London, 1991), pp. 35–51, 52–80, and A. J. McIvor, *Organised Capital. Employers' Associations and Industrial Relations in Northern England, 1880–1939* (Cambridge, 1996). For government pressure towards collective bargaining see R. Davidson, *Whitehall and the Labour Problem in Late-Victorian and Edwardian Britain. A Study in Official Statistics and Social Control* (London, 1985), and R. Lowe, *Adjusting to Democracy. The Role of the Ministry of Labour in British Politics, 1916–1939* (Oxford, 1986). For the impact of the First World War see the relevant sections of Clegg, *A History of British Trade Unions*, listed above. For detailed discussions of events on Clydeside see I. McLean, *The Legend of Red Clydeside* (Edinburgh, 1983), A. J. Reid, 'Dilution, trade unionism and the state in Britain during the First World War', in S. Tolliday and J. Zeitlin, *Shop Floor Bargaining and the State. Historical and Comparative Perspectives* (Cambridge, 1985), pp. 46–74, and the relevant sections of D. Englander, *Landlord and Tenant in Urban Britain, 1838–1918* (Oxford, 1983).

9 Union Recognition among the Process Workers

For all aspects of trade unionism among the process workers in these years see H. A. Clegg, A. Fox and A. F. Thompson, *A History of British Trade Unions since 1889. Volume 1. 1889–1910* (Oxford, 1964), and H. A. Clegg, *A History of British Trade Unions since 1889. Volume 2. 1911–1933* (Oxford, 1985). For the origins of conciliation boards see W. Hamish Fraser, *Trade Unions and Society. The Struggle for Acceptance, 1850–1880* (London, 1974), pp. 98–119, and for the long survival of the sliding scale in iron and steel see F. Wilkinson, 'Collective bargaining in the steel industry in the 1920s', in A. Briggs and J. Saville (eds.), *Essays in Labour History, 1918–1939* (London, 1977), pp. 102–32. For the strong position of the spinners in cotton see A. Fowler and T. Wyke (eds.), *The Barefoot Aristocrats. A History of the Amalgamated Association of Operative Cotton Spinners* (Littleborough, 1987). For the emergence of the national miners' union and proposals for public ownership see the relevant sections of R. Church, A. Hall and J. Kanefsky, *The History of the British Coal Industry. Volume 3. 1830–1913. Victorian Pre-eminence* (Oxford, 1986), and B. Supple, *The History of the British Coal Industry. Volume 4. 1913–1946. The Political Economy of Decline* (Oxford, 1987). For a more detailed account of south Wales in a comparative context see R. Fagge, *Power, Culture and Conflict in the Coalfields. West Virginia and South Wales, 1900–1922* (Manchester, 1996).

10 New Organizations among the General Workers

For all aspects of trade unionism among the general workers in these years see E. J. Hobsbawm, 'General labour unions in Britain, 1889–1914', in *Labouring Men. Studies in the History of Labour* (London, 1964), pp. 179–203, H. A. Clegg, A. Fox and A. F. Thompson, *A History of British Trade Unions since 1889. Volume 1. 1889–1910* (Oxford, 1964), and H. A. Clegg, *A History of*

British Trade Unions since 1889. Volume 2. 1911–1933 (Oxford, 1985). For the agricultural labourers see J. P. D. Dunbabin, *Rural Discontent in Nineteenth-Century Britain* (London, 1974), and A. Howkins, *Poor Labouring Men. Rural Radicalism in Norfolk, 1872–1923* (London, 1985). For the dockers in general see J. Lovell, *Stevedores and Dockers. A Study of Trade Unionism in the Port of London, 1870–1914* (London, 1969), for the Dublin strike of 1913 see A. Mitchell, *Labour in Irish Politics, 1890–1930* (Dublin, 1974), for the Shaw Inquiry see A. Bullock, *The Life and Times of Ernest Bevin. Volume I. Trade Union Leader, 1881–1940* (London, 1960), and for attitudes to decasualization see G. Phillips and N. Whiteside, *Casual Labour. The Unemployment Question in the Port Transport Industry, 1880–1970* (Oxford, 1985). For women in woollen weaving see J. Bornat, 'Lost leaders: women, trade unionism and the case of the General Union of Textile Workers, 1875–1914', in A. V. John (ed.), *Unequal Opportunities. Women's Employment in England, 1800–1918* (Oxford, 1985), pp. 207–33, and for women in jute manufacture see E. Gordon, *Women and the Labour Movement in Scotland, 1850–1914* (Oxford, 1991). For the Women's Trade Union League and the achievement of the Trade Boards see J. A. Schmiechen, *Sweated Industries and Sweated Labour. The London Clothing Trades, 1860–1914* (London, 1984), and for women during the First World War see A. Woollacott, *On Her Their Lives Depend. Munitions Workers in the Great War* (Berkeley, 1994).

11 Trade Unionists and the Origins of the Labour Party

For the effectiveness of the Liberal-Labour strategy and the vitality of popular radicalism see the relevant sections of H. A. Clegg, A. Fox, and A. F. Thompson, *A History of British Trade Unions Since 1889. Volume I: 1889–1910* (Oxford, 1964), H. Pelling, *Popular Politics and Society in Late Victorian Britain* (London, 1968), M. Pugh, *The Making of Modern British Politics, 1867–1939* (Oxford, 1982), D. Howell, *British Workers and the Independent Labour Party, 1888–1906* (Manchester, 1983), and E. F. Biagini, *Liberty, Retrenchment and Reform. Popular Liberalism in the Age of Gladstone, 1860–1880* (Cambridge, 1992). See also J. Lawrence, 'Popular politics and the limitations of party: Wolverhampton, 1867–1900', J. Shepherd, 'Labour and parliament: the Lib-Labs as the first working-class MPs, 1885–1906', and A. J. Reid, 'Old Unionism reconsidered: the radicalism of Robert Knight, 1870–1900', all in E. F. Biagini and A. J. Reid (eds.), *Currents of Radicalism. Popular Radicalism, Organised Labour and Party Politics in Britain, 1850–1914* (Cambridge, 1991), pp. 65–85, 187–213, 214–43. For the impact of these traditions on the development of the early Labour Party see P. Thane, 'Labour and local politics: radicalism, democracy and social reform, 1880–1914', and D. Tanner, 'Ideological debate in Edwardian labour politics: radicalism, Revisionism and socialism', both in Biagini and Reid, *Currents of Radicalism*, listed above, pp. 244–70, 271–93, and A. Chadwick, *Augmenting Democracy. Political Movements and Constitutional Reform during the Rise of Labour, 1900–1924* (Aldershot, 1999). For the political background to the formation of the Labour Representation Committee see H. Pelling, *The Origins of the Labour Party, 1880–1900* (London, 1954), and for its subsequent development, including the Gladstone-MacDonald pact, see F. Bealey and H. Pelling, *Labour and Politics, 1900–1906. A History of the Labour Representation Committee* (London, 1958). For regional variations in the appeal of Liberal, Labour and Conservative politics see H. Pelling, *Social Geography of British Elections, 1885–1910* (London, 1967), and D. Tanner, *Political Change and the Labour Party, 1900–1918* (Cambridge, 1990). For Labour's influence on the pre-war Liberal social reforms see K. D. Brown, *Labour and Unemployment, 1900–1914* (Newton Abbot, 1971), and P. Thane, 'The Labour Party and state "welfare"', in K. D. Brown (ed.), *The First Labour Party, 1906–1914* (London, 1985), pp. 183–216. For the political impact of the First World War and the emergence of an independent Labour Party see the relevant sections of Pugh, *The Making of Modern British Politics*, and Tanner, *Political Change*, listed above.

12 Shop-floor Bargaining among the Assembly Workers

For the emergence and consequences of shop-floor bargaining in the motor industry see S. Tolliday, 'Government, employers and shop floor organization in the British motor industry, 1939–69', in S. Tolliday and J. Zeitlin (eds.), *Shop Floor Bargaining and the State. Historical and Comparative Perspectives* (Cambridge, 1985), pp. 108–47, S. Tolliday, 'Management and labour in Britain, 1896–1939', in S. Tolliday and J. Zeitlin (eds.), *The Automobile Industry and its Workers. Between Fordism and Flexibility* (Cambridge, 1986), pp. 29–56, and S. Tolliday, 'Ford and "Fordism" in postwar Britain: enterprise management and the control of labour, 1937–1987', in S. Tolliday and J. Zeitlin (eds.), *The Power to Manage? Employers and Industrial Relations in Comparative-Historical Perspective* (London, 1991), pp. 81–114. For case studies of the functioning of shop-steward organization in the Coventry area see M. Terry and P. K. Edwards (eds.), *Shopfloor Politics and Job Controls. The Post-War Engineering Industry* (Oxford, 1988). For the spreading visions of 'workers' control' see M. Poole, *Towards a New Indus-*

trial Democracy. Workers' Participation in Industry (London, 1986). For developments among the assembly workers during the Second World War see the relevant sections of H. A. Clegg, *A History of British Trade Unions since 1889. Volume 3. 1934–1951* (Oxford, 1994), and for the nature of employment and trade unionism among women see C. Wightman, *More than Munitions. Women, Work and the Engineering Industries, 1900–1950* (London, 1999). For the limited role of revolutionary agitators see R. Martin, *Communism and the British Trade Unions, 1924–1933. A Study of the National Minority Movement* (Oxford, 1969), N. Fishman, *The British Communist Party and the Trade Unions, 1933–45* (Aldershot, 1995), and J. McIlroy, ' "Always outnumbered, always outgunned": the Trotskyists and the trade unions', in J. McIlroy, N. Fishman and A. Campbell (eds.), *British Trade Unions and Industrial Politics. Volume 2. The High Tide of Trade Unionism, 1964–79* (Aldershot, 1999), pp. 259–96. For the campaign against the Conservatives' act of 1971 see M. Moran, *The Politics of Industrial Relations. The Origins, Life and Death of the 1971 Industrial Relations Act* (London, 1977), and for the pluralist supporters of voluntarism see J. Kelly, 'Social democracy and anti-communism: Allan Flanders and British industrial relations in the early post-war period', in A. Campbell, N. Fishman and J. McIlroy (eds.), *British Trade Unions and Industrial Politics. Volume 1. The Post-War Compromise, 1945–64* (Aldershot, 1999), pp. 192–221, and R. Lewis, 'Method and ideology in the labour law writings of Otto Kahn-Freund', in K. W. Wedderburn, R. Lewis and J. Clark (eds.), *Labour Law and Industrial Relations. Building on Kahn-Freund* (Oxford, 1983), pp. 107–26.

13 Industrial Decline among the Process Workers

For surveys of developments among the miners see B. Supple, *The History of the British Coal Industry. Volume 4. 1913–1946. The Political Economy of Decline* (Oxford, 1987), and W. Ashworth and M. Pegg, *The History of the British Coal Industry. Volume 5. 1946–1982. The Nationalized Industry* (Oxford, 1986). For the events of 1926 see G. A. Phillips, *The General Strike. The Politics of Industrial Conflict* (London, 1976). For the importance of working-men's clubs as a new focus of identity see the relevant sections of H. Beynon and T. Austrin, *Masters and Servants. Class and Patronage in the Making of a Labour Organisation. The Durham Miners and the English Political Tradition* (London, 1994), and for the shift towards more moderate policies among Communist activists see the relevant sections of N. Fishman, *The British Communist Party and the Trade Unions, 1933–45* (Aldershot, 1995). For the impact of nationalization on the railways see T. R. Gourvish,

British Railways, 1948–73. A Business History (Cambridge, 1986). For the terminal decline of cotton see A. Fowler and T. Wyke (eds.), *The Barefoot Aristocrats. A History of the Amalgamated Association of Operative Cotton Spinners* (Littleborough, 1987).

14 Federal Organization among the General Workers

For the tensions within the transport workers over dock decasualization and their eventual resolution see G. Phillips and N. Whiteside, *Casual Labour. The Unemployment Question in the Port Transport Industry, 1880–1970* (Oxford, 1985), and J. Phillips, 'Decasualisation and disruption: industrial relations in the docks, 1945–79', in C. Wrigley (ed.), *A History of British Industrial Relations, 1939–1979. Industrial Relations in a Declining Economy* (Cheltenham, 1996), pp. 165–85. For the limited role of revolutionary agitators see J. Phillips, 'Democracy and trade unionism on the docks', in A. Campbell, N. Fishman and J. McIlroy (eds.), *British Trade Unions and Industrial Politics. Volume I. The Post-War Compromise, 1945–64* (Aldershot, 1999), pp. 293–310. For the role of Communists as a ginger group among the London busworkers see N. Fishman, *The British Communist Party and the Trade Unions, 1933–45* (Aldershot, 1995), and for the long-standing weakness of organization in road haulage before its transformation in the 1970s see P. Smith, *Unionization and Union Leadership. The Road Haulage Industry* (London, 2001). For the problems of black workers see R. Ramdin, *The Making of the Black Working Class in Britain* (Aldershot, 1987). For trade unionism among white-collar workers see D. Lockwood, *The Blackcoated Worker. A Study in Class Consciousness* (London, 1958, 2nd edn, Oxford, 1989), and R. Lumley, *White-Collar Unionism in Britain. A Survey of the Present Position* (London, 1973). For women in the white-collar and public-sector unions see C. Wrigley, 'Women in the labour market and in the unions', in J. McIlroy, N. Fishman and A. Campbell (eds.), *British Trade Unions and Industrial Politics. Volume 2. The High Tide of Trade Unionism, 1964–79* (Aldershot, 1999), pp. 43–69. For surveys of the position among the federal unions in the 1970s see R. Taylor, *The Fifth Estate. Britain's Unions in the Seventies* (1978), and J. Eaton and C. Gill, *The Trade Union Directory. A Guide to all TUC Unions* (2nd edn, London, 1983).

15 Trade Unionists and Labour in Power

For the limitations of direct action and the relations between the unions and the first Labour governments see the relevant sections of H. A. Clegg, *A History of British Trade Unions since 1889. Volume 2. 1911–1933* (Oxford, 1985). For the Communist Party's failure to establish an independent industrial base in the 1920s see R. Martin, *Communism and the British Trade Unions, 1924–1933. A Study of the National Minority Movement* (Oxford, 1969), and for its pockets of local support see S. McIntyre, *Little Moscows. Communism and Working-class Militancy in Inter-war Britain* (London, 1980). For the Labour Party's shift towards a more statist attitude in the 1930s and 1940s see J. Harris, 'Labour's political and social thought', and M. Taylor, 'Labour and the constitution', both in D. Tanner, P. Thane and N. Tiratsoo (eds.), *Labour's First Century* (Cambridge, 2000), pp. 8–45 and pp. 151–80 respectively, and for the development of specific policies during the Second World War see I. Taylor, 'Labour and the impact of war, 1939–45', in N. Tiratsoo (ed.), *The Attlee Years* (London, 1991), pp. 7–28. For the relationships between governments and the unions after 1945 see J. Tomlinson, 'The Labour government and the trade unions, 1945–51', in Tiratsoo, *The Attlee Years*, listed above, pp. 90–105, P. Davies and M. Freedland, *Labour Legislation and Public Policy. A Contemporary History* (Oxford, 1993), R. Taylor, *The Trade Union Question in British Politics. Government and Unions since 1945* (Oxford, 1993), J. Phillips, *The Great Alliance. Economic Recovery and the Problems of Power, 1945–1951* (London, 1996), and N. Whiteside, 'The politics of the "social" and the "industrial" wage, 1945–60', in H. Jones and M. Kandiah (eds.), *The Myth of Consensus. New Views on British History, 1945–64* (Basingstoke, 1996), pp. 120–38.

16 The End or a New Beginning?

For the trade-union and employment legislation of the Thatcher governments see P. Davies and M. Freedland, *Labour Legislation and Public Policy. A Contemporary History* (Oxford, 1993). For changes in workplace organiz- ation and industrial relations see the national data in N. Millward et al., *All Change at Work? British Employment Relations 1980–1998, as portrayed by the Workplace Industrial Relations Survey Series* (London, 2000), comple- mented by the case studies in A. Pendleton and J. Winterton (eds.), *Public Enterprise in Transition. Industrial Relations in State and Privatised Corpor- ations* (London, 1993), and D. Gallie et al. (eds.), *Trade Unionism in Recession*

(Oxford, 1996). For a survey of union responses see J. McIlroy, *Trade Unions in Britain Today* (2nd edn, Manchester, 1995). For the Labour Party's long march back to the centre of British politics see E. Shaw, *The Labour Party since 1979. Crisis and Transformation* (London, 1994).

Notes

1 From Medieval Guilds to Modern Trade Unions

1. Montesquieu, 'Notes sur l'Angleterre', in *Oeuvres Completes*, vol. 3 (edited by A. Masson, Paris, 1955), pp. 283–93, quotation from pp. 283–4.

2. ibid., p. 292.

3. Masters and Yeomen of the Blacksmiths' Company Agreement in 1434, quoted in R. A. Leeson, *Travelling Brothers. The Six Centuries' Road from Craft Fellowship to Trade Unionism* (London, 1979), p. 41.

4. A Trowbridge clothier's journal for 1677, quoted in C. R. Dobson, *Masters and Journeymen. A Prehistory of Industrial Relations, 1717–1800* (London, 1980), pp. 19–20.

5. Press report of a case involving the saddlers in the Middlesex Sessions in October 1777, quoted in ibid., p. 91.

6. Sir John Fielding in 1760, quoted in ibid. p. 69.

7. Tocqueville, *Journeys to England and Ireland* (edited by J. P. Mayer, London, 1958), p. 88.

8. ibid., pp. 47–8.

9. Tocqueville, *Democracy in America* (Everyman edition, London, 1994), vol. 2, p. 324.

PART ONE

The 1770s to the 1820s

2 Local Organization among the Assembly Workers

1. F. Place, *The Autobiography of Francis Place (1771–1854)* (edited by M. Thale, Cambridge, 1972), p. 112.
2. ibid., p. 112.
3. ibid., p. 114.
4. ibid., pp. 115–17.
5. Society of Journeymen Brushmakers Articles of 1806, reprinted in W. Kiddier, *The Old Trade Unions. From the Unprinted Records of the Brushmakers* (London, 1930), p. 37.
6. T. Carter, *Memoirs of a Working Man* (London, 1845), p. 169.
7. Press report of Thompson's trial in December 1840, quoted in R. A. Leeson, *Travelling Brothers. The Six Centuries' Road from Craft Fellowship to Trade Unionism* (London, 1979), p. 131.

3 Problems of Organization among the Process Workers

1. John Doherty, reminiscences in 1831, quoted in R. G. Kirby and A. E. Musson, *The Voice of the People. John Doherty, 1798–1854, Trade Unionist, Radical and Factory Reformer* (Manchester, 1975), p. 22.
2. John Doherty, reminiscences in 1832, quoted in ibid., pp. 3–4.
3. John Doherty, election letter, 1828, quoted in ibid., p. 27.
4. John Doherty, speech to a delegate meeting of the spinners on the Isle of Man in December 1829, quoted in ibid., p. 31.
5. Bolton Association of Weavers Address in May 1799, quoted in D. Bythell, *The Handloom Weavers. A Study in the English Cotton Industry during the Industrial Revolution* (London, 1969), p. 149.
6. General Ludd, letter to Spencer Perceval in February 1812, reproduced in M. I. Thomis, *The Luddites. Machine-Breaking in Regency England* (Newton Abbot, 1971), p. 118.

4 Trade Unionists and Extra-parliamentary Radicalism

1. John Gast, speech in February 1812, quoted in I. J. Prothero, *Artisans and Politics in Early Nineteenth-Century London. John Gast and His Times* (London, 1979), p. 80.

2. John Gast, speech in September 1818, quoted in ibid., p. 98.

3. A reformer's letter to the Manchester press in August 1819, quoted in D. Read, *Peterloo. The 'Massacre' and Its Background* (Manchester, 1958), p. 41.

4. Lord Holland, speech in the House of Lords in 1799, quoted in J. V. Orth, *Combination and Conspiracy. A Legal History of Trade Unionism, 1721–1906* (Oxford, 1991), p. 45.

5. F. Place, *The Autobiography of Francis Place (1771–1854)* (edited by M. Thale, Cambridge, 1972), p. 116.

6. John Doherty, letter to Francis Place, July 1825, quoted in R. G. Kirby and A. E. Musson, *The Voice of the People. John Doherty, 1798–1854, Trade Unionist, Radical and Factory Reformer* (Manchester, 1975), p. 40.

PART TWO

The 1820s to the 1870s

5 Financial Centralization among the Assembly Workers

1. Robert Applegarth, recollection, quoted in A. W. Humphrey, *Robert Applegarth. Trade Unionist, Educationist, Reformer* (London, 1913, reprinted 1984), p. 127.

2. Humphrey, *Robert Applegarth*, p. 18.

3. Robert Applegarth, recollection, quoted in ibid., p. 143.

4. Robert Applegarth, recollection, quoted in ibid., p. 180.

5. Robert Applegarth to a joiners' meeting in Chester in 1866, quoted in ibid., p. 34.

6. Robert Applegarth, aphorism, quoted in ibid., p. 126.

7. Daniel Guile, evidence to the Royal Commission on Trades Unions in 1867–8, quoted in W. Hamish Fraser, *Trade Unions and Society. The Struggle for Acceptance, 1850–1880* (London, 1974), p. 63.

8. Robert Applegarth, evidence to the Royal Commission on Trades Unions in 1867–8, quoted in Humphrey, *Robert Applegarth*, p. 157.

9. H. Broadhurst, *The Story of his Life from a Stonemason's Bench to the Treasury Bench. Told by Himself* (London, 1901), pp. 45–6.

6 State Intervention among the Process Workers

1. Alexander McDonald, address to the Coal and Iron Miners of Scotland in 1855, quoted in G. M. Wilson, *Alexander McDonald. Leader of the Miners* (Aberdeen, 1982), pp. 67–8.

2. Alexander McDonald, evidence to the Royal Commission on Trades Unions in 1867–8, quoted in ibid., p. 11.

3. Alexander McDonald to the members of the Miners' Association of Scotland in 1856, quoted in ibid., p. 74.

4. James Keir Hardie to a meeting of the Lanarkshire Miners' Union at Hamilton in 1879, quoted in ibid., p. 194.

5. Dr John Watts in 1866, quoted in J. K. Walton, *Lancashire. A Social History, 1558–1939* (Manchester, 1987), pp. 242–3.

6. Banners of the Mosley and Roddymoor pits in 1872, described in H. Beynon and T. Austrin, *Masters and Servants. Class and Patronage in the Making of a Labour Organisation. The Durham Miners and the English Political Tradition* (London, 1994), p. 209.

7. Press report of the first Durham Miners' Gala in July 1871, quoted in ibid., pp. 206–7.

7 Trade Unionists and Popular Liberalism

1. George Howell, election address, 1868, quoted in F. M. Leventhal, *Respectable Radical. George Howell and Victorian Working Class Politics* (London, 1971), p. 119.

2. George Howell, 'Autobiography', quoted in ibid., p. 17.

3. George Howell, letter to John Bright in October 1865, quoted in ibid., p. 67.

4. George Howell, letter to George Jackson in May 1868, quoted in ibid., p. 104.

5. Resolution of the Trades Union Congress at Sheffield in 1874, quoted in ibid., p. 175.

6. George Howell, *Labour Legislation, Labour Movements and Labour Leaders* (London, 1902), p. vii.

7. Robert Lowery, 'Passages in the Life of a Temperance Lecturer', in B. Harrison and P. Hollis (eds.), *Robert Lowery. Radical and Chartist* (London, 1979), quotation from p. 109.

8. Manhood Suffrage and Vote by Ballot Association Address to the Trade Unions of the Kingdom in 1862, quoted in A. W. Humphrey, *Robert Applegarth. Trade Unionist, Educationist, Reformer* (London, 1913, reprinted 1984), p. 58.

9. *Newcastle Weekly Chronicle* in November 1868, quoted in E. F. Biagini,

Liberty, Retrenchment and Reform. Popular Liberalism in the Age of Gladstone, 1860–1880 (Cambridge, 1992), p. 278.

10. William Crawford, pamphlet for the Durham Miners' Association in 1884, quoted in J. Spain, 'Trade unionists, Gladstonian Liberals and the labour law reforms of 1875', in E. F. Biagini and A. J. Reid (eds.), *Currents of Radicalism. Popular Radicalism, Organised Labour and Party Politics in Britain, 1850–1914* (Cambridge, 1991), p. 133.

PART THREE

The 1870s to the 1920s

8 National Bargaining among the Assembly Workers

1. John Hill, speech to the Labour conference in 1918, in *Labour Party Annual Report*, June 1918, p. 62.

2. John Hill, speech to the TUC conference in 1918, in *TUC Annual Report*, 1918, p. 192.

3. John Hill, speech to the TUC conference in 1930, in *TUC Annual Report*, 1930, p. 288.

4. John Hill, comments to his members in 1917, in *Boilermakers' Society Annual Report*, 1917, p. xi.

5. John Hill, presidential address to the TUC conference in 1917, in *TUC Annual Report*, 1917, pp. 54, 57–8.

6. The chairman of the Engineering Employers' Federation to a special meeting of his executive in July 1906, quoted in J. Zeitlin, 'The internal politics of employer organisation. The Engineering Employers' Federation, 1896–1939', in S. Tolliday and J. Zeitlin (eds.), *The Power to Manage? Employers and Industrial Relations in Comparative-Historical Perspective* (London, 1991), pp. 52–80, especially p. 59.

7. The secretary of the Shipbuilding Employers' Federation to the secretary of the EEF in September 1911, quoted in ibid., p. 61.

8. John Hill during national negotiations in February 1932, quoted in A. McKinlay, 'Employers and Skilled Workers in the Inter-War Depression. Engineering and Shipbuilding on Clydeside, 1919–1939' (D.Phil. thesis, Oxford University, 1986), p. 236.

9. D. Lloyd George, *War Memoirs. Volume I* (1938), p. 177, quoted in part in H. A. Clegg, *A History of British Trade Unions since 1889. Volume 2: 1911–1933* (Oxford, 1985), p. 123.

9 Union Recognition among the Process Workers

1. Jimmy Thomas, speech to the Labour conference in 1918, in *Labour Party Annual Report*, June 1918, p. 43.

2. J. H. Thomas, *My Story* (London, 1937), p. 16.

3. Jimmy Thomas, speech to the House of Commons in November 1916, quoted in G. Blaxland, *J. H. Thomas. A Life for Unity* (London, 1964), p. 97.

4. Jimmy Thomas, speech to strikers at London stations in 1911, quoted in ibid., p. 75.

5. Jimmy Thomas, speech to strikers on the London underground in 1919, quoted in ibid., pp. 121–2.

6. Jimmy Thomas, presidential address to the railwaymen's conference in 1905, quoted in ibid., p. 48.

7. Jimmy Thomas, interview in the *New York Times* in 1917, quoted in ibid., p. 107.

8. George Greenwell, evidence to the Royal Commission on Trade Unions in 1867–8, quoted in R. Church, A. Hall and J. Kanefsky, *The History of the British Coal Industry. Volume 3. 1830–1913. Victorian Pre-eminence* (Oxford, 1986), pp. 663–4.

9. John Chambers, chairman of the South Yorkshire Coalowners' Association, report in 1899, quoted in ibid., p. 735.

10. The Sankey Commission in 1919, quoted in B. Supple, *The History of the British Coal Industry. Volume 4, 1913–1946. The Political Economy of Decline* (Oxford, 1987), p. 130.

10 New Organizations among the General Workers

1. Mary Macarthur, speech to the Labour conference in 1918, in *Labour Party Annual Report*, June 1918, p. 65.

2. Mary Macarthur, quoted in M. A. Hamilton, *Mary Macarthur. A Biographical Sketch* (London, 1925), p. 23.

3. Mary Macarthur, speech to the National Women's Trade Union League of America in 1909, quoted in ibid., p. 35.

4. Dundee newspaper reports of 1906, quoted in ibid., pp. 53–4.

5. Anonymous commentator, quoted in ibid., p. 57.

6. Mary Macarthur, memorandum on the National Insurance Act in 1914, quoted in ibid., pp. 117–18.

7. H. Llewellyn Smith and V. Nash, *The Story of the Dockers' Strike* (London, 1889), pp. 32–3, quoted in H. A. Clegg, A. Fox and A. F. Thompson,

A History of British Trade Unions since 1889. Volume 1: 1889–1910 (Oxford, 1962), p. 59.

8. Shaw Report in 1920, quoted in G. Phillips and N. Whiteside, *Casual Labour. The Unemployment Question in the Port Transport Industry, 1880–1970* (Oxford, 1985), p. 168, and J. Jones, *Union Man* (London, 1986), p. 29.

9. Press report in February 1906, quoted in E. Gordon, *Women and the Labour Movement in Scotland, 1850–1914* (Oxford, 1991), p. 208.

11 Trade Unionists and the Origins of the Labour Party

1. Arthur Henderson, speech to the Labour conference in 1918, in *Labour Party Annual Report*, January–February 1918, p. 100.

2. Arthur Henderson, acceptance speech in July 1903, quoted in C. Wrigley, *Arthur Henderson* (Cardiff, 1990), p. 34.

3. Arthur Henderson, speech in Lancashire in December 1920, quoted in ibid., p. 137.

4. Arthur Henderson, speech to a Wesleyan Brotherhood Movement meeting in Bradford in February 1908, quoted in ibid., p. 41.

5. Arthur Henderson, article in the ironfounders' monthly report for July 1907, quoted in ibid., pp. 43–4.

6. Arthur Henderson, speech in the House of Commons in May 1906, quoted in ibid., p. 74.

7. Arthur Henderson, speech to a special TUC and Labour Party conference on the League of Nations in April 1919, quoted in ibid., p. 133.

8. William Randal Cremer in *The Labour Tribune* in October 1886, quoted in J. Shepherd, 'Labour and parliament: the Lib-Labs as the first working-class MPs, 1885–1906', in E. F. Biagini and A. J. Reid (eds.), *Currents of Radicalism. Popular Radicalism, Organised Labour and Party Politics in Britain, 1850–1914* (Cambridge, 1991), pp. 187–213, quotation on pp. 206–7.

9. Thomas Burt in the *Contemporary Review* in May 1889, quoted in ibid., p. 207.

10. James Keir Hardie, election handbill in 1888, quoted in H. Pelling, *The Origins of the Labour Party, 1880–1900* (2nd edn, London, 1965), p. 65.

11. Herbert Gladstone, letters to *Daily News* in May 1903, quoted in F. Bealey and H. Pelling, *Labour and Politics, 1900–1906. A History of the Labour Representation Committee* (London, 1958), p. 151.

12. Ramsay MacDonald, speech to a National Liberal Federation symposium in August 1903, quoted in ibid., p. 155.

13. W. C. Anderson, speech to the Labour conference in 1918, in *Labour Party Annual Report*, June 1918, p. 50.

14. 'The Constitution of the Labour Party', Appendix I in *Labour Party Annual Report*, January–February 1918, p. 140.

PART FOUR

The 1920s to the 1970s

12 Shop-floor Bargaining among the Assembly Workers

1. Harold Wilson, memorandum of 1 June 1969, quoted in R. Taylor, *The TUC. From the General Strike to New Unionism* (Basingstoke, 2000), p. 173.
2. This biographical information is largely drawn from an interview with Hugh Scanlon, 'The role of militancy', in *New Left Review*, 46 (1967), pp. 3–15, especially pp. 3–4.
3. ibid., p. 13.
4. ibid., p. 7.
5. H. Scanlon, *The Way Forward for Workers' Control* (Nottingham, 1968), the text of a speech given at the sixth Conference on Workers' Control in Nottingham in March 1968, p. 3. See also H. Scanlon, *Workers' Control and the Transnational Company* (Nottingham, 1972).
6. Scanlon, *The Way Forward*, p. 7.
7. Ivan Yates, Chairman of the Midland Regional Committee of the Engineering Employers' Federation, at a meeting with the national officers of the EEF in October 1957, quoted in E. Wigham, *The Power to Manage. A History of the Engineering Employers' Federation* (London, 1973), pp. 194–5.
8. Interview with Alf Brogan, quoted in S. Tolliday, 'High tide and after: Coventry engineering workers and shopfloor bargaining, 1945–80', in B. Lancaster and T. Mason (eds.), *Life and Labour in a Twentieth Century City. The Experience of Coventry* (Coventry, 1986), pp. 204–43, quotation on p. 211.
9. Interview with Ralph Fuller, quoted in N. Fishman, *The British Communist Party and the Trade Unions, 1933–45* (Aldershot, 1995), p. 214.
10. Central Committee of the Socialist Workers' Party, 'The next six to nine months', in *Internal Bulletin 1, 1978*, quoted in J. McIlroy, '"Always outnumbered, always outgunned": the Trotskyists and the trade unions', in J. McIlroy, N. Fishman and A. Campbell (eds.), *British Trade Unions and Industrial Politics. Volume 2. The High Tide of Trade Unionism. 1964–79* (Aldershot, 1999), pp. 259–96, quotation from p. 283.

13 Industrial Decline among the Process Workers

1. Joe Gormley to the Miners' annual conference in July 1973, quoted in J. Gormley, *Battered Cherub* (London, 1982), p. 123.

2. ibid., p. 196.

3. ibid., p. 34.

4. ibid., p. 44.

5. ibid., p. 91, his emphasis.

6. ibid., p. 131, his emphasis.

7. ibid., p. 182.

8. Frank Betts in the *Nation and Atheneum* in July 1921, quoted in B. Supple, *The History of the British Coal Industry. Volume 4. 1913–1946. The Political Economy of Decline* (Oxford, 1987), p. 485.

9. *The Economist* in January 1945, quoted in ibid., pp. 623, 626.

10. *Wilberforce Inquiry Report* in 1972, quoted in C. Wrigley (ed.), *British Trade Unions, 1945–1995* (Manchester, 1997), p. 156.

14 Federal Organization among the General Workers

1. Jack Jones's recollection of his speech to the biennial delegate conference of the Transport and General Workers' Union in July 1977, in J. Jones, *Union Man* (London, 1986), p. 326.

2. St Luke, chapter 1, verse 51, Authorised Version; B. Disraeli, *Sybil* (London, 1845), book 4, chapter 8.

3. Jones, *Union Man*, p. 35.

4. ibid., p. 107.

5. ibid., p. 186.

6. ibid., p. 193.

7. Ernest Bevin, speech to the special rules conference of the Transport and General Workers' Union in September 1921, quoted in A. Bullock, *The Life and Times of Ernest Bevin. Volume I. Trade Union Leader, 1881–1940* (London, 1960), p. 190.

8. George Bromley, Transport and General Workers' Union, in *Race Today* in July 1974, quoted in R. Ramdin, *The Making of the Black Working Class in Britain* (Aldershot, 1987), p. 272.

9. Mel Read, Association of Scientific, Technical and Managerial Staffs, in a communication with Chris Wrigley in July 1998, quoted in C. Wrigley, 'Women in the labour market and in the unions', in J. McIlroy, N. Fishman and A. Campbell (eds.), *British Trade Unions and Industrial Politics.*

Volume 2. The High Tide of Trade Unionism, 1964–79 (Aldershot, 1999), pp. 43–69, pp. 58–9.

10. Account of a demonstration in October 1976 in J. Dromey and G. Taylor, *Grunwick. The Workers' Story* (London, 1978), quoted in Ramdin, *The Making of the Black Working Class*, p. 292.

15 Trade Unionists and Labour in Power

1. James Callaghan's recollection of his thinking in May 1976, quoted in J. Callaghan, *Time and Chance* (London, 1987), p. 398.

2. ibid., pp. 396, 397.

3. ibid., pp. 44–5.

4. ibid., pp. 237–8.

5. ibid., p. 207.

6. James Callaghan, speech to the Nottinghamshire Miners in May 1969, quoted in K. O. Morgan, *Callaghan. A Life* (Oxford, 1997), pp. 343–4.

7. Callaghan, *Time and Chance*, p. 540.

8. Ernest Bevin (transport workers), speech to the Labour Party conference in October 1927, in *Labour Party Annual Report 1927*, p. 186, quoted in A. Bullock, *The Life and Times of Ernest Bevin. Volume 1. Trade Union Leader, 1881–1940* (London, 1960), p. 390.

9. William Kean (gold and silver trades), speech to the TUC in September 1935, quoted in H. A. Clegg, *A History of British Trade Unions since 1889. Volume 3: 1934–1951* (Oxford, 1994), p. 113.

10. Ernest Bevin (transport workers), speech to the TUC in September 1936, quoted in ibid., p. 129.

11. Unnamed trade-union official interviewed in F. Zweig, *The British Worker* (London, 1952), quoted in R. Taylor, *The Trade Union Question in British Politics. Government and Unions since 1945* (Oxford, 1993), p. 46.

16 The End or a New Beginning?

1. J. Mather, *The European Union and British Democracy. Towards Convergence* (Basingstoke, 2000), p. 40.

2. ibid., p. 52.

3. ibid., pp. 59–60.

4. P. Davies and M. Freedland, *Labour Legislation and Public Policy. A Contemporary History* (Oxford, 1993), p. 599.

5. Paul Edwards in the April 1985 issue of *Personnel Manager*, quoted in

J. McIlroy, *Trade Unions in Britain Today* (2nd edn, Manchester, 1995), p. 112.

6. M. Cully et al., *Britain at Work. As Depicted by the 1998 Workplace Employee Relations Survey* (London, 1999), p. 296.

Index